PHILOSOPHY OF
MATERIAL NATURE

Immanuel Kant

PHILOSOPHY OF
MATERIAL NATURE

the complete texts of

PROLEGOMENA

To Any Future Metaphysics That Will Be Able To Come Forward As Science

The Paul Carus Translation
extensively revised by
JAMES W. ELLINGTON

and

METAPHYSICAL FOUNDATIONS
OF NATURAL SCIENCE

Translation by JAMES W. ELLINGTON

Hackett Publishing Company

Immanuel Kant: 1724-1804

Prolegomena to Any Future Metaphysics was
originally published in 1783
Metaphysical Foundations of Natural Science was
originally published in 1786

Cover design by Richard L. Listenberger
Interior design by Jared Carter, Starr Koester Atkinson

Printed in the United States of America

10 09 08 07 06 05 04 03 02 01 00 99 98 97   3 4 5 6 7 8 9 10

For further information, please address
Hackett Publishing Company, Inc.
Box 44937, Indianapolis, Indiana 46244

Library of Congress Cataloging in Publication Data

Kant, Immanuel, 1724-1804.
The philosophy of material nature.

Includes index.
Contents: Prolegomena to any future metaphysics that will be able to come
forward as science / the Paul Carus translation extensively revised by James W.
Ellington — Metaphysical foundations of natural science / translation by James W.
Ellington.
1. Metaphysics. 2. Knowledge, Theory of. I. Carus, Paul, 1852-1919. II.
Ellington, James W. (James Wesley), 1927-   . III. Kant, Immanuel, 1724-1804.
Metaphysische Anfangsgründe der Naturwissenschaft. English. 1985. IV. Title.

B2787.E5C3 1985   110   85-889
ISBN 0-915145-87-1
ISBN 0-915145-88-X (pbk.)

CONTENTS

Book I

CONTENTS

Book II

TRANSLATOR'S FOREWORD

In the Introduction to the *Critique of Judgment* at Akademie page 194 Kant says that this third *Critique* will be followed by no doctrine, inasmuch as it contains nothing but reflective judgments, whereas the *Critique of Pure Reason* and the *Critique of Practical Reason* contain determinant judgments. Accordingly, both of these Critiques are followed by two bodies of doctrine: the metaphysics of nature and the metaphysics of morals. The latter doctrine was in fact entitled the *Metaphysics of Morals* and appeared in 1797. But what about the metaphysics of nature? It is mentioned by Kant in several places scattered about in his writings: *Critique of Pure Reason*, B869–70 and B874; *Prolegomena to Any Future Metaphysics*, Ak. 295; *Grounding for the Metaphysics of Morals*, Ak. 388; *Critique of Judgment*, Ak. 181. This body of doctrine was not entitled the Metaphysics of Nature but the *Metaphysical Foundations of Natural Science*, which appeared in 1786.

It does indeed follow upon the *Critique of Pure Reason* in that the principles of the understanding *(Grundsätze des reinen Verstandes)*, which in the "Transcendental Analytic" of this first *Critique* are principles for determining objects in general, are in the *Metaphysical Foundations* principles for determining material objects in particular. This entails the fact that the *Metaphysical Foundations* cannot be fully understood unless one is also familiar with the first half of the *Critique*. To combine the *Critique* (or even just the "Aesthetic" and the "Analytic") with the *Metaphysical Foundations* would make for a very lengthy volume. To combine the *Prolegomena* with the *Metaphysical Foundations* yields a much more manageable book, and that is what has been done here. Ideally, the latter should be combined with the *Critique* (or at least with the "Aesthetic" and "Analytic" of it) but the *Prolegomena* will do. After all, the First Part and the Second Part of the *Pro-*

legomena present to the reader in summary form the results of the elaborate inquiries of the "Aesthetic" and "Analytic". This combination was made once before by Ernest Belfort Bax for Bohn's Philosophical Library at London in 1883 (now long out of print, not entirely satisfactory translations of the two works to begin with).

My translation of the *Prolegomena* (which appeared first in 1977 in the Hackett series of philosophical classics) is a rather extensive revision of the Paul Carus rendition (Open Court Press, Chicago, 1902). Carus made extensive use of John P. Mahaffy's English version of the *Prolegomena* (London, 1872), and Mahaffy made use of John Richardson's rendering (London, 1819). I used the German text that appears in Vol. IV (Berlin, 1911) of the Royal Prussian Academy of Sciences' edition of Kant's works. The translation of the *Metaphysical Foundations* first appeared in 1970 in the Library of Liberal Arts series. For this I used the German text as it appears in Vol. IV of the Academy edition. Page numbers of that edition, the standard reference for Kant's work, here appear as marginal numbers for both the *Prolegomena* and *Metaphysical Foundations*. All material added by me in text or notes has been bracketed. My Introduction to the *Prolegomena* and my Essay at the end of the *Metaphysical Foundations* are for the most part reprints from the 1970 Library of Liberal Arts edition. The Introduction to the *Metaphysical Foundations* appears for the first time in this volume.

University of Connecticut   JAMES W. ELLINGTON
Storrs

TRANSLATOR'S INTRODUCTION

The *Metaphysical Foundations of Natural Science* is a neglected work. This is unfortunate, because it tells us many interesting things and has an important function in the overall structure of Kant's philosophy of material nature (the inorganic world studied in physical science). Many people seem to think that mining the "Second Part" (How Is Pure Natural Science Possible?) of the *Prolegomena to Any Future Metaphysics* and the "Transcendental Analytic" of the *Critique of Pure Reason* is the most profitable venture for learning what Kant thinks about the philosophical presuppositions of physics (perhaps mainly, or at least in part, because no accurate English translation of the *Metaphysical Foundations* has been available). It is quite true that the "Second Part" of the *Prolegomena* and the "Transcendental Analytic" of the *Critique* contain his most general thoughts on the subject, but the *Metaphysical Foundations* is an indispensable stage in the passage from the highly abstract transcendental discussion of the "Second Part" and the "Analytic" to the more concrete treatment of nature in empirical physics.

In this carefully structured philosophical system of corporeal nature, the *Metaphysical Foundations* fits in between the "Second Part" of the *Prolegomena* and the "Analytic" of the *Critique* on the one hand and the *Transition from the Metaphysical Foundations of Natural Science to Physics* on the other hand. Most people are even less familiar with this latter work than with the *Metaphysical Foundations*. The *Transition* is unfinished, making up a part of a project that Kant was working on at the time of his death (see below, *Metaphysical Foundations of Natural Science*, page 215) and which survived as a stack of handwritten sheets. Editors later gathered these into thirteen fascicles, collectively called the *Opus Postumum*, to be found in Volumes XXI and XXII of the Royal Prussian Academy of Sciences edition of Kant's writings. The relationship among these three works is a hierarchical one. The overall organization of the *Metaphysical Foundations* depends upon a plan laid out in the *Prolegomena* and in the *Critique*. And, as one might expect, there are frequent references in the *Metaphysical Foundations* to the *Critique* (see below, *Metaphysical Foundations of Natural Science* pages 6, 11, 15–16, 102, 104–105, 106–107, 118–120, for example). Therefore, some familiarity with the "Second Part" of the *Prolegomena* and the "Analytic" of the *Critique* is necessary if one is to understand the *Metaphysical Foundations*. The *Transition*, in turn, depends on the *Metaphysical Foundations*. The essay at the end of the translation of the *Metaphysical Foundations of Natural Science* is intended for those who are interested in the definitive architectonic interconnections among the *Prolegomena* and *Critique*, the *Metaphysical Foundations*, and the *Transition*.

Here in this Introduction our aim is not so ambitious. In order to get some idea of the architectonic relations involved, let us consider an example. When a rock is thrown in a direction parallel to the ground, we know by experience that its path is a curvilinear line ending on the ground some yards away; how many yards away depends on how strong the pitcher is. The exact nature of the curvilinear path depends on the mass of the rock, the velocity it attains by means of the force the pitcher imparts when he throws it, the resistance of the air through which it passes, and the pull of gravity on it. When these things are known, we can plot the exact path by laws of physics, which are generalizations from many experiments. But we are also told that if the air exerted no resistance and if gravity exerted no pull, then the rock would keep on going forever in a straight line (provided no hills got in the way before it cleared the planet earth and no celestial objects blocked its path after it left the earth). This is Newton's first law of motion, which says that every object continues in a state of rest or of uniform motion (constant velocity or zero acceleration) in a straight line unless acted on by some outside force—a curious law that would seem to hold for some science-fiction world rather than our own. In our world the atmosphere always offers some resistance and gravity always pulls, with the result that any rock we ever throw always comes to earth. Thus Newton's law seems to be of a character different from that of the aforementioned laws determining the paths of projectiles. Furthermore, there are philosophers who tell us that every change has a cause. This law is even more general than Newton's first law of motion, for this one covers not only the case of material bodies that stay put or else keep going in a straight line with uniform velocity unless some external cause acts on them, but also the case of living things that act according to an internal cause (a lion rushes after an antelope not because a big puff of wind propels him but because he has a desire to eat).

Kant carefully distinguished these three different kinds of laws. Laws of the first kind are the empirical ones of physics, which are validated by experiment. The second he called metaphysical; the third transcendental. These last two kinds are not established by experience. Metaphysical and transcendental principles require a priori, philosophical justifications showing how it is that principles which in their origin owe nothing to experience are nevertheless applicable to experience. For example, according to the transcendental principle of efficient causation, all things change in conformity with the law of the connection of cause and effect. Take the case of a warm room and a glowing stove. I come out of the cold into a warm room; I feel the warmth and later notice a glowing stove. But I do not say that the warm room is the cause of the glowing stove; rather, the other way around. When we are confronted with certain successions of events, we rework the subjective order of our perceiving these events in accordance with the principle of causation and set up an objective order of the events—the stove causes the room to be warm. This universal law of efficient causation is imposed a priori upon objects by the mind itself. The various a priori forms of thought according to which we order our perceptions are explored by Kant in the *Critique of Pure Reason,* where he explains how they, though not having their origin in experience, are yet the very conditions that make experience possible as an objective synthesis of subjective sense impressions.

These metaphysical and transcendental principles are a priori in the strict sense. They are not only prior to experience, but

are independent of experience in the sense that they are the
necessary grounds which make experience itself possible; they
have their origin in the very nature of the thinking faculty itself.
One sometimes hears that hypotheses are a priori in the sense that
they are prior to the experience that confirms or rejects them;
however, these are not independent of experience, because all
sorts of analogies, knowledge of other physical laws, educated
guesses, and even plain hunches go into their manufacture. For
instance, when Copernicus first thought that the planets might be
moving about the sun instead of the sun and other planets moving
about the earth, he was advancing a hypothesis that later proved
to be a confirmable description of the solar system; but this
hypothesis was a priori only in a weak sense. Kant would say that
such specific hypotheses are *regulative* principles that guide empirical enquiry, but that the aforementioned strictly a priori principles are *constitutive* of experience.

What, now, are these various transcendental and metaphysical principles? Let us take up the transcendental ones first.

In the *Critique* and *Prolegomena* Kant treats of the most
formal functions of thought. Representations, or what a philosopher such as Locke would call ideas, are combined in consciousness (the transcendental unity of apperception) to give us
objectively valid knowledge of things, e.g., the earth is a rotating body. The fundamental ways in which thoughts are so
combined comprise the logical functions of judgment. These are
the familiar universal, particular, singular, affirmative, negative, etc. to be found in the *Prolegomena* (at Ak. 302–303) and
in the *Critique* (at B 95). When these twelve logical forms of
judgment are employed so as to constitute the knowledge of
some object, they function as categories and not simply as logical forms of thought in general. The following example points
up the differences between a category and a logical function of
judgment: according to the categorical form of judgment I can
say that "all bodies are divisible", but I can also say that
"something divisible is a body"; however, when the concept of
body is subsumed under the category of substance, the empirical intuition of body must always be considered as subject and
never as predicate. Similarly, the other categories are used to
determine the empirical knowledge of some object.

The laws according to which the categories must apply to all objects of experience are called the principles of pure understanding *(Grundsätze des reinen Verstandes)*. Following the order of the categories, these transcendental principles comprise a system. The **Axioms of Intuition** tell us that the intuitions of phenomena are extensive magnitudes; this means that objects are spread out in space and last through time. The **Anticipations of Perception** tell us that objects also have intensive magnitude. Since the sensible perception of objects always involves sensation (as well as the temporal and spatial intuitions treated in the Axioms), and sensation has a degree starting from the complete absence of any sensation (pure intuition) and proceeding to sensations of indefinitely increasing intensity—given through sense perception—a corresponding intensive magnitude must be ascribed to objects. And so, even though all sensations as such are given only a posteriori, the fact that they have a degree can be known a priori. Accordingly, color, sound, taste, and even resistance and weight must have intensive magnitude. These Axioms and Anticipations are concerned with homogeneous elements of experience which do not necessarily belong to one another; the following **Analogies of Experience** are concerned with relations of heterogeneous elements which do necessarily belong to one another. The First Analogy of Experience tells us that substance is the permanent substratum underlying all change; in every alteration there is an exchange of one state of a thing for another state of that thing, but the thing itself must remain the same. According to the Second Analogy all changes of phenomena take place in conformity with the law of the connection of cause and effect. The Third Analogy tells us that substances stand in a relation of reciprocal causality regarding their accidents. The **Postulates of Empirical Thought** are not concerned with the necessary traits of objects (as are the Axioms, Anticipations, and Analogies), but, rather, with the existence of objects in relation to the mind that knows them. The First Postulate says that if things are to be *possible,* then the concept of these things must agree with the formal conditions of experience, i.e., with the forms of thought that together constitute the transcendental unity of apperception. The Second Postulate tells us that what is connected with that which is given in sensation is *actual;* this means that we must have sense perception of things in order to know their actuality. The Third Postulate says that the *necessary* is that whose connection with the actual is determined according to the Analogies. The necessity here applies only to the changing states of substances and not to the substances themselves, since substances do not come to be and pass away. If we have actual experience of the cause of something, then by thought we can affirm the necessary existence of the effect.

Obviously, the *Critique* and *Prolegomena* treat only of the most general aspects of things. For example, through the category of substance I think of an unchanging subject to which changing predicates belong. Now, if this category is not to remain a mere abstract form of thought, there must be something permanent presented in experience corresponding to this formal concept of substance. The experience of bodies in space, with their changing characteristics, is the content that gives this abstract concept meaning and truth. In other words, the transcendental concepts and principles treated in the *Critique* and *Prolegomena* must be applied to our experience of bodies (matter) if they are not to remain mere abstractions.

Now, this is one of the jobs of the *Metaphysical Foundations of Natural Science;* it outlines the general ways in which the categories can be applied to matter. Matter affects the external senses (and hence becomes an object of experience) only through its motion. Consequently, the metaphysics of corporeal nature is concerned with the motion of matter. But empirical physics is concerned with this also. How do the two differ? Metaphysics is concerned with the range of the possible motions of any matter (i.e., of matter in general); physics is concerned with the actual motion of particular matter (e.g., the paths of projectiles). Even though metaphysics treats of concepts that can only be given empirically (matter and motion), it is nonetheless an a priori science, because it determines matter by means of the formal categories (as we shall soon see) instead of by empirically given predicates as does physics. If I may cite our earlier example, according to Kant's second law of mechanics (see below, *Metaphysical Foundations of Natural Science,* p. 104), every body remains motionless or else moves with uni-

form velocity in a straight line as long as no external cause
changes its condition of rest or uniform motion. On the other
hand, a rock thrown in a line initially parallel to the ground
actually describes an arc, which is determinable once we know
the force with which it was thrown, the resistance of the air,
and the pull of gravity on it; all these variables are ascertained
by empirical measurement.

There are, then, some things (possibilities) that can be known
about objects of experience without regard to their particular
traits (actualities), which are treated in physics. The *Critique*
and the *Metaphysical Foundations* are both concerned with
these possible characteristics of phenomenal objects, but in different degrees. The transcendental concept of substance is one
of an unchanging subject to which changing predicates belong;
this is the most general notion that we can have of a phenomenal object. The metaphysical concept of matter narrows this
notion down; substance is determined by the possible spatial
perception of matter. In other words, the metaphysical concept
of matter introduces a sensible content (or "intuition" in
Kant's terminology). Intuition is either empirical or pure.
Through empirical intuition the physicist knows about the *actual* behavior of some definite matter (the path of a thrown
rock). The metaphysician knows about the *possible* behavior
(motion) of matter in general through mathematical construction (pure intuition). The mathematical constructions Kant
deals with are mainly geometrical constructions in Euclidean
space; for example, when two motions of one material body
that is taken as a mathematical point are represented by two
lines, each of which expresses velocity and direction and such
that the two lines enclose an angle, then the composite motion
of the point can be represented by the diagonal (expressing velocity and direction) of the parallelogram produced by drawing
lines parallel to the original two lines. (Please notice that this
law does not tell us what the lengths of the sides of the parallelogram will be or what the angle between the sides will be;
only experience can do that in a particular case under consideration. This law is a rule for generating infinitely many cases
involving all manner of angles between the lines and all lengths
of the lines.)

The metaphysics of corporeal nature, then, deals with the principles of the application of transcendental concepts to matter and with the principles of the mathematical construction of such concepts as belong to the possibility of matter in general. These metaphysical principles constitute a complete system when the empirically given concept of matter is determined by the categories. These principles do not enable us to foretell or predetermine what concrete facts will be given us by experience; but they should enable us to know in a necessary way the general aspects of every possible object of physics until experience gives us the actual presence of some of these material objects, and they should guide us in formulating the questions for whose answers we devise experiments.

These metaphysical principles fall into four groups corresponding to the categorical heads: quantity, quality, relation, and modality. I shall not list them in detail but merely indicate the general aspects of matter with which they deal. In **Phoronomy** only motion is treated. Here movability in space is the only property attributed to matter; accordingly, matter is regarded as a mathematical point. Motion is considered as a quantum measured by velocity and direction. In **Dynamics** matter is regarded as the movable insofar as it fills a space. Matter does so by means of a special moving force—through the force of repulsion one body resists the approach of another. But if this force were not balanced by any other force, matter would disperse itself to infinity. The force of attraction counteracts repulsion. The attractive force depends on the mass of the matter in a given space; the repulsive force rests on the degree to which the space is filled, and this degree can be specifically very different. Consider, for instance, a given quantity of air in a given volume. Its attraction depends on its mass and is constant, yet it manifests more or less elasticity according to its greater or lesser heating. And so a spectrum of material samples, all with the same mass (and hence with the same attraction), may vary widely in repulsion running, for instance, from the density of platinum to the rarity of helium. Therefore every space can be thought of both as full and yet as filled in varying degrees. In **Mechanics** bodies already in motion are regarded as possessing moving forces (repulsive or attractive) in order actively to impart their motions to other bodies. The three mechanical laws state that, first, in all changes of corporeal nature the quantity of matter taken as a whole remains the same, unincreased and undiminished; second, every change of matter has an external cause; and, third, in all communication of motion, action and reaction are always equal to one another. **Phenomenology** is concerned with the way in which the subject's private experience of motion can become public experience of it. The subject's private experience of something movable becomes public when this movable thing is determined by the predicate of motion. For example, in the case of the rotation of the earth on its axis, it is all the same to the subject whether the earth stands still and the heavens revolve about it or the earth rotates and the heavens stand still. Either situation would give the same appearance of motion. But in reality which one does move? This appearance becomes public experience when the *actuality* of the earth's rotation is proved by, say, the Foucault pendulum. In the case of rectilinear motion there is the *possibility* that the change of place be attributed either to the matter (i.e., space at rest and matter moving with respect to it) or to the space (i.e., matter at rest and space moving with respect to it). Further, there is also the case where both the matter and the space must *necessarily* be represented as moved at the same time: in every motion of a body whereby it is moving with regard to another body, an opposite and equal motion of the other body is necessary.

We can be sure that in general the motion of matter is caused by fundamental forces of repulsion and attraction. But the specific variety and behavior of matter can be accounted for only by particular forces discovered by experience. In the *Transition,* Kant aims to systematize rationally the empirical forces that determine the particular nature and behavior of matter as given in experience. The *Transition* is to serve as a propaedeutic for physics by preordering and prearranging the empirical search for forces in their actual realization. First, an a priori system of possible forces manifested by experience is fixed in accordance with the table of the categories. Second, the general properties of matter are set up in a similar fashion. Third, the foundation of the unity of experience and matter is set up by proving the existence of the ether.

Thus Kant builds up his system of nature in stages, beginning in the *Prolegomena* and the *Critique* with the most formal aspects of phenomena, and continuing through the *Metaphysical Foundations* and the *Transition* to those aspects that are less formal. After this would come physics, which is an empirical science and not an a priori, philosophical one at all.

Since the categories specify the a priori functions of the understanding completely (as I shall show in the Essay appearing after the translation of the *Metaphysical Foundations of Natural Science*), these philosophical sciences are complete systems inasmuch as these categories determine phenomenal objects in general in the *Prolegomena* and the *Critique*, and matter in general in the *Metaphysical Foundations*, as we have already seen. Empirical physics can never be complete: nature's secrets are inexhaustible in that the multitude of natural objects and their discoverable features are endless (see below, *Metaphysical Foundations*, p. 11). (In this respect Kant differs sharply from certain other dealers in the a priori—e.g., Schelling—who thought that the whole of physics could be completely and exhaustively spun out of the mind itself.) Neither can a system of the mathematical principles of corporeal nature attain completeness, even though these principles are a priori. The reason is similar to that which makes completeness unattainable in empirical physics: any mathematical science involves an endless multiplicity of possible pure intuitions.

Kant stresses that any such mathematical system of corporeal nature depends on the metaphysical system (see below, *Metaphysical Foundations*, pp. 9–10, 15, 16–17). The principles of the latter system indicate (among other things) what mathematical constructions are appropriate and useful for application to natural phenomena. Kant gives several examples (see *ibid.*, pp. 25–27, 35–38, 49–56, 70–76), only one of which I shall mention here (see *ibid.*, pp. 70–71). Consider a force that diffuses itself through space in order to act on a distant body. How is one to represent this diffusion? One common way, borrowed from optics, is to let rays diverge from a central point (the location of the force) so that an infinite number of concentric spherical surfaces are indicated thereby. Kant considers this a bad representation because the lines so drawn can never fill the space they pass through nor the spherical surface they reach, because of their divergence. A much better way is suggested by the diffusion of the illumination of a light. This illumination diffuses itself in spherical surfaces that ever increase with the square of the distance from the source. Any one of these infinitely larger spheres is uniformly illuminated, while the degree of illumination of any one of them is inversely proportional to its distance from the light source. Accordingly, a force diffuses itself uniformly throughout space, and the degree of its action on a distant body is inversely proportional to the spatial distance through which it has had to diffuse itself in order to act on this distant body. Thus a philosophical consideration of the nature of diffusing forces indicates the appropriate mathematical construction. And so the principles of the *Metaphysical Foundations* make possible a subsequent system of the mathematical principles of corporeal nature. It is not the business of metaphysics to discover applications of mathematics to phenomena (mathematical physics does that), but, rather, to pass judgment on the legitimacy and propriety of such application. The function of metaphysics as conceived by Kant is critical rather than heuristic.

Prolegomena

Prolegomena

zu

einer jeden

künftigen Metaphysik

die

als Wissenschaft

wird auftreten können,

von

Immanuel Kant.

Riga,

bey Johann Friedrich Hartknoch.

1783.

PREFACE

These *Prolegomena* are not for the use of pupils but of future teachers, and even the latter should not expect that they will be serviceable for the systematic exposition of a ready-made science, but merely for the discovery of the science itself.

There are scholars for whom the history of philosophy (both ancient and modern) is philosophy itself; for these the present *Prolegomena* are not written. They must wait till those who endeavor to draw from the fountain of reason itself have completed their work; it will then be the turn of such scholars to inform the world of what has been done. Unfortunately, nothing can be said which, in their opinion, has not been said before, and truly the same prophecy applies to all future time; for since the human reason has for many centuries speculated upon innumerable objects in various ways, it is hardly to be expected that we should not be able to discover analogies for every new idea among the old sayings of past ages.

My object is to persuade all those who think metaphysics worth studying that it is absolutely necessary to pause a moment and, disregarding all that has been done, to propose first the preliminary question, "Whether such a thing as metaphysics be at all possible?"

If it is a science, how does it happen that it cannot, like other sciences, obtain universal and permanent recognition? If not, how can it maintain its pretensions and keep the human under- standing in suspense with hopes never ceasing, yet never fulfilled? Whether then we demonstrate our knowledge or our ignorance in this field, we must come once for all to a definite conclusion respecting the nature of this so-called science, which cannot possibly remain on its present footing. It seems almost ridiculous, while every other science is continually advancing, that in this, which pretends to be wisdom incarnate, for whose oracle every one inquires, we should constantly move round the same spot, without gaining a single step. And so its supporters having melted away, we do not find that men who are confident of their ability to shine in other sciences venture their reputation here, where everybody, however ignorant in other matters, presumes to deliver a final verdict, inasmuch as in this domain there is as yet no standard weight and measure to distinguish soundness from shallow talk.

After all, it is nothing extraordinary in the elaboration of a science, when men begin to wonder how far it has advanced, that the question should at last occur as to whether and how in general such a science is possible? Human reason so delights in constructions that it has several times built up a tower and then razed it to examine the nature of the foundation. It is never too late to become reasonable and wise; but if the insight comes late, there is always more difficulty in starting the change.

The question whether a science be possible presupposes a doubt as to its actuality. But such a doubt offends the man whose entire goods may perhaps consist in this supposed jewel; hence he who raises the doubt must expect opposition from all sides. Some, in the proud consciousness of their possessions, which are ancient and therefore considered legitimate, will take their metaphysical compendia in their hands and look down on him with contempt; others who never see anything except it be identical with what they have somewhere else seen before will not understand him, and everything will remain for a time as if nothing had happened to excite the concern or the hope for an impending change.

Nevertheless, I venture to predict that the independent reader of these *Prolegomena* will not only doubt his previous science, but ultimately be fully persuaded that it cannot exist unless the demands here stated on which its possibility depends be satisfied; and, as this has never been done, that there is, as yet, no such thing as metaphysics. But as it can never cease to be in demand[1]—since the interests of human reason in general are

257

1. Says Horace:
   Rusticus expectat, dum defluat amnis, at ille labitur et labetur

intimately interwoven with it—he must confess that a radical reform, or rather a rebirth of the science according to a new plan, is unavoidable, however much men may struggle against it for a while.

Since the *Essays* of Locke and Leibnitz, or rather since the origin of metaphysics so far as we know its history, nothing has ever happened which could have been more decisive to its fate than the attack made upon it by David Hume. He threw no light on this kind of knowledge; but he certainly struck a spark from which light might have been obtained, had it caught some inflammable substance and had its smouldering fire been carefully nursed and developed.

Hume started mainly from a single but important concept in metaphysics, namely, that of the connection of cause and effect (including its derivative concepts of force and action, etc.). He challenged reason, which pretends to have given birth to this concept of herself, to answer him by what right she thinks anything could be so constituted that if that thing be posited, something else also must necessarily be posited; for this is the meaning of the concept of cause. He demonstrated irrefutably that it was entirely impossible for reason to think *a priori* and by means of concepts such a combination as involves necessity. We cannot at all see why, in consequence of the existence of one thing, another must necessarily exist, or how the concept of such a combination can arise *a priori*. Hence he inferred that reason was altogether deluded with reference to this concept, which she erroneously considered as one of her children, whereas in reality it was nothing but a bastard of imagination, impregnated by experience, which subsumed certain representations under the law of association, and mistook a subjective necessity (custom) for an objective necessity arising from insight. Hence he inferred that reason had no power to think such connections, even in general, because her concepts would then be purely fictitious and all her pretended *a priori* cognitions nothing but common experiences marked with a false stamp. This is as much as to say

258

---

in omne volubilis aevum. ["A peasant waits for the river to flow away, but it flows on and will so flow forever."] *Epistle* I, 2, 42f.

that there is not, and cannot be, any such thing as metaphysics at all.[2] However hasty and mistaken Hume's conclusion may appear, it was at least founded upon investigation, and this investigation deserved the concentrated attention of the brighter spirits of his day as well as determined efforts on their part to discover, if possible, a happier solution of the problem in the sense proposed by him, all of which would have speedily resulted in a complete reform of the science. But Hume suffered the usual misfortune of metaphysicians, of not being understood. It is positively painful to see how utterly his opponents, Reid, Oswald, Beattie, and lastly Priestley, missed the point of the problem; for while they were ever taking for granted that which he doubted, and demonstrating with zeal and often with impudence that which he never thought of doubting, they so misconstrued his valuable suggestion that everything remained in its old condition, as if nothing had happened. The question was not whether the concept of cause was right, useful, and even indispensable for our knowledge of nature, for this Hume had never doubted; but whether that con-

259 cept could be thought by reason *a priori,* and consequently whether it possessed an inner truth, independent of all experience, implying a more widely extended usefulness, not limited merely to objects of experience. This was Hume's problem. It was a question concerning the *origin* of the concept, not concerning its indispensability in use. Were the former decided, the conditions of its use and the sphere of its valid application would have been determined as a matter of course.

But to satisfy the conditions of the problem, the opponents of the great thinker should have penetrated very deeply into the

2. Nevertheless Hume called such destructive philosophy metaphysics and attached to it great value. "Metaphysics and morals," he says, "are the most important branches of science; mathematics and natural philosophy are not half so important." [*Essays Moral, Politcal, and Literary* (edited by Green and Grose) vol. I, p. 187. Essay XIV: Of the Rise and Progress of the Arts and Sciences] But the acute man merely regarded the negative use arising from the moderation of extravagant claims of speculative reason, and the complete settlement of the many endless and troublesome controversies that mislead mankind. He overlooked the positive injury which results if reason be deprived of its most important prospects, which can alone supply to the will the highest aim for all its endeavors.

nature of reason, so far as it is concerned with pure thought—a task which did not suit them. They found a more convenient method of being defiant without any insight, viz., the appeal to *common sense*. It is indeed a great gift of heaven to possess right or (as they now call it) plain common sense. But this common sense must be shown in deeds by well-considered and reasonable thoughts and words, not by appealing to it as an oracle when no rational justification of oneself can be advanced. To appeal to common sense when insight and science fail, and no sooner—this is one of the subtle discoveries of modern times, by means of which the most superficial ranter can safely enter the lists with the most thorough thinker and hold his own. But as long as a particle of insight remains, no one would think of having recourse to this subterfuge. Seen in a clear light, it is but an appeal to the opinion of the multitude, of whose applause the philosopher is ashamed, while the popular charlatan glories and confides in it. I should think that Hume might fairly have laid as much claim to common sense as Beattie and, in addition, to a critical reason (such as the latter did not possess), which keeps common sense in check and prevents it from speculating, or, if speculations are under discussion, restrains the desire to decide because it cannot satisfy itself concerning its own principles. By this means alone can common sense remain sound. Chisels and hammers may suffice to work a piece of wood, but for etching we require an etcher's needle. Thus common sense and speculative understanding are both useful, but each in its own 260 way: the former in judgments which apply immediately to experience; the latter when we judge universally from mere concepts, as in metaphysics, where sound common sense, so called in spite of the inappropriateness of the word, has no right to judge at all.

I openly confess that my remembering David Hume was the very thing which many years ago first interrupted my dogmatic slumber and gave my investigations in the field of speculative philosophy a quite new direction. I was far from following him in the conclusions to which he arrived by considering, not the whole of his problem, but a part, which by itself can give us no information. If we start from a well-founded, but undeveloped, thought which another has bequeathed to us, we may well hope by continued reflection to advance further than the acute man to whom we owe the first spark of light.

So I tried first whether Hume's objection could not be put into a general form, and soon found that the concept of the connection of cause and effect was by no means the only concept by which the understanding thinks the connection of things *a priori,* but rather that metaphysics consists altogether of such concepts. I sought to ascertain their number; and when I had satisfactorily succeeded in this by starting from a single principle, I proceeded to the deduction of these concepts, which I was now certain were not derived from experience, as Hume had tried, but sprang from the pure understanding. This deduction (which seemed impossible to my acute predecessor and had never even occured to any one else, though no one had hesitated to use the concepts without investigating the basis of their objective validity) was the most difficult task ever undertaken in the service of metaphysics; and the worst was that metaphysics, such as it then existed, could not assist me in the least because this deduction alone can render metaphysics possible. But as soon as I had succeeded in solving Hume's problem, not merely in a particular case, but with respect to the whole faculty of pure reason, I could proceed safely, though slowly, to determine the whole sphere of pure reason completely and from universal principles, in its boundaries as well as in its contents. This was required for metaphysics in order to construct its system according to a sure plan.

261

But I fear that the working out of Hume's problem in its widest extent (namely, my *Critique of Pure Reason*) will fare as the problem itself fared when first proposed. It will be misjudged because it is misunderstood, and misunderstood because men choose to skim through the book and not to think through it—a disagreeable task, because the work is dry, obscure, opposed to all ordinary notions, and moreover long-winded. Now I confess that I did not expect to hear from philosophers complaints of want of popularity, entertainment, and facility when the existence of a highly prized and indispensable cognition is at stake, which cannot be established otherwise than by the strictest rules of scholarly precision. Popularity may follow, but is inadmissible at the beginning. Yet as regards a certain obscurity, arising partly from the diffuseness of the plan, owing to which the principal points of the investigation are easily lost sight of, the complaint is just, and I intend to remove it by the present *Prolegomena.*

The first-mentioned work, which discusses the pure faculty of reason in its whole extent and bounds, will remain the foundation, to which the *Prolegomena,* as a preliminary exercise, refer; for that critique must exist as a science, systematic and complete as to its smallest parts, before we can think of letting metaphysics appear on the scene, or even have the most distant hope of so doing.

We have been long accustomed to seeing antiquated knowledge produced as new by taking it out of its former context, and fitting it into a systematic dress of any fancy pattern under new titles. Most readers will set out by expecting nothing else from the *Critique;* but these *Prolegomena* may persuade him that it is a perfectly new science, of which no one has ever even thought, the very idea of which was unknown, and for which nothing hitherto accomplished can be of the smallest use, except it be the suggestion of Hume's doubts. Yet even he did not suspect such a formal science, but ran his ship ashore, for safety's sake, landing on scepticism, there to let it lie and rot; whereas my object is rather to give it a pilot who, by means of safe navigational principles drawn from a knowledge of the globe and provided with a complete chart and compass, may steer the ship safely whither he listeth.

262

If in a new science that is wholly isolated and unique in its kind we started with the prejudice that we can judge of things by means of would-be knowledge previously acquired, even though this is precisely what has first to be called in question; then we should only fancy we saw everywhere what we had already known, because the expressions have a similar sound. Yet everything would appear utterly metamorphosed, senseless, and unintelligible, because we should have as a foundation our own thoughts, made by long habit a second nature, instead of the author's. However, the longwindedness of the work, so far as it depends on the science itself and not on the exposition, its consequent unavoidable dryness, and its scholastic precision are qualities which can only benefit the science, though they may discredit the book.

Few writers are gifted with the subtlety and, at the same time, with the grace of David Hume, or with the depth, as well as the elegance, of Moses Mendelssohn. Yet I flatter myself that I might have made my own exposition popular, if my object had been merely to sketch out a plan and leave its completion to others, instead of having my heart in the welfare of the science to which I had devoted myself so long; in truth, it required no little constancy, and even self-denial, to postpone the sweets of an immediate success to the prospect of a slower, but more lasting, reputation.

Making plans is often the occupation of an opulent and boastful mind, which thus obtains the reputation of a creative genius by demanding what it cannot itself supply, by censuring what it 263 cannot improve, and by proposing what it knows not where to find. And yet something more should belong to a sound plan of a general critique of pure reason than mere conjectures, if this plan is to be other than the usual declamations of pious aspirations. But pure reason is a sphere so separate and self-contained that we cannot touch a part without affecting all the rest. We can therefore do nothing without first determining the position of each part and its relation to the rest. For inasmuch as our judgment cannot be corrected by anything outside of pure reason, so the validity and use of every part depends upon the relation in which it stands to all the rest within the domain of reason, just as in the structure of an organized body the end of each member can only be deduced from the full conception of the whole. It may, then, be said of such a critique that it is never trustworthy except it be perfectly complete, down to the smallest elements of pure reason. In the sphere of this faculty you can determine either everything or nothing.

But although a mere sketch preceding the *Critique of Pure Reason* would be unintelligible, unreliable, and useless, it is all the more useful as a sequel which enables us to grasp the whole, to examine in detail the chief points of importance in the science, and to improve in many respects our exposition, as compared with the first execution of the work.

That work being completed, I offer here such a plan which is sketched out after an analytical method, while the *Critique* itself had to be executed in the synthetical style, in order that the science may present all its articulations, as the structure of a peculiar cognitive faculty, in their natural combination. But should any reader find this plan, which I publish as the *Prolegomena to Any Future Metaphysics,* still obscure, let him consider that not every one is bound to study metaphysics, that

many minds will succeed very well in the exact and even in deep
sciences more closely allied to intuition while they cannot succeed in investigations dealing exclusively with abstract concepts.
In such cases men should apply their talents to other subjects.   264
But he who undertakes to judge or, still more, to construct a system of metaphysics must satisfy the demands here made, either
by adopting my solution or by thoroughly refuting it and substituting another. To evade it is impossible. In conclusion, let it
be remembered that this much-abused obscurity (frequently
serving as a mere pretext under which people hide their own
indolence or dullness) has its uses, since all who in other
sciences observe a judicious silence speak authoritatively in metaphysics and make bold decisions, because their ignorance is not
here contrasted with the knowledge of others. Yet it does contrast with sound critical principles, which we may therefore com-
mend in the words of Virgil:

Ignavum, fucos, pecus a praesepibus arcent.[3]

---

3. ["They keep out of the hives the drones, an indolent bunch."] *Georgics,*
IV, 168.

Preamble on the Peculiarities of all
Metaphysical Cognition

§1. OF THE SOURCES OF METAPHYSICS

If it becomes desirable to present any cognition as science, it will be necessary first to determine exactly its differentia, which no other science has in common with it and which constitutes its peculiarity; otherwise the boundaries of all sciences become confused, and none of them can be treated thoroughly according to its nature.

The peculiar features of a science may consist of a simple difference of object, or of the sources of cognition, or of the kind of cognition, or perhaps of all three conjointly. On these features, therefore, depends the idea of a possible science and its territory.

First, as concerns the sources of metaphysical cognition, its very concept implies that they cannot be empirical. Its principles (including not only its basic propositions but also its basic concepts) must never be derived from experience. It must not be physical but metaphysical knowledge, i.e., knowledge lying beyond experience. It can therefore have for its basis neither external experience, which is the source of physics proper, nor internal, which is the basis of empirical psychology. It is therefore *a priori* cognition, coming from pure understanding and 266 pure reason.

But so far metaphysics would not be distinguishable from pure mathematics; it must therefore be called pure philosophical cognition; and for the meaning of this term I refer to the *Critique of Pure Reason* ("Methodology," Chap. I, Sect. 1), where the distinction between these two employments of reason is sufficiently explained. So much for the sources of metaphysical cognition.

§ 2. CONCERNING THE KIND OF COGNITION WHICH CAN ALONE BE CALLED METAPHYSICAL

a. Of the Distinction between Analytic and Synthetic Judgments in General.—The peculiarity of its sources demands that metaphysical cognition must consist of nothing but *a priori* judgments. But whatever be their origin or their logical form, there is a distinction in judgments, as to their content, according to which they are either merely *explicative*, adding nothing to the content of the cognition, or *ampliative*, increasing the given cognition: the former may be called *analytic*, the latter *synthetic*, judgments.

Analytic judgments express nothing in the predicate but what has been already actually thought in the concept of the subject, though not so clearly and with the same consciousness. If I say: "All bodies are extended," I have not amplified in the least my concept of body, but have only analyzed it, as extension was really thought to belong to that concept before the judgment was made, though it was not expressed; this judgment is therefore analytic. On the other hand, this judgment, "Some bodies have weight," contains in its predicate something not actually thought in the universal concept of body; it amplifies my knowledge by adding something to my concept, and must therefore be called synthetic.

267

b. The Common Principle of all Analytic Judgments is that of Contradiction.—All analytic judgments depend wholly on the principle of contradiction, and are in their nature *a priori* cognitions, whether the concepts that supply them with matter be empirical or not. For the predicate of an affirmative analytic judgment is already thought in the concept of the subject, of which it cannot be denied without contradiction. In the same way its opposite is necessarily denied of the subject in an analytic, but negative, judgment, by the same principle of contradiction. Such is the case of the judgments: "All bodies are extended," and "No bodies are unextended (i.e., simple)."

For this very reason all analytic judgments are *a priori* even when the concepts are empirical, as, for example, "Gold is a yellow metal"; for to know this I require no experience beyond my concept of gold, which contained the thought that this body is yellow and metal. It is, in fact, this thought that constituted my concept; and I need only analyze it, without looking beyond it elsewhere.

c. Synthetic Judgments Require a Different Principle from that of Contradiction.—There are synthetic *a posteriori* judgments of empirical origin; but there are also others which are certain *a priori,* and which spring from pure understanding and reason. Yet they both agree in this, that they cannot possibly spring from the principle of analysis, namely, the principle of contradiction, alone, but require another quite different principle. But whatever principle they may be deduced from, they must be subject to the principle of contradiction, which must never be violated, even though everything cannot be deduced from it. I shall first classify synthetic judgments.

1. *Judgments of Experience* are always synthetic. For it would be absurd to base an analytic judgment on experience, as our concept suffices for the purpose without requiring any testimony from experience. That a body is extended is a judgment which holds *a priori,* and is not a judgment of experience. For before appealing to experience, we already have all the conditions for the judgment in the concept, from which we have then but to elicit the predicate according to the principle of contradiction, and thereby to become conscious of the necessity of the judgment, which experience could not at all teach us.

2. *Mathematical Judgments* are all synthetic. This fact seems hitherto to have altogether escaped the observation of those who have analyzed human reason; it even seems directly opposed to all their conjectures, though it is incontestably certain and most important in its consequences. For as it was found that the conclusions of mathematicians all proceed according to the principle of contradiction (as is demanded by all apodeictic certainty), men persuaded themselves that the fundamental propositions were known from the principle of contradiction. This was a great mistake, for a synthetic proposition can indeed be comprehended according to the principle of contradiction, but only by presupposing another synthetic proposition from which it follows, but never in and by itself.

First of all, we must observe that properly mathematical propositions are always judgments *a priori,* and not empirical, because they carry with them necessity, which cannot be obtained

268

from experience. But if this be not conceded to me, very well; I shall confine my assertion to *pure mathematics,* the very concept of which implies that it contains pure *a priori* and not empirical cognition.

It might at first be thought that the proposition $7 + 5 = 12$ is a mere analytic judgment, following from the concept of the sum of seven and five, according to the principle of contradiction. But on closer examination it appears that the concept of the sum of $7 + 5$ contains merely their union in a single number, without its being at all thought what the particular number is that unites them. The concept of twelve is by no means thought by merely 269 thinking of the combination of seven and five; and, analyze this possible sum as we may, we shall not discover twelve in the concept. We must go beyond these concepts by calling to our aid some intuition corresponding to one of them, i.e., either our five fingers or five points (as Segner[4] has it in his *Arithmetic*); and we must add successively the units of the five given in the intuition to the concept of seven. Hence our concept is really amplified by the proposition $7 + 5 = 12$, and we add to the first concept a second one not thought in it. Arithmetical judgments are therefore synthetic, and the more plainly according as we take larger numbers; for in such cases it is clear that, however closely we analyze our concepts without calling intuition to our aid, we can never find the sum by such mere analysis.

Any principle of pure geometry is no less synthetic. That a straight line is the shortest path between two points is a synthetic proposition. For my concept of straight contains nothing of quantity, but only a quality. The concept of the shortest is therefore altogether additional and cannot be obtained by any analysis of the concept of the straight line. Here, too, intuition must come to aid us. It alone makes the synthesis possible.

(Some other principles, assumed by geometers, are indeed actually analytic and depend on the principle of contradiction; but they only serve, as identical propositions, as a method of concatenation, and not as principles, e.g., $a = a$, the whole is equal to itself, or $a + b > a$, the whole is greater than its part. And yet even these, though they are recognized as valid from mere con-

4. [J. A. Segner: *Elementa Arithmeticae et Geometriae*, Göttingen, 1739.]

cepts, are only admitted in mathematics because they can be presented in some intuition.)
What actually makes us believe that the predicate of such apodeictic judgments is already contained in our concept, and that the judgment is therefore analytic, is the duplicity of the expression. We must think a certain predicate as joined to a given concept, and this necessity inheres in the concepts themselves. But the question is not what we must join in thought *to* the given concept, but what we actually think together with and in it, though obscurely; and so it is manifest that the predicate belongs to this concept necessarily indeed, yet not directly but indirectly by means of a necessarily present intuition.[5]

The essential and distinguishing feature of pure mathematical   272
cognition among all other *a priori* cognitions is that it cannot at all proceed from concepts, but only by means of the construction of concepts (see *Critique of Pure Reason,* "Methodology," Chap. I, Sect. 1). As therefore in its judgments it must proceed beyond the concept to that which its corresponding intuition contains, these judgments neither can, nor ought to arise analytically, by dissecting the concept, but are all synthetic.

I cannot refrain from pointing out the disadvantage resulting to philosophy from the neglect of this easy and apparently insignificant observation. Hume, feeling the call (which is worthy of a philosopher) to cast his eye over the whole field of *a priori* cognitions in which human understanding claims such mighty possessions, heedlessly severed from it a whole, and indeed its most valuable, province, viz., pure mathematics. For he imagined that its nature, or, so to speak, the constitution of this province, depended on totally different principles, namely, on the principle of contradiction alone, and although he did not divide judgments in this manner formally and universally and did not use the same terminology as I have done here, what he said was equivalent to this: that pure mathematics contains only analytic, but metaphysics synthetic, *a priori* judgments. In this, however, he was greatly mistaken, and the mistake had a decidedly in-

---

5. [In the next several pages the order of the German text as it appears in the *Philosophische Bibliothek* Edition of Kant's *Works* is followed rather than the *Akademie* Edition.]

jurious effect upon his whole conception. But for this, he would have extended his question concerning the origin of our synthetic judgments far beyond the metaphysical concept of causality and included in it the possibility of mathematics *a priori* also; for this latter he must have assumed to be equally synthetic. And then he could not have based his metaphysical judgments on mere experience without subjecting the axioms of mathematics equally to experience, a thing which he was far too acute to do. The good company into which metaphysics would thus have been brought would have saved it from the danger of a contemptuous ill-treatment; for the thrust intended for it must have reached mathematics, which was not and could not have been Hume's intention. Thus that acute man would have been led into considerations which must needs be similar to those that now occupy us, but which would have gained inestimably from his inimitably elegant style.

[3.] *Metaphysical Judgments,* properly so-called, are all synthetic. We must distinguish judgments belonging to metaphysics from metaphysical judgments properly so-called. Many of the former are analytic, but they only afford the means to metaphysical judgments, which are the whole aim of the science and which are always synthetic. For if there be concepts belonging to metaphysics (as, for example, that of substance), the judgments springing from simple analysis of them also belong to metaphysics, as, for example, substance is that which only exists as subject, etc. By means of several such analytic judgments we seek to arrive at the definition of a concept. But as the analysis of a pure concept of the understanding (such as metaphysics contains) does not proceed in any different manner from the dissection of any other, even empirical, concepts, not belonging to metaphysics (such as, air is an elastic fluid, the elasticity of which is not destroyed by any known degree of cold), it follows that the concept indeed, but not the analytic judgment, is properly metaphysical. This science has something special and peculiar to itself in the production of its *a priori* cognitions, which must therefore be distinguished from the features it has in common with other rational knowledge. Thus the judgment that all the substance in things is permanent is a synthetic and properly metaphysical judgment.

If the *a priori* concepts which constitute the materials and

building blocks of metaphysics have first been collected according to fixed principles, then their analysis will be of great value. It might be taught as a particular part (as a *philosophia definitiva*), containing nothing but analytic judgments pertaining to metaphysics, and could be treated separately from the synthetic,   274
which constitute metaphysics proper. For indeed these analyses are not elsewhere of much value except in metaphysics, i.e., as regards the synthetic judgments which are to be generated out of these previously analyzed concepts.

The conclusion drawn in this section then is that metaphysics is properly concerned with synthetic propositions *a priori*, and these alone constitute its end, for which it indeed requires various dissections of its concepts, viz., analytic judgments, but wherein the procedure is not different from that in every other kind of cognition, in which we merely seek to render our concepts distinct by analysis. But the generation of *a priori* cognition by intuition as well as by concepts, in fine, of synthetic propositions *a priori* in philosophical cognition, constitutes the essential content of metaphysics.

§ 3. A REMARK ON THE GENERAL DIVISION OF JUDGMENTS   270
INTO ANALYTIC AND SYNTHETIC

This division is indispensable as concerns the critique of human understanding and therefore deserves to be classical in it, though otherwise it is of little use. But this is the reason why dogmatic philosophers, who always seek the sources of metaphysical judgments in metaphysics itself and not outside of it in the pure laws of reason generally, altogether neglected this apparently obvious distinction. Thus the celebrated Wolff and his acute follower Baumgarten came to seek the proof of the principle of sufficient reason, which is clearly synthetic, in the principle of contradiction. In Locke's *Essay,* however, I find an indication of my division. For in the fourth book (chap. iii., § 9, seq.), having discussed the various connections of representations in judgments, and their sources, one of which he makes "identity or contradiction" (analytic judgments) and another the coexistence of representations in a subject (synthetic judgments), he confesses (§10) that our (*a priori*) knowledge of the latter is very narrow and almost nothing. But in his remarks on this species of cognition, there is so little of what is definite and reduced to rules that we cannot wonder if no one, not even Hume, was led to make investigations concerning judgments of this kind. For such universal and yet determinate principles are not easily learned from other men who have only had them obscurely in their minds. One must hit on them first by one's own reflection; then one finds them elsewhere, where one could not possibly have found them at first because the authors themselves did not know that such an idea lay at the basis of their observations. Men who never think independently have nevertheless the acuteness to discover everything, after it has been once shown them, in what was said long since, though no one could ever see it there before.

271   § 4. THE GENERAL QUESTION OF THE PROLEGOMENA:
                    IS METAPHYSICS AT ALL POSSIBLE?

Were a metaphysics that could maintain its place as a science really in existence, were we able to say: here is metaphysics, learn it, and it will convince you irresistibly and irrevocably of its truth then the above question would be pointless, and there would only remain that other question (which would rather be a test of our acuteness than a proof of the existence of the thing itself): how is the science possible, and how does reason come to attain it? But human reason has not been so fortunate in this case. There is no single book to which you can point, as you do to Euclid, and say: this is metaphysics; here you may find the noblest aim of this science, namely, the knowledge of a highest being, and of a future existence, proved from principles of pure reason. We can be shown indeed many judgments, apodeictically certain, and never questioned; but these are all analytic, and rather concern the materials and the scaffolding for metaphysics than the extension of knowledge, which is our proper object in studying it (§ 2). Even supposing you point to synthetic judgments (such as the principles of sufficient reason, which you have never proved, as you ought to, from pure reason *a priori*, though we gladly concede its truth), you lapse, when you try to use them for your principal purpose, into such inadmissible and uncertain assertions that in all ages one metaphysics has contradicted another, either in its assertions or their proofs, and thus has itself destroyed its own claim to lasting assent. Nay, the very attempts to set up such a science are the main cause of the early appearance of scepticism, a way of thinking in which reason treats itself with such violence that it could never have arisen save from complete despair of ever satisfying our most important aspirations. For long before men began to inquire into nature methodically, they consulted abstract reason, which had to some extent been exercised by means of ordinary experience; for reason is ever present, while laws of nature must usually be discovered with labor. So metaphysics floated to the surface, like foam, which dissolved the moment it was scooped off. But immediately there appeared a new supply on the surface, to be ever eagerly gathered up by some; while others, instead of seeking in the depths the cause of the phenomenon, thought they showed their wisdom by ridiculing the idle labor of their neighbors.

Weary therefore of dogmatism, which teaches us nothing, and 274 of scepticism, which does not even promise us anything, not even to rest in permitted ignorance; disquieted by the importance of knowledge so much needed; and, lastly, rendered suspicious by long experience of all knowledge which we believe we possess or which offers itself under the title of pure reason— we have left but one critical question upon whose answer depends our future conduct, viz., *is metaphysics at all possible?* But this question must be answered not by sceptical objections to the asseverations of some actual system of metaphysics (for we do not as yet admit such a thing to exist), but from the conception, as yet only problematic, of a science of this sort.

In the *Critique of Pure Reason* I have treated this question synthetically, by making inquiries into pure reason itself and endeavoring in this source to determine the elements as well as the laws of its pure use according to principles. The task is difficult and requires a resolute reader to penetrate by degrees into a system based on no data except reason itself, and which therefore seeks, without resting upon any fact, to unfold knowledge from its original germs. These *Prolegomena,* however, are designed for preparatory exercises; they are intended to point out what must be done in order to make a science actual if it is possible, rather than to expound it. They must therefore rest upon 275 something already known as trustworthy, from which we can set out with confidence and ascend to sources as yet unknown, the discovery of which will not only explain to us what we knew but exhibit a sphere of many cognitions which all spring from the same sources. The method of such *Prolegomena*, especially of those designed as a preparation for future metaphysics, is consequently analytical.

But it happens, fortunately, that though we cannot assume metaphysics to be an actual science, we can say with confidence that certain pure *a priori* synthetic cognitions are actual and given, namely, pure mathematics and pure physics; for both contain propositions which are everywhere recognized as apodeictically certain, partly by mere reason, partly by universal agreement from experience, and yet as independent of experience. We have therefore some, at least uncontested, synthetic knowledge *a priori*, and need not ask *whether* it be possible (for it is actual) but *how* it is possible, in order that we may deduce from the principle which makes the given knowledge possible the possibility of all the rest.

§ 5. THE GENERAL QUESTION: HOW IS COGNITION FROM PURE REASON POSSIBLE?

We have above learned the significant distinction between analytic and synthetic judgments. The possibility of analytic propositions was easily comprehended, being entirely founded on the principle of contradiction. The possibility of synthetic *a posteriori* judgments, of those which are gathered from experience, also requires no special explanation; for experience is nothing but a continual joining together (synthesis) of perceptions. There remain therefore only synthetic propositions *a priori,* of which the possibility must be sought or investigated, because they must depend upon other principles than that of contradiction.

276   But here we need not first establish the possibility of such propositions so as to ask whether they are possible. For there are enough of them which indeed are of undoubted certainty, and as our present method is analytical, we shall start from the fact that such synthetic but purely rational cognition actually exists; but

we must now inquire into the ground of this possibility and ask *how* such cognition is possible, in order that we may, from the principles of its possibility, be enabled to determine the conditions of its use, its sphere, and its limits. The proper problem upon which all depends, when expressed with scholastic precision, is therefore:

How are synthetic propositions *a priori* possible?

For the sake of popularity I have above expressed this problem somewhat differently, as an inquiry into purely rational cognition, which I could do for once without detriment to the desired insight, because, as we have only to do here with metaphysics and its sources, the reader will, I hope, after the foregoing remarks, keep in mind that when we speak of purely rational cognition we do not mean analytic but synthetic cognition.[6]

Metaphysics stands or falls with the solution of this problem; its very existence depends upon it. Let anyone make metaphysical assertions with ever so much plausibility, let him overwhelm us with conclusions; but if he has not first been able to answer this question satisfactorily, I have the right to say: this is all vain, baseless philosophy and false wisdom. You speak through pure reason and claim, as it were, to create cognitions *a priori* not only by dissecting given concepts, but also by asserting connections which do not rest upon the principle of contradiction, and which you believe you conceive quite independently of all experience; how do you arrive at this, and how will you justify such pretensions? An appeal to the consent of the common sense of mankind cannot be allowed, for that is a witness whose authority

277

6. It is unavoidable that as knowledge advances certain expressions which have become classical after having been used since the infancy of science will be found inadequate and unsuitable, and a newer and more appropriate application of the terms will give rise to confusion. [This is the case with the term "analytic."] The analytical method, insofar as it is opposed to the synthetical, is very different from an aggregate of analytic propositions. It signifies only that we start from what is sought, as if it were given, and ascend to the only conditions under which it is possible. In this method we often use nothing but synthetic propositions, as in mathematical analysis, and it were better to term it the regressive method, in contradistinction to the synthetical or progressive. A principal part of logic too is distinguished by the name of analytic, which here signifies the logic of truth in contrast to dialectic, without considering whether the cognitions belonging to it are analytic or synthetic.

depends merely upon rumor. Says Horace:

Quodcunque ostendis mihi sic, incredulus odi.[7]

The answer to this question is as indispensable as it is difficult; and though the principal reason that it was not attempted long ago is that the possibility of the question never occurred to anybody, there is yet another reason, viz., that a satisfactory answer to this one question requires a much more persistent, profound, and painstaking reflection than the most diffuse work on metaphysics, which on its first appearance promised immortality to its author. And every intelligent reader, when he carefully reflects what this problem requires, must at first be struck with its difficulty, and would regard it as insoluble and even impossible did there not actually exist pure synthetic cognitions *a priori*. This actually happened to David Hume, though he did not conceive the question in its entire universality as is done here and as must be done, if the answer is to be decisive for all metaphysics. For how is it possible, says that acute man, that when a concept is given me I can go beyond it and connect with it another which is not contained in it, in such a manner as if the latter *necessarily* belonged to the former? Nothing but experience can furnish us with such connections (thus he concluded from the difficulty which he took to be an impossibility), and all that vaunted necessity or, what is the same thing, all cognition assumed to be *a priori* is nothing but a long habit of accepting something as true, and hence of mistaking subjective necessity for objective.

278 　Should my reader complain of the difficulty and the trouble which I occasion him in the solution of this problem, he is at liberty to solve it himself in an easier way. Perhaps he will then feel under obligation to the person who has undertaken for him a labor of so profound research and will rather be surprised at the facility with which, considering the nature of the subject, the solution has been attained. Yet it has cost years of work to solve the problem in its whole universality (using the term in the mathematical sense, viz., for that which is sufficient for all cases), and finally to exhibit it in the analytical form, as the reader will find it here.

7. ["Whatever is shown me thus, I do not believe and do hate."] *Epistle* II, 3, 188.

All metaphysicians are therefore solemnly and legally suspended from their occupations till they shall have satisfactorily answered the question: *How are synthetic cognitions a priori possible?* For the answer contains the only credentials which they must show when they have anything to offer us in the name of pure reason. But if they do not possess these credentials, they can expect nothing else of reasonable people, who have been deceived so often, than to be dismissed without further ado.

If they, on the other hand, desire to carry on their business, not as a science, but as an art of wholesome persuasion suitable for the common sense of man, they cannot in fairness be prevented from pursuing this trade. They will then speak the modest language of a rational belief; they will grant that they are not allowed even to conjecture, far less to know, anything which lies beyond the bounds of all possible experience, but only to assume (not for speculative use, which they must abandon, but for practical use only) the existence of something that is possible and even indispensable for the guidance of the understanding and of the will in life. In this manner alone can they be called useful and wise men, and the more so as they renounce the title of metaphysicians. For the latter profess to be speculative philosophers; and since, when judgments *a priori* are under discussion, poor probabilities cannot be admitted (for what is declared to be known *a priori* is thereby announced as necessary), such men cannot be permitted to play with conjectures, but their assertions must be either science or else nothing at all. 279

It may be said that the entire transcendental philosophy, which necessarily precedes all metaphysics, is nothing but the complete solution of the problem here propounded, in systematic order and completeness, and that we have hitherto never had any transcendental philosophy. For what goes by its name is properly a part of metaphysics, whereas the former science has first to settle the possibility of the latter and must therefore precede all metaphysics. And it is not surprising that when a whole science, deprived of all help from other sciences and consequently in itself quite new, is required to answer a single question satisfactorily, we should find the answer troublesome and difficult, nay, even shrouded in obscurity.

As we now proceed to this solution according to the analytical method, in which we assume that such cognitions from pure reason actually exist, we can only appeal to two sciences of theoretical cognition (which alone is under consideration here), namely, pure mathematics and pure natural science. For these alone can exhibit to us objects in intuition and consequently (if there should occur in them a cognition *a priori*) can show the truth or conformity of the cognition to the object *in concreto*, that is, its actuality, from which we could proceed to the ground of its possibility by the analytical method. This facilitates our work greatly, for here universal considerations are not only applied to facts, but even start from them, while in a synthetic procedure they must strictly be derived *in abstracto* from concepts.

But in order to ascend from these actual and, at the same time, well-grounded pure cognitions *a priori* to a possible cognition of the kind that we are seeking, viz., to metaphysics as a science, we must comprehend that which occasions it, namely, the mere natural (though not above suspicion as to its truth) cognition *a priori* which lies at the foundation of that science, the elaboration of which without any critical investigation of its possibility is commonly called metaphysics. In a word, we must comprehend the natural conditions of such a science as a part of our inquiry, and thus the transcendental problem will be gradually answered by a division into four questions:

280

all dependent on synthetic a priori judgments

1. *How is pure mathematics possible?*
2. *How is pure natural science possible?*
3. *How is metaphysics in general possible?*
4. *How is metaphysics as a science possible?*

It may be seen that the solution of these problems, though chiefly designed to exhibit the essential content of the *Critique*, has yet something peculiar, which for itself alone deserves attention. This is the search for the sources of given sciences in reason itself, so that its faculty of knowing something *a priori* may by its own deeds be investigated and measured. By this procedure these sciences gain, if not with regard to their contents, yet as to their proper use; and while they throw light on the higher question concerning their common origin, they give, at the same time, an occasion for better explaining their own nature.

FIRST PART OF THE
MAIN TRANSCENDENTAL QUESTION

How is Pure Mathematics Possible?

§ 6. Here is a great and established branch of knowledge, encompassing even now a wonderfully large domain and promising an unlimited extension in the future, and carrying with it thoroughly apodeictical certainty, i.e., absolute necessity, which therefore rests upon no empirical grounds. Consequently it is a pure product of reason, and moreover is thoroughly synthetic. [Here the question arises:] "How then is it possible for human reason to produce such cognition entirely *a priori?*" Does not this faculty [which produces mathematics], as it neither is nor can be based upon experience, presuppose some ground of cognition *a priori,* which lies deeply hidden but which might reveal itself by these its effects, if their first beginnings were but diligently ferreted out?

§ 7. But we find that all mathematical cognition has this 281 peculiarity: it must first exhibit its concept in intuition, and do so *a priori,* in an intuition that is not empirical but pure. Without this mathematics cannot take a single step; hence its judgments are always *intuitive;* whereas philosophy must be satisfied with *discursive* judgments from mere concepts, and though it may illustrate its apodeictic doctrines through intuition, can never derive them from it. This observation on the nature of mathematics gives us a clue to the first and highest condition of its possibility, which is that some pure intuition must form its basis, in which all its concepts can be exhibited or constructed, *in concreto* and yet *a priori.*[8] If we can discover this pure intuition and its possibility, we may thence easily explain how synthetic propositions *a priori* are possible in pure mathematics, and consequently

8. [See *Critique of Pure Reason,* B 741.]

how this science itself is possible. For just as empirical intuition [viz., sense-perception] enables us without difficulty to enlarge the concept which we frame of an object of intuition by new predicates which intuition itself presents synthetically in experience, so pure intuition also does likewise, only with this difference: that in the latter case the synthetic judgment is *a priori* certain and apodeictic, in the former only *a posteriori* and empirically certain, because the *a posteriori* case contains only that which occurs in contingent empirical intuition, but the *a priori* case contains that which must necessarily be discovered in pure intuition. Here intuition, being an intuition *a priori*, is inseparably joined with the concept before all experience or particular perception.

§ 8. But with this step our perplexity seems rather to increase than to lessen. For the question now is, "How is it possible to intuit anything *a priori?*" An intuition is such a representation as would immediately depend upon the presence of the object. Hence it seems impossible to intuit anything *a priori* originally, because intuition would in that event have to take place without either a former or a present object to refer to, and hence could not be intuition. Concepts indeed are such that we can easily form some of them *a priori*, viz., such as contain nothing but the thought of an object in general; and we need not find ourselves in an immediate relation to the object. Take, for instance, the concepts of quantity, of cause, etc. But even these require, in order to be meaningful and significant, certain concrete use— that is, an application to some intuition by which an object of them is given us. But how can the intuition of the object precede the object itself?

§ 9. If our intuition had to be of such a nature as to represent things as they are in themselves, there would not be any intuition *a priori*, but intuition would be always empirical. For I can only know what is contained in the object in itself if it is present and given to me. It is indeed even then inconceivable how the intuition of a present thing should make me know this thing as it is in itself, as its properties cannot migrate into my faculty of representation. But even if this possibility be granted, an intuition of that sort would not take place *a priori*, that is, before the object were presented to me; for without this latter fact no ground of a relation between my representation and the object can be conceived, unless it rested on inspiration. Therefore in one way only can my intuition anticipate the actuality of the object, and be a cognition *a priori*, viz., *if my intuition contains nothing but the form of sensibility, which in me as subject precedes all the actual impressions through which I am affected by objects.* For that objects of sense can only be intuited according to this form of sensibility I can know *a priori.* Hence it follows that propositions which concern this form of sensuous intuition only are possible and valid for objects of the senses; as also, conversely, that intuitions which are possible *a priori* can never concern any other things than objects of our senses.

§ 10. Accordingly, it is only the form of sensuous intuition by which we can intuit things *a priori*, but by which we can know objects only as they *appear* to us (to our senses), not as they are in themselves; and this assumption is absolutely necessary if synthetic propositions *a priori* be granted as possible or if, in case they actually occur, their possibility is to be conceived and determined beforehand.

Now, the intuitions which pure mathematics lays at the foundation of all its cognitions and judgments which appear at once apodeictic and necessary are space and time. For mathematics must first present all its concepts in intuition, and pure mathematics in pure intuition, i.e., it must construct them. If it proceeded in any other way, it would be impossible to make a single step; for mathematics proceeds, not analytically by dissection of concepts, but synthetically, and if pure intuition be wanting there is nothing in which the matter for synthetic judgments *a priori* can be given. Geometry is based upon the pure intuition of space. Arithmetic attains its concepts of numbers by the successive addition of units in time, and pure mechanics especially can attain its concepts of motion only by employing the representation of time. Both representations, however, are merely intuitions; for if we omit from the empirical intuitions of bodies and their alterations (motion) everything empirical, i.e., belonging to sensation, space and time still remain, and are therefore pure intuitions that lie *a priori* at the basis of the empirical. Hence they can never be omitted; but at the same time, by their being pure intuitions *a priori*, they prove that they are mere

283

forms of our sensibility, which must precede all empirical intuition, i.e., perception of actual objects, and in conformity with which objects can be known *a priori* but only as they appear to us.

§ 11. The problem of the present section is therefore solved. Pure mathematics, as synthetic cognition *a priori*, is possible only by referring to no other objects than those of the senses. At the basis of their empirical intuition lies a pure intuition (of space and time), which is *a priori*. This is possible because the latter intuition is nothing but the mere form of sensibility, which precedes the actual appearance of the objects, since in fact it makes them possible. Yet this faculty of intuiting *a priori* concerns not the matter of the appearance (that is, the sensation in it, for this constitutes what is empirical), but its form, viz., space and time. Should any man venture to doubt that both are not determinations of things in themselves but are merely determinations of their relation to sensibility, I should be glad to know how it can be possible to know *a priori* how their intuition will be characterized before we have any acquaintance with them and before they are presented to us. Such, however, is the case with space and time. But this is quite conceivable as soon as both count for nothing more than formal conditions of our sensibility, while the objects count merely as appearance; for then the form of the appearance, i.e., pure intuition, can by all means be represented as proceeding from ourselves, that is, *a priori*.

§ 12. In order to add something by way of illustration and confirmation, we need only watch the ordinary and unavoidably necessary procedure of geometers. All proofs of the complete congruence of two given figures (where the one can in every respect be substituted for the other) ultimately come down to the fact that they may be made to coincide. This is evidently nothing but a synthetic proposition resting upon immediate intuition; and this intuition must be pure and given *a priori*, else the proposition could not hold as apodeictically certain but would have empirical certainty only. In that case it could only be said that it is always found to be so and holds good only as far as our perception reaches. That complete space (which is not itself the boundary of another space) has three dimensions and that space in general cannot have more is based on the proposition that not more than three lines can intersect at right angles in one point.

284

This proposition cannot at all be shown from concepts, but rests   285
immediately on intuition, and indeed on pure intuition *a priori*
because it is apodeictically certain. That we can require a line to
be drawn to infinity (*in indefinitum*) or that a series of changes
(for example, spaces traversed by motion) shall be infinitely
continued presupposes a representation of space and time,
which can only attach to intuition, namely, so far as it in itself is
bounded by nothing, for from concepts it could never be inferred. Consequently, the basis of mathematics actually is pure
intuitions, which make its synthetic and apodeictically valid
propositions possible. Hence our transcendental deduction of
the concepts of space and of time explains at the same time the
possibility of pure mathematics. Without some such deduction
its truth may be granted, but its existence could by no means be
understood, and we must assume "that everything which can be
given to our senses (to the external senses in space and to the
internal sense in time) is intuited by us as it appears to us, not as
it is in itself."

§ 13. Those who cannot yet rid themselves of the notion that
space and time are actual qualities inherent in things in themselves may exercise their acumen on the following paradox.
When they have in vain attempted its solution and are free from
prejudices at least for a few moments, they will suspect that the
reduction of space and time to mere forms of our sensuous
intuition may perhaps be well founded.

If two things are quite equal in all respects as much as can be
ascertained by all means possible, quantitatively and qualitative-
ly, it must follow that the one can in all cases and under all circumstances replace the other, and this substitution would not
occasion the least recognizable difference. This in fact is true of
plane figures in geometry; but some spherical figures exhibit,
notwithstanding a complete internal agreement, such a
difference in their external relation that the one figure cannot
possibly be put in the place of the other. For instance, two
spherical triangles on opposite hemispheres which have an arc of
the equator as their common base may be quite equal, both as   286
regards sides and angles, so that nothing is to be found in either,
if it be described for itself alone and completed, that would not
equally be applicable to both; and yet the one cannot be put in

the place of the other (on the opposite hemisphere). Here, then, is an internal difference between the two triangles; this difference our understanding cannot show to be internal but only manifests itself by external relations in space. But I shall adduce examples, taken from common life, that are more obvious still.

What can be more similar in every respect and in every part more alike to my hand and to my ear than their images in a mirror? And yet I cannot put such a hand as is seen in the mirror in the place of its original; for if this is a right hand, that in the mirror is a left one, and the image or reflection of the right ear is a left one, which never can serve as a substitute for the other. There are in this case no internal differences which our understanding could determine by thinking alone. Yet the differences are internal as the senses teach, for, notwithstanding their complete equality and similarity, the left hand cannot be enclosed in the same bounds as the right one (they are not congruent); the glove of one hand cannot be used for the other. What is the solution? These objects are not representations of things as they are in themselves, and as some pure understanding would cognize them, but sensuous intuitions, that is, appearances, whose possibility rests upon the relation of certain things unknown in themselves to something else, viz., to our sensibility. Space is the form of the external intuition of this sensibility, and the internal determination of any space is possible only by the determination of its external relation to the whole of space, of which it is a part (in other words, by its relation to external sense). That is to say, the part is possible only through the whole, which is never the case with things in themselves as objects of the mere understanding, but can well be the case with mere appearances. Hence the difference between similar and equal things which are not congruent (for instance, helices winding in opposite ways) cannot be made intelligible by any concept, but only by the relation to the right and the left hands, which immediately refers to intuition.

REMARK I

287   Pure mathematics, and especially pure geometry, can only

have objective reality on condition that it refers merely to objects of sense. But in regard to the latter the principle holds good that our sense representation is not a representation of things in themselves, but of the way in which they appear to us. Hence it follows that the propositions of geometry are not determinations of a mere creation of our poetic imagination, which could therefore not be referred with assurance to actual objects; but rather that they are necessarily valid of space, and consequently of all that may be found in space, because space is nothing but the form of all external appearances, and it is this form alone in which objects of sense can be given to us. Sensibility, the form of which is the basis of geometry, is that upon which the possibility of external appearance depends. Therefore these appearances can never contain anything but what geometry prescribes to them. It would be quite otherwise if the senses were so constituted as to represent objects as they are in themselves. For then it would not by any means follow from the representation of space, which with all its properties serves the geometer as an *a priori* foundation, that this foundation together with what is inferred from it must be so in nature. The space of the geometer would be considered a mere fiction, and it would not be credited with objective validity because we cannot see how things must of necessity agree with an image of them which we make spontaneously and previous to our acquaintance with them. But if this image, or rather this formal intuition, is the essential property of our sensibility by means of which alone objects are given to us, and if this sensibility represents not things in themselves but their appearances, then we shall easily comprehend, and at the same time indisputably prove, that all external objects of our world of sense must necessarily coincide in the most rigorous way with the propositions of geometry. This is so because sensibility by means of its form of external intuition (space), with which the geometer is concerned, makes those objects possible as mere appearances. It will always remain a remarkable phenomenon in the history of philosophy that there was a time when even mathematicians who at the same time were philosophers began to doubt, not of the correctness of their geometrical propositions so far as they merely concerned space, but of their objective validity and the applicability to   288 nature of this concept itself and all its geometrical determinations. They showed much concern whether a line in nature might not consist of physical points, and consequently that true space in the object might consist of simple parts, while the space which the geometer has in his mind cannot be such. They did not recognize that this thought space renders possible the physical space, i.e., the extension of matter itself, and that this pure space is not at all a quality of things in themselves but a form of our sensuous faculty of representation, and that furthermore all objects in space are mere appearances, i.e., not things in themselves but representations of our sensuous intuition. But such is the case, for the space of the geometer is exactly the form of sensuous intuition which we find *a priori* in us, and contains the ground of the possibility of all external appearances (according to their form); and the latter must necessarily and most precisely agree with the propositions of the geometer, which he draws not from any fictitious concept but from the subjective basis of all external appearances, viz., sensibility itself. In this and no other way can geometry be made secure as to the undoubted objective reality of its propositions against all the chicaneries of a shallow metaphysics, however strange this may seem to a metaphysics that does not go back to the sources of its concepts.

REMARK II

Whatever is given us as object must be given us in intuition. All our intuition, however, takes place only by means of the senses; the understanding intuits nothing but only reflects. And as we have just shown that the senses never and in no manner enable us to know things in themselves, but only their appearances, which are mere representations of the sensibility, we conclude that "all bodies, together with the space in which they are, must be considered nothing but mere representations in us, and exist nowhere but in our thoughts." Now is not this manifest idealism?

Idealism consists in the assertion that there are none but thinking beings; all other things which we believe are perceived 289 in intuition are nothing but representations in the thinking beings, to which no object external to them in fact corresponds.

On the contrary, I say that things as objects of our senses existing outside us are given, but we know nothing of what they may be in themselves, knowing only their appearances, i.e., the representations which they cause in us by affecting our senses. Consequently, I grant by all means that there are bodies without us, that is, things which, though quite unknown to us as to what they are in themselves, we yet know by the representations which their influence on our sensibility procures us, and which we call bodies. This word merely means the appearance of the thing, which is unknown to us but is not therefore less real. Can this be termed idealism? It is the very contrary.

Long before Locke's time, but assuredly since him, it has been generally assumed and granted without detriment to the actual existence of external things that many of their predicates may be said to belong, not to the things in themselves, but to their appearances, and to have no proper existence outside our representation. Heat, color, and taste, for instance, are of this kind. Now, if I go further and, for weighty reasons, rank as mere appearances also the remaining qualities of bodies, which are called primary—such as extension, place, and, in general, space, with all that which belongs to it (impenetrability or materiality, shape, etc.)—no one in the least can adduce the reason of its being inadmissible. As little as the man who admits colors not to be properties of the object in itself but only to be modifications of the sense of sight should on that account be called an idealist, so little can my doctrine be named idealistic merely because I find that more, nay, *all the properties which constitute the intuition of a body belong merely to its appearance.* The existence of the thing that appears is thereby not destroyed, as in genuine idealism, but it is only shown that we cannot possibly know it by the senses as it is in itself.

I should be glad to know what my assertions must be in order to avoid all idealism. Undoubtedly, I should say that the representation of space is not only perfectly conformable to the relation which our sensibility has to objects—that I have said—but that it is completely like the object—an assertion in which I can find as little meaning as if I said that the sensation of red has a similarity to the property of cinnabar which excites this sensation in me.

290

REMARK III

Hence we may at once dismiss an easily foreseen but futile objection, "that by our admitting the ideality of space and of time the whole sensible world would be turned into mere illusion." After all philosophical insight into the nature of sensuous cognition was spoiled by making the sensibility merely a confused mode of representation, according to which we still know things as they are, but without being able to reduce everything in this our representation to a clear consciousness; whereas on the contrary proof is offered by us that sensibility consists, not in this logical distinction of clearness and obscurity, but in the genetic one of the origin of cognition itself. For sensuous perception represents things not at all as they are, but only the mode in which they affect our senses; and consequently by sensuous perception appearances only, and not things themselves, are given to the understanding for reflection. After this necessary correction, an objection rises from an unpardonable and almost intentional misconception, as if my doctrine turned all the things of the world of sense into mere illusion.

When an appearance is given us, we are still quite free as to how we should judge the matter. The appearance depends upon the senses, but the judgment upon the understanding; and the only question is whether in the determination of the object there is truth or not. But the difference between truth and dreaming is not ascertained by the nature of the representations which are referred to objects (for they are the same in both cases), but by their connection according to those rules which determine the coherence of the representations in the concept of an object, and by ascertaining whether they can subsist together in experience or not. And it is not the fault of the appearances if our cognition 291 takes illusion for truth, i.e., if the intuition, by which an object is given us, is taken for the concept of the thing or even of its existence, which the understanding only can think. The senses represent to us the paths of the planets as now progressive, now retrogressive; and therein is neither falsehood nor truth, because as long as we hold this to be nothing but appearance we do not judge of the objective nature of their motion. But as a false judgment may easily arise when the understanding is not on its guard against this subjective mode of representation being considered objective, we say they appear to move backward; it is not the senses however which must be charged with the illusion, but the understanding, whose province alone it is to make an objective judgment on appearances.

Thus, even if we did not at all reflect on the origin of our representations, whenever we connect our intuitions of sense (whatever they may contain) in space and in time, according to the rules of the coherence of all cognition in experience, illusion or truth will arise according as we are negligent or careful. It is merely a question of the use of sensuous representations in the understanding, and not of their origin. In the same way, if I consider all the representations of the senses, together with their form, space and time, to be nothing but appearances, and space and time to be a mere form of the sensibility, which is not to be met with in objects out of it, and if I make use of these representations in reference to possible experience only, there is nothing in my regarding them as appearances that can lead astray or cause illusion. For all that, they can correctly cohere according to rules of truth in experience. Thus all the propositions of geometry hold good of space as well as of all the objects of the senses, consequently, of all possible experience, whether I consider space as a mere form of the sensibility or as something adhering to the things themselves. In the former case, however, I comprehend how I can know *a priori* these propositions concerning all the objects of external intuition. Otherwise, everything else as regards all possible experience remains just as if I had not departed from the ordinary view.

But if I venture to go beyond all possible experience with my concepts of space and time, which I cannot refrain from doing if I proclaim them qualities inherent in things in themselves (for what should prevent me from letting them hold good of the same things, even though my senses might be different, and unsuited to them?), then a grave error may arise due to illusion, in which I proclaim to be universally valid what is merely a subjective condition of the intuition of things and certain only for all objects of sense, viz., for all possible experience; I would refer this condition to things in themselves, and not limit it to the conditions of experience.

292

My doctrine of the ideality of space and of time, therefore, far from reducing the whole sensible world to mere illusion, is the only means of securing the application of one of the most important cognitions (that which mathematics propounds *a priori*) to actual objects and of preventing its being regarded as mere illusion. For without this observation it would be quite impossible to make out whether the intuitions of space and time, which we borrow from no experience and which yet lie in our representation *a priori*, are not mere phantasms of our brain to which no objects correspond, at least not adequately; and, consequently, whether we have been able to show geometry's unquestionable validity with regard to all the objects of the sensible world just because they are mere appearances.

Secondly, though these my principles make appearances of the representations of the senses, they are so far from turning the truth of experience into mere illusion that they are rather the only means of preventing the transcendental illusion, by which metaphysics has been deceived hitherto and misled into childish efforts of catching at bubbles, because appearances, which are mere representations, were taken for things in themselves. Here originated the remarkable event of the antinomy of reason, which I shall mention later on and which is cancelled by the single observation that appearance, as long as it is employed in experience, produces truth, but the moment it transgresses the bounds of experience, and consequently becomes transcendent, produces nothing but illusion.

293   Inasmuch, therefore, as I leave to things as we obtain them by the senses their actuality and only limit our sensuous intuition of these things to this—that it represents in no respect, not even in the pure intuitions of space and of time, anything more than mere appearance of those things, but never their constitution in themselves—so is this position of mine not a sweeping illusion invented by me for nature. My protestation, too, against all charges of idealism is so valid and clear as even to seem superfluous, were there not incompetent judges who, while they would have an old name for every deviation from their perverse though common opinion and never judge of the spirit of philosophic nomenclature, but cling to the letter only, are ready to put their own conceits in the place of well-defined concepts, and

thereby deform and distort them. I have myself given this my theory the name of transcendental idealism, but that cannot authorize anyone to confound it either with the empirical idealism of Descartes (indeed, his was only an insoluble problem, owing to which he thought every one at liberty to deny the existence of the corporeal world because it could never be proved satisfactorily), or with the mystical and visionary idealism of Berkeley (against which and other similar phantasms, our *Critique* contains the proper antidote). My idealism concerns not the existence of things (the doubting of which, however, constitutes idealism in the ordinary sense), since it never came into my head to doubt it; but it concerns the sensuous representation of things, to which space and time especially belong. Regarding space and time and, consequently, regarding all appearances in general, I have only shown that they are neither things (but are mere modes of representation) nor are they determinations belonging to things in themselves. But the word "transcendental," which for me never means a reference of our cognition to things, but only to our faculty of cognition, was meant to obviate this misconception. Yet rather than give further occasion to it by this word, I now retract it and desire this idealism of mine to be called "critical." But if it be really an objectionable idealism to convert actual things (not appearances) into mere representations, by what name shall we call that which, conversely, changes mere representations into things? It may, I think, be called *dreaming* idealism, in contradistinction to the former, which may be called *visionary* idealism, both of which are to be   294
refuted by my transcendental, or better, *critical* idealism.

SECOND PART OF THE
MAIN TRANSCENDENTAL QUESTION

How is Pure Natural Science Possible?

§ 14. *Nature* is the *existence* of things, so far as it is determined according to universal laws. Should nature signify the existence of things in themselves, we could never cognize it either *a priori* or *a posteriori*. Not *a priori,* for how can we know what belongs to things in themselves, since this never can be done by the dissection of our concepts (in analytic judgments)? For I do not want to know what is contained in my concept of a thing (for that belongs to its logical being), but what in the actuality of the thing is superadded to my concept and by what the thing itself is determined in its existence outside the concept. My understanding and the conditions on which alone it can connect the determinations of things in their existence do not prescribe any rule to things in themselves; these do not conform to my understanding, but it would have to conform to them; they would therefore have to be first given to me in order to gather these determinations from them, wherefore they would not be cognized *a priori.*

A cognition of the nature of things in themselves *a posteriori* would be equally impossible. For if experience is to teach us laws to which the existence of things is subject, these laws, if they refer to things in themselves, would have to refer to them of necessity even outside our experience. But experience teaches us what exists and how it exists, but never that it must necessarily exist so and not otherwise. Experience therefore can never teach us the nature of things in themselves.

§ 15. We nevertheless actually possess a pure natural science in which are propounded, *a priori* and with all the necessity 295 requisite to apodeictic propositions, laws to which nature is subject. I need only call to witness that propaedeutic to natural knowledge which, under the title of universal natural science,[9] precedes all physics (which is founded upon empirical principles). In it we have mathematics applied to appearances, and also merely discursive principles (from concepts),[10] which constitute the philosophical part of the pure cognition of nature. But there is much in it which is not quite pure and independent of empirical sources, such as the concept of *motion,* that of *impenetrability* (upon which the empirical concept of matter rests), that of *inertia,* and many others, which prevent its being called a quite pure [transcendental] natural science. Besides, it only refers to objects of the external senses, and therefore does not give an example of a universal natural science in the strict sense; for such a science must bring nature in general, whether it regards the object of the external senses or that of the internal sense (the object of physics as well as psychology), under universal laws. But among the principles of this universal physics there are a few which actually have the required universality; for instance, the propositions that "substance is permanent," and that "every event is determined by a cause according to constant laws," etc. These are actually universal laws of nature, which subsist completely *a priori.* There is then in fact a pure [transcendental] natural science, and the question arises: how is it possible?

§ 16. The word *nature* assumes yet another meaning, which determines the object, whereas in the former sense it only denotes the conformity to law of the determinations of the existence of things generally. Nature considered *materialiter* is the *totality of all objects of experience.* And with this only are we now concerned; for, besides, things which can never be objects of experience, if they were to be cognized as to their nature, would oblige us to have recourse to concepts whose meaning could never be given *in concreto* (by any example of possible experience). Consequently, we would have to form for ourselves a list of concepts of their nature, the reality whereof (i.e., whether they actually referred to objects or were mere creations of 296 thought) could never be determined. The cognition of what can-

---

9. [Contained in Kant's *Metaphysical Foundations of Natural Science* (1786)]

10. [Rather than intuitive principles, like mathematics]

not be an object of experience would be hyperphysical, and with things hyperphysical we are here not concerned, but only with the cognition of nature, the actuality of which can be confirmed by experience, though this cognition is possible *a priori* and precedes all experience.

§ 17. The formal aspect of nature in this narrower sense is therefore the conformity to law of all the objects of experience and, so far as it is cognized *a priori,* their necessary conformity. But it has just been shown that the laws of nature can never be cognized *a priori* in objects so far as they are considered, not in reference to possible experience, but as things in themselves. And our inquiry here extends, not to things in themselves (the properties of which we pass by), but to things as objects of possible experience, and the totality of these is properly what we here call nature. And now I ask, when the possibility of cognition of nature *a priori* is in question, whether it is better to arrange the problem thus: how can we cognize *a priori* that things as objects of experience necessarily conform to law? or thus: how is it possible to cognize *a priori* the necessary conformity to law of experience itself as regards all its objects generally?

Closely considered, the solution of the question represented in either way amounts, with regard to the pure cognition of nature (which is the point of the question at issue), entirely to the same thing. For the subjective laws, under which alone an empirical cognition of things is possible, hold good of these things as objects of possible experience (not as things in themselves, which are not considered here). Either of the following statements means quite the same: a judgment of perception can never rank as experience without the law that, whenever an event is observed, it is always referred to some antecedent, which it follows according to a universal rule; or else, everything of which experience teaches that it happens must have a cause.

297   It is, however, more convenient to choose the first formula. For we can *a priori* and before all given objects have a cognition of those conditions on which alone experience of them is possible, but never of the laws to which things may in themselves be subject, without reference to possible experience. We cannot, therefore, study the nature of things *a priori* otherwise than by investigating the conditions and the universal (though sub-

jective) laws, under which alone such a cognition as experience (as to mere form) is possible, and we determine accordingly the possibility of things as objects of experience. For if I should choose the second formula and seek the *a priori* conditions under which nature as an object of experience is possible, I might easily fall into error and fancy that I was speaking of nature as a thing in itself, and then move round in endless circles, in a vain search for laws concerning things of which nothing is given me.

Accordingly, we shall here be concerned merely with experience and the universal conditions of its possibility, which are given *a priori*. Thence we shall determine nature as the whole object of all possible experience. I think it will be understood that I here do not mean the rules of the observation of a nature that is already given, for these already presuppose experience. I do not mean how (through experience) we can study the laws of nature; for these would not then be laws *a priori* and would yield us no pure natural science; but [I mean to ask] how the conditions *a priori* of the possibility of experience are at the same time the sources from which all the universal laws of nature must be derived.

§ 18. In the first place we must state that while all judgments of experience are empirical (i.e., have their ground in immediate sense-perception), yet conversely, all empirical judgments are not therefore judgments of experience; but, besides the empirical, and in general besides what is given to sensuous intuition, special concepts must yet be superadded—concepts which have their origin quite *a priori* in the pure understanding, and under which every perception must be first of all subsumed and then by their means changed into experience.

Empirical judgments, so far as they have objective validity, are *judgments of experience;* but those which are only subjectively valid I name mere *judgments of perception.* The latter require no pure concept of the understanding, but only the logical connection of perception in a thinking subject. But the former always require, besides the representation of the sensuous intuition, special *concepts originally generated in the understanding,* which make the judgment of experience objectively valid. 298

All our judgments are at first merely judgments of perception;

they hold good only for us (i.e., for our subject), and we do not till afterwards give them a new reference (to an object) and want that they shall always hold good for us and in the same way for everybody else; for if a judgment agrees with an object, all judgments concerning the same object must likewise agree with one another, and thus the objective validity of the judgment of experience signifies nothing else than its necessary universal validity. And, conversely, if we have reason to hold a judgment to be necessarily universally valid (which never rests on perception, but on the pure concept of the understanding under which the perception is subsumed), we must consider it to be objective also, that is, that it expresses not merely a reference of our perception to a subject, but a quality of the object. For there would be no reason for the judgments of other men necessarily to agree with mine, if it were not the unity of the object to which they all refer and with which they accord; hence they must all agree with one another.

§ 19. Therefore objective validity and necessary universal validity (for everybody) are equivalent concepts, and though we do not know the object in itself, yet when we consider a judgment as universally valid, and hence necessary, we understand it thereby to have objective validity. By this judgment we cognize the object (though it remains unknown as it is in itself) by the universally valid and necessary connection of the given perceptions. As this is the case with all objects of sense, judgments of experience take their objective validity, not from the immediate cognition of the object (which is impossible), but merely from the condition of the universal validity of empirical judgments, which, as already said, never rests upon empirical or, in short, sensuous conditions, but upon a pure concept of the understanding. The object in itself always remains unknown; but when by the concept of the understanding the connection of the representations of the object, which are given by the object to our sensibility, is determined as universally valid, the object is determined by this relation, and the judgment is objective.

To illustrate the matter: when we say, "The room is warm, sugar sweet, and wormwood nasty,"[11] we have only subjectively

11. I freely grant that these examples do not represent such judgments of perception as ever could become judgments of experience, even though a con-

valid judgments. I do not at all expect that I or any other person shall always find it as I now do; each of these sentences only expresses a reference of two sensations to the same subject, i.e., myself, and that only in my present state of perception; consequently, they are not intended to be valid of the object. Such are judgments of perception. Judgments of experience are of quite a different nature. What experience teaches me under certain circumstances, it must always teach me and everybody; and its validity is not limited to the subject nor to its state at a particular time. Hence I pronounce all such judgments as being objectively valid. For instance, when I say the air is elastic, this judgment is as yet a judgment of perception only—I do nothing but refer two sensations in my senses to one another. But if I would have it called a judgment of experience, I require this connection to stand under a condition which makes it universally valid. I desire therefore that I and everybody else should always necessarily connect the same perceptions under the same circumstances.

§ 20. We must therefore analyze experience in general in   300 order to see what is contained in this product of the senses and of the understanding, and how the judgment of experience itself is possible. The foundation is the intuition of which I become conscious, i.e., perception *(perceptio)*, which pertains merely to the senses. But in the next place, there is judging (which belongs only to the understanding). But this judging may be twofold: first, I may merely compare perceptions and connect them in a consciousness of my state; or, secondly, I may connect them in consciousness in general. The former judgment is merely a judgment of perception and is of subjective validity only; it is merely a connection of perceptions in my mental state, without reference to the object. Hence it is not, as is commonly imagined, enough for experience to compare perceptions and connect

---

cept of the understanding were superadded, because they refer merely to feeling, which everybody knows to be merely subjective and which, of course, can never be attributed to the object and, consequently, never can become objective. I only wished to give here an example of a judgment that is merely subjectively valid, containing no ground for necessary universal validity and thereby for a relation to the object. An example of the judgments of perception which become judgments of experience by superadded concepts of the understanding will be given in the next note.

them in consciousness through judgment; there arises no universal validity and necessity, by virtue of which alone consciousness can become objectively valid and be called experience.

Quite another judgment therefore is required before perception can become experience. The given intuition must be subsumed under a concept which determines the form of judging in general with regard to the intuition, connects the empirical consciousness of the intuition in consciousness in general, and thereby procures universal validity for empirical judgments. A concept of this nature is a pure *a priori* concept of the understanding, which does nothing but determine for an intuition the general way in which it can be used for judging. Let the concept be that of cause; then it determines the intuition which is subsumed under it, e.g., that of air, with regard to judging in general, viz., the concept of air as regards its expansion serves in the relation of antecedent to consequent in a hypothetical judgment. The concept of cause accordingly is a pure concept of the understanding, which is totally disparate from all possible perception and only serves to determine the representation contained under it with regard to judging in general, and so to make a universally valid judgment possible.

301 Before, therefore, a judgment of perception can become a judgment of experience, it is requisite that the perception should be subsumed under some such concept of the understanding; for instance, air belongs under the concept of cause, which determines our judgment about it with regard to its expansion as hypothetical.[12] Thereby the expansion of the air is represented, not as merely belonging to the perception of the air in my present state or in several states of mine, or in the state of perception of others, but as belonging to it necessarily. The judgment that air is elastic becomes universally valid and a judgment of experience only because certain judgments precede it which subsume

12. As an easier example, we may take the following: when the sun shines on the stone, it grows warm. This judgment, however often I and others may have perceived it, is a mere judgment of perception and contains no necessity; perceptions are only usually conjoined in this manner. But if I say: the sun warms the stone, I add to the perception a concept of the understanding, viz., that of cause, which necessarily connects with the concept of sunshine that of heat, and the synthetic judgment becomes of necessity universally valid, viz., objective, and is converted from a perception into experience.

the intuition of air under the concepts of cause and effect; and they thereby determine the perceptions, not merely as regards one another in me, but as regards the form of judging in general (which is here hypothetical), and in this way they render the empirical judgment universally valid.

If all our synthetic judgments are analyzed so far as they are objectively valid, it will be found that they never consist of mere intuitions connected only (as is commonly supposed) by comparison into a judgment; but that they would be impossible were not a pure concept of the understanding superadded to the concepts abstracted from intuition, under which pure concept these latter concepts are subsumed and in this manner only combined into an objectively valid judgment. Even the judgments of pure mathematics in their simplest axioms are not exempt from this condition. The principle that a straight line is the shortest distance between two points presupposes that the line is subsumed under the concept of quantity, which certainly is no mere intuition but has its seat in the understanding alone and serves to determine the intuition (of the line) with regard to the judgments which may be made about it in respect to the quantity, that is, to plurality (as *judica plurativa*.)[13] For under them it is understood that in a given intuition there is contained a plurality of homogeneous parts.

§ 21. To prove, then, the possibility of experience so far as it rests upon pure *a priori* concepts of the understanding, we must first represent what belongs to judgments in general and the various moments (functions) of the understanding in them, in a complete table. For the pure concepts of the understanding must run parallel to these moments, inasmuch as such concepts are nothing more than concepts of intuitions in general, so far as these are determined by one or other of these moments of judging, in themselves, i.e., necessarily and universally. Hereby also

302

13. This name seems preferable to the term *particularia*, which is used for these judgments in logic. For the latter already contains the thought that they are not universal. But when I start from unity (in singular judgments) and proceed to totality, I must not [even indirectly and negatively] include any reference to totality. I think plurality merely without totality, and not the exclusion of totality. This is necessary, if the logical moments are to underlie the pure concepts of the understanding. In logical usage one may leave things as they were.

the *a priori* principles of the possibility of all experience, as objectively valid empirical cognition, will be precisely determined. For they are nothing but propositions which subsume all perception (conformably to certain universal conditions of intuition) under those pure concepts of the understanding.

LOGICAL TABLE OF JUDGMENTS

1	2
As to Quantity	*As to Quality*
Universal	Affirmative
Particular	Negative
Singular	Infinite

3	4
As to Relation	*As to Modality*
Categorical	Problematic
Hypothetical	Assertoric
Disjunctive	Apodeictic

303

TRANSCENDENTAL TABLE OF THE CONCEPTS OF THE UNDERSTANDING

1	2
As to Quantity	*As to Quality*
Unity (Measure)	Reality
Piurality (Quantity)	Negation
Totality (Whole)	Limitation

3	4
As to Relation	*As to Modality*
Substance	Possibility
Cause	Existence
Community	Necessity

PURE PHYSIOLOGICAL[14] TABLE OF THE UNIVERSAL
PRINCIPLES OF NATURAL SCIENCE

1 Axioms of Intuition	2 Anticipations of Perception
3 Analogies of Experience	4 Postulates of Empirical Thought in General

§ 21a. In order to comprise the whole matter in one idea, it is   304
first necessary to remind the reader that we are discussing, not
the origin of experience, but what lies in experience. The former
pertains to empirical psychology and would even then never be
adequately developed without the latter, which belongs to the
critique of cognition, and particularly of the understanding.

Experience consists of intuitions, which belong to the sensibility, and of judgments, which are entirely a work of the understanding. But the judgments which the understanding makes
entirely out of sensuous intuitions are far from being judgments
of experience. For in the one case the judgment connects only
the perceptions as they are given in sensuous intuition, while in
the other the judgments must express what experience in general and not what the mere perception (which possesses only subjective validity) contains. The judgment of experience must
therefore add to the sensuous intuition and its logical connection
in a judgment (after it has been rendered universal by comparison) something that determines the synthetic judgment as
necessary and therefore as universally valid. This can be nothing
but that concept which represents the intuition as determined in
itself with regard to one form of judgment rather than another,
viz., a concept of that synthetic unity of intuitions which can
only be represented by a given logical function of judgments.

14. [See last sentence of § 23.]

§ 22. The sum of the matter is this: the business of the senses is to intuit, that of the understanding is to think. But thinking is uniting representations in a consciousness. This unification originates either merely relative to the subject and is contingent and subjective, or it happens absolutely and is necessary or objective. The uniting of representations in a consciousness is judgment. Thinking therefore is the same as judging, or referring representations to judgments in general. Hence judgments are either merely subjective when representations are referred to a consciousness in one subject only and are united in it, or they are objective when they are united in a consciousness in general, that is, necessarily. The logical moments of all judgments are so many possible ways of uniting representations in consciousness. But if they serve as concepts, they are concepts of the necessary unification of representations in a consciousness and so are principles of objectively valid judgments. This uniting in a consciousness is either analytic by identity, or synthetic by the combination and addition of various representations one to another. Experience consists in the synthetic connection of appearances (perceptions) in consciousness, so far as this connection is necessary. Hence the pure concepts of the understanding are those under which all perceptions must first be subsumed before they can serve for judgments of experience, in which the synthetic unity of the perceptions is represented as necessary and universally valid.[15]

305

§ 23. Judgments, when considered merely as the condition of the unification of given representations in a consciousness, are

15. But how does the proposition that judgments of experience contain necessity in the synthesis of perceptions agree with my statement so often before inculcated that experience, as cognition *a posteriori,* can afford contingent judgments only? When I say that experience teaches me something, I mean only the perception that lies in experience—for example, that heat always follows the shining of the sun on a stone; consequently, the proposition of experience is always so far contingent. That this heat necessarily follows the shining of the sun is contained indeed in the judgment of experience (by means of the concept of cause), yet is a fact not learned by experience; for, conversely, experience is first of all generated by this addition of the concept of the understanding (of cause) to perception. How perception attains this addition may be seen by referring in the *Critique* itself to the section on the transcendental faculty of judgment, B 176 *et seq.*

rules. These rules, so far as they represent the unification as necessary, are rules *a priori,* and so far as they cannot be deduced from higher rules, are principles. But in regard to the possibility of all experience, merely in relation to the form of thinking in it, no conditions of judgments of experience are higher than those which bring the phenomena, according to the different form of their intuition, under pure concepts of the understanding, and   306 render the empirical judgments objectively valid. These are therefore the *a priori* principles of possible experience.

The principles of possible experience are then at the same time universal laws of nature, which can be cognized *a priori.* And thus the problem in our second question: How is pure natural science possible? is solved. For the systematization which is required for the form of a science is to be met with in perfection here, because, beyond the above-mentioned formal conditions of all judgments in general and of all rules in general, that are offered in logic, no others are possible, and these constitute a logical system. The concepts grounded thereupon, which contain the *a priori* conditions of all synthetic and necessary judgments, accordingly constitute a transcendental system. Finally, the principles by means of which all appearances are subsumed under these concepts constitute a physiological system, that is, a system of nature, which precedes all empirical cognition of nature, first makes it possible, and hence may in strictness be called the universal and pure natural science.

§ 24. The first[16] of the physiological principles[17] subsumes all appearances, as intuitions in space and time, under the concept of *quantity,* and is so far a principle of the application of mathematics to experience. The second[18] subsumes the strictly empirical element, viz., sensation, which denotes the real in intuitions, not indeed directly under the concept of *quantity,* because sensation is not an intuition that *contains* either space or time, though

16. The three following paragraphs will hardly be understood unless reference be made to what the *Critique* itself says on the subject of the principles; they will, however, be of service in giving a general view of the principles, and in fixing the attention on the main moments. [See *Critique,* B 187–294.]

17. [The Axioms of Intuition. See *Critique,* B 202–207.]

18. [The Anticipations of Perception. See *ibid.,* B 207–218.]

it puts the object corresponding to sensation in both space and time. But still there is between reality (sense-representation) and zero, or total lack of intuition in time, a difference which has a quantity. For between any given degree of light and darkness, between any degree of heat and complete cold, between any degree of weight and absolute lightness, between any degree of 307 occupied space and of totally empty space, ever smaller degrees can be thought, just as even between consciousness and total unconsciousness (psychological darkness) ever smaller degrees obtain. Hence there is no perception that can show an absolute absence; for instance, no psychological darkness that cannot be regarded as a consciousness only surpassed by a stronger consciousness. This occurs in all cases of sensation; and so the understanding can anticipate sensations, which constitute the peculiar quality of empirical representations (appearances), by means of the principle that they all have a degree, consequently, that what is real in all appearance has a degree. Here is the second application of mathematics (*mathesis intensorum*) to natural science.

§ 25. As regards the relation of appearances merely with a view to their existence, the determination is not mathematical but dynamical, and can never be objectively valid and fit for experience, if it does not come under *a priori* principles[19] by which the cognition of experience relative to appearances first becomes possible. Hence appearances must be subsumed under the concept of substance, which as a concept of the thing itself is the foundation of all determination of existence; or, secondly—so far as a succession is found among appearances, that is, an event—under the concept of an effect with reference to cause; or, lastly—so far as coexistence is to be known objectively, that is, by a judgment of experience—under the concept of community (action and reaction). Thus *a priori* principles form the basis of objectively valid, though empirical, judgments—that is, of the possibility of experience so far as it must connect objects as existing in nature. These principles are properly the laws of nature, which may be called dynamical.

Finally[20] the cognition of the agreement and connection, not

19. [The Analogies of Experience. See *ibid.,* B 218–265.]

20. [The Postulates of Empirical Thought. See *ibid.,* B 265–294.]

only of appearances among themselves in experience, but of
their relation to experience in general, belongs to judgments of
experience. This relation contains either their agreement with
the formal conditions which the understanding cognizes, or their
coherence with the material of the senses and of perception, or   308
combines both into one concept and consequently contains possibility, actuality, and necessity according to universal laws of
nature. This would constitute the physiological doctrine of
method (distinction between truth and hypotheses, and the
bounds of the reliability of the latter).

§ 26. The third table of principles drawn from the nature of
the understanding itself according to the critical method shows
an inherent perfection, which raises it far above every other
table which has hitherto, though in vain, been tried or may yet
be tried by analyzing the objects themselves dogmatically. It exhibits all synthetic *a priori* principles completely and according to
one principle, viz., the faculty of judging in general, which constitutes the essence of experience as regards the understanding,
so that we can be certain that there are no more such principles.
This affords a satisfaction such as can never be attained by the
dogmatic method. Yet this is not all; there is a still greater merit
in it.

We must carefully bear in mind the ground of proof which
shows the possibility of this cognition *a priori* and, at the same
time, limits all such principles to a condition which must never
be lost sight of, if they are not to be misunderstood and extended in use beyond what is allowed by the original sense which
the understanding places in them. This limit is that they contain
nothing but the conditions of possible experience in general so
far as it is subjected to laws *a priori*. Consequently, I do not say
that things *in themselves* possess a quantity, that their reality
possesses a degree, their existence a connection of accidents in a
substance, etc. This nobody can prove, because such a synthetic
connection from mere concepts, without any reference to sensuous intuition on the one side or connection of such intuition
in a possible experience on the other, is absolutely impossible.
The essential limitation of the concepts in these principles, then,
is that all things stand necessarily *a priori* under the aforementioned conditions only *as objects of experience*.

Hence there follows, secondly, a specifically peculiar mode of proof of these principles; they are not directly referred to appearances and to their relation, but to the possibility of experience, of which appearances constitute the matter only, not the form. Thus they are referred to objectively and universally valid synthetic propositions, in which we distinguish judgments of experience from those of perception. This takes place because appearances, as mere intuitions *occupying a part of space and time,* come under the concept of quantity, which synthetically unites their multiplicity *a priori* according to rules. Again, insofar as the perception contains, besides intuition, sensation, and between the latter and nothing (i.e., the total disappearance of sensation), there is an ever-decreasing transition, it is apparent that the real in appearances must have a degree, so far as it (viz., the sensation) *does not itself occupy any part of space or of time.*[21] Still the transition to sensation from empty time or empty space is only possible in time. Consequently, although sensation, as the quality of empirical intuition in respect of its specific difference from other sensations, can never be cognized *a priori,* yet it can, in a possible experience in general, as a quantity of perception be intensively distinguished from every other similar perception. Hence the application of mathematics to nature, as regards the sensuous intuition by which nature is given to us, is first made possible and determined.

Above all, the reader must pay attention to the mode of proof of the principles which occur under the title of Analogies of Experience. For these do not refer to the generation of intuitions, as do the principles of applying mathematics to natural science in general, but to the connection of their existence in experience; and this can be nothing but the determination of their existence

---

21. Heat and light are in a small space just as large, as to degree, as in a large one; in like manner the internal representations, pain, consciousness in general, whether they last a short or a long time, need not vary as to the degree. Hence the quantity is here in a point and in a moment just as great as in any space or time, however great. Degrees are thus quantities not in intuition but in mere sensation (or the quantity of the content of an intuition). Hence they can only be estimated quantitatively by the relation of 1 to 0, viz., by their capability of decreasing by infinite intermediate degrees to disappearance, or of increasing from naught through infinite gradations to a determinate sensation in a certain time. *Quantitas qualitatis est gradus* [the quantity of quality is degree].

in time according to necessary laws, under which alone the connection is objectively valid and thus becomes experience. The proof, therefore, does not turn on the synthetic unity in the connection of things in themselves, but merely of perceptions, and of these, not in regard to their content, but to the determination of time and of the relation of their existence in it according to universal laws. If the empirical determination in relative time is indeed to be objectively valid (i.e., experience), these universal laws thus contain the necessity of the determination of existence in time generally (viz., according to a rule of the understanding *a priori*). Since these are prolegomena I cannot further descant on the subject, but my reader (who has probably long been accustomed to consider experience as a mere empirical synthesis of perceptions, and hence has not considered that it goes much beyond them since it imparts to empirical judgments universal validity, and for that purpose requires a pure and *a priori* unity of the understanding) is recommended to pay special attention to this distinction of experience from a mere aggregate of perceptions and to judge the mode of proof from this point of view.

§ 27. Now we are prepared to remove Hume's doubt. He justly maintains that we cannot comprehend by reason the possibility of causality, that is, of the reference of the existence of one thing to the existence of another which is necessitated by the former. I add that we comprehend just as little the concept of subsistence, that is, the necessity that at the foundation of the existence of things there lies a subject which cannot itself be a predicate of any other thing; nay, we cannot even form a concept of the possibility of such a thing (though we can point out examples of its use in experience). The very same incomprehensibility affects the community of things, as we cannot comprehend how from the state of one thing an inference to the state of quite another thing beyond it, and *vice versa,* can be drawn, and how substances which have each their own separate existence should depend upon one another necessarily. But I am very far from holding these concepts to be derived merely from   311
experience, and the necessity represented in them to be fictitious and a mere illusion produced in us by long habit. On the contrary, I have amply shown that they and the principles derived from them are firmly established *a priori* before all expe-

rience and have their undoubted objective rightness, though only with regard to experience.

§ 28. Though I have no conception of such a connection of things in themselves, how they can either exist as substances, or act as causes, or stand in community with others (as parts of a real whole) and I can just as little think such properties in appearances as such (because those concepts contain nothing that lies in the appearances, but only what the understanding alone must think), we have yet a concept of such a connection of representations in our understanding and in judgments generally. This is the concept that representations belong in one sort of judgments as subject in relation to predicates; in another as ground in relation to consequent; and, in a third, as parts which constitute together a total possible cognition. Further we know *a priori* that without considering the representation of an object as determined with regard to one or the other of these moments, we can have no valid cognition of the object; and, if we should occupy ourselves with the object in itself, there is not a single possible attribute by which I could know that it is determined with regard to one or the other of these moments, that is, belonged under the concept of substance, or of cause, or (in relation to other substances) of community, for I have no conception of the possibility of such a connection of existence. But the question is not how things in themselves but how the empirical cognition of things is determined, as regards the above moments of judgments in general, that is, how things, as objects of experience, can and must be subsumed under these concepts of the understanding. And then it is clear that I completely comprehend, not only the possibility, but also the necessity, of subsuming all appearances under these concepts, that is, of using them as principles of the possibility of experience.

312   § 29. In order to put to a test Hume's problematic concept (his *crux metaphysicorum*), the concept of cause, we have, in the first place, given *a priori* by means of logic the form of a conditional judgment in general, i.e., we have one given cognition as antecedent and another as consequent. But it is possible that in perception we may meet with a rule of relation which runs thus: that a certain appearance is constantly followed by another (though not conversely); and this is a case for me to use the

hypothetical judgment and, for instance, to say that if the sun shines long enough upon a body it grows warm. Here there is indeed as yet no necessity of connection, or concept of cause. But I proceed and say that if this proposition, which is merely a subjective connection of perceptions, is to be a judgment of experience, it must be regarded as necessary and universally valid. Such a proposition would be that the sun is by its light the cause of heat. The empirical rule is now considered as a law, and as valid not merely of appearances but valid of them for the purposes of a possible experience which requires universal and therefore necessarily valid rules. I therefore easily comprehend the concept of cause as a concept necessarily belonging to the mere form of experience, and its possibility as a synthetic unification of perceptions in a consciousness in general; but I do not at all comprehend the possibility of a thing in general as a cause, inasmuch as the concept of cause denotes a condition not at all belonging to things, but to experience. For experience can only be an objectively valid cognition of appearances and of their succession, only so far as the antecedent appearances can be conjoined with the consequent ones according to the rule of hypothetical judgments.

§ 30. Hence if the pure concepts of the understanding try to go beyond objects of experience and be referred to things in themselves *(noumena),* they have no meaning whatever. They serve, as it were, only to spell out appearances, so that we may be able to read them as experience. The principles which arise from their reference to the sensible world only serve our understanding for use in experience. Beyond this they are arbitrary combinations without objective reality; and we can neither cognize their possibility *a priori,* nor verify their reference to objects, let alone make such reference understandable, by any example, because examples can only be borrowed from some possible experience, and consequently the objects of these concepts can be found nowhere but in a possible experience. 313

This complete (though to its originator unexpected) solution of Hume's problem rescues for the pure concepts of the understanding their *a priori* origin and for the universal laws of nature their validity as laws of the understanding, yet in such a way as to limit their use to experience, because their possibility depends solely on the reference of the understanding to experience, but with a completely reversed mode of connection which never occured to Hume: they are not derived from experience, but experience is derived from them.

This is, therefore, the result of all our foregoing inquiries: "All synthetic principles *a priori* are nothing more than principles of possible experience" and can never be referred to things in themselves, but only to appearances as objects of experience. And hence pure mathematics as well as pure natural science can never be referred to anything more than mere appearances, and can only represent either that which makes experience in general possible, or else that which, as it is derived from these principles, must always be capable of being represented in some possible experience.

§ 31. And thus we have at last something determinate upon which to depend in all metaphysical enterprises, which have hitherto, boldly enough but always at random, attempted everything without discrimination. That the goal of their exertions should be set up so close struck neither the dogmatic thinkers nor those who, confident in their supposed sound common sense, started with concepts and principles of pure reason (which were legitimate and natural, but destined for mere empirical use) in search of insights for which they neither knew nor could 314 know any determinate bounds, because they had never reflected nor were able to reflect on the nature or even on the possibility of such a pure understanding.

Many a naturalist of pure reason (by which I mean the man who believes he can decide in matters of metaphysics without any science) may pretend that he, long ago, by the prophetic spirit of his sound sense, not only suspected but knew and comprehended what is here propounded with so much ado, or, if he likes, with prolix and pedantic pomp: "that with all our reason we can never reach beyond the field of experience." But when he is questioned about his rational principles individually, he must grant that there are many of them which he has not taken from experience and which are therefore independent of it and valid *a priori*. How then and on what grounds will he restrain both himself and the dogmatist, who makes use of these concepts and principles beyond all possible experience because they are recognized to be independent of it? And even he, this adept in sound sense, in spite of all his assumed and cheaply acquired wisdom, is not exempt from wandering inadvertently beyond objects of experience into the field of chimeras. He is often deeply enough involved in them, though in announcing everything as mere probability, rational conjecture, or analogy, he gives by his popular language a color to his groundless pretensions.

§ 32. Since the oldest days of philosophy, inquirers into pure reason have thought that, besides the things of sense, or appearances *(phenomena)*, which make up the sensible world, there were certain beings of the understanding *(noumena)*, which should constitute an intelligible world. And as appearance and illusion were by those men identified (a thing which we may well excuse in an undeveloped epoch), actuality was only conceded to the beings of the understanding.

And we indeed, rightly considering objects of sense as mere appearances, confess thereby that they are based upon a thing in itself, though we know not this thing as it is in itself but only 315
know its appearances, viz., the way in which our senses are affected by this unknown something. The understanding therefore, by assuming appearances, grants also the existence of things in themselves, and thus far we may say that the representation of such things as are the basis of appearances, consequently of mere beings of the understanding, is not only admissible but unavoidable.

Our critical deduction by no means excludes things of that sort *(noumena)*, but rather limits the principles of the Aesthetic[22] in such a way that they shall not extend to all things (as everything would then be turned into mere appearance) but that they shall hold good only of objects of possible experience. Hereby, then, beings of the understanding are admitted, but with the inculcation of this rule which admits of no exception: that we neither know nor can know anything determinate whatever about these pure beings of the understanding, because our pure concepts of the understanding as well as our pure intuitions extend to

22. [The principles of sensibility (space and time). See *Critique of Pure Reason,* B 33-B 73.]

nothing but objects of possible experience, consequently to mere things of sense; and as soon as we leave this sphere, these concepts retain no meaning whatever.

§ 33. There is indeed something seductive in our pure concepts of the understanding which tempts us to a transcendent use—a use which transcends all possible experience. Not only are our concepts of substance, of power, of action, of reality, and others, quite independent of experience, containing nothing of sense appearance, and so apparently applicable to things in themselves *(noumena)*, but, what strengthens this conjecture, they contain a necessity of determination in themselves, which experience never attains. The concept of cause contains a rule according to which one state follows another necessarily; but experience can only show us that one state of things often or, at most, commonly follows another, and therefore affords neither strict universality nor necessity.

Hence concepts of the understanding seem to have a deeper meaning and content than can be exhausted by their merely empirical use, and so the understanding inadvertently adds for itself to the house of experience a much more extensive wing which it fills with nothing but beings of thought, without ever observing that it has transgressed with its otherwise legitimate concepts the bounds of their use.

316

§ 34. Two important and even indispensable, though very dry, investigations therefore became indispensable in the *Critique of Pure Reason* [viz., the two chapters "The Schematism of the Pure Concepts of the Understanding" and "The Ground of the Distinction of All Objects in General into Phenomena and Noumena"]. In the former there is shown that the senses furnish, not the pure concepts of the understanding *in concreto,* but only the schema for their use, and that the object conformable to it occurs only in experience (as the product of the understanding from materials of sensibility). In the latter there is shown that, although our pure concepts of the understanding and our principles are independent of experience, and despite the apparently greater sphere of their use, still nothing whatever can be thought by them beyond the field of experience, because they can do nothing but merely determine the logical form of the judgment with regard to given intuitions. But as there is no intuition at all beyond the field of sensibility, these pure concepts, since they cannot possibly be exhibited *in concreto,* are void of all meaning; consequently all these *noumena,* together with their sum total, the intelligible world,[23] are nothing but representations of a problem, the object of which in itself is quite possible but the solution, from the nature of our understanding, totally impossible. For our understanding is not a faculty of intuition but of the connection of given intuitions in an experience. Experience must therefore contain all the objects for our concepts; but 317 beyond it no concepts have any meaning, since no intuition can be subsumed under them.

§ 35. The imagination may perhaps be forgiven for occasional vagaries and for not keeping carefully within the limits of experience, since it gains life and vigor by such flights and since it is always easier to moderate its boldness than to stimulate its languor. But the understanding which ought to *think* can never be forgiven for indulging in vagaries; for we depend upon it alone for assistance to set bounds, when necessary, to the vagaries of the imagination.

But the understanding begins its aberrations very innocently and modestly. It first discerns the elementary cognitions which inhere in it prior to all experience, but yet must always have their application in experience. It gradually drops these limits; and what is there to prevent it, inasmuch as it has quite freely derived its principles from itself? And then it proceeds first to newly thought out forces in nature, then to beings outside nature—in short, to a world for whose construction the materials cannot be wanting, because fertile fiction furnishes them abundantly, and though not confirmed is yet never refuted by

23. We speak of the "intelligible world," not (as the usual expression is) "intellectual world." For cognitions are intellectual through the understanding and refer to our world of sense also; but objects, insofar as they can be represented merely by the understanding, and to which none of our sensible intuitions can refer, are termed "intelligible." But as some possible intuition must correspond to every object, we would have to think an understanding that intuits things immediately; but of such we have not the least concept, nor of *beings of the understanding* to which it should be applied.

experience. This is the reason why young thinkers are so partial to metaphysics in the truly dogmatical manner, and often sacrifice to it their time and their talents, which might be otherwise better employed.

But there is no use in trying to moderate these fruitless endeavors of pure reason by all manner of cautions as to the difficulties of solving questions so occult, by complaints of the limits of our reason, and by degrading our assertions into mere conjectures. For if their impossibility is not distinctly shown, and reason's knowledge of itself does not become a true science, in which the field of its right use is distinguished, so to say, with geometrical certainty from that of its worthless and idle use, these fruitless efforts will never be entirely abandoned.

318   § 36. *How is nature itself possible?* This question—the highest point that transcendental philosophy can ever reach, and to which, as its boundary and completion, it must proceed—properly contains two questions.

FIRST: How is nature possible in general in the *material* sense, i.e., according to intuition, as the totality of appearances; how are space, time, and that which fills both—the object of sensation—possible in general? The answer is: by means of the constitution of our sensibility, according to which it is in its special way affected by objects which are in themselves unknown to it and totally distinct from those appearances. This answer is given in the *Critique* itself in the Transcendental Aesthetic, and in these *Prolegomena* by the solution of the first main question.

SECONDLY: How is nature possible in the *formal* sense, as the totality of the rules under which all appearances must come in order to be thought as connected in an experience? The answer must be this: it is only possible by means of the constitution of our understanding, according to which all those representations of sensibility are necessarily referred to a consciousness, and by which the peculiar way in which we think (viz., by rules) and hence also experience are possible, but must be clearly distinguished from an insight into the objects in themselves. This answer is given in the *Critique* itself in the Transcendental Logic, and in these *Prolegomena* in the course of the solution of the second main question.

But how this peculiar property of our sensibility itself is possible, or that of our understanding and of the apperception which is necessarily its basis and also that of all thinking, cannot be further analyzed or answered, because it is of them that we are in need for all our answers and for all our thinking about objects.

There are many laws of nature which we can only know by means of experience; but conformity to law in the connection of appearances, i.e., nature in general, we cannot discover by any experience, because experience itself requires laws which are *a priori* at the basis of its possibility. 319

The possibility of experience in general is therefore at the same time the universal law of nature, and the principles of experience are the very laws of nature. For we know nature as nothing but the totality of appearances, i.e., of representations in us; and hence we can only derive the law of their connection from the principles of their connection in us, that is, from the conditions of their necessary unification in a consciousness, which constitutes the possibility of experience.

Even the main proposition expounded throughout this section—that universal laws of nature can be cognized *a priori*—leads of itself to the proposition that the highest legislation of nature must lie in ourselves, i.e., in our understanding; and that we must not seek the universal laws of nature in nature by means of experience, but conversely must seek nature, as to its universal conformity to law, in the conditions of the possibility of experience, which lie in our sensibility and in our understanding. For how would it otherwise be possible to know *a priori* these laws, as they are not rules of analytic cognition but truly synthetic extensions of it? Such a necessary agreement of the principles of possible experience with the laws of the possibility of nature can only proceed from one of two reasons: either these laws are drawn from nature by means of experience, or conversely nature is derived from the laws of the possibility of experience in general and is quite the same as the mere universal conformity to law of the latter. The former is self-contradictory, for the universal laws of nature can and must be cognized *a priori* (that is, independent of all experience) and must be the foundation of all empirical use of the understanding; the latter alternative therefore alone remains.[24]

320   But we must distinguish the empirical laws of nature, which always presuppose particular perceptions, from the pure or universal laws of nature, which, without being based on particular perceptions, contain merely the conditions of their necessary unification in experience. With regard to the latter, nature and possible experience are quite the same, and as the conformity to law in the latter depends upon the necessary connection of appearances in experience (without which we cannot cognize any object whatever in the sensible world), consequently upon the original laws of the understanding, it seems at first strange, but is not the less certain, to say: *the understanding does not derive its laws (a priori) from, but prescribes them to, nature.*

§ 37. We shall illustrate this seemingly bold proposition by an example, which will show that laws which we discover in objects of sensuous intuition (especially when these laws are cognized as necessary) are already held by us to be such as have been placed there by the understanding, in spite of their being similar in all points to the laws of nature which we ascribe to experience.

§ 38. If we consider the properties of the circle, by which this figure at once combines into a universal rule so many arbitrary determinations of the space in it, we cannot avoid attributing a nature to this geometrical thing. Two lines, for example, which intersect each other and the circle, howsoever they may be drawn, are always divided so that the rectangle constructed with the segments of the one is equal to that constructed with the segments of the other. The question now is: Does this law lie in the circle or in the understanding? That is, does this figure, independently of the understanding, contain in itself the ground of the law; or does the understanding, having constructed according to its concepts (of the equality of the radii) the figure itself, intro-

24. Crusius alone thought of a compromise: that a spirit who can neither err nor deceive implanted these laws in us originally. But since false principles often intrude themselves, as indeed the very system of this man shows in not a few examples, we are involved in difficulties as to the use of such a principle in the absence of sure criteria to distinguish the genuine origin from the spurious, for we never can know certainly what the spirit of truth or the father of lies may have instilled into us.

duce into it this law of the chords intersecting in geometrical pro- 321
portion? When we follow the proofs of this law, we soon perceive that it can only be derived from the condition on which the
understanding founds the construction of this figure, viz., the
equality of the radii. But if we enlarge this concept to pursue
further the unity of manifold properties of geometrical figures
under common laws and consider the circle as a conic section,
which of course is subject to the same fundamental conditions of
construction as other conic sections, we shall find that all the
chords which intersect within the circle, ellipse, parabola, and
hyperbola always intersect so that the rectangles of their segments are not indeed equal but always bear a constant ratio to
one another. If we proceed still further to the fundamental
doctrines of physical astronomy, we find a physical law of reciprocal attraction extending over the whole material nature, the
rule of which is that it decreases inversely as the square of the
distance from each attracting point, just as the spherical surfaces
through which this force diffuses itself increase; and this law
seems to be necessarily inherent in the very nature of things, so
that it is usually propounded as cognizable *a priori.* Simple as the
sources of this law are, merely resting upon the relation of
spherical surfaces of different radii, its consequence is so excellent with regard to the variety and regularity of its agreement
that not only are all possible orbits of the celestial bodies conic
sections, but such a relation of these orbits to each other results
that no other law of attraction than that of the inverse square of
the distance can be thought as fit for a cosmical system.

Here, accordingly, is nature resting on laws which the understanding cognizes *a priori,* and chiefly from universal principles
of the determination of space. Now I ask: do the laws of nature
lie in space, and does the understanding learn them by merely
endeavoring to find out the enormous wealth of meaning that
lies in space; or do they inhere in the understanding and in the
way in which it determines space according to the conditions of
the synthetic unity in which its concepts are all centered? Space
is something so uniform and as to all particular properties so
indeterminate that we should certainly not seek a store of laws of
nature in it. Whereas that which determines space to assume the
form of a circle, or the figures of a cone and a sphere is the un- 322

derstanding, so far as it contains the ground of the unity of their constructions. The mere universal form of intuition, called space, must therefore be the substratum of all intuitions determinable to particular objects; and in it, of course, the condition of the possibility and of the variety of these intuitions lies. But the unity of the objects is entirely determined by the understanding, and according to conditions which lie in its own nature; and thus the understanding is the origin of the universal order of nature, in that it comprehends all appearances under its own laws and thereby brings about, in an *a priori* way, experience (as to its form), by means of which whatever is to be cognized only by experience is necessarily subjected to its laws. For we are not concerned with the nature of things in themselves, which is independent of the conditions both of our sensibility and our understanding, but with nature as an object of possible experience; and in this case the understanding, because it makes experience possible, thereby insists that the sensuous world is either not an object of experience at all, or else is nature.

Appendix to Pure Natural Science

§ 39. *Of the system of the categories.* There can be nothing more desirable to a philosopher than to be able to derive the scattered multiplicity of the concepts or the principles which had occurred to him in concrete use from a principle *a priori*, and to unite everything in this way in one cognition. He formerly only believed that those things which remained after a certain abstraction, and seemed by comparison among one another to constitute a particular kind of cognitions, were completely collected; but this was only an *aggregate*. Now he knows that just so many, neither more nor less, can constitute this kind of cognition, and perceives the necessity of his division; this constitutes comprehension. And only now has he attained a *system*.

To search in our ordinary knowledge for the concepts which do not rest upon particular experience and yet occur in all knowledge from experience, of which they constitute as it were the mere form of connection, presupposes neither greater reflection

323

nor deeper insight than to detect in a language the rules of the actual use of words generally and thus to collect elements for a grammar (in fact both inquiries are very closely related), even though we are not able to give a reason why each language has just this and no other formal constitution, and still less why exactly so many, neither more nor less, of such formal determinations in general can be found in it.

Aristotle collected ten pure elementary concepts under the name of categories.[25] To these, which were also called predicaments, he found himself obliged afterwards to add five post-predicaments,[26] some of which however *(prius, simul,* and *motus)* are contained in the former; but this rhapsody must be considered (and commended) as a mere hint for future inquirers, not as a regularly worked out idea, and hence it has, in the present more advanced state of philosophy, been rejected as quite useless.

After long reflection on the pure elements of human knowledge (those which contain nothing empirical), I at last succeeded in distinguishing with certainty and in separating the pure elementary concepts of sensibility (space and time) from those of the understanding. Thus the 7th, 8th, and 9th categories had to be excluded from the old list. And the others were of no service to me because there was no principle on which the understanding could be fully mapped out and all the functions, whence its pure concepts arise, determined exhaustively and with precision.

But in order to discover such a principle, I looked about for an act of the understanding which comprises all the rest and is differentiated only by various modifications or moments, in bringing the manifold of representation under the unity of thinking in general. I found this act of the understanding to consist in judging. Here, then, the labors of the logicians were ready at hand, though not yet quite free from defects; and with this help I was enabled to exhibit a complete table of the pure functions of the understanding, which were however undetermined 324 in regard to any object. I finally referred these functions of judging to objects in general, or rather to the condition of determin-

25. 1. *Substantia.* 2. *Qualitas.* 3. *Quantitas.* 4. *Relatio.* 5. *Actio.* 6. *Passio.* 7. *Quando.* 8. *Ubi.* 9. *Situs.* 10. *Habitus.*

26. *Oppositum, Prius, Simul, Motus, Habere.*

ing judgments as objectively valid; and so there arose the pure concepts of the understanding, concerning which I could make certain that these, and this exact number only, constitute our whole cognition of things from pure understanding. I was justified in calling them by their old name of *categories*, while I reserved for myself the liberty of adding, under the title of *predicables*, a complete list of all the concepts deducible from them by combinations, whether among themselves, or with the pure form of the appearance, i.e., space or time, or with its matter, so far as it is not yet empirically determined (viz., the object of sensation in general), as soon as a system of transcendental philosophy should be completed, with the construction of which I was engaged in the *Critique of Pure Reason* itself.

Now the essential point in this system of categories, which distinguishes it from the old rhapsody (which proceeded without any principle) and for which point alone this system deserves to be considered as philosophy, consists in this: that, by means of it, the true meaning of the pure concepts of the understanding and the condition of their use could be exactly determined. For here it became obvious that they are themselves nothing but logical functions, and as such do not constitute the least concept of an object in itself, but require some sensuous intuition as a basis. These concepts, therefore, only serve to determine empirical judgments (which are otherwise undetermined and indifferent with respect to all functions of judging) as regards these functions, thereby procuring them universal validity, and by means of them, making judgments of experience in general possible.

Such an insight into the nature of the categories, which limits them at the same time to use merely in experience, never occurred either to their first author, or to any of his successors; but without this insight (which exactly depends upon their derivation or deduction), they are quite useless and only a miserable list of names, without explanation or rule for their use. Had the ancients ever conceived such a notion, doubtless the whole study of pure rational knowledge, which under the name of metaphysics has for centuries spoiled many a sound mind, 325 would have reached us in quite another shape and would have enlightened the human understanding instead of actually exhausting it in obscure and vain subtleties and rendering it useless for true science.

This system of categories makes all treatment of every object of pure reason itself systematic, and affords a direction or clue how and through what points of inquiry any metaphysical consideration must proceed in order to be complete; for it exhausts all the moments of the understanding, under which every other concept must be brought. In like manner the table of principles has been formulated, the completeness of which we can only vouch for by the system of the categories. Even in the division of the concepts which are to go beyond the physiological application of the understanding,[27] it is still the same clue, which, as it must always be determined *a priori* by the same fixed points of the human understanding, always forms a closed circle. There is no doubt that the object of a pure concept, either of the understanding or of reason, so far as it is to be estimated philosophically and on *a priori* principles, can in this way be completely cognized. I could not therefore omit to make use of this clue with regard to one of the most abstract ontological divisions, viz., the various distinctions of the concepts of something and of nothing, and to construct accordingly[28] a regular and necessary table of their divisions.[29]

27. [Cf. *Critique of Pure Reason*, B 402 and B 442–3.]

28. [Cf. *ibid.*, B 348.]

29. On the table of the categories many neat observations may be made, for instance: (1) that the third arises from the first and the second, joined in one concept; (2) that in those of quantity and of quality there is merely a progress from unity to totality or from something to nothing (for this purpose the categories of quality must stand thus: reality, limitation, total negation), without *correlata* or *opposita*, whereas those of relation and of modality have them; (3) that, as in logic categorical judgments are the basis of all others, so the category of substance is the basis of all concepts of actual things; (4) that, as modality in a judgment is not a distinct predicate, so by the modal concepts a determination is not superadded to things, etc. Such observations are of great use. If we, besides, enumerate all the predicables, which we can find pretty completely in any good ontology (for example, Baumgarten's), and arrange them in classes under the categories, in which operation we must not neglect to add as complete a dissection of all these concepts as possible, there will then arise a merely analytic part of metaphysics, which does not contain a single synthetic proposition and might precede the second (the synthetic), and would, by its precision and completeness, be not only useful, but, in virtue of its system, be even to some extent elegant.

326   And this system, like every other true one founded on a universal principle, shows its inestimable usefulness in that it excludes all foreign concepts which might otherwise intrude
among the pure concepts of the understanding, and determines
the place of every cognition. Those concepts, which under the
name of *concepts of reflection* have been likewise arranged in a
table according to the clue of the categories, intrude into
ontology without having any privilege or legitimate claim to be
among the pure concepts of the understanding. The latter are
concepts of connection, and thereby of the objects themselves,
whereas the former are only concepts of a mere comparison of
concepts already given, and therefore are of quite another
nature and use. By my systematic division[30] they are saved from
this confusion. But the utility of this separate table of the categories will be still more obvious when, as will soon happen, we separate the table of the transcendental concepts of reason from the
concepts of the understanding. The concepts of reason being of
quite another nature and origin, their table must have quite
another form from that of the concepts of understanding. This
so necessary separation has never yet been made in any system
of metaphysics, where as a rule these ideas of reason are all
mixed up with the concepts of the understanding, like children
belonging to one family—a confusion that was unavoidable in
the absence of a definite system of categories.

   30. [See *Critique of Pure Reason*, B 316.]

How is Metaphysics in General Possible?

§ 40. Pure mathematics and pure natural science had no need for such a deduction (as has been made for both) for the sake of their own safety and certainty. For the former rests upon its own evidence, and the latter (though sprung from pure sources of the understanding) upon experience and its thorough confirmation. Pure natural science cannot altogether refuse and dispense with the testimony of experience; hence with all its certainty it can never, as philosophy, rival mathematics. Both sciences therefore stood in need of this inquiry, not for themselves, but for the sake of another science, namely, metaphysics.

Metaphysics has to do not only with concepts of nature, which always find their application in experience, but also with pure rational concepts, which never can be given in any possible experience whatsoever. Consequently, the objective reality of these concepts (viz., that they are not mere chimeras) and also the truth or falsity of metaphysical assertions cannot be discovered or confirmed by any experience. This part of metaphysics, however, is precisely what constitutes its essential end, to which the rest is only a means, and thus this science is in need of such a deduction for its own sake. The third question now proposed relates therefore. as it were, to the root and peculiarity of metaphysics, i.e., the occupation of reason merely with itself and the supposed knowledge of objects arising immediately from this brooding over its own concepts, without requiring experience or indeed being able to reach that knowledge through experience.[31]

31. If we can say that a science is actual, at least in the idea of all men, as soon as it appears that the problems which lead to it are proposed to everybody by the nature of human reason, and hence that at all times many (though faulty) endeavors are unavoidably made in its behalf; then we are bound to say that metaphysics is subjectively (and indeed necessarily) actual, and then we justly ask how is it (objectively) possible.

Without solving this question, reason will never be satisfied. The empirical use to which reason limits the pure understanding does not fully satisfy reason's own proper destination. Every
328 single experience is only a part of the whole sphere of its domain, but the absolute totality of all possible experience is itself not experience. Yet it is a necessary problem for reason, the mere representation of which requires concepts quite different from the pure concepts of the understanding, whose use is only immanent, i.e., refers to experience so far as it can be given. Whereas the concepts of reason aim at the completeness, i.e., the collective unity, of all possible experience, and thereby go beyond every given experience. Thus they become *transcendent*.

As the understanding stands in need of categories for experience, reason contains in itself the ground of ideas, by which I mean necessary concepts whose object *cannot* be given in any experience. The latter are inherent in the nature of reason, as the former are in that of the understanding. While the ideas carry with them an illusion likely to mislead, this illusion is unavoidable though it certainly can be kept from misleading us.

Since all illusion consists in holding the subjective ground of our judgments to be objective, a self-knowledge of pure reason in its transcendent (hyperbolical) use is the only safeguard against the aberrations into which reason falls when it mistakes its destination, and transcendently refers to the object in itself that which only concerns reason's own subject and its guidance in all immanent use.

§ 41. The distinction of *ideas,* i.e., of pure concepts of reason, from the categories, or pure concepts of the understanding, as cognitions of a quite different species, origin, and use is so important a point in founding a science which is to contain the system of all these *a priori* cognitions that, without this distinction,
329 metaphysics is absolutely impossible or is at best a random, bungling attempt to build a castle in the air without a knowledge of the materials or of their fitness for one purpose or another. Had the *Critique of Pure Reason* done nothing but first point out this distinction, it would thereby have contributed more to clear up our conception of, and to guide our inquiry in, the field of metaphysics than all the vain efforts which have hitherto been made to satisfy the transcendent problems of pure reason; for one

never even suspected that he was in quite another field from that of the understanding, and hence that he was classing concepts of the understanding and those of reason together, as if they were of the same kind.

§ 42. All pure cognitions of the understanding have the feature that the concepts can be given in experience, and the principles can be confirmed by it; whereas the transcendent cognitions of reason cannot either, as ideas, be given in experience or, as propositions, ever be confirmed or refuted by it. Hence whatever errors may slip in unawares can only be discovered by pure reason itself—a discovery of much difficulty, because this very reason naturally becomes dialectical by means of its ideas; and this unavoidable illusion cannot be limited by any objective and dogmatic inquiries into things, but only by a subjective investigation of reason itself as a source of ideas.

§ 43. In the *Critique of Pure Reason* it was always my greatest care to endeavor, not only carefully to distinguish the several kinds of cognition, but to derive concepts belonging to each one of them from their common source. I did this in order that by knowing whence they originated, I might determine their use with safety and also have the invaluable, but never previously anticipated, advantage of knowing the completeness of my enumeration, classification, and specification of concepts *a priori,* and of knowing it according to principles. Without this, meta- 330 physics is mere rhapsody, in which no one knows whether he has enough or whether and where something is still wanting. We can indeed have this advantage only in pure philosophy, but of this philosophy it constitutes the very essence.

As I had found the origin of the categories in the four logical functions of all judgments of the understanding, it was quite natural to seek the origin of the ideas in the three functions of syllogisms. For as soon as these pure concepts of reason (the transcendental ideas) are given, they could hardly, except they be held innate, be found anywhere else than in the same activity of reason, which, so far as it regards mere form, constitutes the logical element of syllogisms; but, so far as it represents judgments of the understanding as determined with respect to one or another form *a priori,* constitutes transcendental concepts of pure reason.

The formal difference of syllogisms makes their division into categorical, hypothetical, and disjunctive necessary. The concepts of reason founded on them contain therefore, first, the idea of the complete subject (the substantial); secondly, the idea of the complete series of conditions; thirdly, the determination of all concepts in the idea of a complete complex of that which is possible.[32] The first idea is psychological, the second cosmological, the third theological; and, as all three give occasion to dialectic, yet each in its own way, the division of the whole dialectic of pure reason into its paralogism, its antinomy, and its ideal was arranged accordingly. Through this derivation we may feel assured that all the claims of pure reason are completely represented and that none can be wanting, because the faculty of reason itself, whence they all take their origin, is thereby completely surveyed.

331   § 44. In these general considerations it is also remarkable that the ideas of reason, unlike the categories, are of no service to the use of our understanding in experience, but quite dispensable, and become even an impediment to the maxims of a rational cognition of nature. Yet in another aspect still to be determined they are necessary. Whether the soul is or is not a simple substance is of no consequence to us in the explanation of its phenomena. For we cannot render the concept of a simple being understandable sensuously and concretely by any possible experience. The concept is therefore quite void as regards all hoped-for insight into the cause of appearances and cannot at all serve as a principle of the explanation of that which internal or external experience supplies. Likewise the cosmological ideas of the beginning of the world or of its eternity *(a parte ante)* cannot be of any service to us for the explanation of any event in the world

32. In disjunctive judgments we consider all possibility as divided in respect to a particular concept. By the ontological principle of the thoroughgoing determination of a thing in general, I understand the principle that either the one or the other of all possible contradictory predicates must be assigned to any object. This is at the same time the principle of all disjunctive judgments, constituting the foundation of the totality of all possibility, and in it the possibility of every object in general is considered as determined. This may serve as a brief explanation of the above proposition: that the activity of reason in disjunctive syllogisms is formally the same as that by which it fashions the idea of a totality of all reality, containing in itself the positive member of all contradictory predicates.

itself. And finally we must, according to a right maxim of the philosophy of nature, refrain from all explanation of the design of nature as being drawn from the will of a Supreme Being, because this would not be natural philosophy but an admission that we have come to the end of it. The use of these ideas, therefore, is quite different from that of those categories by which (and by the principles built upon which) experience itself first becomes possible. But our laborious analytic of the understanding would be superfluous if we had nothing else in view than the mere cognition of nature as it can be given in experience; for reason does its work, both in mathematics and in natural science, quite safely and well without any of this subtle deduction. Therefore our critique of the understanding combines with the ideas of pure reason for a purpose which lies beyond the empirical use of the understanding; but we have above declared the use of the understanding in this respect to be totally inadmissible and without any object or meaning. Yet there must be a harmony between the nature of reason and that of the understanding, and the former must contribute to the perfection of the latter and cannot possibly upset it.

The solution of this question is as follows. Pure reason does not in its ideas point to particular objects which lie beyond the   332
field of experience, but only requires completeness of the use of the understanding in the complex of experience. But this completeness can be a completeness of principles only, not of intuitions and of objects. In order, however, to represent the ideas definitely, reason conceives them after the fashion of the cognition of an object. This cognition is, as far as these rules are concerned, completely determined; but the object is only an idea invented for the purpose of bringing the cognition of the understanding as near as possible to the completeness indicated by that idea.

PREFATORY REMARK TO THE DIALECTIC OF PURE REASON

§ 45. We have above shown in §§ 33 and 34 that the purity of the categories from all admixture of sensuous determinations may mislead reason into extending their use beyond all experience to things in themselves; for though these categories themselves find no intuition which can give them meaning or sense *in concreto,* they, as mere logical functions, can represent a thing in general, but not give by themselves alone a determinate concept of anything. Such hyperbolical objects are distinguished by the appellation of *noumena,* or pure beings of the understanding (or better, beings of thought)—such as, for example, "substance," but conceived without permanence in time; or "cause," but not acting in time, etc. Here predicates that only serve to make the conformity-to-law of experience possible are applied to these concepts, and yet they are deprived of all the conditions of intuition on which alone experience is possible, and so these concepts lose all significance.

There is no danger, however, of the understanding spontaneously making an excursion so very wantonly beyond its own bounds into the field of the mere beings of thought, unless being impelled by alien laws. But when reason, which cannot be fully satisfied with any empirical use of the rules of the understanding, as being always conditioned, requires a completion of this chain of conditions, then the understanding is forced out of its sphere. And then reason partly represents objects of experience
333 in a series so extended that no experience can grasp it, partly even (with a view to complete the series) it seeks entirely beyond experience *noumena,* to which it can attach that chain; and so, having at last escaped from the conditions of experience, reason makes its hold complete. These are then the transcendental ideas, which, (though in accord with the true but hidden ends of the natural determination of our reason) may aim, not at extravagant concepts, but at an unbounded extension of their empirical use, yet seduce the understanding by an unavoidable illusion to a transcendent use, which, though deceitful, cannot be restrained within the bounds of experience by any resolution, but only by scientific instruction and with much difficulty.

I. THE PSYCHOLOGICAL IDEAS[33]

§ 46. People have long since observed that in all substances the subject proper, that which remains after all the accidents (as

33. See *Critique of Pure Reason,* "The Paralogisms of Pure Reason," A 341/B 399—A 405/B 432.

predicates) are abstracted, hence the substantial itself, remains unknown, and various complaints have been made concerning these limits to our insight. But it will be well to consider that the human understanding is not to be blamed for its inability to know the substance of things, i.e., to determine it by itself, but rather for demanding to cognize it determinately as though it were a given object, it being a mere idea. Pure reason requires us to seek for every predicate of a thing its own subject, and for this subject, which is itself necessarily nothing but a predicate, its subject, and so on indefinitely (or as far as we can reach). But hence it follows that we must not hold anything at which we can arrive to be an ultimate subject, and that substance itself never can be thought by our understanding, however deep we may penetrate, even if all nature were unveiled to us. For the specific nature of our understanding consists in thinking everything discursively, i.e., by concepts, and so by mere predicates, to which, therefore, the absolute subject must always be wanting. Hence all the real properties by which we cognize bodies are mere accidents, not even excepting impenetrability, which we can only represent to ourselves as the effect of a force for which the sub-   334 ject is unknown to us.

Now we appear to have this substance in the consciousness of ourselves (in the thinking subject), and indeed in an immediate intuition; for all the predicates of an internal sense refer to the *ego,* as a subject, and I cannot conceive myself as the predicate of any other subject. Hence completeness in the reference of the given concepts as predicates to a subject—not merely an idea, but an object—that is, the *absolute subject* itself, seems to be given in experience. But this expectation is disappointed. For the ego is not a concept,[34] but only the indication of the object of the internal sense, so far as we cognize it by no further predicate. Consequently, it cannot be itself a predicate of any other thing; but just as little can it be a determinate concept of an absolute subject, but is, as in all other cases, only the reference of the

34. Were the representation of the apperception (the ego) a concept by which anything could be thought, it could be used as a predicate of other things or contain predicates in itself. But it is nothing more than the feeling of an existence without the slightest concept and is only the representation of that to which all thinking stands in relation *(relatione accidentis).*

internal phenomena to their unknown subject. Yet this idea (which serves very well as a regulative principle totally to destroy all materialistic explanations of the internal phenomena of the soul) occasions by a very natural misunderstanding a very specious argument, which infers the nature of the soul from this supposed cognition of the substance of our thinking being. This argument is specious insofar as the knowledge of this substance falls quite without the complex of experience.

§ 47. But though we may call this thinking self (the soul) substance, as being the ultimate subject of thinking which cannot be further represented as the predicate of another thing, it remains quite empty and inconsequential if permanence—the quality which renders the concept of substances in experience fruitful—cannot be proved of it.

335   But permanence can never be proved of the concept of a substance as a thing in itself, but only for the purposes of experience. This is sufficiently shown by the first Analogy of Experience,[35] and whoever will not yield to this proof may try for himself whether he can succeed in proving, from the concept of a subject which does not exist itself as the predicate of another thing, that its existence is thoroughly permanent and that it cannot either in itself or by any natural cause come into being or pass out of it. These synthetic a priori propositions can never be proved in themselves, but only in reference to things as objects of possible experience.

§ 48. If, therefore, from the concept of the soul as a substance we would infer its permanence, this can hold good as regards possible experience only, not of the soul as a thing in itself and beyond all possible experience. Now life is the subjective condition of all our possible experience; consequently we can only infer the permanence of the soul in life, for the death of man is the end of all the experience that concerns the soul as an object of experience, except the contrary be proved—which is the very question in hand. The permanence of the soul can therefore only be proved (and no one cares for that) during the life of man, but not, as we desire to do, after death. This is so because the concept of substance, insofar as it is to be considered as necessarily

35. Cf. Critique, B 224–232.

combined with the concept of permanence, can be so combined only according to the principles of possible experience, and therefore for the purposes of experience only.[36]

§ 49. That there is something real outside us which not only 336 corresponds but must correspond to our external perceptions can likewise be proved to be, not a connection of things in themselves, but for the sake of experience. This means that there is something empirical, i.e., some appearance in space outside us, that admits of a satisfactory proof; for we have nothing to do with other objects than those which belong to possible experience, because objects which cannot be given us in any experience are nothing for us. Empirically outside me is that which is intuited in space; and space, together with all the appearances which it contains, belongs to the representations whose connection, according to laws of experience, proves their objective truth, just as the connection of the appearances of the internal sense proves the actuality of my soul (as an object of the internal sense). By means of external experience I am conscious of the actuality of bodies as external appearances in space, in the same manner as by means of internal experience I am conscious of the existence of my soul in time; but this soul is cognized only as an

36. It is indeed very remarkable how carelessly metaphysicians have always passed over the principle of the permanence of substances without ever attempting a proof of it; doubtless because they found themselves abandoned by all proofs as soon as they began to deal with the concept of substance. Common sense, which felt distinctly that without this presupposition no union of perceptions in experience is possible, supplied the want by a postulate. From experience itself it never could derive such a principle, partly because material objects (substances) cannot be so traced in all their alterations and dissolutions that the matter can always be found undiminished, partly because the principle contains *necessity*, which is always the sign of an *a priori* principle. People then boldly applied this postulate to the concept of soul as a *substance*, and concluded a necessary continuance of the soul after the death of man (especially as the simplicity of this substance, which is inferred from the indivisibility of consciousness, secured it from destruction by dissolution). Had they found the genuine source of this principle—a discovery which requires deeper researches than they were ever inclined to make—they would have seen that the law of the permanence of substances finds a place for the purposes of experience only, and hence can hold good of things so far as they are to be cognized and conjoined with others in experience, but never independently of all possible experience, and consequently cannot hold good of the soul after death.

object of the internal sense by appearances that constitute an internal state and of which the being in itself, which forms the basis of these appearances, is unknown. Cartesian idealism therefore does nothing but distinguish external experience from

337 dreaming and the conformity to law (as a criterion of its truth) of the former from the irregularity and the false illusion of the latter. In both it presupposes space and time as conditions of the existence of objects, and it only inquires whether the objects of the external senses which we, when awake, put in space are as actually to be found in it as the object of the internal sense, the soul, is in time; that is, whether experience carries with it sure criteria to distinguish it from imagination. This doubt, however, may easily be disposed of, and we always do so in common life by investigating the connection of appearances in both space and time according to universal laws of experience; and we cannot doubt, when the representation of external things throughout agrees therewith, that they constitute truthful experience. Material idealism, in which appearances are considered as such only according to their connection in experience may accordingly be very easily refuted; and it is just as sure an experience that bodies exist outside us (in space) as that I myself exist according to the representation of the internal sense (in time), for the concept "outside us" only signifies existence in space. However, as the ego in the proposition "I am" means not only the object of internal intuition (in time) but the subject of consciousness, just as body means not only external intuition (in space) but the thing in itself which is the basis of this appearance, then the question whether bodies (as appearances of the external sense) exist as bodies in nature apart from my thoughts may without any hesitation be denied. But the question whether I myself as an appearance of the internal sense (the soul according to empirical psychology) exist apart from my faculty of representation in time is an exactly similar question and must likewise be answered in the negative. And in this manner everything, when it is reduced to its true meaning, is decided and certain. The formal (which I have also called transcendental) actually abolishes the material, or Cartesian, idealism. For if space be nothing but a form of my sensibility, it is as a representation in me just as actual as I myself am, and nothing but the empirical truth of the appearances in it remains for consideration. But if this is not the case, if space and the appearances in it are something existing outside us, then all the criteria of experience outside our perception can never prove the actuality of these objects outside us.

II. THE COSMOLOGICAL IDEAS[37]   338

§ 50. This product of pure reason in its transcendent use is its most remarkable phenomenon. It serves as a very powerful agent to rouse philosophy from its dogmatic slumber and to stimulate it to the arduous task of undertaking a criticism of reason itself.

I term this idea cosmological because it always takes its object only from the sensible world and does not need any other world than that whose object is given to sense; consequently, it remains in this respect in its native home, does not become transcendent, and is therefore so far not an idea; whereas to conceive the soul as a simple substance, on the contrary, means to conceive such an object (the simple) as cannot be presented to the senses. Notwithstanding, the cosmological idea extends the connection of the conditioned with its condition (whether mathematical or dynamical) so far that experience never can keep up with it. It is therefore with regard to this point always an idea, whose object never can be adequately given in any experience.

§ 51. In the first place, the use of a system of categories becomes here so obvious and unmistakable that, even if there were not several other proofs of it, this alone would sufficiently prove it indispensable in the system of pure reason. There are only four such transcendent ideas, as many as there are classes of categories; in each of which, however, they refer only to the absolute completeness of the series of the conditions for a given conditioned. In conformity with these cosmological ideas, there are only four kinds of dialectical assertions of pure reason, which, being dialectical, prove that to each of them, on equally specious principles of pure reason, a contradictory assertion stands opposed. As all the metaphysical art of the most subtle distinction cannot prevent this opposition, it compels the philos-

37. Cf. *Critique*, "The Antinomy of Pure Reason," B 432–595.

339   opher to recur to the first sources of pure reason itself. This antinomy, not arbitrarily invented but founded in the nature of
human reason, and hence unavoidable and never ceasing, contains the following four theses together with their antitheses:

1
Thesis
The world has, as to time and space, a beginning (limit).
Antithesis
The world is, as to time and space, infinite.

2
Thesis
Everything in the world is constituted out of the simple.
Antithesis
There is nothing simple, but everything is composite.

3
Thesis
There are in the world causes through freedom.
Antithesis
There is no freedom, but all is nature.

4
Thesis
In the series of world-causes there is some necessary being.
Antithesis
There is nothing necessary in the world, but in this series all is
contingent.

§ 52a. Here is the most singular phenomenon of human reason, no other instance of which can be shown in its any other
use. If we, as is commonly done, represent to ourselves the appearances of the sensible world as things in themselves, if we
assume the principles of their combination as principles universally valid of things in themselves and not merely of experience,
as is usually, nay, without our *Critique,* unavoidably done, there
arises an unexpected conflict which never can be removed in the
common dogmatic way; because the thesis, as well as the anti-

thesis, can be shown by equally clear, evident, and irresistible proofs—for I pledge myself as to the correctness of all these proofs—and reason therefore sees that it is divided against itself, a state at which the sceptic rejoices, but which must make the critical philosopher pause and feel ill at ease.

§ 52b. We may blunder in various ways in metaphysics without any fear of being detected in falsehood. For we never can be refuted by experience if we but avoid self-contradiction, which in synthetic though purely fictitious propositions may be done whenever the concepts which we connect are mere ideas that cannot be given (as regards their whole content) in experience. For how can we make out by experience whether the world is from eternity or had a beginning, whether matter is infinitely divisible or consists of simple parts? Such concepts cannot be given in any experience, however extensive, and consequently the falsehood either of the affirmative or the negative propostion cannot be discovered by this touchstone.

The only possible way in which reason could have revealed unintentionally its secret dialectic, falsely announced as dogmatics, would be when it were made to ground an assertion upon a universally admitted principle and to deduce the exact contrary with the greatest accuracy of inference from another which is equally granted. This is actually here the case with regard to four natural ideas of reason, whence four assertions on the one side and as many counter-assertions on the other arise, each consistently following from universally acknowledged principles. Thus they reveal, by the use of these principles, the dialectical illusion of pure reason, which would otherwise forever remain concealed.

This is therefore a decisive experiment, which must necessarily expose any error lying hidden in the assumptions of reason.[38]

340

341

---

38. I therefore would be pleased to have the critical reader to devote to this antinomy of pure reason his chief attention, because nature itself seems to have established it with a view to stagger reason in its daring pretentions and to force it to self-examination. For every proof which I have given both of the thesis and the antithesis, I pledge myself to be responsible, and thereby to show the certainty of the inevitable antinomy of reason. When the reader is brought by this curious phenomenon to fall back upon the proof of the presumption upon which it rests, he will feel himself obliged to investigate the ultimate foundation of all the cognition of pure reason with me more thoroughly.

Contradictory propositions cannot both be false, unless the concept lying at the ground of both of them is self-contradictory; for example, the propositions, "A square circle is round," and "A square circle is not round," are both false. For, as to the former, it is false that the circle is round because it is quadrangular; and it is likewise false that it is not round, i.e., angular, because it is a circle. For the logical criterion of the impossibility of a concept consists in this, that if we presuppose it, two contradictory propositions both become false; consequently, as no middle between them is conceivable, nothing at all is thought by that concept.

§ 52c. The first two antinomies, which I call mathematical because they are concerned with the addition or division of the homogeneous, are founded on such a contradictory concept; and hence I explain how it happens that both the thesis and antithesis of the two are false.

When I speak of objects in time and in space, it is not of things in themselves, of which I know nothing, but of things in appearance, i.e., of experience, as a particular way of cognizing objects which is only afforded to man. I must not say of that which I think in time or in space, that in itself, and independent of these my thoughts, it exists in space and in time, for in that case I would contradict myself, because space and time, together with the appearances in them, are nothing existing in themselves and outside of my representations, but are themselves only 342 modes of representation, and it is palpably contradictory to say that a mere mode of representation exists outside our representation. Objects of the senses therefore exist only in experience, whereas to give them a self-subsisting existence apart from experience or prior to it is merely to represent to ourselves that experience actually exists apart from experience or prior to it.

Now if I ask about the magnitude of the world, as to space and time, it is equally impossible, with regard to all my concepts, to declare it infinite or to declare it finite. For neither assertion can be contained in experience, because experience either of an infinite space or of an infinite time elapsed, or again, of the boundary of the world by an empty space or by an antecedent empty time, is impossible; these are mere ideas. This magnitude of the world, be it determined in either way, would therefore have to exist in the world itself apart from all experience. But this contradicts the concept of a world of sense, which is merely a complex of the appearances whose existence and connection occur only in our representations, i.e. , in experience; since this latter is not an object in itself but a mere mode of representation. Hence it follows that, as the concept of an absolutely existing world of sense is self-contradictory, the solution of the problem concerning its magnitude, whether attempted affirmatively or negatively, is always false.

The same holds of the second antinomy, which relates to the division of appearances. For these are mere representations; and the parts exist merely in their representation, consequently in the division (i.e., in a possible experience where they are given) and the division reaches only as far as such experience reaches. To assume that an appearance, e.g., that of a body, contains in itself before all experience all the parts which any possible experience can ever reach is to impute to a mere appearance, which can exist only in experience, an existence previous to experience. In other words, it would mean that mere representations exist before they can be found in our faculty of representation. Such an assertion is self-contradictory, as also every solution of our misunderstood problem, whether we maintain that bodies in themselves consist of an infinite number of parts or of a finite number of simple parts.

§ 53. In the first (the mathematical) class of antinomies the falsehood of the presupposition consists in representing in one concept something self-contradictory as if it were compatible (i.e., an appearance as an object in itself). But as to the second (the dynamical) class of antinomies, the falsehood of the presupposition consists in representing as contradictory what is compatible. Consequently, whereas in the first case the opposed assertions were both false, in this case, on the other hand, where they are opposed to one another by mere misunderstanding, they may both be true.

Any mathematical connection necessarily presupposes homogeneity of what is connected (in the concept of magnitude), while the dynamical one by no means requires this. When we have to deal with extended magnitudes, all the parts

343

must be homogeneous with one another and with the whole. But in the connection of cause and effect homogeneity may indeed likewise be found but is not necessary, for the concept of causality (by means of which something is posited through something else quite different from it) does not in the least require it.

If the objects of the world of sense are taken for things in themselves and the above-mentioned laws of nature for the laws of things in themselves, the contradiction would be unavoidable. So also, if the subject of freedom were, like other objects, represented as mere appearance, the contradiction would be just as unavoidable; for the same predicate would at once be affirmed and denied of the same kind of object in the same sense. But if natural necessity is referred merely to appearances and freedom merely to things in themselves, no contradiction arises if we at the same time assume or admit both kinds of causality, however difficult or impossible it may be to make the latter kind conceivable.

In appearance every effect is an event, or something that happens in time; the effect must, according to the universal law of nature, be preceded by a determination of the causality of its cause (a state of the cause) on which the effect follows according to a constant law. But this determination of the cause to causal action must likewise be something that takes place or happens; 344   the cause must have begun to act, otherwise no succession between it and the effect could be thought. Otherwise the effect, as well as the causality of the cause, would have always existed. Therefore the determination of the cause to act must also have originated among appearances and must consequently, just like its effect, be an event, which must again have its cause, and so on; hence natural necessity must be the condition according to which efficient causes are determined. Whereas if freedom is to be a property of certain causes of appearances, it must, as regards the latter as events, be a faculty of starting them spontaneously, i.e., without the causality of the cause itself needing to begin and hence needing no other ground to determine its beginning. But then the cause, as to its causality, must not stand under time-determinations of its state, i.e., it cannot be an appearance, and must be considered a thing in itself, while only its effects would be appearances.[39] If without contradiction we can think of the beings of understanding as exercising such an influence on appearances, then natural necessity will attach to all connections of cause and effect in the sensuous world, though, on the other hand, freedom can be granted to the cause which is itself not an appearance (but the foundation of appearance). Nature and freedom therefore can without contradiction be attributed to the very same thing, but in different relations—on one side as an appearance, on the other as a thing in itself.

We have in us a faculty which not only stands in connection with its subjective determining grounds that are the natural causes of its actions and is so far the faculty of a being that itself belongs to appearances, but is also related to objective grounds that are only ideas so far as they can determine this faculty; this connection is expressed by *ought.* This faculty is called *reason,* and, so far as we consider a being (man) entirely according to this objectively determinable reason, he cannot be considered as a being of sense; but, rather, this property is that of a thing in itself, and we cannot comprehend the possibility of this property—I mean how the *ought* (which might never yet have taken place) should determine its activity and could become the cause of actions whose effect is an appearance in the sensible world. Yet the causality of reason would be freedom with regard to the effects in the sensuous world, so far as we can consider *objective grounds,* which are themselves ideas, as their determinants. For

345

39. The idea of freedom occurs only in the relation of the intellectual, as cause, to the appearance, as effect. Hence we cannot attribute freedom to matter in regard to the incessant action by which it fills its space, though this action takes place from an internal principle. We can likewise find no concept of freedom suitable to purely rational beings, for instance, to God, so far as his action is immanent. For his action, though independent of external determining causes, is determined in his eternal reason, that is, in the divine *nature.* It is only, if *something is to start* by an action, and so the effect occurs in the sequence of time, or in the world of sense (e.g., the beginning of the world), that we can put the question whether the causality of the cause must in its turn have been started or whether the cause can originate an effect without its causality itself beginning. In the former case the concept of this causality is a concept of natural necessity; in the latter, that of freedom. From this the reader will see that as I explained freedom to be the faculty of starting an event spontaneously, I have exactly hit the concept which is the problem of metaphysics.

its action in that case would not depend upon subjective conditions, consequently not upon those of time, and of course not upon the law of nature which serves to determine them, because grounds of reason give the rule universally to actions, according to principles, without influence of the circumstances of either time or place.

What I adduce here is merely meant as an example to make the thing intelligible, and does not necessarily belong to our problem, which must be decided from mere concepts independently of the properties which we meet in the actual world.

Now I may say without contradiction that all the actions of rational beings, so far as they are appearances (encountered in some experience), are subject to the necessity of nature; but the same actions, as regards merely the rational subject and its faculty of acting according to mere reason, are free. For what is required for the necessity of nature? Nothing more than the determinability of every event in the world of sense according to constant laws, i.e., a reference to cause in the appearance; in this process the thing in itself at its foundation and its causality remain unknown. But, I say, the law of nature remains, whether the rational being is the cause of the effects in the sensuous world from reason, i.e., through freedom, or whether it does not determine them on grounds of reason. For if the former is the case, the action is performed according to maxims, the effect of which as appearance is always conformable to constant laws; if the latter is the case, and the action not performed on principles of reason, it is subject to the empirical laws of sensibility, and in both cases the effects are connected according to constant laws; more than this we do not require or know concerning natural necessity. But in the former case reason is the cause of these laws of nature, and therefore free; in the latter, the effects follow according to mere natural laws of sensibility, because reason does not influence it; but reason itself is not determined on that account by the sensibility (which is impossible) and is therefore free in this case too. Freedom is therefore no hindrance to natural law in appearances; neither does this law abrogate the freedom of the practical use of reason, which is connected with things in themselves as determining grounds.

Thus practical freedom, viz., the freedom in which reason

possesses causality according to objectively determining grounds, is rescued; and yet natural necessity is not in the least curtailed with regard to the very same effects, as appearances. The same remarks will serve to explain what we had to say concerning transcendental freedom and its compatibility with natural necessity (in the same subject, but not taken in one and the same reference). For, as to this, every beginning of the action of a being from objective causes regarded as determining grounds is always a first beginning, though the same action is in the series of appearances only a subordinate beginning, which must be preceded by a state of the cause which determines it and is itself determined in the same manner by another immediately preceding. Thus we are able, in rational beings, or in beings generally so far as their causality is determined in them as things in themselves, to think of a faculty of beginning of themselves a series of states without falling into contradiction with the laws of nature. For the relation of the action to objective grounds of reason is not a time-relation; in this case that which determines the causality does not precede in time the action, because such determining grounds represent, not a reference to objects of sense, e.g., to causes in the appearances, but to determining causes as things in themselves, which do not stand under conditions of time. And in this way the action, with regard to the causality of reason, can be considered as a first beginning, while in respect to the series of appearances as a merely subordinate 347 beginning. We may therefore without contradiction consider it in the former aspect as free, but in the latter (insofar as it is merely appearance) as subject to natural necessity.

As to the fourth antinomy, it is solved in the same way as the conflict of reason with itself in the third. For, provided the cause *in* the appearance is distinguished from the cause *of* the appearances (so far as it can be thought as a thing in itself), both propositions are perfectly reconcilable: the one, that there is nowhere in the sensuous world a cause (according to similar laws of causality) whose existence is absolutely necessary; the other, that this world is nevertheless connected with a necessary being as its cause (but of another kind and according to another law). The incompatibility of these two propositions rests entirely upon the misunderstanding of extending what is valid merely of appearances to things in themselves and in general of mixing both in one concept.

§ 54. This, then, is the exposition, and this is the solution of the whole antinomy in which reason finds itself involved in the application of its principles to the sensible world. The former alone (the mere exposition) would be a considerable service in the cause of our knowledge of human reason, even though the solution might fail to fully satisfy the reader, who has here to combat a natural illusion which has been but recently exposed to him and which he had hitherto always regarded as true. For one result at least is unavoidable. As it is quite impossible to prevent this conflict of reason with itself—so long as the objects of the sensible world are taken for things in themselves and not for mere appearances, which they are in fact—the reader is thereby compelled to examine over again the deduction of all our *a priori* cognition and the proof which I have given of my deduction in order to come to a decision on the question. This is all I require at present; for when in this occupation he shall have thought himself deep enough into the nature of pure reason, those con-348 cepts by which alone the solution of the conflict of reason is possible will become sufficiently familiar to him. Without this preparation I cannot expect an unreserved assent even from the most attentive reader.

III. THE THEOLOGICAL IDEA[40]

§ 55. The third transcendental idea, which affords material for the most important but, if pursued only speculatively, transcendent and thereby dialectical use of reason, is the ideal of pure reason. Reason in this case does not, as with the psychological and the cosmological ideas, start from experience and err by exaggerating its grounds in striving to attain, if possible, the absolute completeness of their series. Rather, it totally breaks with experience and from mere concepts of what constitutes the absolute completeness of a thing in general (hence by means of the idea of a most perfect primal being) proceeds to determine the possibility and therefore the actuality of all other things. And so the mere presupposition of a being which, al-

40. Cf. *Critique*, "The Ideal of Pure Reason," B 595–670.

though not in the series of experiences is thought for the purposes of experience and for the sake of conceiving its connection, order, and unity, i.e., the idea, is more easily distinguished from the concept of the understanding here than in the former cases. Hence we can easily expose the dialectical illusion which arises from our making the subjective conditions of our thinking objective conditions of objects themselves, and from making an hypothesis necessary for the satisfaction of our reason into a dogma. As the observations of the *Critique* on the pretensions of trancendental theology are intelligible, clear, and decisive, I have nothing more to add on the subject.

GENERAL REMARK ON THE TRANSCENDENTAL IDEAS

§ 56. The objects which are given us by experience are in many respects inconceivable, and many questions to which the law of nature leads us when carried beyond a certain point 349 (though still quite conformably to the laws of nature) admit of no answer, as, for example, the question as to why material objects attract one another? But if we entirely quit nature or, in pursuing its combinations, exceed all possible experience, and so enter the realm of mere ideas, we cannot then say that the object is inconceivable and that the nature of things proposes to us insoluble problems. For we are not then concerned with nature or with given objects at all, but with mere concepts which have their origin solely in our reason, and with mere beings of thought; and all the problems that arise from our concepts of them must be solved, because of course reason can and must give a full account of its own procedure.[41] As the psychological,

41. Herr Platner, in his *Aphorisms*, acutely says (§§ 728, 729), "If reason be a criterion, no concept which is incomprehensible to human reason can be possible. Incomprehensibility has place in what is actual only. Here incomprehensibility arises from the insufficiency of the acquired ideas." It sounds paradoxical, but is otherwise not strange to say that in nature there is much that is incomprehensible (e.g., the faculty of generation); but if we mount still higher and go even beyond nature, everything again becomes conceivable. For we then quit entirely the objects which can be given us and occupy ourselves merely about ideas, in which occupation we can easily conceive the law that reason prescribes by them to the understanding for its use in experience, because the law is reason's own product.

cosmological, and theological ideas are nothing but pure concepts of reason, which cannot be given in any experience, the questions which reason asks us about them are put to us, not by the objects, but by mere maxims of our reason for the sake of its own satisfaction. They must all be capable of satisfactory answers, which are provided by showing that they are principles which bring our use of the understanding into thorough agreement, completeness, and synthetical unity, and that they thus hold good of experience only, but of experience as a whole. Although an absolute whole of experience is impossible, the idea of a whole of cognition according to principles in general must impart to our knowledge a peculiar kind of unity, that of a system, without which it is nothing but piecework and cannot be used for the highest purpose (which is always only the system of all purposes); I do not here refer only to the practical, but also to the highest purpose of the speculative use of reason.

350

The transcendental ideas therefore express the peculiar application of reason as a principle of systematic unity in the use of the understanding. Yet if we assume this unity of the mode or cognition to pertain to the object of cognition, if we regard that which is merely *regulative* to be *constitutive,* and if we persuade ourselves that we can by means of these ideas enlarge our cognition transcendently or far beyond all possible experience, while it only serves to render experience within itself as nearly complete as possible, i.e., to limit its progress by nothing that cannot belong to experience—if we do all this, then we suffer from a mere misunderstanding in our estimate of the proper application of our reason and of its principles and suffer from a dialectic which confuses the empirical use of reason and also sets reason at variance with itself.

CONCLUSION

On The Determination of the Bounds of Pure Reason

§ 57. The clearest arguments having been adduced, it would be absurd for us to hope that we can know more of any object than belongs to the possible experience of it or lay claim to the least knowledge of how anything not assumed to be an object of possible experience is determined according to the constitution that it has in itself. For how could we determine anything in this way, since time, space, and all the concepts of the understanding, and still more all the concepts formed by empirical intuition (or perception) in the sensible world have and can have no other use than to make experience possible? And if this condition is omitted from the pure concepts of the understanding, they do not determine any object and have no meaning whatever.

But it would be, on the other hand, a still greater absurdity if we conceded no things in themselves or declared our experience 351 to be the only possible mode of knowing things, our intuition of them in space and in time to be the only possible intuition, our discursive understanding to be the archetype of every possible understanding, and to have the principles of the possibility of experience taken for universal conditions of things in themselves.

Our principles, which limit the use of reason to possible experience, might in this way become transcendent and the limits of our reason be set up as limits of the possibility of things in themselves (as Hume's *Dialogues*[42] may illustrate) if a careful critique did not guard the bounds of our reason with respect to its empirical use and set a limit to its pretensions. Scepticism originally arose from metaphysics and its lawless dialectic. At first it might, merely to favor the empirical use of reason, announce everything that transcends this use as worthless and deceitful;

42. [David Hume, *Dialogues Concerning Natural Religion* (1779)]

but by and by, when it was noticed that the very same principles that are used in experience insensibly and apparently with the same right led still further than experience extends, then men began to doubt even the propositions of experience. But here there is no danger, for common sense will doubtless always assert its rights. A certain confusion, however, arose in science, which cannot determine how far reason is to be trusted, and why only so far and no further; and this confusion can only be cleared up and all future relapses obviated by a formal determination, on principle, of the boundary of the use of our reason.

We cannot indeed, beyond all possible experience, form a definite notion of what things in themselves may be. Yet we are not at liberty to abstain entirely from inquiring into them; for experience never satisfies reason fully but, in answering questions, refers us further and further back and leaves us dissatisfied with regard to their complete solution. This anyone may gather from the dialectic of pure reason, which therefore has its good subjective grounds. Having acquired, as regards the nature of our soul, a clear conception of the subject, and having come to the conviction that its appearances cannot be explained materialistically, 352 who can refrain from asking what the soul really is and, if no concept of experience suffices for the purpose, from accounting for it by a concept of reason (that of a simple immaterial being), though we cannot by any means prove its objective reality? Who can satisfy himself with mere empirical knowledge in all the cosmological questions of the duration and of the magnitude of the world, of freedom or of natural necessity, since every answer given on principles of experience begets a fresh question, which likewise requires its answer and thereby clearly shows the insufficiency of all physical modes of explanation to satisfy reason? Finally, who does not see in the thoroughgoing contingency and dependence of all his thoughts and assumptions on mere principles of experience the impossibility of stopping there? And who does not feel himself compelled, notwithstanding all interdictions against losing himself in transcendent ideas, to seek rest and contentment, beyond all the concepts which he can vindicate by experience, in the concept of a being, the possibility of which cannot be conceived but at the same time cannot be refuted, because it relates to a mere being of the understanding and without it reason must needs remain forever dissatisfied?

Bounds (in extended beings) always presuppose a space existing outside a certain definite place and inclosing it; limits do not require this, but are mere negations which affect a quantity so far as it is not absolutely complete. But our reason, as it were, sees in its surroundings a space for the cognition of things in themselves, though we can never have determinate concepts of them and are limited to appearances only.

As long as the cognition of reason is homogeneous, determinate bounds to it cannot be thought. In mathematics and natural science human reason admits of limits but not of bounds, viz., that something indeed lies outside it, at which it can never arrive, but not that it will at any point find completion in its internal progress. The enlarging of insights in mathematics and the possibility of new discoveries are infinite; and the same is the case with the discovery of new properties of nature, of new forces and laws, by continued experience and its rational unification. But limits cannot fail to be seen here; for mathematics refers to appearances only, and what cannot be an object of sensuous intuition (such as the concepts of metaphysics and of morals) lies entirely without its sphere. It can never lead to them, but neither does it require them. There is therefore a continuous progress and approach to these sciences; and there is, as it were, a point or line of contact. Natural science will never reveal to us the internal constitution of things, which, though not appearance, yet can serve as the ultimate ground for explaining appearances. Nor does that science need this for its physical explanations. Nay, even if such grounds should be offered from other sources (for instance, the influence of immaterial beings), they must be rejected and not used in the progress of its explanations. For these explanations must only be grounded upon that which as an object of sense can belong to experience, and be brought into connection with our actual perceptions according to empirical laws.

But metaphysics leads us towards bounds in the dialectical attempts of pure reason (not undertaken arbitrarily or wantonly, but stimulated thereto by the nature of reason itself). And the transcendental ideas, as they do not admit of evasion and yet are never capable of realization, serve to point out to us actually not

353

only the bounds of the use of pure reason, but also the way to determine them. Such is the end and the use of this natural predisposition of our reason, which has brought forth metaphysics as its favorite child, whose generation, like every other in the world, is not to be ascribed to blind chance but to an original germ, wisely organized for great ends. For metaphysics, in its fundamental features, perhaps more than any other science, is placed in us by nature itself and cannot be considered the production of an arbitrary choice or a casual enlargement in the progress of experience from which it is quite disparate.

Reason with all its concepts and laws of the understanding, which are adequate to it for empirical use, i.e., within the sensible world, finds for itself no satisfaction because ever-recurring questions deprive us of all hope of their complete solution. The transcendental ideas, which have that completion in view, are 354 such problems of reason. But it sees clearly that the sensible world cannot contain this completion; neither, consequently, can all the concepts which serve merely for understanding the world of sense, e.g., space and time, and whatever we have adduced under the name of pure concepts of the understanding. The sensible world is nothing but a chain of appearances connected according to universal laws; it has therefore no subsistence by itself; it is not the thing in itself, and consequently must point to that which contains the basis of this appearance, to beings which cannot be cognized merely as appearances, but as things in themselves. In the cognition of them alone can reason hope to satisfy its desire for completeness in proceeding from the conditioned to its conditions.

We have above (§§ 33, 34) indicated the limits of reason with regard to all cognition of mere beings of thought. Now, since the transcendental ideas have urged us to approach them and thus have led us, as it were, to the spot where the occupied space (viz., experience) touches the void (that of which we can know nothing, viz., noumena), we can determine the bounds of pure reason. For in all bounds there is something positive (e.g., a surface is the boundary of corporeal space, and is therefore itself a space; a line is a space, which is the boundary of the surface, a point the boundary of the line, but yet always a place in space), whereas limits contain mere negations. The limits pointed out in those paragraphs are not enough after we have discovered that beyond them there still lies something (though we can never cognize what it is in itself). For the question now is, What is the attitude of our reason in this connection of what we know with what we do not, and never shall, know? This is an actual connection of a known thing with one quite unknown (and which will always remain so), and though what is unknown should not become the least more known—which we cannot even hope— yet the notion of this connection must be definite, and capable of being rendered distinct.

We must therefore think an immaterial being, a world of understanding, and a Supreme Being (all mere noumena), because in them only, as things in themselves, reason finds that completion and satisfaction, which it can never hope for in the derivation of appearances from their homogeneous grounds, and because these actually have reference to something distinct from them (and totally heterogeneous), as appearances always presuppose an object in itself and therefore suggest its existence whether we can know more of it or not.

355

But as we can never cognize these beings of understanding as they are in themselves, that is, determinately, yet must assume them as regards the sensible world and connect them with it by reason, we are at least able to think this connection by means of such concepts as express their relation to the world of sense. Yet if we represent to ourselves a being of the understanding by nothing but pure concepts of the understanding, we then indeed represent nothing determinate to ourselves, and consequently our concept has no significance; but if we think of it by properties borrowed from the sensible world, then it is no longer a being of understanding but is conceived as a phenomenon and belongs to the sensible world. Let us take an instance from the concept of the Supreme Being.

The deistic concept is quite a pure concept of reason, but represents only a thing containing all realities, without being able to determine any one of them; because for that purpose an example must be taken from the world of sense, in which case I should have an object of sense only, not something quite heterogeneous which can never be an object of sense. Suppose I attribute to the Supreme Being understanding, for instance; I have no concept of an understanding other than my own, one that must receive its intuitions by the senses and which is occupied in bringing them under rules of the unity of consciousness. Then the elements of my concept would always lie in the appearance; I should, however, by the insufficiency of the appearances be required to go beyond them to the concept of a being which neither depends upon appearances nor is bound up with them as conditions of its determination. But if I separate understanding from sensibility to obtain a pure understanding, then nothing remains but the mere form of thinking without intuition, by which form alone I can cognize nothing determinate and consequently no object. For that purpose I should have to think another understanding, such as would intuit its objects but of which I have not the least concept, because the human understanding is discursive, and can cognize only by means of general concepts. And the very same difficulties arise if we attribute a will to the Supreme Being; for I have this concept only by drawing it from my inner experience, and therefore from my dependence for satisfaction upon objects whose existence I require; and so the concept rests upon sensibility, which is wholly incompatible with the pure concept of the Supreme Being.

356

Hume's objections to deism are weak, and affect only the proofs, and not the deistic assertion itself. But as regards theism, which depends on a stricter determination of the concept of the Supreme Being, which in deism is merely transcendent, they are very strong and, as this concept is formed, in certain (in fact in all common) cases irrefutable. Hume always insists that by the mere concept of an original being to which we apply only ontological predicates (eternity, omnipresence, omnipotence) we think nothing determinate, and that properties which can yield a concept *in concreto* must be superadded. He insists also that it is not enough to say that it is cause, but we must explain the nature of its causality, e.g., that of an understanding and of a will. He then begins his attacks on the essential point itself, i.e., theism, as he had previously directed his battery only against the proofs of deism, an attack which is not very dangerous to it in its consequences. All his dangerous arguments refer to anthropomorphism, which he holds to be inseparable from theism and to make it contradictory in itself; but if the former can be aban-

doned, the latter must vanish with it and nothing remain but
deism, of which nothing can come, which is of no value and
which cannot serve as any foundation to religion or morals. If
this anthropomorphism were really unavoidable, no proofs
whatever of the existence of a Supreme Being, even were they
all granted, could determine for us the concept of this Being
without involving us in contradictions.

If we connect with the command to avoid all transcendent
judgments of pure reason the command (which apparently conflicts with it) to proceed to concepts that lie beyond the field of
its immanent (empirical) use, we discover that both can subsist
together, but only at the boundary of all permitted use of reason.
For this boundary belongs to the field of experience as well as to   357
that of the beings of thought, and we are thereby taught how
these remarkable ideas serve merely for marking the bounds of
human reason. On the one hand, they give warning not
boundlessly to extend cognition by experience, as if nothing but
world remained for us to cognize, and yet, on the other hand,
not to transgress the bounds of experience and to think of judging about things beyond them as things in themselves.

But we stop at this boundary if we limit our judgment merely
to the relation which the world may have to a being whose very
concept lies beyond all the cognition which we can attain within
the world. For we then do not attribute to the Supreme Being
any of the properties in themselves by which we represent
objects of experience, and thereby avoid *dogmatic* anthropomorphism; but we attribute them to his relation to the world and
allow ourselves a *symbolic* anthropomorphism, which in fact concerns language only and not the object itself.

If I say that we are compelled to consider the world *as if* it
were the work of a Supreme Understanding and Will, I really say
nothing more than that a watch, a ship, a regiment bears the
same relation to the watchmaker, the shipbuilder, the com-
manding officer as the world of sense (or whatever constitutes
the substratum of this complex of appearances) does to the
unknown, which I do not hereby cognize as it is in itself but as it
is for me, i.e., in relation to the world of which I am a part.

§ 58. Such a cognition is one of analogy and does not signify
(as is commonly understood) an imperfect similarity of two

things, but a perfect similarity of relations between two quite dis-
358   similar things.[43] By means of this analogy, however, there remains a concept of the Supreme Being sufficiently determined
for us, though we have left out everything that could determine
it absolutely and *in itself;* for we determine it as regards the world
and therefore as regards ourselves, and more do we not require.
The attacks which Hume makes upon those who would determine this concept absolutely, by taking the materials for so
doing from themselves and the world, do not affect us; and he
cannot object to us that we have nothing left if we take away the
objective anthropomorphism from our concept of the Supreme
Being.

For let us assume at the outset (as Hume in his *Dialogues*
makes Philo grant Cleanthes), as a necessary hypothesis, the
deistic concept of the First Being, in which this Being is thought
by the mere ontological predicates of substance, of cause, etc.
This must be done because reason, actuated in the sensible
world by mere conditions which are themselves in turn always
conditioned, cannot otherwise have any satisfaction; and it
therefore can be done without falling into anthropomorphism
(which transfers predicates from the world of sense to a being
quite distinct from the world) because those predicates are mere
categories which, though they do not give a determinate concept
of this being, yet give a concept not limited to any conditions of
sensibility. Thus nothing can prevent our predicating of this
being a causality through reason with regard to the world, and

43. Thus there is an analogy between the juridical relation of human actions
and the mechanical relation of moving forces. I never can do anything to
another man without giving him a right to do the same to me on the same conditions; just as no body can act with its moving force on another body without
thereby causing the other to react equally against it. Here right and moving
force are quite dissimilar things, but in their relation there is complete
similarity. By means of such an analogy, I can obtain a relational concept of
things which are absolutely unknown to me. For instance, as the promotion of
the welfare of children (= a) is to the love of parents (= b), so the welfare of
the human species (= c) is to that unknown in God (= x), which we call love;
not as if it had the least similarity to any human inclination, but because we can
posit its relation to the world to be similar to that which things of the world bear
one another. But the relational concept in this case is a mere category, viz., the
concept of cause, which has nothing to do with sensibility.

thus passing to theism, without being obliged to attribute to this being itself this kind of reason, as a property inhering in it. For   **359** as to the former, the only possible way of pushing the use of reason (as regards all possible experience in complete harmony with itself) in the world of sense to the highest point is to assume a supreme reason as a cause of all the connections in the world. Such a principle must be quite advantageous to reason and can hurt it nowhere in its application to nature. As to the latter, reason is thereby not transferred as a property to the First Being in itself, but only to its relation to the world of sense, and so anthropomorphism is entirely avoided. For nothing is considered here but the cause of the rational form which is found everywhere in the world, and reason is attributed to the Supreme Being so far as it contains the ground of this rational form in the world, but according to analogy only, i.e., so far as this expression shows merely the relation which the Supreme Cause, unknown to us, has to the world in order to determine everything in it conformably to reason in the highest degree. We are thereby kept from using reason as an attribute in order to think God, but not kept from thinking the world in such a manner as is necessary to have the greatest possible use of reason within it according to principle. We thereby acknowledge that the Supreme Being is quite inscrutable and even unthinkable in any determinate way as to what it is in itself. We are thereby kept, on the one hand, from making a transcendent use of the concepts which we have of reason as an efficient cause (by means of the will), in order to determine the Divine Nature by properties which are only borrowed from human nature, and from losing ourselves in gross and extravagant concepts; and, on the other hand, from deluging the contemplation of the world with hyperphysical modes of explanation according to our concepts of human reason which we transfer to God, and so from losing for this contemplation its proper role, according to which it should be a rational study of mere nature and not a presumptuous derivation of its appearances from a Supreme Reason. The expression suited to our feeble concepts is that we conceive the world *as if* it came, regarding its existence and its inner determination, from a Supreme Reason. By this conception we both cognize the constitution which belongs to the world itself with-

out pretending to determine the nature of its cause in itself, and
we transfer the ground of this constitution (of the rational form
360   of the world) to the *relation* of the Supreme Cause to the world,
without finding the world sufficient by itself for that purpose.[44]

Thus the difficulties which seem to oppose theism disappear
by combining with Hume's principle, "not to carry the use of
reason dogmatically beyond the field of all possible experience,"
this other principle, which he quite overlooked, "not to consider
the field of experience as one which bounds itself in the eyes of
our reason." The *Critique of Pure Reason* here points out the true
mean between dogmatism, which Hume combats, and skepti-
cism, which he would substitute for it—a mean which is not like
other means that we find advisable to determine for ourselves as
it were mechanically (by adopting something from one side and
something from the other), and by which nobody is taught a better way, but such a one as can be exactly determined on principles.

§ 59. At the beginning of this note I made use of the
metaphor of a boundary in order to establish the limits of reason
in regard to its suitable use. The world of sense contains merely
appearances, which are not things in themselves; but the understanding must assume these latter ones, viz., noumena, because
it knows the objects of experience to be mere appearances. In
our reason both are comprised together, and the question is,
How does reason proceed to set boundaries to the understanding as regards both these fields? Experience, which contains all
that belongs to the sensible world, does not bound itself; it only
proceeds in every case from the conditioned to some other
equally conditioned thing. Its boundary must lie quite without it,
361   and this is the field of the pure beings of the understanding. But
this field, so far as the determination of the nature of these

44. I may say that the causality of the Supreme Cause holds the same place
with regard to the world that human reason does with regard to its works of art.
Here the nature of the Supreme Cause itself remains unknown to me; I only
compare its effects (the order of the world), which I know, and their conformity to reason to the effects of human reason, which I also know; and hence I
term the former reason, without attributing .o it on that account what I understand in man by this term, or attaching to it anything else known to me as its
property.

beings is concerned, is an empty space for us; and if dogmatically determined concepts are being considered, we cannot pass beyond the field of possible experience. But as a boundary is itself something positive, which belongs to what lies within as well as to the space that lies without the given complex, it is still an actual positive cognition which reason only acquires by enlarging itself to this boundary, yet without attempting to pass it because it there finds itself in the presence of an empty space in which it can think forms of things but not things themselves. But the setting of a boundary to the field of experience by something which is otherwise unknown to reason, is still a cognition which belongs to it even at this point, and by which it is neither confined within the sensible nor strays beyond the sensible, but only limits itself, as befits the knowledge of a boundary, to the relation between what lies beyond it and what is contained within it.

Natural theology is such a concept at the boundary of human reason, being constrained to look beyond this boundary to the idea of a Supreme Being (and, for practical purposes, to that of an intelligible world also), not in order to determine anything relatively to this mere being of the understanding, which lies beyond the world of sense, but in order to guide the use of reason within the world of sense according to principles of the greatest possible (theoretical as well as practical) unity. For this purpose reason makes use of the reference of the world of sense to an independent reason as the cause of all that world's connections. Thereby reason does not merely invent a being, but, as beyond the sensible world there must be something that can be thought only by the pure understanding, reason determines that something in this particular way, though only of course according to analogy.

And thus there remains our original proposition, which is the result of the whole *Critique:* "that reason by all its *a priori* principles never teaches us anything more than objects of possible experience, and even of these nothing more than can be cognized in experience." But this limitation does not prevent reason from leading us to the objective boundary of experience, viz., to the reference to something which is not itself an object of experience but must be the highest ground of all experience. Reason

362 does not, however, teach us anything concerning the thing in itself; it only instructs us as regards its own complete and highest use in the field of possible experience. But this is all that can be reasonably desired in the present case, and with it we have cause to be satisfied.

§ 60. Thus we have fully exhibited metaphysics according to its subjective possibility, as it is actually given in the natural predisposition of human reason and in that which constitutes the essential end of its pursuit. We have found that this merely natural use of such a predisposition of our reason, if no discipline arising only from a scientific critique bridles and sets limits to it, involves us in transcendent dialectical inferences, that are in part merely illusory and in part even self-contradictory, and that this fallacious metaphysics is not only unnecessary as regards the promotion of our knowledge of nature but even disadvantageous to it. There yet remains a problem worthy of inquiry, which is to find out the natural ends intended by this disposition to transcendent concepts in our reason, because everything that lies in nature must be originally intended for some useful purpose.

Such an inquiry is of a doubtful nature, and I acknowledge that what I can say about it is conjecture only, like every speculation about the first ends of nature. This conjecture may be allowed to me in this case alone, because the question does not concern the objective validity of metaphysical judgments but our natural predisposition to them, and therefore does not belong to the system of metaphysics but to anthropology.

When I compare all the transcendental ideas, the totality of which constitutes the particular problem of natural pure reason, compelling it to quit the mere contemplation of nature, to transcend all possible experience, and in this endeavor to produce the thing (be it knowledge or fiction) called metaphysics; I think I perceive that the aim of this natural tendency is to free our concepts from the fetters of experience and from the limits of the mere contemplation of nature so far as at least to open to us a field containing mere objects for the pure understanding which no sensibility can reach, not indeed for the purpose of speculatively occupying ourselves with them (for there we can

363 find no ground to stand on), but in order that practical principles might find some such scope for their necessary expectation and

hope and might expand to the universality which reason unavoidably requires from a moral point of view.

So I find that the psychological idea (however little it may reveal to me the nature of the human soul, which is elevated above all concepts of experience) shows the insufficiency of these concepts plainly enough and thereby deters me from materialism, a psychological concept which is unfit for any explanation of nature and which in addition confines reason in practical respects. The cosmological ideas, by the obvious insufficiency of all possible cognition of nature to satisfy reason in its legitimate inquiry, serve in the same manner to keep us from naturalism, which asserts nature to be sufficient for itself. Finally, all natural necessity in the sensible world is conditional, as it always presupposes the dependence of things upon others, and unconditional necessity must be sought only in the unity of a cause different from the world of sense. But as the causality of this cause, in its turn, were it merely nature, could never render the existence of the contingent (as its consequent) comprehensible, reason frees itself by means of the theological idea from fatalism (both as a blind natural necessity in the coherence of nature itself, without a first principle, and as a blind causality of this principle itself) and leads to the concept of a cause possessing freedom and hence of a Supreme Intelligence. Thus the transcendental ideas serve, if not to instruct us positively, at least to destroy the impudent and restrictive assertions of materialism, of naturalism, and of fatalism, and thus to afford scope for the moral ideas beyond the field of speculation. These considerations, I should think, explain in some measure the natural predisposition of which I spoke.

The practical value which a merely speculative science may have lies outside the bounds of this science, and can therefore be considered as a scholium merely, and like all scholia does not form part of the science itself. This application, however, surely lies within the bounds of philosophy, especially of philosophy drawn from the pure sources of reason, where its speculative use in metaphysics must necessarily be at one with its practical use in morals. Hence the unavoidable dialectic of pure reason, con- 364 sidered in metaphysics as a natural tendency, deserves to be explained not as a mere illusion, which is to be removed, but also, if possible, as a natural provision as regards its end, though this task, a work of supererogation, cannot justly be assigned to metaphysics proper.

The solutions of these questions which are treated in the *Critique*[45] should be considered a second scholium, which, however, has a greater affinity with the subject of metaphysics. For there certain rational principles are expounded which determine *a priori* the order of nature or rather of the understanding, which seeks nature's laws through experience. They seem to be constitutive and legislative with regard to experience, though they spring from mere reason, which cannot be considered, like the understanding, as a principle of possible experience. Now whether or not this harmony rests upon the fact that, just as nature does not inhere in appearances or in their source (the sensibility) itself, but only in the relation of the latter to the understanding, so also a thoroughgoing unity in the use of the understanding to bring about an entirety of all possible experience (in a system) can only belong to the understanding when in relation to reason, with the result that experience is in this way mediately subordinate to the legislation of reason: this question may be discussed by those who desire to trace the nature of reason even beyond its use in metaphysics into the general principles for making systematic a history of nature in general. I have presented this task as important, but not attempted its solution in the book itself.[46]

365   And thus I conclude the analytical solution of the main question which I had proposed: "How is metaphysics in general possible?" by ascending from the data of its actual use, at least in its consequences, to the grounds of its possibility.

45. *Critique of Pure Reason,* "The Regulative Employment of the Ideas of Pure Reason," B 670–696

46. Throughout in the *Critique* I never lost sight of the plan not to neglect anything, were it ever so recondite, that could render the inquiry into the nature of pure reason complete. Everybody may afterwards carry his researches as far as he pleases, when he has been merely shown what yet remains to be done. This can reasonably be expected of him who has made it his business to survey the whole field, in order to consign it to others for future cultivation and allotment. And to this branch both the scholia belong, which will hardly recommend themselves by their dryness to amateurs, and hence are added here for connoisseurs only.

SOLUTION OF THE GENERAL QUESTION
OF THE PROLEGOMENA

"How is Metaphysics Possible as Science?"

Metaphysics, as a natural disposition of reason, is actual; but if considered by itself alone (as the analytical solution of the third principal question showed), it is dialectical and illusory. If we think of taking principles from it, and in using them follow the natural, but on that account not less false, illusion, we can never produce science, but only a vain dialectical art, in which one school may outdo another but none can ever acquire a just and lasting approbation.

In order that as a science metaphysics may be entitled to claim, not mere fallacious plausibility, but insight and conviction, a critique of reason must itself exhibit the whole stock of *a priori* concepts, their division according to their various sources (sensibility, understanding, and reason), together with a complete table of them, the analysis of all these concepts, with all their consequences and especially the possibility of synthetic cognition *a priori* by means of the deduction of these concepts, the principles and bounds of their use, all in a complete system. Critique, therefore, and critique alone contains in itself the whole well-proved and well-tested plan, and even all the means required to establish metaphysics as a science; by other ways and means it is impossible. The question here, therefore, is not so much how this performance is possible as how to set it going and induce men of clear heads to quit their hitherto perverted and fruitless cultivation for one that will not deceive, and how such a union for the common end may best be directed.

This much is certain: whoever has once tasted critique will be 366 ever after disgusted with all dogmatical twaddle which he formerly put up with because his reason had to have something and could find nothing better for its support. Critique stands in the same relation to the common metaphysics of the schools as chemistry does to alchemy, or as astronomy to the astrology of the fortune teller. I pledge myself that nobody who has thought through and grasped the principles of critique, even only in these *Prolegomena,* will ever return to that old and sophistical pseudo-science; but he will, rather, with a certain delight look forward to a metaphysics which is now indeed in his power, requiring no more preparatory discoveries, and now at last affording permanent satisfaction to reason. For here is an advantage upon which, of all possible sciences, metaphysics alone can with certainty reckon: that it can be brought to such completion and fixity as to require no further change or be capable of any augmentation by new discoveries, because here reason has the sources of its knowledge in itself, not in objects and their observation, by which its stock of knowledge could be further increased. When, therefore, it has exhibited the fundamental laws of its faculty completely and so determinately as to avoid all misunderstanding, there remains nothing more for pure reason to cognize *a priori;* nay, there is even no ground to raise further questions. The sure prospect of knowledge so determinate and so compact has a peculiar charm, even though we should set aside all its advantages, of which I shall hereafter speak.

All false art, all vain wisdom, lasts its time but finally destroys itself, and its highest culture is also the epoch of its decay. That this time is come for metaphysics appears from the state into which it has fallen among all learned nations, despite all the zeal with which other sciences of every kind are pursued. The old arrangement of our university studies still preserves its shadow; now and then an academy of science tempts men by offering prizes to write essays on it, but it is no longer numbered among sound sciences; and let anyone judge for himself how a sophisticated man, if he were called a great metaphysician, would receive the compliment, which may be well meant but is scarcely envied by anybody.

367   Yet, though the period of the downfall of all dogmatic metaphysics has undoubtedly arrived, we are yet far from being able to say that the period of its regeneration is come by means of a thorough and complete critique of reason. All transitions from an inclination to its contrary pass through the stage of indifference, and this moment is the most dangerous for an

author but, in my opinion, the most favorable for the science. For when party spirit has died out by a total dissolution of former connections, minds are in the best state to listen to several proposals for an organization according to a new plan.

When I say that I hope these *Prolegomena* will excite investigation in the field of critique and afford a new and promising object to sustain the general spirit of philosophy, which seems on its speculative side to want sustenance, I can imagine beforehand that everyone whom the thorny paths of my *Critique* have tired and put out of humor will ask me upon what I found this hope. My answer is: upon the irresistible law of necessity.

That the human spirit will ever give up metaphysical researches is as little to be expected as that we should prefer to give up breathing altogether, in order to avoid inhaling impure air. There will, therefore, always be metaphysics in the world; nay, everyone, especially every reflective man, will have it and, for want of a recognized standard, will shape it for himself after his own pattern. What has hitherto been called metaphysics cannot satisfy any critical mind, but to forego it entirely is impossible; therefore a critique of pure reason itself must now be attempted or, if one exists, investigated and brought to the full test, because there is no other means of supplying this pressing want which is something more than mere thirst for knowledge.

Ever since I have come to know critique, whenever I finish reading a book of metaphysical contents which, by the determination of its concepts, by variety, order, and an easy style, was not only entertaining but also helpful, I cannot help asking, 368 "Has this author indeed advanced metaphysics a single step?" The learned men whose works have been useful to me in other respects and always contributed to the culture of my mental powers will, I hope, forgive me for saying that I have never been able to find either their essays or my own less important ones (though self-love may recommend them to me) to have advanced the science of metaphysics in the least, and why? Here is the very obvious reason: metaphysics did not then exist as a science, nor can it be gathered piecemeal; but its germ must be fully preformed in critique. But in order to prevent all misconception, we must remember what has already been said—that by the analytic treatment of our concepts the understanding gains indeed a great deal, but the science (of metaphysics) is thereby not in the least advanced because these analyses of concepts are nothing but the materials from which the intention is to carpenter our science. Let the concepts of substance and of accident be ever so well analyzed and determined; all this is very well as a preparation for some future use. But if we cannot prove that in all which exists the substance endures and only the accidents vary, our science is not the least advanced by all our analyses. Metaphysics has hitherto never been able to prove *a priori* either this proposition or that of sufficient reason, still less any more complex theorem such as belongs to psychology or cosmology, or indeed any synthetic proposition. By all its analyzing, therefore, nothing is affected, nothing obtained or forwarded; and the science, after all this bustle and noise, still remains as it was in the days of Aristotle, though far better preparations were made for it than of old if only the clue to synthetic cognitions had been discovered.

If anyone thinks himself offended, he is at liberty to refute my charge by producing a single synthetic proposition belonging to metaphysics which he would prove dogmatically *a priori;* for until he has actually performed this feat, I shall not grant that he has truly advanced the science, even though this proposition should be sufficiently confirmed by common experience. No demand can be more moderate or more equitable and, in the (inevitably certain) event of its nonperformance, no assertion more just than that hitherto metaphysics has never existed as a science.

369

But there are two things which, in case the challenge be accepted, I must deprecate: first, trifling about probability and conjecture, which are suited as little to metaphysics as to geometry; and secondly, a decision by means of the magic wand of socalled sound common sense, which does not convince everyone but accommodates itself to personal peculiarities.

For as to the former, nothing can be more absurd than in metaphysics, a philosophy from pure reason, to try to ground our judgments upon probability and conjecture. Everything that is to be cognized *a priori* is thereby announced as apodeictically certain, and must therefore be proved in this way. We might as well try to ground geometry or arithmetic upon conjectures. As to the calculus of probabilities in the latter, it does not contain

probable but perfectly certain judgments concerning the degree
of the possibility of certain cases under given uniform conditions, which, in the sum of all possible cases, must infallibly happen according to the rule, though it is not sufficiently determined as regards every single instance. Conjectures (by means
of induction and analogy) can be suffered in an empirical natural
science only, yet even there at least the possibility of what we
assume must be quite certain.

The appeal to common sense is even more absurd, when concepts and principles are said to be valid, not insofar as they hold
with regard to experience, but outside the conditions of experience. For what is common sense? It is normal good sense, so far
as it judges rightly. What is normal good sense? It is the faculty
of the knowledge and use of rules *in concreto,* as distinguished
from the speculative understanding, which is a faculty of knowing rules *in abstracto.* Common sense can hardly understand the
rule that every event is determined by means of its cause and
can never comprehend it thus generally. It therefore demands an
example from experience; and when it hears that this rule means
nothing but what it always thought when a pane was broken or a   370
kitchen-utensil missing, it then understands the principle and
grants it. Common sense, therefore, is only of use so far as it can
see its rules (though they actually are *a priori*) confirmed by experience; consequently, to comprehend them *a priori,* or independently of experience, belongs to the speculative understanding and lies quite beyond the horizon of common sense. But the
province of metaphysics is entirely confined to the latter kind of
knowledge, and it is certainly a bad sign of common sense to appeal to it as a witness, for it cannot here form any opinion
whatever, and men look down upon it with contempt until they
are in trouble and can find in their speculation neither advice nor
help.

It is a common subterfuge of those false friends of common
sense (who occasionally prize it highly, but usually despise it) to
say that there must surely be at all events some propositions
which are immediately certain and of which there is no occasion
to give any proof, or even any account at all, because we otherwise could never stop inquiring into the grounds of our judgments. But if we except the principle of contradiction, which is

not sufficient to show the truth of synthetic judgments, they can never adduce, in proof of this privilege, anything else indubitable which they can immediately ascribe to common sense, except mathematical propositions, such as twice two make four, between two points there is but one straight line, etc. But these judgments are radically different from those of metaphysics. For in mathematics I can by thinking construct whatever I represent to myself as possible by a concept: I add to the first two the other two, one by one, and myself make the number four, or I draw in thought from one point to another all manner of lines, equal as well as unequal; yet I can draw one only which is like itself in all its parts. But I cannot, by all my power of thinking, extract from the concept of a thing the concept of something else whose existence is necessarily connected with the former, but I must call upon experience. And though my understanding furnishes me *a priori* (yet only in reference to possible experience) with the concept of such a connection (i.e., causation), I cannot exhibit it *a priori* in intuition, like the concepts of mathematics, and so show its possibility *a priori*. This concept, together with the principles of its application, always requires, if it is to hold *a priori*—as is requisite in metaphysics—a justification and deduction of its possibility, because we cannot otherwise know how far it holds good and whether it can be used in experience only or beyond it also. Therefore in metaphysics, as a speculative science of pure reason, we can never appeal to common sense, but may do so only when (in certain matters) we are forced to surrender it and renounce all pure speculative cognition, which must always be theoretic knowledge, and therefore are forced to forego metaphysics itself and its instruction for the sake of adopting a rational faith which alone may be possible for us, sufficient to our wants, and perhaps even more salutary than knowledge itself. For then the shape of the thing is quite altered. Metaphysics must be science, not only as a whole but in all its parts; otherwise it is nothing at all, because as speculation of pure reason it finds a hold only on universal insights. Beyond its field, however, probability and common sense may be used advantageously and justly, but on quite special principles, the importance of which always depends on their reference to the practical.

This is what I hold myself justified in requiring for the possibility of metaphysics as a science.

371

APPENDIX

On What Can Be Done to Make Metaphysics As a Science Actual

Since all the ways heretofore taken have failed to attain the goal, and since without a preceding critique of pure reason it is not likely ever to be attained, the attempt before us has a right to an accurate and careful examination, unless it be thought more advisable to give up all pretensions to metaphysics, to which, if 372 men would but consistently adhere to their purpose, no objection can be made. If we take the course of things as it is, not as it ought to be, there are two sorts of judgments: (1) one a judgment which precedes investigation (in our case one in which the reader from his own metaphysics pronounces judgment on the *Critique of Pure Reason,* which was intended to discuss the very possibility of metaphysics); (2) the other a judgment subsequent to investigation. In the latter, the reader is enabled to ignore for a while the consequences of the critical researches that may be repugnant to his formerly adopted metaphysics, and first examines the grounds whence those consequences are derived. If what common metaphysics propounds were demonstrably certain (like geometry) the former way of judging would hold good. For if the consequences of certain principles are repugnant to established truths, these principles are false and without further inquiry to be repudiated. But if metaphysics does not possess a stock of indisputably certain (synthetic) propositions, and should it even be the case that there are a number of them, which, though among the most plausible, are by their consequences in mutual conflict, and if no sure criterion of the truth of peculiarly metaphysical (synthetic) propositions is to be met with in it, then the former way of judging is not admissible, but the investigation of the principles of the *Critique* must precede all judgments as to its value.

A Specimen of a Judgment about the Critique
Prior to Its Examination.

Such a judgment is to be found in the *Göttingische gelehrte
Anzeigen,* in the supplement to the third part, of January 19,
1782, pages 40 *et seq.*[47]

When an author who is familiar with the subject of his work
and endeavors to present his independent reflections in its
elaboration falls into the hands of a reviewer who, in his turn, is
keen enough to discern the points on which the worth or
worthlessness of the books rests, who does not cling to words
but goes to the heart of the subject, sifting and testing the principles which the author takes as his point of departure, the
severity of the judgment may indeed displease the author, but
the public does not care, as it gains thereby. And the author him-
373 self may be satisfied at having an opportunity of correcting or explaining his positions at an early date by the examination of a
competent judge, in such a manner that if he believes himself
fundamentally right, he can remove in time any stumbling-block
that might hurt the success of his work.

I find myself, with my reviewer, in quite another position. He
seems not to see at all the real matter of the investigation, with
which (successfully or unsuccessfully) I have been occupied. It is
either impatience at thinking out a lengthy work, or vexation at a
threatened reform of a science in which he believed he had
brought everything to perfection long ago, or, what I am reluc-
tant to suppose, real narrow-mindedness that prevents him from
ever carrying his thoughts beyond his school metaphysics. In
short, he passes impatiently in review a long series of propositions, of which, without knowing their premises, one can
comprehend nothing, intersperses here and there his censure,
the reason of which the reader understands just as little as the
propositions against which it is directed; and hence [his report]
can neither serve the public nor damage me in the judgment of
experts. I should, for these reasons, have passed over this judgment altogether, were it not that it may afford me occasion for

47. [This review was given by Christian Garve.]

some explanations which may in some cases save the readers of these *Prolegomena* from a misconception.

In order to take a position from which my reviewer could most easily set the whole work in a most unfavorable light, without venturing to trouble himself with any special investigation, he begins and ends by saying: "This work is a system of transcendental (or, as he translates it, of higher[48]) idealism."

A glance at this line soon showed me the sort of criticism that 374 I had to expect, much as though the reviewer were one who had never seen or heard of geometry, having found a Euclid and coming upon various figures in turning over its leaves, were to say, on being asked his opinion of it: "The work is a textbook of drawing; the author introduces a peculiar terminology in order to give dark, incomprehensible directions, which in the end teach nothing more than what everyone can effect by a fair natural accuracy of eye, etc."

Let us see, in the meantime, what sort of an idealism it is that goes through my whole work, although it does not by a long way constitute the soul of the system.

The dictum of all genuine idealists, from the Eleatic school to Bishop Berkeley, is contained in this formula: "All cognition through the senses and experience is nothing but sheer illusion, and only in the ideas of the pure understanding and reason is there truth."

The principle that throughout dominates and determines my idealism is, on the contrary: "All cognition of things merely from pure understanding or pure reason is nothing but sheer illusion, and only in experience is there truth."

---

48. By no means "higher." High towers and metaphysically great men resembling them, round both of which there is commonly much wind, are not for me. My place is the fruitful bathos of experience; and the word "transcendental," the meaning of which is so often indicated by me but not once grasped by my reviewer (so carelessly has he regarded everything), does not signify something passing beyond all experience but something that indeed precedes it *a priori*, but that is intended simply to make cognition of experience possible. If these concepts overstep experience, their use is termed "transcendent," which must be distinguished from the immanent use, i.e., use restricted to experience. All misunderstandings of this kind have been sufficiently guarded against in the work itself, but my reviewer found his advantage in misunderstanding me.

But this is directly contrary to idealism proper. How came I then to use this expression for quite an opposite purpose, and how came my reviewer to see it everywhere?

The solution of this difficulty rests on something that could have been very easily understood from the context of the work, if the reader had only desired to do so. Space and time, together with all that they contain, are not things in themselves or their qualities but belong merely to the appearances of the things in themselves; up to this point I am one in confession with the above idealists. But these, and among them more particularly Berkeley, regarded space as a mere empirical representation that, like the appearances it contains, is, together with its deter-

375   minations, known to us only by means of experience or perception. I, on the contrary, prove in the first place that space (and also time, which Berkeley did not consider) and all its determinations can be cognized *a priori* by us, because, no less than time, it inheres in us as a pure form of our sensibility before all perception of experience and makes possible all intuition of sensibility, and therefore all appearances. It follows from this that, as truth rests on universal and necessary laws as its criteria, experience, according to Berkeley, can have no criteria of truth because its appearances (according to him) have nothing *a priori* at their foundation, whence it follows that experience is nothing but sheer illusion; whereas with us, space and time (in conjunction with the pure concepts of the understanding) prescribe their law *a priori* to all possible experience and, at the same time, afford the certain criterion for distinguishing truth from illusion therein.[49]

My so-called (properly critical) idealism is of quite a special kind, in that it reverses the usual idealism and through my kind all *a priori* cognition, even that of geometry, first receives objective reality, which, without my demonstrated ideality of space and time, could not be maintained by the most zealous realists.

49. Idealism proper always has a mystical tendency, and can have no other; but mine is solely designed for the purpose of comprehending the possibility of our *a priori* cognition of objects of experience, which is a problem never hitherto solved or even suggested. In this way all mystical idealism falls to the ground, for (as may be seen in Plato) it inferred from our cognitions *a priori* (even from those of geometry) another intuition different from that of the senses (namely, an intellectual intuition), because it never occurred to anyone that the senses themselves might intuit *a priori*.

This being the state of the case, I could wish, in order to avoid all misunderstanding, to have named this concept of mine otherwise, but to alter it altogether is probably impossible. It may therefore be permitted me in future, as has been above intimated, to term it "formal" or, better still, "critical" idealism, to distinguish it from the dogmatic idealism of Berkeley and from the skeptical idealism of Descartes.

Beyond this, I find nothing remarkable in the judgment of my book. The reviewer makes sweeping criticisms, a mode prudently chosen, since it does not betray one's own knowledge or igno- 376 rance; a single thorough criticism in detail, had it touched the main question, as is only fair, would have exposed either my error or my reviewer's measure of insight into this kind of inquiry. It was, moreover, not a badly conceived plan, in order at once to take from readers (who are accustomed to form their conceptions of books from newspaper reports) the desire to read the book itself, to pour out one after the other in one breath a number of propositions which, torn from their connection with their premises and explanations, must necessarily sound senseless, especially considering how antipathetic they are to all school-metaphysics; to exhaust the reader's patience *ad nauseam,* and then, having made me acquainted with the lucid propostion that persistent illusion is truth, to conclude with the crude paternal moralization: to what end, then, the quarrel with accepted language; to what end, and whence, the idealistic distinction? A judgment which seeks all that is characteristic of my book, first supposed to be metaphysically heterodox, in a mere innovation of the nomenclature proves clearly that my would-be judge has understood nothing of the subject and, in addition, has not understood himself.[50]

50. The reviewer often fights with his own shadow. When I oppose the truth of experience to dream, he never thinks that I am here speaking simply of the well-known *somnio objective sumto* ["dreams taken objectively"—Christian Wolff's *German Metaphysics,* § 142] of the Wolffian philosophy, which is merely formal, and with which the distinction between sleeping and waking is in no way concerned—a distinction which can indeed have no place in a transcendental philosophy. For the rest, he calls my deduction of the categories and table of the principles of the understanding "common well-known axioms of logic and ontology, expressed in an idealistic manner." The reader need only consult these *Prolegomena* upon this point to convince himself that a more miserable and historically incorrect judgment could hardly be made.

My reviewer speaks like a man who is conscious of important and superior insight which he keeps hidden, for I am aware of nothing recent with respect to metaphysics that could justify his tone. But he is quite wrong to withhold his discoveries from the world, for there are doubtless many who, like myself, have not been able to find in all the fine things that have for long past 377 been written in this department anything that has advanced the science by so much as a finger's breadth. We find indeed the giving a new point to definitions, the supplying of lame proofs with new crutches, the adding to the crazy-quilt of metaphysics fresh patches or changing its pattern; but all this is not what the world requires. The world is tired of metaphysical assertions; what is wanted is the possibility of this science, the sources from which certainty therein can be derived, and certain criteria by which it may distinguish the dialectical illusion of pure reason from truth. To this the critic seems to possess a key, otherwise he would never have spoken out in such a high tone.

But I am inclined to suspect that no such requirement of the science has ever entered his thoughts, for in that case he would have directed his judgment to this point, and even a mistaken attempt in such an important matter would have won his respect. If that be the case, we are once more good friends. He may penetrate as deeply as he likes into his metaphysics, without any one hindering him; only as concerns that which lies outside metaphysics, its sources, which are to be found in reason, he cannot form a judgment. That my suspicion is not without foundation is proved by the fact that he does not mention a word about the possibility of synthetic knowledge *a priori,* the special problem upon the solution of which the fate of metaphysics wholly rests and upon which my *Critique* (as well as the present *Prolegomena)* entirely hinges. The idealism he encountered and which he hung upon was only taken up in the doctrine as the sole means of solving the above problem (although it received its confirmation on other grounds), and hence he must have shown either that the above problem does not possess the importance I attribute to it (even in these *Prolegomena*) or that, by my concept of appearances, it is either not solved at all or can be better solved in another way; but I do not find a word of this in the criticism. The reviewer, then, understands nothing of my work and possibly also nothing of the spirit and essential nature of metaphysics itself; and it is not, what I would rather assume, the haste of a reviewer to finish his review, incensed at the labor of plodding through so many obstacles, that threw an unfavorable shadow over the work lying before him and made its fundamental features unrecognizable.

There is a great deal to be done before a learned journal, it   378 matters not with what care its writers may be selected, can maintain its otherwise well-merited reputation in the field of metaphysics as elsewhere. Other sciences and branches of knowledge have their standard. Mathematics has it in itself, history and theology in secular or sacred books, natural science and the art of medicine in mathematics and experience, jurisprudence in law books, and even matters of taste in the examples of the ancients. But for the judgment of the thing called metaphysics, the standard has yet to be found. I have made an attempt to determine it, as well as its use. What is to be done, then, until it be found, when works of this kind have to be judged? If they are of a dogmatic character, one may do what one likes; no one will play the master over others here for long before someone else appears to deal with him in the same manner. If, however, they are critical in character, not indeed with reference to other works but to reason itself, so that the standard of judgment cannot be assumed but has first of all to be sought for, then, though objection and blame may indeed be permitted, yet a certain degree of leniency is indispensable, since the need is common to us all and the lack of the necessary insight makes the high-handed attitude of judge unwarranted.

In order, however, to connect my defense with the interest of the philosophical commonwealth, I propose a test, which must be decisive as to the mode whereby all metaphysical investigations may be directed to their common purpose. This is nothing more that what mathematicians have done in establishing the advantage of their methods by competition. I challenge my critic to demonstrate, as is only just, on *a priori* grounds, in his own way, any single really metaphysical principle asserted by him. Being metaphysical, it must be synthetic and cognized *a priori* from concepts, but it may also be any one of the most indispensable propositions, as, for instance, the principle of the permanence of substance or of the necessary determination of events in the world by their causes. If he cannot do this (silence however is confession), he must admit that, since metaphysics without apodeictic certainty of propositions of this kind is nothing at all, its possibility or impossibility must before all things be 379 established in a critique of pure reason. Thus he is bound either to confess that my principles in the *Critique* are correct, or he must prove their invalidity. But as I can already foresee that, confidently as he has hitherto relied on the certainty of his principles, when it comes to a strict test he will not find a single one in the whole range of metaphysics he can boldly bring forward, I will concede to him an advantageous condition, which can only be expected in such a competition, and will relieve him of the *onus probandi* by laying it on myself.

He finds in these *Prolegomena* and in my *Critique*[51] eight propositions, of which one in each pair contradicts the other, but each of which necessarily belongs to metaphysics, by which it must either be accepted or rejected (although there is not one that has not in its time been accepted by some philosopher). Now he has the liberty of selecting any one of these eight propositions at his pleasure and accepting it without any proof, of which I shall make him a present, but only one (for waste of time will be just as little serviceable to him as to me), and then of attacking my proof of the opposite proposition. If I can save this one and at the same time show that, according to principles which every dogmatic metaphysics must necessarily recognize, the contrary of the proposition adopted by him can be just as clearly proved, it is thereby established that metaphysics has an hereditary failing not to be explained, much less set aside, until we ascend to its birthplace, pure reason itself. And thus my *Critique* must either be accepted or a better one take its place; at least it must be studied, which is the only thing I now require. If, on the other hand, I cannot save my demonstration, then a synthetic proposition *a priori* from dogmatic principles is to be reckoned to the score of my opponent, and I shall deem my impeachment of ordinary metaphysics unjust and pledge myself to

51. [The theses and antitheses of "The Antinomy of Pure Reason" in the *Critique*, B 454–489]

recognize his censure of my *Critique* as justified (although this would not be the consequence by a long way). To this end it would be necessary, it seems to me, that he should step out of his incognito. Otherwise I do not see how it could be avoided that, instead of dealing with one, I should be honored or besieged by several challenges coming from anonymous and **380** unqualified opponents.

Proposals as to an Investigation of the
Critique *upon which a Judgement May Follow*

I feel obliged to the learned public even for the silence with which it for a long time honored my *Critique,* for this proves at least a postponement of judgment and some supposition that, in a work leaving all beaten tracks and striking out on a new path, in which one cannot at once perhaps so easily find one's way, something may perchance lie from which an important but at present dead branch of human knowledge may derive new life and productiveness. Hence may have originated a solicitude for the as yet tender shoot, lest it be destroyed by a hasty judgment. A specimen of a judgment, delayed for the above reasons, is now before my eye in the *Gothaische gelehrte Zeitung,* [52] the thoroughness of which (leaving out of account my praise, which might be suspicious) every reader will himself perceive from the clear and unperverted presentation of a fragment of one of the first principles of my work.

Since an extensive structure cannot be judged at once as a whole from a hurried glance, I propose that it be tested piece by piece from its foundation up, and in this, the present *Prolegomena* may be used as a general outline with which the work itself may conveniently be compared. This suggestion, if it were founded on nothing more than my conceit of importance, such as vanity ordinarily attributes to all of one's own productions, would be immodest and would deserve to be rejected with indig-

---

52. [The issue of August 24, 1782]

nation. But now the interests of all speculative philosophy have arrived at the point of total extinction, while human reason hangs upon them with inextinguishable affection; and only after having been endlessly disappointed, does it vainly attempt to change this into indifference.

In our thinking age, it is not to be supposed but that many deserving men would use any good opportunity of working for the common interest of an ever more enlightened reason, if there were only some hope of attaining the goal. Mathematics, natural science, laws, arts, even morality, etc. do not completely fill the soul; there is always a space left over reserved for pure and speculative reason, the emptiness of which prompts us to seek in vagaries, buffooneries, and mysticism for what seems to be employment and entertainment, but what actually is mere pastime undertaken in order to deaden the troublesome voice of reason, which, in accordance with its nature, requires something that can satisfy it and does not merely subserve other ends or the interests of our inclinations. A consideration, therefore, which is concerned only with this extent of reason as it subsists for itself has, as I may reasonably suppose, a great fascination for everyone who has attempted thus to extend his concept, and I may even say a greater fascination than any other theoretical branch of knowledge, for which he would not willingly exchange it because here all other branches of knowledge and even purposes must meet and unite themselves in a whole.

I offer, therefore, these *Prolegomena* as a plan and guide for this investigation, and not the work itself. Although I am even now perfectly satisfied with the latter as far as contents, order, and mode of presentation, and the care that I have expended in weighing and testing every sentence before writing it down are concerned (for it has taken me years to satisfy myself fully, not only as regards the whole, but in some cases even as to the sources of one particular proposition); yet I am not quite satisfied with my exposition in some sections of the Doctrine of Elements,[53] as for instance in the deduction of the concepts of the understanding or in the chapter on the paralogisms of pure

381

53. [The first part of the *Critique of Pure Reason*, the second part being the Methodology]

reason,[54] because a certain diffuseness takes away from their clearness, and in place of them what is here said in the *Prolegomena* respecting these sections may be made the basis of the test.

It is the boast of the Germans that, where steady and continuous industry are requisite, they can carry things further than other nations. If this opinion be well founded, an opportunity, a task, presents itself; the successful issue of this task can scarcely be doubted and all thinking men can equally take part in it, though they have hitherto been unsuccessful in accomplishing it and in thus confirming the above good opinion. This is chiefly because the science in question is of such a special kind that it can all at once be brought to completion and to that permanent 382 state beyond which it can never be developed, in the least degree enlarged by later discoveries, or changed if we leave out of account adornment by greater clearness in some places or additional utility for all sorts of purposes. This is an advantage no other science has or can have, because there is none so completely isolated and independent of others and so exclusively concerned with the faculty of cognition pure and simple. And the present moment seems not to be unfavorable to my expectation; for in Germany no one seems now to know how to occupy himself, apart from the so-called useful sciences, so as to pursue not mere play but a business possessing an enduring purpose.

To discover how the endeavors of the learned may be united in such a purpose I must leave to others. In the meantime, it is not my intention to persuade anyone merely to follow my theses or even to flatter me with the hope that he will do so; but attacks, repetitions, limitations, or confirmation, completion, and extension, as the case may be, should be appended. If the matter be but investigated from its foundation, it cannot fail that a system, albeit not my own, shall be erected that shall be a possession for future generations for which they may have reason to be grateful.

It would lead us too far here to show what kind of metaphysics may be expected when the principles of criticism have been per-

---

54. [These sections were almost entirely rewritten in the second edition of the *Critique* (1787).]

fected and how, though the old false feathers have been pulled out, it need by no means appear poor and reduced to an insignificant figure but may be in other respects richly and respectably adorned. But other and great uses which would result from such a reform strike one immediately. The ordinary metaphysics had its uses, in that it sought out the elementary concepts of the pure understanding in order to make them clear through analysis and determinate through explications. In this way it was a training for reason, in whatever direction it might be turned. But this was all the good it did. This merit was subsequently destroyed when it favored conceit by venturesome assertions, sophistry by subtle dodges and prettifying, and shallowness by the ease with which it decided the most difficult problems by means of a little

383   school wisdom, which is only the more seductive the more it has the choice, on the one hand, of taking on something of the language of science and, on the other, from that of popular discourse—thus being everything to everybody but in reality being nothing at all. By criticism, however, a standard is given to our judgment whereby knowledge may be with certainty distinguished from pseudo-knowledge and firmly founded, being brought into full operation in metaphysics—a mode of thought extending by degrees its beneficial influence over every other use of reason, at once infusing into it the true philosophical spirit. But the service that metaphysics performs also for theology, by making it independent of the judgment of dogmatic speculation and thereby securing it completely against the attacks of all such opponents, is certainly not to be valued lightly. For ordinary metaphysics, although it promised theology much advantage, could not keep this promise, and by summoning speculative dogmatics to its assistance did nothing but arm enemies against itself. Mysticism, which can prosper in a rationalistic age only when it hides itself behind a system of school metaphysics, under the protection of which it may venture to rave with a semblance of rationality, is driven from theology, its last hiding place, by critical philosophy. Last, but not least, it cannot be otherwise than important to a teacher of metaphysics to be able to say with universal assent that what he expounds is *science*, and that by it actual service will be rendered to the commonweal.

GERMAN-ENGLISH LIST OF TERMS

A

Aesthetik	aesthetic
Akzidenz	accident
Allgemeingültig- keit	universal validity
Allheit	totality
Analogie	analogy
Analogien der Erfahrung	analogies of expe- rience
Analytik	analytic
analytische Methode	analytic method
analytische Sätze	analytic proposi- tions
Anfang	beginning
Anschauung	intuition
Anthropologie	anthropology
Anthropomor- phismus	anthropomorphism
Antinomie der reinen Vernunft	antinomy of pure reason
Antizipationen der Wahrnehmung	anticipations of perception
Apperzeption	apperception
Arithmetik	arithmetic
Astronomie	astronomy
Attraktion	attraction
Aufgabe	problem
Axiom	axiom
Axiome der An- schauung	axioms of intuition

B

Bedingung	condition
Begriff	concept
Beharrlichkeit	permanence

Bewegung	motion
Bewußtsein	consciousness

C

Chemie	chemistry

D

Dasein	existence
Deduktion	deduction, jus- tification
Deismus	deism
Denken	thinking
Dialektik	dialectic
Ding an sich	thing in itself
discursiv	discursive
Dogmatik	dogmatics
dogmatisch	dogmatic
Dogmatismus	dogmatism
Dynamik	dynamics
dynamische Grund- sätze	dynamic principles

E

Einbildungskraft	imagination
Einfache, das	simple
Einheit	unity
Einschränkung	limitation
Elementarbegriff	elementary concept
Elementarerkennt- nis	elementary cogni- tion
Empfindung	sensation
Erfahrung	experience
Erfahrungsurteil	judgment of expe- rience
Erkenntnis	cognition, knowl- edge

Erläuterungsurteil	explicative judgment
Erscheinung	appearance
Erweiterungsurteil	ampliative judgment
Etwas	something
extensiv	extensive

F

Fatalismus	fatalism
Form	form
Frage	question
Freiheit	freedom

G

Gefühl	feeling
Gegenstand	object
gemeiner Menschenverstand	common sense
Gemeinschaft	community
Geometrie	geometry
Gesetz	law
Gewohnheit	habit
Glaube	belief
Gott	God
Grad	degree
Grammatik	grammar
Grenze	bounds
Größe	quantity
Grundsatz	principle
Gültigkeit	validity

H

Handlung	action
höchstes Wesen	Supreme Being
hyperphysisch	hyperphysical
Hypothese	hypothesis

I

Ich, das	ego
Ideal	ideal
Idealismus	idealism
Idealität	ideality
Idee	idea
Identität	identity

immanent	immanent
Induktion	induction
intellektuel	intellectual
Intelligenz	intelligence
intelligible	intelligible
intensiv	intensive
intuitiv	intuitive

K

Kategorie	category
Kausalität	causality
Kegelschnitte	conic sections
Konstruktion	construction
Körper	body
Kraft	force
Kritik	critique, criticism

L

Leben	life
Logik	logic
Logiker	logician
logisch	logical

M

Materialismus	materialism
Materie	matter
Mathematik	mathematics
mathematische Grundsätze	mathematical principles
Mechanik	mechanics
Metaphysik	metaphysics
Metaphysiker	metaphysician
metaphysisch	metaphysical
Methode	method
Methodenlehre	doctrine of method
Modalität	modality
Möglichkeit	possibility
Momente	moments
Moral	morals
moralisch	moral

N

Natur	nature
Naturalismus	naturalism
Naturgeschichte	history of nature
Naturgesetz	law of nature

Naturnotwendigkeit	natural necessity
Naturphilosophie	philosophy of nature
Natursystem	system of nature
Naturwissenschaft	natural science
Negation	negation
Nichts	nothing
Notwendigkeit	necessity
Noumena	noumena
Null	zero

O

| Ontologie | ontology |
| ontologisch | ontological |

P

Paralogismus	paralogism
Phänomenologie	phenomenology
Philosophie	philosophy
Phoronomie	phoronomy
Physik	physics
physiologisch	physiological
Postprädikamente	post-predicaments
Postulate	postulates
Prädikabilien	predicables
Prädikamente	predicaments
Prinzip	principle
Psychologie	psychology
psychologisch	psychological

Q

| Qualität | quality |
| Quantität | quantity |

R

Raum	space
Realisten	realists
Realität	reality
Reflexionsbegriffe	concepts of reflection
Regel	rule
Relation	relation

| Religion | religion |
| Rhapsodie | rhapsody |

S

Schein	illusion
Schema	schema
Schematismus	schematism
Schwärmerei	vagaries
Seele	soul
Sinne	sense
Sinnenwelt	sensible world
Sinnlichkeit	sensibility
Skeptizismus	scepticism
Sollen, das	ought
Subjekt	subject
Substanz	substance
Synthesis	synthesis
synthetisch	synthetic
synthetische Sätze	synthetic propositions
System	system

T

Tafel	table
Teilbarkeit	divisibility
Theismus	theism
Theologie	theology
Tod	death
Trägheit	inertia
transscendent	transcendent
transscendental	transcendental
Transscendental-philosophie	transcendental philosophy

U

Unbegreiflichkeit	incomprehensibility
Undurchdring-lichkeit	impenetrability
Unendlichkeit	infinity
Unmöglichkeit	impossibility
Ursache	cause
Urteil	judgment
Urteilen, das	judging
Urwesen	original being

V

Vereinigung	unification
Vernunft	reason
Vernunftbegriffe	concepts of reason
Vernunftgründe	grounds of reason
Verstand	understanding
Verstandesbegriffe	concepts of the understanding
Verstandeswesen	beings of the understanding
Vielheit	plurality
Vollkommenheit	completeness
Vorstellung	representation

W

Wahrheit	truth
Wahrnehmung	perception
Wahrnehmungsurteil	judgment of perception

Wahrscheinlichkeit	probability
Welt	world
Widerspruch	contradiction
Wirklichkeit	actuality
Wirkung und Gegenwirkung	action and reaction
Wissen	knowing
Wissenschaft	science

Z

Zeit	time
Zufall	contingent
zureichender Grund	sufficient reason
Zusammengesetztes	composite
Zusammensetzung	combination
Zweck	purpose

INDEX

127

Astrology (*Astrologie*), 366
Astronomy (*Astronomie*), 366; physical, 321
Attraction (*Attraktion*), law of, 321
Axiom (*Axiom*), mathematical, 273, 301
Axioms of intuition (*Axiome der Anschauung*), xiii, 303, 306

Baumgarten, A. G., 270, 325n
Beattie, James, 258, 259
Beginning (*Anfang*) of time and space, 339-340; of the world, 344; of an action, 346
Beings of the understanding (*Verstandeswesen*), 314, 315, 344, 355; *see also* Noumena, Thing in itself
Belief (*Glaube*), rational, 278, 371
Berkeley, George, 293, 374-375
Body (*Körper*), 289, 337
Bounds (*Grenze*), contrasted with limits (*Schranke*), 352, 353, 354, 356-357, 360-361; determination of the bounds of pure reason, 350-365

Categories (*Kategorien*) of the understanding, system of, 322-326; table of, 303, 325; Aristotle's list of, 323; origin of Kant's table of, 323-324; true meaning of, 324; use of, xii, 325, 338; *see also* Concepts of the understanding
Causality (*Kausalität*), xi, xiii, 260, 307, 310, 312, 315, 343, 370-371; Hume's treatment of, 257-258, 260, 272, 310; through reason (rather than understanding), 356, 358, 360n
Cause (*Ursache*), category of, 303; concept of, 295, 301, 305n, 315, 332, 343-344, *see also* Causality; supreme, 357n, 360, 360n, *see also* God; through freedom, 363
Chemistry (*Chemie*), 366
Cognition (*Erkenntnis*), metaphysical and physical, 265; metaphysical, 266-274; pure philosophical, 266; theoretic, 279; synthetic a priori, 277, 365; idea of a whole of, 349
Combination (*Zusammensetzung*) of rep-

resentations in synthetic knowledge, 305
Common sense (*gemeiner Menschenverstand*), 259, 277, 369-371
Community (*Gemeinschaft*), category of, 303; principle of, xiii, 307, 310, 311
Completeness (*Vollkommenheit*) of transcendental and metaphysical systems of material nature, xviii; as contrasted with incompleteness of mathematical and physical systems of material nature, xviii
Composite (*Zusammengesetztes*), in contrast to the simple, 339
Concept (*Begriff*), 281, 284, 290; mathematical construction of, 269, 370; formal concepts of understanding, 260, 302-306
Concepts of reason (*Vernunftbegriffe*), *see* Ideas
Concepts of reflection (*Reflexionsbegriffe*), 326
Concepts of the understanding (*Verstandesbegriffe*), pure, 302, 305; table of, 302-303; determine intuitions for judging, 300-301; are merely of immanent use, 315, 329, 350, 354, 355; their true meaning, 312-317, 318, 324; *see also* Categories of the understanding
Condition (*Bedingung*), infinite series of, 332, 338, 348, 354, 360; formal condition of judging, 305, 306, 307
Conic sections (*Kegelschnitte*), 321
Consciousness (*Bewußtsein*), xii, 300, 304, 312; of self, 334; degrees of, 307, 309n; indivisibility of, 335n
Constitutive use of reason's ideas, *see* Idea
Construction (*Konstruktion*), mathematical, xv, xvi, xviii-xix, 268-269, 281, 283, 321, 370-371
Contingent (*Zufall*), in contrast to the necessary, 339, 363
Contradiction, principle of (*Widerspruchs, Satz des*), is the principle of analytic judgments, 267, 270, 275, 277, 370; *see also* Principle of sufficient reason

Metaphysical
Foundations
of Natural
Science

CONTENTS

TRANSLATOR'S INTRODUCTION

The new physical science of the renaissance aimed to reduce all change in nature to the motion of matter, expressible in mathematical equations. Material atomism proved to be very convenient for this purpose. The world can be thought of as composed of large clusters of indivisible, homogeneously dense atoms, which differ from one another only in size and shape. The atoms themselves are so small that they can be regarded as mathematical points, while bodies composed of them can be regarded as sums of points. The relations among atoms and bodies can thereupon be regarded as geometrical ones. Newton, for example, could explain the paths of projectiles and the motions of the planets by means of his principle of universal gravitation, and could then extend the realm of terrestrial mechanics to that of celestial. By contrast, the medieval science of the scholastics relied on a more elaborate analysis involving not only matter and the efficient causes moving it but also qualitative formal causes and final causes (or purposes) as well. In fact the resuscitation of the atomism of Leucippus, Democritus, Epicurus, and Lucretius provided a convenient foil to the medieval scholasticism derived from Aristotle. One of the pioneers of modern science, Sir Francis Bacon, in his *Novum Organum*, Book I, Parts 51 and 63, expresses a preference for the philosophy of Democritus to that of Aristotle. Revolutions in thought not infrequently occur by a return to and adaptation of some mode of thought long in disuse.

Pierre Gassendi, a Frenchman living in the middle of the seventeenth century, was perhaps the most ardent reviver of Epicurean atomism. He maintained in his *Syntagma Philosophicum* that all atoms are homogenous in substance but differ from one another in size, shape, and weight. Atoms compose bodies, which move in empty space (void). God created the atoms and set them in motion; subsequently they move by repulsion and attraction.

Robert Boyle, the English philosopher-scientist coming just a bit later, admitted his debt to Gassendi. But he thought that motion or rest was a basic attribute of the atoms, in addition to size, shape, and weight. Also, he elaborated in greater detail than Gassendi the principles according to which the atoms associate to form the variety of bodies in the world. Boyle profoundly influenced the thought of the greatest of all the seventeenth century natural philosophers—Sir Isaac Newton.

Another strong influence on Newton was Galileo. He counted magnitude, shape, motion or rest as the primary qualities of matter, though not because he had studied Gassendi or Boyle inasmuch as he predated them by quite a few years. He thought that new configurations of matter arise through quantitative change of these primary qualities among themselves. Such change can be expressed mathematically and predicted accordingly. All change in the universe is ultimately reducible to the motion of quantity in space—a view which makes Galileo, perhaps more than anyone else, the true founder of the new physical science. Matter itself is atomic, and the atoms are indivisible and infinitely small.

The stage is now set for the "incomparable Mr. Newton", if I may use the English philosopher John Locke's famous epithet for him. According to Newton the atoms are particles of matter that are hard, indivisible, impenetrable, and possessed of extension, density, mobility, and inertia. They vary in size and shape, and these variations are responsible for their different colors. A mass is any aggregate of atoms and is measured by its density and bulk. The weight of such a mass conveys the notion of force. He did not consider moving force (e.g., gravitation) to be a fundamental property of matter but thought matter to be inert but mobile.

The question then arises as to why matter moves at all and why particles attract one another. Inertia is an entirely passive property of matter. He reasoned, then, that matter must be moved by an active principle external to it. From various scholia and queries in the *Principia* and *Optics* one can infer that this active principle is God. He is the ultimate cause of gravitational motion by virtue of His acting through the immaterial medium of space by means of effluences. Newton got the idea of effluence from his contemporary, the English philosopher Henry More. Newton thought of the atoms as being material, spatially extended, and impenetrable substances. Effluences are immaterial (or spiritual) but yet spatially extended and penetrable substances. God, the angels, and souls (human and animal) are immaterial and unextended substances. Today, most scientists take only the first kind of substance seriously, but Newton took the other two kinds seriously also. Effluences are spiritual forces, which are the principles of the motion and attraction of atomic matter, which is inherently inert. Space has the important function of being the contact point between finite bodies and effluences. Newton says that space is God's sensorium, meaning that space is the medium by which God comes in contact with finite objects (both living and nonliving). Newton thus propounded a true attraction that operates by immediate contact. He did not regard attraction (as Kant was to do) as a basic property of matter itself. If it were, then God would have nothing to do; and Newton ardently hoped that his *Principia* would provide an adequate proof for the existence of a theistic God.

This is a brief history of the material atomism of the seventeenth century, culminating in Newton. It was this material atomism to which Kant so strongly objected. He usually refers to this atomism as the mathematico-mechanical theory of matter. According to Kant's view of this theory, all matter is made up of atoms, which are physically indivisible. This means that the matter comprising an atom coheres with a force that cannot be overcome by any existing force in nature. Accordingly, the atoms are absolutely impenetrable. Matter so conceived is absolutely homogeneous as to density. Atoms differ from one another only with regard to their sizes and shapes. Bodies as aggregates of such atoms differ in density according to the amount of empty space (void) interspersed among the atoms. Kant objects that such absolute impenetrability and such empty space as are here assumed by the atomists can never be proved by any experience whatsoever. These are metaphysical assumptions which no experiment can substantiate. No doubt the Brownian motion of fine particles of dust seen in sunbeams suggested to Leucippus and Democritus between 450 and 420 B.C. that matter may ultimately be composed of atoms. But so far no one has succeeded in proving conclusively that matter has an atomic structure—neither the relatively simple structure propounded by the Greeks and the seventeenth century atomists, nor the much more elaborate structure advanced by Bohr, Heisenberg, and others in the twentieth century. Kant acknowledged that the mathematico-mechanical theory of matter (as he called the atomic theory) lent itself admirably to the mathematical elaboration of a great many physical laws that were experimentally verifiable. But the claim that absolutely impenetrable atoms endure forever in absolute time and move about in absolutely empty space gave Kant (and others—e.g., Bishop Berkeley) pause for thought.

Kant thought of matter as continuous quantity; the atomists thought of it as discrete quantity. He was not the first person to advance a continuum theory of matter. In the first half of the sixth century B.C. Thales, Anaximander, and Anaximenes viewed matter as continuous quantity and assumed that if matter is divided into infinitely small pieces then such a piece will still retain all the properties of the basic material. Atomists such as Democritus and Leucippus, on the other hand, held that matter is composed of discrete, indivisible particles that differ in kind. Thales thought water to be the underlying principle of matter. Anaximander opted for an anonymous, indeterminate substrate that manifested itself as earth, air, fire, or water. Anaximenes held that air was basic and that through the processes of rarefaction and condensation it was transformed into the various forms of matter. A century after these men Empedocles maintained that there were four basic kinds of matter: fire, earth, air, and water. These four combined through the agency of love and strife (or attraction and repulsion in later terms) to form familiar objects.

In the seventeenth century Descartes argued that there were at least two different fundamental kinds of matter—one kind that was subtle, ethereal, and almost weightless and another kind that was heavy and solid. He then accounted for the varieties of bodies by assuming that they contained different proportions of ether and solid matter. In this way he had no need to assume the existence of the void (or empty space).

Kant, as we shall soon see, held that matter is continuous quantity involving a proportion between the two fundamental forces of attraction and repulsion. The varieties of matter can be accounted for by noting that the attraction depends on the mass of the matter in a given space and is constant, while repulsion depends on the variable degree to which the given space is filled. In Kant's dynamic theory, matter is reduced to force. In the mechanical theory of the atomists, matter is discrete; and the forces must be superadded.

Not only did material atomism give Kant pause for thought, but immaterial atomism did so as well. This latter is usually referred to as monadology, and its most famous proponent was Leibniz, who influenced Kant in many ways. Kant was like Leibniz in that both put emphasis on force rather than on particles of impenetrable mass. In Leibniz's essay *What is Nature?* (1698) prime matter is distinguished from secondary matter. These are not two different kinds of matter; the distinction, rather, indicates the two different aspects of one matter. Prime matter is merely passive and possesses only geometrical spatial extension and mass. It is not composed of atoms of either mass or minimum extension because the mathematical spatial continuum is not composed of discrete points—i.e., there are no gaps between the points. Secondary matter is not merely passive but possesses a primitive moving force. This means that for matter to be matter there must be in addition to the properties of extension and mass also moving force. Force endows matter with activity, and indeed matter is always active and alive. Such moving force he calls the substantial principle of matter, and this principle is what is called soul in biological beings and substantial form in corporeal things (rocks, metals, gases, etc.). These souls and substantial forms he also calls monads, which are infinitely many. Each monad has no parts and is hence unitary. And so one may say that prime matter is not atomic, while secondary matter is atomic (but the atoms here are spiritual). If matter is to be changeable (as prime matter would be), then it cannot be everywhere the same. The heterogeneity of matter is accounted for by the various degrees and directions of the tendencies which are modifications inherent in the monads. Our senses and imagination make us aware of prime matter; secondary matter is known by the intellect.

This is a rather exotic theory (some critics have even called it rococo), but nonetheless it influenced many subsequent thinkers. One of the most important of these was Roger Joseph Boscovich, a Jesuit of Dalmatian origin. His *magnum opus,* entitled *A Theory of Natural Philosophy,* appeared first in 1758. He was elected to the Royal Society in London and granted membership in the French Academy at Paris. In the nineteenth century Lord Kelvin and Michael Faraday expressed their great debt to Boscovich. In his famous work he declares his theory of matter to be midway between that of Newton and Leibniz. All matter is composed of indivisible, nonextended points, which are never in immediate contact. (Newton thought his indivisible, extended atoms could touch one another.) Matter is interspersed in a void and floats in it. (Leibniz thought there was no void.) The points are never completely at rest (like Leibniz). There are mutual forces between the points; at very small distances the force is repulsive, while at larger distances the force then becomes attractive and varies as the inverse square of the distance. (Newton thought that an attractive force attained between his atoms at very small distances and changed over to a repulsive force at greater distances.) This theory is as close to a continuum theory as it is to a discrete, atomic theory inasmuch as matter is envisaged as consisting of dimensionless points that act on one another by mutual forces. If Leibniz's theory has been called rococo, what is one to call the hybrid theory of Boscovich?

Such is the milieu in which Kant found himself during the last half of the eighteenth century, when he was doing all of his important work in the philosophy of science. All physics presupposes philosophy of science inasmuch as the latter discipline is concerned with the very foundations on which physics builds. The physicist and the philosopher may be separate persons, or they may coincide as in the cases of Newton and Einstein. Kant knew physics but was not an experimental physicist. As a philosopher, he was deeply concerned with the nature of time, space, matter, force, and motion—the very things with which natural philosophy concerns itself. The experimental physicist is often content to ignore or neglect such considerations or else to borrow them from some natural philosopher. Kant exerted all his energies to ascertain the ultimate principles of material nature, and he was at the very forefront of human knowledge regarding such principles. He was not interested in gleaning facts and data; rather, he speculated concerning the grand scheme in which the facts gleaned by others are arrayed. He has sometimes been accused (as by Erich Adickes in his *Kant als Naturforscher*) of being an armchair scientist. He might more accurately be called an armchair philosopher speculating on the fundamental bases of science.

Let us now consider in some detail Kant's fundamental thoughts regarding the key concepts of the science of material nature. The first to be considered are space and time. Kant as a young man was much interested in the disputes between Leibniz and Newton regarding the nature of space and time. He carefully examined the famous exchange of letters between

Leibniz and Samuel Clark, a defender of Newton's philosophy.[1] Leibniz claimed that the universe is made up of an infinitude of monads, which are simple, immaterial (spiritual) substances. Every monad is endowed with some degree of consciousness. He conceived of space as a set of relations which the monads have to one another; it is the order of coexistent things. He thought of time as the relations of the successive states of consciousness of a single monad. Physical bodies, on this theory, are groups of monads. Mathematically considered, every monad is a dimensionless point. Length, breadth, and position can be represented as relations of monads. Space, then, is a continuous, three-dimensional system of mathematical points corresponding to the order of a plenum of distinct monads. Time has but one dimension; succession and coexistence are the only temporal relations, corresponding, as they do, to the order of perceptions in the consciousness of a monad. For Leibniz, then, space and time were relations among things (monads) which would have no existence whatever if there were no monads.

By contrast, Newton held that space and time are infinite and independent of the physical bodies that exist in space and time. For him space and time were things, and they would exist even if there were no bodies. He held that there are absolute positions in space and time which are independent of the material entities occupying them and, furthermore, that empty space (void) and empty time are possible. Leibniz denied both tenets. Neither Leibniz nor Clarke was able fully to undermine the position of the other, and the result was an impasse.

In his early years Kant pondered the nature of space and time first from the point of view of Leibniz and then of Newton, but eventually he found both positions unsatisfactory. In his

[1]The material in the next several pages (xii–xxvi) appeared originally in my article on Kant in Volume Seven, pages 225–231 of the *Dictionary of Scientific Biography* (copyright 1973 by the American Council of Learned Societies). It is reprinted here by permission from Charles Scribner's Sons Publishers, New York.

Thoughts of the True Estimation of Living Forces (1747) he took Leibniz's view and tried to explain the nature of space by means of the forces of unextended substances (monads) that cause such substances to interact. He attempted to account for the threefold dimensionality of space by appealing to the laws that govern such interactions; but he was not very successful, as he himself admitted.

In his *On the First Ground of the Distinction of Regions in Space* (1768) Kant took Newton's view that space is absolute and argued against Leibniz's relational theory of space. He used the example of a pair of human hands. They are perfect counterparts of one another, yet they are incongruent (like left- and right-hand spirals). The two hands are identical as far as their spatial relations are concerned, but they are, nevertheless, spatially different. Therefore, space is not just the relationship of the parts of the world to one another.

When Kant was inaugurated as professor of logic and metaphysics in 1770, he submitted a dissertation, in accordance with the custom of the time. It was entitled *On the Form and Principles of the Sensible and Intelligible World.* Here his views on space and time had developed to a point that was very close to the views enunciated in the *Critique of Pure Reason* (1781). Space and time are the schemata and conditions of all human knowledge based on sensible intuition. Our concepts of space and time are acquired from the action of the mind in coördinating its sensa according to unchanging laws. The sensa are produced in the mind by the presence of some physical object or objects. Space and time are now based epistemologically on the nature of the mind rather than ontologically on the nature of things, either as a relation among monads (Leibniz) or as a thing (Newton's absolute space). Kant had turned from modes of being to ways of knowing. This new epistemological view of space and time provided him with a way of reconciling the opposed views of Leibniz and Newton. Space and time are indeed the relational orders of contemporaneous objects and successive states, inasmuch as space and time are the conditions of intuitive representations of objects, rather than being mere relations of independent substances (monads). Space and time are indeed absolute wholes in which physical objects are located, inasmuch as they are forms of sensible intuition lying ready in the mind, rather than being independently existing containers for physical objects.

Kant's views in the *Critique* differ from those of the *Dissertation* in that space and time are held in the former to be passive forms of intuition by means of which a manifold of sensa are presented to the understanding, which has the active function of synthesizing this manifold. Space is the form of all appearances of the external senses, just as time is the form of all appearances of the internal sense. As such, space and time are nothing but properties of the human mind. Everything in our knowledge that belongs to spatial intuition contains nothing but relations: locations in an intuition (extension), change of location (motion), and the laws of moving forces according to which change of location is determined. The representations of the external senses are set in time, which contains nothing but relations of succession, coexistence, and duration.

Geometry is based on the pure intuition of space. To say that a straight line is the shortest distance between two points involves an appeal to spatial intuition. The concept of straight is merely qualitative. The concept of shortest is not already contained in the concept of straight but is an addition to straight through recourse to the pure intuition of space. Accordingly, the propositions of geometry are not analytic but a priori synthetic. So are the propositions of arithmetic. The concept of number is achieved by the successive addition of units in the pure intuition of time. Leibniz had claimed that the propositions of mathematics are analytic. For Kant even some of the propositions of mechanics are a priori synthetic because pure mechanics cannot attain its concepts of motion without employing the representation of time.

As we have seen, Kant rejected Newton's absolute space conceived as an independently existing whole containing all physical objects. In the *Metaphysical Foundations of Natural Science* (1786) he pointed out a meaning for "absolute space" which makes it a legitimate idea. At the beginning of "Phoronomy" in that treatise, he distinguishes relative space from absolute space. Relative (or material or empirical) space is the sum total of all objects of experience (bodies). Such space is movable because it is defined by material entities (bodies). If the motion of a movable space is to be perceived, that space must be contained in another, larger space in which it is to move. This larger space must be contained in another, still larger one, and so on to infinity. Absolute space is merely that largest space which includes all relative ones and in which the relative ones move. As such, absolute (empty) space cannot be perceived because it is not defined by material entities, as relative (empirical) spaces are, and so exists merely in idea, with no actual ontological status. Kant claimed that Newton mistakenly endowed such absolute space with ontological significance.

So much for time and space; now let us consider matter. The terms "physical things," "material entities," "bodily objects" are for Kant all roughly equivalent and indicate what he usually calls "matter" or "body." Toward the end of the "Dynamics" in the *Metaphysical Foundations of Natural Science* he does say that a body is matter between determinate boundaries and thus has definite shape. "Matter" is therefore a more general term than "body," but he often uses the two interchangeably. What, indeed, is matter for Kant? In the development of his thought at the stage of the *Dissertation,* he distinguished a sensible world from an intelligible one. The former is the world that sense reveals, and the latter is what the intellect reveals. He called the former world phenomenal and the latter noumenal. The former is the world of things as they appear, while the latter consists in things as they are. Sensibility with its two pure forms, space and time, provides the foundation for the validity of physics and geometry; however, the scope of the application of these two sciences is restricted to phenomena. Intellect with its pure concepts of substance, cause, possibility, existence, and necessity provides the foundation for the validity of the metaphysics of monads; this science yields an intellectual knowledge of such substances (monads) as they are in themselves, but there is no sensible knowledge of monads. The concepts of matter and body are empirical, sensible ones belonging to physics but not to metaphysics.

By the time Kant's thought attained full maturity in the *Critique of Pure Reason,* the pure concepts of substance, cause, possibility, existence, and necessity had become coterminous with the two pure forms of intuition, space and time, in having a valid application to nothing but phenomena. The intelligible world of monads, conceived in the *Dissertation* as a known realm of things-in-themselves, becomes in the *Critique* an unknowable realm of noumena underlying the knowable realm of phenomena. One has a detailed and actual knowledge of matter and body but only a problematic knowledge of monads and noumena. The noumena did not wither away completely in the *Critique.* If they had, Kant would have been an idealist like Berkeley or a phenomenalist like Hume. Rather, Kant was a type of realist not unlike Descartes or Locke in his claim that appearances are not all that there is but are all that one has an actual and detailed knowledge of. There is a reality behind the appearance, but one has only a problematic concept of this reality. He often characterized this position of the *Critique* as transcendental idealism in order to distinguish this brand of idealism from the extreme form typified by Berkeley.

And so matter can be defined, in most general terms, as an appearance given in space. When one turns to a more particular characterization of matter, one finds that Kant's mature theory of matter developed as an opposition to the atomist view of matter held by Newton and the monadist view of matter held by Leibniz. For Newton matter is composed of physical atoms, which are things-in-themselves. He seems to espouse some form of simple realism and doubtless would have held that these atoms would move about in empty space even if there were no sentient beings anywhere to perceive them. The atoms are absolutely impenetrable, and this means that the matter constituting an atom coheres with a force that cannot be overcome by any existing force in nature. Atoms are absolutely homogeneous as to density. They differ from one another only in size and shape. Bodies are aggregates of such atoms and differ in density according to how much empty space, or void, is interspersed among the atoms.

In the "Dynamics" of the *Metaphysical Foundations* Kant objected to such absolute impenetrability as being an occult quality that no experiment or experience whatsoever could substantiate. We have seen earlier what Kant thought about absolute empty space. Newton thus regarded matter as an interruptum. So also did Kant in his early work, *Physical Monadology* (1756). But in the Critical thought of the *Metaphysical Foundations,* he rejected all forms of atomism and monadology. He maintained that matter is a continuum, as we shall see.

Motive forces were for him the fundamental attributes of matter, a position which he held even in the days of the *Physical Monadology.* By contrast, Newton had taken a different view on the relation between forces and matter. For him atoms are inert but mobile. Because inertia is an entirely passive property of the atoms, they must be moved by an active principle external to them. God is the ultimate cause of gravitational motion by virtue of His acting through the immaterial medium of absolute space, as one can infer from various scholia in the *Principia* and queries in the *Opticks.* Accordingly, Newton did not regard attraction (as Kant did) as a basic property of matter itself. For Kant only two kinds of moving forces are possible: repulsive and attractive. If two bodies (regarded as mathematical points) are being considered, then any motion that the one body can impress on the other must be imparted in the straight line joining the two points. They either recede from one another or approach one another; there are no other possibilities. Since forces are what cause bodies to move, the only kinds of forces are therefore repulsive and attractive.

When one body tries to enter the space occupied by another

body, the latter resists the intrusion and the former is moved in the opposite direction. The repulsive (or expansive) force exerted here is also called elastic. For Kant all matter is originally elastic, infinitely compressible but impenetrable—one body cannot compress another to the extent that the first occupies all the space of the second. He called such elasticity "relative impenetrability" and contrasted it with the absolute impenetrability posited by atomism. The relative kind has a degree that can be ascertained by experience—for instance, gold is more penetrable than iron—whereas the absolute kind is open to no experience whatsoever. On the atomic theory, bodies are compressed when the empty space among the atoms constituting bodies is eliminated and the atoms stand tightly packed. But once so packed, they admit of no further compression.

Unless there were another force acting in an opposite direction to repulsion, that is, acting for approach, matter would disperse itself to infinity. By means of universal attraction all matter acts directly on all other matter and so acts at all distances. This force is usually called gravitation, and the endeavor of a body to move in the direction of the greater gravitation is called its weight. If matter possessed only gravitational force, it would all coalesce in a point. The very possibility of matter as an entity filling space in a determinate degree depends on a balance between repulsion and attraction. Sensation makes us aware of repulsion when we feel or see some physical object and ascertain its size, shape, and location. Repulsion is directly attributed to matter. Attraction is attributed to matter by inference, since gravitation alone makes us aware of no object of determinate size and shape but reveals only the endeavor of our body to approach the center of the attracting body.

True attraction is action at a distance. The earth attracts the moon through space that may be regarded as wholly empty. And so gravity acts directly in a place where it is not. Descartes and others thought this to be a contradictory notion and tried to reduce all attraction to repulsive force in contact. Attraction is therefore nothing but apparent attraction at a distance. Descartes propounded the theory of a plenum with fourteen vortices to account for the celestial motions of the planets about the sun and the moons about the planets. Newton objected to such plenum and vortices because he thought that the friction between the celestial bodies and this hypothesized swirling fluid medium would slow down the celestial motions and eventually terminate them. He, like Kant, espoused a true attraction rather than an apparent one.

If Kant had ever critically examined Newton's suggestions as to the ultimate cause of gravitation, he doubtless would have had emphatic objections. He showed in the *Critique of Pure Reason* that God's existence cannot be established by theoretic reason. For him attraction is a property of matter itself. He argued against Descartes's apparent attraction by pointing out that such attraction operates by means of the repulsive forces of pressure and impact so as to produce the endeavor to approach, just as in the case when one billiard ball approaches another after the first has been hit by a cue. But there would not be even any impact or pressure unless matter cohered in such a way as to make such impact and pressure possible. Matter would disperse itself to infinity if it possessed nothing but repulsive force. Hence, there must be a true attraction acting contrary to repulsion in order for impact and pressure to bring about even apparent attraction.

Thus, matter in general was reduced by Kant to the moving forces of repulsion and attraction. He appealed to these forces to account for the specific varieties of matter. Attraction depends on the mass of the matter in a given space and is constant. Repulsion depends on the degree to which the given space is filled; this degree can vary widely. For example, the attraction of a given quantity of air in a given volume depends on its mass and is constant, while its elasticity is directly proportional to its temperature and varies accordingly. This means that repulsion can, with regard to one and the same attractive force, be originally different in degree in different matters. Consequently, a spectrum of different kinds of matter each having the same mass (and therefore having the same attraction) can vary widely in repulsion—running, for instance, from the density of osmium to the rarity of the ether. And so every space can be thought of as full and yet as filled in varying measure.

Kant claimed that matter is continuous quantity involving a proportion between the two fundamental forces of attraction and repulsion. For an atomist like Newton matter is discrete quantity, and the force of attraction in his theory is superadded through the agency of God. The varying densities of elements and compounds of matter are for Newton a function of the amount of empty space interspersed among the atoms. Empty space, according to Kant, is a fiction that can be discerned by no sense experience whatever. The senses reveal to us only full spaces. Kant's theory of matter committed him to accept the existence of an ether.

The ether was mentioned in many of his writings. In his doctoral dissertation, *A Brief Account of Some Reflections on Fire* (1755), Kant said in proposition VIII that the matter of heat (or the caloric) is nothing but the ether (or the matter of light) which is compressed within the interstices of bodies by means of their strong attraction. In the *Metaphysical Foundations of Natural Science* he accepted the existence of the ether cautiously, as a hypothesis that he found more plausible than the atomists' hypothesis of the reality of absolutely impenetrable atoms and absolutely empty space. Toward the end of chapter 2 the ether is characterized as a matter that entirely fills space, leaving no void. It is so rarefied that it fills its space with far less quantity of matter than any of the bodies known to us fill their spaces. In relation to its attractive force the repulsive force of the ether must be incomparably greater than in any other kind of matter known to us.

Between 1790 and 1803 Kant worked on what is now called the *Opus postumum*. At his death this unfinished work survived as a stack of handwritten pages, which were eventually gathered by editors into thirteen fascicles *(Convolute)*. Sections of it constitute coherent wholes, others provide illustrations, and still others are repetitions of earlier works. The *Opus* appears in Volumes XXI and XXII of the Royal Prussian Academy edition of Kant's works. Part of the *Opus* contains the *Transition From the Metaphysical Foundations of Natural Science to Physics*. The theory of the ether figures in almost all parts of the *Transition* but especially in *Convolute* X, XI, and XII of the *Opus*. There the ether is characterized as a matter that occupies absolutely every part of space, that penetrates the entire material domain, that is identical in all its parts, and that is endowed with a spontaneous and perpetual motion.

Kant based his proof of the ether's existence on the unity of experience. Space, which is unitary, is the form of all experience; hence experience is unitary. Experience is a system made up of a manifold of sense perceptions synthesized in space by the intellect. These perceptions are caused by the actions of the material forces that fill space. Accordingly, the motive forces of matter must collectively be capable of constituting a system in order to conform to the unity of possible experience. Such a system is possible only if one admits, as the basis of these forces, the existence of an ether that has the properties listed above. Therefore, the existence of the ether is the a priori condition of the system of experience. Many critics have found this proof unconvincing, as well they might. The *Transition*, as it has come down to us, is merely a series of sketches for a work that was never finished. Accordingly, it suggests about as many unanswered questions as it provides solutions.

Kant in his mature period opposed not only atomism but also all forms of monadology. He was like Leibniz and unlike Newton in that he put the emphasis, both in his youth and in his maturity, on force rather than on atomic particles of impenetrable mass. In the *Physical Monadology* (1756) he even claimed (following Leibniz) that bodies are composed of monads, which are indivisible simple substances. The space that bodies fill is infinitely divisible and is not composed of original simple parts because space does not have any substantiality; it is only the appearance of the external relations bound up with the unity of the monad. So conceived, the infinite divisibility of space is not opposed to the simplicity of monads. Matter is not infinitely divisible, whereas space is. But by the time his thought had arrived at the critical phase represented by the *Critique of Pure Reason* and the *Metaphysical Foundations,* Kant had repudiated both the view (derived from Leibniz) that bodies are composed of monads and the view (espoused by Leibniz) that space is a relation among monads. Perceptible matter was now continuous quantity, and space was a form of sensible intuition. What did he think now about the infinite divisibility of matter and space? One must turn to the Second Antinomy in the "Dialectic" of the *Critique* and the "Dynamics" of the *Metaphysical Foundations* to learn the answer.

The outcome of these discussions is this: Matter as appearance is infinitely divisible and therefore consists of infinitely many parts, but matter as appearance does not consist of the simple (either atoms or monads); matter as thing-in-itself does not consist of infinitely many parts (either atoms or monads), but matter as thing-in-itself does consist of the simple. It was pointed out earlier that according to Kant's position of transcendental idealism, we have actual cognition of things as appearances and a problematic concept of the reality behind the appearance. Accordingly, matter can be regarded as appearance or as the reality (thing-in-itself) behind the appearance.

Intuitive space is divisible to infinity. Any matter filling such space is also divisible to infinity. But this means that matter as appearance is infinitely divisible; it does not mean that matter as thing-in-itself consists of infinitely many parts (as an atomist or a monadist might claim). Only the division of the appearance can be infinitely continued, not the division of the thing-in-itself. Any whole as thing-in-itself must already contain all the parts into which it can be divided. But the division process can never be finished. And so the thought that matter as thing-in-itself contains infinitely many parts is self-contradictory.

Furthermore, it cannot be maintained that matter as appearance is made up of the simple. The composite of things-in-themselves must consist of the simple, since the parts must be given before all composition. But the composite in the appearance does not consist of the simple, because an appearance can never be given in any way other than as composite (extended in space); its parts can be given only through the process of division, and therefore not before the composite but only in it (and thus the atomist and monadist are foiled again).

Even though matter as appearance is mathematically divisible into infinitely many parts, no real distance of parts is to be assumed. Physicists usually represent the repulsive forces of the parts of elastic matters (for instance, a gas) when these matters are in a state of greater or lesser compression as increasing or decreasing in a certain proportion to the distance of their parts from one another. This is necessary for the mathematical construction of the concept corresponding to such a state of elastic matters; in this construction all contact of parts is represented as an infinitely small distance. The posited spatial distance of the parts should be understood, however, as nothing but a mathematical convenience, necessary convenience though it is. In reality, matter is continuous quantity, and there is no spatial distance between its parts; they are always in contact.

Time, space, matter, force—Kant's views on these fundamental concepts of natural science have now been examined; but motion has not yet been considered in any detail. In contrast with Newton, Kant claimed in the "Phenomenology" of the *Metaphysical Foundations,* as well as in the earlier *New Conception of Motion and Rest* (1758), that all motion is relative. The motion of a body is the change of its external relations to a given space. If a ball rolls on a table top, it changes its position relative to various points on the top. But we have the same change of positions if the ball remains at rest and the table moves under it in the opposite direction with the same velocity. Hence, the rectilinear motion of a body with regard to an empirical space can be viewed as either the body moving by reference to the space at rest or as the body at rest and the space moving relative to it. It is impossible to think of a body in rectilinear motion relative to no material space outside of it. Matter can be thought of as moved or at rest only in relation to matter and never by reference to mere space without matter. Furthermore, there is no fixed empirical point by reference to which absolute motion and absolute rest can be determined. The center of the sun might be fixed as the center of our solar system, but our solar system moves relative to other solar systems in the Milky Way, and the Milky Way moves relative to other galaxies, and so on.

Accordingly, there is no empirical space defined by matter that can provide a reference system for all possible rectilinear motions of bodies in the universe. Therefore, all motion or rest is merely relative, and neither is absolute. But the empirical space (for instance, the table top) in relation to which a body (for instance, the ball) moves or remains at rest must itself be referred to another (absolute) space at rest within which this given empirical space is movable. If one did not invoke such immovable, absolute space, one would be claiming that the given empirical space is immovable and hence absolute; but by experience all material spaces are movable. This ultimate absolute space by reference to which all empirical spaces are movable (and hence relative) exists merely in thought and not in fact, since only empirical (material) spaces actually exist. But such absolute (immovable, immaterial) space is nevertheless a necessary idea which serves as a rule for considering all motion therein as relative. Everything empirical is movable in such ideal absolute space; and all such motions in it are valid as merely relative to one another, while none is valid as absolute. And so the rectilinear motion of a body in relative space is reduced to absolute space when one thinks of the body as in itself at rest but thinks of the relative space as moved in the opposite direction in absolute space.

The circular motion of a body might seem, at first glance, to be an absolute motion. In contrast with the foregoing case of rectilinear motion, it is not all the same whether the earth is regarded as rotating on its axis while the heavens remain still or the earth is regarded as staying still while the heavens rotate about it. Both give the same appearance of motion. But the former case is the true one, while the second one is false. To prove that the earth rotates, Kant says that if one puts a stone at some distance from the surface of the earth and drops it, then the stone will not remain over the same point on the earth's surface in its fall but will wander from west to east. Accordingly, the rotation of the earth on its axis (or the rotation of any other body) is not to be represented as externally relative. But does this mean that the motion is absolute? Even though circular motion exhibits no real change of place with regard to the space outside of the rotating body, such motion does exhibit a continuous dynamic change of the relation of matter within its space. If the earth were to stop spinning, it would contract in size. The present size of the earth involves a balance between centrifugal forces and attracting ones. Hence, the actuality of the earth's rotation rests on the tendency of the parts of the earth on opposite sides of the axis of rotation to recede from one another. The rotation is actual in absolute space, since this rotation is referred to the space within, and not to that outside of, the rotating body. And so rotation is not absolute motion but is a continuous change of the relations of matters (or parts of the rotating body) to one another; this change is represented in absolute space (the space within the rotating body), and for this reason such change is actually only relative motion.

The case of the translation of a body relative to a material reference system and the case of a rotating body have now been considered. What about the third and last case, in which one body hits another? Is this motion absolute? In this case both the matter and the (relative) space must necessarily be represented as moved at the same time; in every motion of a body whereby it is moving with regard to another body, an opposite and equal motion of the other body is necessary. One body cannot by its motion impart motion to another body that is absolutely at rest; this second body must be moved (together with its relative space) in the opposite direction with just that quantity of motion equal to that quantity of motion it is to receive through the agency of the first body and in the direction of this first one. Both bodies, subsequently, put themselves relative to one another—that is, in the absolute space lying between their two centers—in a state of rest. But with reference to the relative space outside of the impacting bodies, the bodies move after impact with equal velocity in the direction in which the first body is moving. This same law holds if the impact involves a second body that is not at rest but moving. There is no absolute motion in this third case, even though a body in absolute space is thought of as moved with regard to another body. The motion in this case is relative not to the space surrounding the bodies but only to the space between them. When this latter space is regarded as absolute, it alone determines their external relation to one another. And so this motion is merely relative.

In the case of rectilinear motion, the change of place may be attributed either to the matter (that is, space at rest and matter moving with respect to it) or to the space (that is, matter at rest and space moving with respect to it). In the case of rotatory motion, the change of place must be attributed to the matter. In the case of colliding bodies, both the matter and the (relative) space must necessarily be represented as moved at the same time. Motion is relative in all three cases by reference to absolute space: in the first case by reference to absolute space outside of the body, in the second to absolute space inside of the body, and in the third to absolute space between two bodies.

Since Kant's time there have been many variations in views regarding time, space, matter, force, motion. Of these let us consider only matter, a topic that interested Kant so much. Atomic theories have been elaborated in great detail. In the early twentieth century it seemed to Rutherford and Bohr that all atoms of matter might be composed of electrons, protons, and neutrons. Negatively charged electrons move in distinct orbits about a positively charged nucleus, which is made up of positively charged protons and uncharged neutrons. But this

picture did not hold for very long. It was learned that when the
nucleus is bombarded by various particles, protons and neutrons are found to be not the only particles contained in the
nucleus; a host of other particles have been observed emerging
from the nucleus—pions, muons, neutrinos, etc. In all, some
150 "elementary" particles have been discovered. Various
theories have been advanced to try to attain some order in this
bewildering array of particles. Murray Gell-Mann has suggested
that all such particles may in the final analysis be composed of
quarks, which are elementary. A proton, for instance, is made
up of three quarks. Geoffrey Chew has advanced the notion that
one particle may be no more basic than another but that particles may be mixtures of one another. The atomistic lines of
thought involved here are far more elegant than anything Newton could have even dreamed of.

Even before quarks and mixtures, some thinkers did not subscribe to the atomistic approach. Einstein suggested that there
might be special kinds of fields which have modes of motion
such that there would be pulse-like concentrations of fields.
These would cohere in a stable fashion and act almost exactly
like small moving bodies. The so-called fundamental particles
may be nothing but such modes of motion of the fields; in other
words, fields are more basic than the so-called particles. John C.
Graves on page 114 of his excellent book, *The Conceptual
Foundations of Contemporary Relativity Theory* (Cambridge,
Massachusetts: MIT Press, 1971), says: "I have introduced this
brief discussion of dynamism [as represented by the thought of
Leibniz, Boscovich, and Kant] for two reasons: (1) in order to
show that the interpretation of the Newtonian particles which
became orthodox and which thereby provided many of the
conceptual difficulties in developing the plan of general relativity was by no means the only possible one; that indeed
dynamism may have remained closer to the *physical* requirements; and (2) because the concepts of the dynamists may
prove useful in giving an adequate interpretation of geomet-
rodynamics. It is fascinating to speculate whether some of the

paradoxes of present-day quantum mechanics would seem so paradoxical if physicists had interpreted the notion of atoms from the start in some sort of dynamist terms, instead of as hard little bodies with sharply defined boundaries and positions in a causally inert absolute space. If such a conception had been more effective, it would be legitimate to criticize Newton and his philosophic followers on the same grounds as Descartes: that they stayed too close to the apparent disclosures of perception rather than the exigencies of the underlying physical level which his theory was trying to explicate." The age-old debate between atomists and continuum theorists has not ended.

Successful theories often (or maybe I should say usually) become dogmatic and resistant to change. Newtonian views won out over Cartesian and Leibnizian ones and reigned triumphant for almost two centuries before they were seriously questioned in the late nineteenth and early twentieth centuries and eventually replaced by the theory of relativity and by quantum mechanics. When an established theory runs into trouble accounting for newly discovered phenomena, it is usually patched up. Eventually such a theory becomes something of a dinosaur— not unlike the Ptolemaic theory of astronomy with its epicycles. In the latter part of the nineteenth century Newtonian mechanics was found to be an awkward fit not only for the phenomena of the macroscopic realm but especially for the microscopic. Just as Einstein's relativity theory won out in the former realm, so the Bohr-Heisenberg quantum mechanics won out in the latter. The quantum mechanics devised to account for the orbital behavior of electrons about a nucleus was without doubt one of the most outstanding achievements of the early twentieth century, but the Bohr-Heisenberg theory has been running into trouble since the 1930s in the domains of nuclear physics and of particles physics. It has been amended and patched up in various ways, but can anyone today claim that it is a satisfactory theory? This mechanics runs into the greatest difficulties in nuclear physics and in particle physics in the treatment of phenomena involving very high energies (of the order of 100 million electron volts or more) and very short distances (of the order of 10^{-13} cm. or less).

Two of the most outspoken and cogent critics of the Bohr-Heisenberg theory have been Louis de Broglie and David Bohm. Both men would like to replace the probabilistic theory of Bohr and Heisenberg by a more deterministic one. Einstein also favored this attempt. So far no one has succeeded in devising a satisfactory new system that will comprehend the domains of the atom, the nucleus, and the particles. Many are looking for it; eventually the breakthrough will come. Who knows? Perhaps a return to some continuum view as suggested by Einstein and much earlier championed by Kant in his opposition to Newton will help implement the discovery of a new comprehensive theory of nature which will embrace not only the phenomena of the microscopic universe but that of the macroscopic as well.

Metaphysical
Foundations
of Natural
Science

Metaphysische Anfangsgründe

der

Naturwissenschaft

von

Immanuel Kant

Riga,

bey Johann Friedrich Hartknoch

1786.

If the word "nature" is taken merely in its formal signification (inasmuch as the word "nature" signifies the primal, internal principle of everything that belongs to the existence of a thing[1]), then there can be as many natural sciences as there are specifically different things, and each of these things must contain its specific internal principle of the determinations belonging to its existence. On the other hand, "nature" is also taken in a material signification to be not a quality but the sum total of all things insofar as they can be objects of our senses and hence also objects of experience, under which is therefore to be understood the whole of all appearances, i.e., the sense-world with the exclusion of all objects that are not sensible. Nature taken in this signification of the word has two main parts according to the main distinction of our senses: the one contains the objects of the external senses, the other the object of the internal sense. Therefore, a twofold doctrine of nature is possible: a *doctrine of body* and a *doctrine of soul*. The first considers extended nature, and the second, thinking nature.

Every doctrine, if it is to be a system, i.e., a whole of cognition ordered according to principles, is called science. And since principles can be either of the empirical or of the rational connection of cognitions in a whole, so natural sci- 468 ence, be it the doctrine of body or the doctrine of soul, would have to be divided into historical and rational natural science, were it not that the word "nature" (because this

[1] Essence is the primal, internal principle of everything that belongs to the possibility of a thing. Therefore, one can attribute to geometrical figures only an essence and not a nature (since there is thought in their concept nothing which expresses an existence).

word designates the derivation of the manifold belonging to the existence of things from their internal principle) necessitates a rational cognition of the coherence of things, so far as this cognition is to deserve the name of natural science. Therefore, the doctrine of nature might better be divided into the historical doctrine of nature, which contains nothing but the systematically ordered facts regarding natural things (which again would consist of the description of nature as a system of classes of natural things ordered according to similarities, and the history of nature as a systematic presentation of natural things in different times and in different places), and natural science. Now, natural science would in turn be natural science either properly or improperly so called; the first would treat its object wholly according to a priori principles, and the second, according to laws of experience.

Only that whose certainty is apodeictic can be called science proper; cognition that can contain merely empirical certainty is only improperly called science. That whole of cognition which is systematic can therefore be called science, and, when the connection of cognition in this system is a coherence of grounds and consequents, rational science. But when these grounds or principles are ultimately merely empirical, as, for example, in chemistry, and when the laws from which reason explains the given facts are merely laws of experience, then they carry with themselves no consciousness of their necessity (are not apodeictically certain), and thus the whole does not in a strict sense deserve the name of science. Therefore, chemistry should be called systematic art rather than science.

A rational doctrine of nature, then, deserves the name of natural science only when the natural laws that underlie it are cognized a priori and are not mere laws of experience. Natural cognition of the first kind is called pure, but that of the second kind is called applied rational cognition. Since the word "nature" already carries with it the concept of laws and since this concept carries with it the concept of the necessity of all the determinations of a thing which belong to its existence, it is easily seen why natural science must derive   *469* the legitimacy of its designation only from a pure part of natural science, namely, from that part which contains the a priori principles of all remaining natural explications, and why natural science is only by virtue of this pure part science proper. And so every doctrine of nature must according to the demands of reason ultimately aim at natural science and terminate in it, inasmuch as the necessity of laws attaches inseparably to the concept of nature and must therefore be thoroughly understood. Hence the most complete explication of certain phenomena by chemical principles always leaves dissatisfaction in its wake, inasmuch as through these contingent laws learned by mere experience no a priori grounds can be adduced.

Thus all natural science proper requires a pure part, upon which the apodeictic certainty sought by reason in such science can be based. And since this pure part is according to its principles completely different by comparison with that part whose principles are only empirical, there is the greatest advantage (indeed according to the nature of the case there is, as regards the method, an indispensable duty) in expounding this pure part separately and entirely unmixed with the empirical part and in expounding this pure part as far as possible in its completeness, in order that one may be able to determine exactly what reason can accomplish of itself and where its capacity begins to require the assistance of principles of experience. Pure rational cognition from mere concepts is called pure philosophy, or metaphysics; on the other hand, that pure rational cognition which is based only upon the construction of concepts by means of the presentation of the object in a priori intuition is called mathematics.[2]

Natural science properly so called presupposes metaphys-

[2] [Cf. *Critique of Pure Reason*, B 740–755.]

ics of nature; for laws, i.e., principles of the necessity of what belongs to the existence of a thing, are occupied with a concept which does not admit of construction, because existence cannot be presented in any a priori intuition.[3] Therefore, natural science proper presupposes metaphysics of nature. Now, the latter must indeed always contain nothing but principles which are not empirical (for that reason it bears the name of a metaphysics). But either it can treat of the laws which make possible the concept of a nature in general even without reference to any determinate object of experience, and therefore undetermined regarding the nature of this or that thing of the sense-world—and in this case it is 470 the transcendental part of the metaphysics of nature[4]—or it occupies itself with the special nature of this or that kind of things, of which an empirical concept is given in such a way that besides what lies in this concept, no other empirical principle is needed for cognizing the things. For example, it lays the empirical concept of a matter or of a thinking being at its foundation and searches the range of cognition of which reason is a priori capable regarding these objects. Such a science must still be called a metaphysics of nature, namely, of corporeal or of thinking nature; however, it is then not a general but a special metaphysical natural science (physics and psychology), in which the aforementioned transcendental principles are applied to the two species of sense-objects.

I maintain, however, that in every special doctrine of nature only so much science proper can be found as there is mathematics in it. For in accordance with the foregoing considerations, science proper, especially science of nature, requires a pure part, which lies at the foundation of the empirical part and is based upon an a priori cognition of natural things.

[3] [Cf. *ibid.*, B 740–755.]

[4] [This transcendental part is contained in the *Critique of Pure Reason*, B 170–294, "The Analytic of Principles" (Book II of the Transcendental Analytic).]

Now, to cognize anything a priori is to cognize it from its mere possibility. But the possibility of determinate natural things cannot be cognized from their mere concepts; from these concepts the possibility of the thought (that it does not contradict itself) can indeed be cognized, but not the possibility of the object as a natural thing, which can be given (as existing) outside of the thought. Therefore, in order to cognize the possibility of determinate natural things, and hence to cognize them a priori, there is further required that the intuition corresponding to the concept be given a priori, i.e., that the concept be constructed. Now, rational cognition through the construction of concepts is mathematical. A pure philosophy of nature in general, i.e., one that only investigates what constitutes the concept of a nature in general, may indeed be possible without mathematics; but a pure doctrine of nature concerning determinate natural things (doctrine of body and doctrine of soul) is possible only by means of mathematics. And since in every doctrine of nature only so much science proper is to be found as there is a priori cognition in it, a doctrine of nature will contain only so much science proper as there is applied mathematics in it.

So long, then, as there is for the chemical actions of matters on one another no concept which admits of being constructed, i.e., no law of the approach or withdrawal of the *471* parts of matters can be stated according to which (as, say, in proportion to their densities and suchlike) their motions together with the consequences of these can be intuited and presented a priori in space (a demand that will hardly ever be fulfilled), chemistry can become nothing more than a systematic art or experimental doctrine, but never science proper; for the principles of chemistry are merely empirical and admit of no presentation a priori in intuition. Consequently, the principles of chemical phenomena cannot make the possibility of such phenomena in the least conceivable inasmuch as they are incapable of the application of mathematics.[5]

But the empirical doctrine of the soul must always remain yet even further removed than chemistry from the rank of what may be called a natural science proper. This is because mathematics is inapplicable to the phenomena of the internal sense and their laws, unless one might want to take into consideration merely the law of continuity in the flow of this sense's internal changes. But the extension of cognition so attained would bear much the same relation to the extension of cognition which mathematics provides for the doctrine of body, as the doctrine of the properties of the straight line bears to the whole of geometry. The reason for the limitation on this extension of cognition lies in the fact that the pure internal intuition in which the soul's phenomena are to be constructed is time, which has only one dimension. But not even as a systematic art of analysis or as an experimental doctrine can the empirical doctrine of the soul ever approach chemistry, because in it the manifold of internal observation is separated only by mere thought, but cannot be kept separate and be connected again at will; still less does another thinking subject submit to our investigations in such a way as to be conformable to our purposes, and even the observation itself alters and distorts the state of the object observed. It can, therefore, never become anything more than a historical (and as such, as much as possible) systematic natural doctrine of the internal sense, i.e., a natural description of the soul, but not a science of the soul, nor even a psychological experimental doctrine. This is the reason why in the title of this work, which, properly speaking, contains the principles of the doctrine of body, we have employed, in accordance with the usual practice, the general name of natural science; for this designation in the strict sense belongs

[5] [The beginnings of the modern science of chemistry were made by Lavoisier shortly before the *Metaphysical Foundations* appeared in 1786. Kant did not foresee the development of atomic physics, which was to make chemistry a science.]

to the doctrine of body alone and hence causes no ambiguity.

But in order to make possible the application of mathe-   *472* matics to the doctrine of body, which can become natural science only by means of such application, principles of the construction of concepts that belong to the possibility of matter in general must precede. Hence a complete analysis of the concept of a matter in general must be laid at the foundation of the doctrine of body. This is the business of pure philosophy, which for this purpose makes use of no particular experiences but uses only what it finds in the separated (although in itself empirical) concept [of matter] with regard to pure intuitions in space and time (according to laws which already depend essentially on the concept of nature in general); hence such a doctrine is an actual metaphysics of corporeal nature.

All natural philosophers who wanted to proceed mathematically in their work had therefore always (though unknown to themselves) made use of metaphysical principles, and had to make use of them, even though they otherwise solemnly repudiated any claim of metaphysics on their science. Doubtless they understood by metaphysics the illusion of inventing possibilities at will and playing with concepts which perhaps do not at all admit of presentation in intuition and have no other certification of their objective reality than the fact that they merely do not stand in contradiction with themselves. All true metaphysics is taken from the essential nature of the thinking faculty itself and therefore is by no means invented. This is because metaphysics is not borrowed from experience but contains the pure operations of thought, and hence contains concepts and principles a priori, which first of all bring the manifold of empirical representations into legitimate connection, whereby such a manifold can become empirical *cognition*, i.e., experience. Those mathematical physicists could not at all, then, dispense with metaphysical principles, and among these principles, not with such as make the concept of their own special object, namely, matter, available a priori for application to external experience (as in the cases of the concept of motion, of the filling of space, of inertia, etc.). However, they rightly held that letting merely empirical principles prevail in these questions would be not at all compatible with the apodeictic certainty which they wanted to give to their natural laws; therefore, they preferred to postulate such laws without investigating their a priori sources.

473   But of the greatest importance for the benefit of the sciences is severing heterogeneous principles from one another and bringing each kind into a separate system, so that each may constitute a science of its own kind in order thereby to avoid the uncertainty which arises from confusing such heterogeneous principles; for a person cannot well distinguish to which of the two kinds of principles are to be attributed, on the one hand, the limitations, and, on the other, the errors which might occur in their use. For this reason I have deemed it necessary that from the pure part of natural science (*physica generalis*), where metaphysical and mathematical constructions are accustomed to traverse one another, the metaphysical constructions, and with them also the principles of the construction of these metaphysical concepts (and hence the principles of the possibility of a mathematical doctrine of nature itself), be [separated and] presented in one system.[6] This separation, beside the aforementioned advantage which such a separation provides, has in addition a special charm afforded by the unity of knowledge when a person takes care that the boundaries of the sciences do not run into one another but occupy their properly divided fields.

There may serve as a second ground for recommending this procedure the fact that in all that is called metaphysics

[6] [Kant means that he is going to gather the metaphysical principles into one system, namely, *The Metaphysical Foundations of Natural Science;* and this system then makes possible a subsequent mathematical system of nature such as Newton's.]

the absolute completeness of the sciences may be hoped for, which is of such a sort as can be promised in no other kind of cognitions; and therefore just as in the metaphysics of nature in general,[7] so here also the completeness of the metaphysics of corporeal nature may be confidently expected. The reason for this is that in metaphysics the object is considered merely as it must be represented in accordance with the universal laws of thought, while in other sciences, as it must be represented in accordance with data of intuition (pure as well as empirical). Hence the former, inasmuch as the object must always be compared with all the necessary laws of thought, must furnish a definite number of cognitions, which can be fully exhausted; but the latter, inasmuch as such sciences offer an infinite manifold of intuitions (pure or empirical), and therefore of objects of thought, can never attain absolute completeness but can be extended to infinity, as in pure mathematics and the empirical doctrine of nature. Moreover, I believe that I have completely exhausted this metaphysical doctrine of body, as far as such a doctrine ever extends; but I believe that I have accomplished thereby no very great work.

The schema for the completeness of a metaphysical system, whether of nature in general or of corporeal nature in particular, is the table of the categories.[8] For there are no   *474*

---

[7] [Contained in the *Critique of Pure Reason,* B 170–294.]

[8] I find doubts expressed in the review of Professor Ulrich's* [book entitled]   *474*
Institutiones Logicae et Metaphysicae [*Instructions in Logic and Metaphysics*] found in the *Allgemeine Literaturzeitung* [*General Literary Journal*], No. 295 [1785], not against this table of the pure concepts of the understanding, but against the conclusions drawn therefrom as to the limitations of the whole faculty of pure reason and therefore of all metaphysics. In these doubts the deeply probing reviewer [anonymous] declares himself to be in agreement with his no less examining author [Ulrich]. Since these doubts are supposed to touch the main foundation of my system, as set forth in the *Critique* [*of Pure Reason*], they should be reasons for thinking that my system, as far as its main goal is concerned, far from carried with it that

---

* [Johann August Heinrich Ulrich (1746–1813), professor of philosophy in Jena.]

more pure concepts of the understanding, which can con-
475 cern the nature of things. Under the four classes of quantity,
quality, relation, and finally modality, all determinations of
476 the universal concept of a matter in general and, therefore,
everything that can be thought a priori respecting it, that can
be presented in mathematical construction, or that can be
given in experience as a determinate object of experience,
must be capable of being brought. There is no more to do

---

apodeictic conviction requisite for compelling an unqualified acceptance. This
main foundation is said to be my deduction of the pure concepts of the
understanding, expounded partly in the *Critique* and partly in the *Prolegomena,* but which in that part of the *Critique* that should have been the clearest
is said to be the most obscure or indeed to move in a circle, etc. I direct
my answers to these objections only to their chief point, namely, that without
a completely clear and adequate deduction of the categories the system of
the *Critique of Pure Reason* would totter on its foundation. I maintain, on the
contrary, that for those who subscribe to my propositions as to the sensibility
of all our intuition and as to the adequacy of the table of the categories insofar as they are determinations of our consciousness borrowed from the logical functions of judgments in general (as the reviewer does), the system of
the *Critique* must carry with it apodeictic certainty, because it is built on the
proposition that the whole speculative use of our reason never reaches beyond
objects of possible experience. For if it can be proved *that* the categories,
which reason must make use of in all its cognition, can have no other employment whatever than that merely with reference to objects of experience
(in such a way that in this experience the categories make possible merely the
form of thought), then the answer to the question *how* they make such form
of thought possible is indeed important enough for completing this deduction, where possible; but with reference to the main purpose of the system,
namely, the determination of the boundary of pure reason, the answer to *how*
is in no way necessary but is merely meritorious. For this purpose the deduction is already carried far enough when it shows that categories, which are
thought, are nothing but mere forms of judgments insofar as these forms are
applied to intuitions (which with us are always sensible only), and that by
such application our intuitions first of all obtain objects and become cognitions; showing these things already suffices to establish with complete certainty the whole system of the *Critique* proper. Thus Newton's system of
universal gravitation is well established, even though it carries with it the
difficulty that one cannot explain how attraction at a distance is possible.
But difficulties are not doubts. Now, that the foundation remains even without the complete deduction of the categories can be shown from what is
conceded, thus.

475   1. Conceded: The table of the categories completely contains all the pure
concepts of the understanding as well as all the formal operations of the

in the way of discovery or addition; but improvement can be made where anything might be lacking in clearness or thoroughness.

Therefore, the concept of matter had to be carried out through all the four functions of the concepts of the understanding (in four chapters), in each of which a new determination of matter was added. The fundamental determination of a something that is to be an object of the external senses

---

understanding in judgments, from which such pure concepts are derived and from which they also differ in nothing except that in the concept of the understanding, an object is thought as determined in regard to one or the other function of judgments. (E.g., in the categorical judgment "the stone is hard", the "stone" is employed as subject and "hard" as predicate, so that it remains permissible for the understanding to interchange the logical function of these concepts and say "something hard is a stone". On the other hand, when I represent to myself in the object as determined that the stone in every possible determination of an object, and not of the mere concept, must be thought only as subject and the hardness only as predicate, the same logical functions now become pure concepts of the understanding for cognizing objects, namely, substance and accident).

2. Conceded: The understanding by its nature carries with it a priori synthetic principles, by which it subordinates to the categories all objects that might be given to it. Consequently, there must also be a priori intuitions, which contain the requisite conditions for the application of the pure concepts of the understanding, inasmuch as without intuition there is no object with regard to which the logical function can be determined as category, and consequently there is no cognition of any object. Therefore, without pure intuition there is no principle which a priori determines the logical function for such cognition.

3. Conceded: These pure intuitions can never be anything but mere forms of the appearances of the external senses or of the internal sense (space and time), and consequently can be forms only of objects of possible experiences.

It follows that no employment of pure reason can ever concern anything but objects of experience; and inasmuch as nothing empirical can be the condition in a priori principles, these cannot be anything more than principles of the possibility of experience generally. This alone is the true and adequate foundation of the determination of the boundary of pure reason, but is not the solution of the problem as to *how* experience is possible by means of these categories, and only by means of them. Although even without this problem the structure stands firm, this problem nevertheless has great importance, and, as I now see, equally great facility, inasmuch as it can be solved almost by a single conclusion from the precisely determined definition of a judgment in general (an act by which given representations first become cognitions of an object). The obscurity which in this part of the   *476*

must be motion, for thereby only can these senses be affected. The understanding leads all other predicates which pertain to the nature of matter back to motion; thus natural science is throughout either a pure or an applied doctrine of motion. *The Metaphysical Foundations of Natural Science* may be brought, then, under four main chapters. The first may be called *Phoronomy;* and in it motion is considered as pure quantum, according to its composition, without any quality of the matter. The second may be termed *Dynamics,* and in it motion is regarded as belonging to the quality of the matter under the name of an original moving force. The third emerges under the name of *Mechanics,* and in it matter with this dynamical quality is considered as by its own

477

---

deduction attaches to my previous treatment, and which I do not disclaim, is attributable to the usual fortune of the understanding in inquiry, the shortest way being commonly not the first which it becomes aware of. Therefore I shall take the earliest opportunity* to make up this defect (which concerns only the manner of the presentation and not the ground of explanation, which is already given correctly there) without my acute reviewer's being placed in the—doubtless to himself—disagreeable necessity of taking refuge in a pre-established harmony because of the surprising agreement of appearances with the laws of the understanding, even though the latter have sources quite different from the former—a remedy far worse than the evil which it is intended to cure and against which it really can avail nothing at all. For from such a preestablished harmony there cannot come the objective necessity that characterizes the pure concepts of the understanding (and the principles of their application to appearances). For example, in the concept of cause as connected with effect, everything remains merely subjectively necessary but is objectively merely chance connection, just as Hume has it when he calls such connection mere illusion through custom. No system in the world can derive this objective necessity otherwise than from the a priori principles lying at the foundation of the possibility of thought itself, by which alone the cognition of objects whose appearance is given us, i.e., experience, is possible. And supposing that the manner as to *how* experience is thereby possible in the first place could never be adequately explained; it would nevertheless remain indisputably certain *that* experience is possible only through those concepts and, conversely, that those concepts likewise are capable of no meaning or employment in any other reference than to objects of experience.

---

* [In the second edition (1787) of the *Critique,* B 129–169.]

motion to be in relation.[9] The fourth is called *Phenomenology;* and in it màtter's motion or rest is determined merely with reference to the mode of representation, or modality, i.e., as an appearance of the external senses.

But beside the internal necessity of distinguishing the metaphysical foundations of the doctrine of body not only from physics, which employs empirical principles, but even from physics' rational premises, which concern the employment of mathematics in physics, there is furthermore an external and, though only accidental, yet important reason for separating its thorough working-out from the general system of metaphysics,[10] and for presenting it systematically as a special whole. For it is permissible to delineate the boundaries of a science not merely according to the constitution of its object and the specific mode of cognition of its object, but also according to the aim that is kept in view as to the further use of the science itself; and one finds that metaphysics has engaged so many heads up till now and will continue to engage them not in order to extend natural knowledge (which comes about much more easily and certainly by observation, experiment, and the application of mathematics to external phenomena), but in order to attain to a knowledge of what lies entirely beyond all the boundaries of experience, namely, God, freedom, and immortality. If these things are so, then one gains when he frees general metaphysics from a shoot springing indeed from its own root but only hindering its regular growth, and plants this shoot apart, without mistaking its origination from metaphysics or ignoring its entire outgrowth from the system of general metaphysics. Doing this does not affect the completeness of the system of general metaphysics but facilitates the uniform progress

[9] [That is, various material objects through their proper motions stand in relation with one another.]

[10] [Contained in the *Critique of Pure Reason.*]

478   of this science toward its goal, if, in all cases where the general doctrine of body is needed, one can call upon the separate system of such a doctrine without encumbering the larger system of metaphysics in general with this general doctrine of body. Furthermore, it is indeed very remarkable (but cannot here be thoroughly entered into) that general metaphysics in all cases where it requires instances (intuitions) in order to provide meaning for its pure concepts of the understanding must always take such instances from the general doctrine of body, i.e., from the form and principles of external intuition;[11] and if these instances are not at hand in their entirety, it gropes, uncertain and trembling, among mere meaningless concepts. Hence there are the well-known disputes, or at least the obscurity in questions, concerning the possibility of an opposition of realities, the possibility of intensive magnitude, etc., with regard to which the understanding is taught only through instances from corporeal nature what the conditions are under which the concepts of the understanding can alone have objective reality, i.e., meaning and truth. And so a separate metaphysics of corporeal nature does excellent and indispensable service to general metaphysics, inasmuch as the former provides instances (cases *in concreto*) in which to realize the concepts and propositions of the latter (properly, transcendental philosophy), i.e., to give to a mere form of thought sense and meaning.

I have in this treatise followed the mathematical method, if not with all strictness (for which more time would have been required than I had to devote to it), at least imitatively. I have done this not in order to obtain a better reception for it through a display of profundity, but because I believe that such a system is quite capable of a mathematical treatment, and that perfection may in time be attained by a cleverer hand when, stimulated by this sketch, mathematical investi-

---

[11] [Cf. *ibid.*, B 288–294.]

gators of nature may find it not unimportant to treat the metaphysical portion—which cannot be got rid of anyway—as a special fundamental part of general physics, and to bring it into unison with the mathematical doctrine of motion.

Newton, in the preface to his *Mathematical Principles of Natural Philosophy* (after having remarked that geometry requires only two mechanical actions, which it postulates, namely, to describe a straight line and a circle), says: Geometry is proud of being able to produce so much with so little taken from elsewhere.[12] On the other hand, one might say   *479* of metaphysics: It stands astonished that with so much offered it by pure mathematics, it can effect so little. Nevertheless, this little is something which even mathematics indispensably requires in its application to natural science; and since mathematics must here necessarily borrow from metaphysics,[13] it need not be ashamed to let itself be seen in the company of the latter.

---

[12] *Gloriatur geometria, quod tam paucis principiis aliunde petitis tam multa praestet.* Newton, *Prin. Phil. Nat. Math. Praefat.*

[13] [See below, Akademie edition numbers 485–486 (pp. 25–27), Ak. 493–495, 503–508, 518–523. Subsequent cross references to this translation will be made to the marginal Akademie numbers.]

FIRST CHAPTER
Metaphysical Foundations of Phoronomy

EXPLICATION[14] 1

Matter is the movable in space. That space which is itself movable is called material, or also relative, space; that in which all motion must ultimately be thought (which is itself therefore absolutely immovable) is called pure, or also absolute, space.

Observation 1

Nothing but motion is to be discussed in phoronomy; therefore, no other property than movability is here attributed to the subject of motion, namely, matter. Matter thus endowed can itself be taken, then, as a point. In phoronomy one abstracts from every internal characteristic, hence also from the quantity, of the movable and concerns himself only with motion and what can be regarded as quantity therein (velocity and direction). If the expression "body" is nevertheless sometimes used here, it occurs only to anticipate to some

---

[14] [*Erklärung.* In view of the mathematical format of the book, it might seem that "definition" would be a better translation. However, compare *Critique of Pure Reason*, B 755–760.]

extent the application of the principles of phoronomy to the subsequent more determinate concepts of matter, so that the discourse may be less abstract and more comprehensible.

Observation 2   *481*

If I am to explicate the concept of matter not by a predicate that applies to it as object but only by its relation to the faculty of cognition in which the representation can first of all be given to me, then matter is every object of the external senses; and this would be its mere metaphysical explication. But space would be simply the form of all external sensible intuition (whether such intuition in itself accrues also to the external object that we call matter or remains only in the nature of our sense does not at all here enter into question). In contrast to. form, matter would be what in external intuition is an object of sensation and consequently would be the properly empirical part of sensible and external intuition, because matter cannot be given at all a priori. In all experience something must be sensed, and this is the real of sensible intuition. Consequently, the space in which we are to set up experience regarding motions must also be capable of being sensed, i.e., must be indicated by what can be sensed; and this space as the sum total of all objects of experience and itself an object of experience is called empirical space. Now, such space insofar as it is material is itself movable. But a movable space, if its motion is to be capable of being perceived, presupposes again another enlarged material space in which it is movable, and this enlarged space presupposes just as well another, and so on to infinity.

Hence all motion that is an object of experience is merely relative. The space in which motion is perceived is a relative space, which itself moves again, perhaps in an opposite direction, in an enlarged space; therefore, matter moved in reference to the first space may be termed at rest in relation to the second. These variations of the concept of motions continue infinitely with the change of the relative space. To assume an absolute space—i.e., such a space as can be no object of experience because it is not material—as itself given means to assume something that cannot be perceived either in itself or in its consequences (motion in absolute space) for the sake of the possibility of experience, which must [in actuality] always be constituted without such a space. Therefore, absolute space is in itself nothing and is no object at all, but signifies merely every other relative space that I can at any time think of outside a given space, and that I merely can extend beyond each given space to infinity as being such a space as includes this given one, and in which I can assume this given one to be moved. Because I have the enlarged, though still material space only in thought, and because nothing is known to me regarding the matter which indicates this space, so I abstract from the matter and therefore repre-

482 sent the space as a pure, nonempirical, and absolute one. I can compare every empirical space with this absolute one and can represent the former as movable in the latter, which is hence always taken as immovable. To make this absolute space an actual thing means to mistake the logical universality of any space, with which I can compare each empirical space as being included in it, for a physical universality of actual compass, and to misunderstand reason in its idea.

In conclusion I observe further that inasmuch as the movability of an object in space cannot be cognized a priori and without instruction from experience, such movability just for that reason could not be counted by me in the *Critique of Pure Reason* among the pure concepts of the understanding; and observe that this concept as empirical can find a place only in a natural science insofar as it is applied metaphysics, which occupies itself with a concept given through experience, though according to a priori principles.

EXPLICATION 2

The motion of a thing is the change of its external relations to a given space.

Observation 1

I have already laid the concept of motion at the basis of the concept of matter. For since I wanted to determine the very concept of matter independently of the concept of extension and thus could consider matter as a point, so I was permitted to allow the use of the common explication of motion as change of place. Now, inasmuch as the concept of matter is to be explicated universally, and hence is to be explicated in a way suitable also for moved bodies, that definition is inadequate. The place of every body is a point. If one wants to determine the distance of the moon from the earth, then he wants to know the distance between their places. And to this end one does not measure from any arbitrary point of the surface or interior of the earth to any arbitrary point of the moon, but takes the shortest line from the center of the one to the center of the other; hence in each of these bodies there is only one point that constitutes its place. Now, a body can move without changing its place, as does the earth in turning on its axis. But its relation to external space hereby changes nonetheless; for it turns, e.g., in twenty-four hours, its various sides toward the moon, and from this turning all kinds of variable effects result on the earth. Only of a movable, i.e., physical, point can one say: motion is always a change of place. Contrary to this explication, one might remember that internal motion, e.g., fermentation, is not in-   *483* cluded in it; but the thing that one says is moved must according to this explication be regarded as a unit. The fact that matter, e.g., a cask of beer, is moved therefore means something other than the fact that the beer in the cask is in motion. The motion of a thing is not identical with the motion in this thing, but the case under consideration here is only the former. However, the application of the former concept of motion to the latter case is subsequently easy.

Observation 2

Motions may be progressive or rotatory (without change of place). They may either enlarge their space or be limited to a given space. Those that enlarge their space are rectilinear motions or even curvilinear ones that do not return in upon themselves. Those limited to a given space are such as return in upon themselves, and these are again either circular or oscillatory, i.e., round or swaying motions. The first cover the very same space always in the same direction, the second the same space always alternately in an opposite direction, like a swaying pendulum. To both belong, in addition, trembling (*motus tremulus*), which is not a progressive motion of a body but a reciprocating motion of a matter that does not thereby change its position as a whole, such as the vibrations of a struck bell or the tremblings of the air set in motion by the peal. I merely make mention of these different kinds of motion in phoronomy because in the case of all that are not progressive the word "velocity" is generally used in another sense than in the case of those that are, as the following observation shows.

Observation 3

In every motion, velocity and direction are the two moments for consideration, when one abstracts from all other properties of the movable. I presuppose here the usual definition of both, but that of direction requires in addition various limitations. A body moved in a circle changes its direction continuously, so that until its return to the point from which it started, all direction is comprised in a plane of merely possible directions; and yet one says that it moves always in the same direction, e.g., a planet from evening till morning.

But what is here the side toward which the motion is directed?[15] This question is related to the following one: upon what rests the internal difference of spirals which are otherwise similar and even equal, except that one species winds to the right and the other to the left? Or upon what rests the internal difference of the winding of pole beans and of hops, the 484 former running around its pole like a corkscrew, or, as sailors would express it, against the sun, the latter running around its pole with the sun? The concept of this internal difference is one that indeed admits of being constructed, but as concept does not at all admit of being clarified by universal marks in the discursive mode of cognition. In things themselves (e.g., in the case of those rare human beings in whom, upon dissection, all their parts agree according to the physiological rule with those of other human beings, but all the viscera are found displaced to the right or to the left, contrary to the usual order) there can be no conceivable difference in the internal consequences. And yet there is a real mathematical and indeed internal difference, whereby two circular motions differing in direction but in all other respects alike nevertheless do correspond, although they are not completely identical. I have elsewhere[16] pointed out that since this difference admits indeed of being given in intuition, but does not at all admit of being brought to clear concepts and therefore of being intelligibly explicated (*dari, non intelligi*[17]), it affords a good confirmative ground of proof for the proposition that space in general does not belong to the properties or relations of things in themselves, which would

[15] [Today in this case one would say, what is here the sense of the motion.]

[16] [See *Prolegomena*, §13, Akademie edition 285–286.]

[17] ["Given, but not understood."]

necessarily have to admit of reduction to objective concepts, but belongs merely to the subjective form of our sensible intuition of things or relations, which must remain wholly unknown to us as regards what they may be in themselves. But this is a digression from our present business, in which we must quite necessarily treat space as a property of the things we are considering, namely, corporeal entities, because these themselves are only phenomena of the external senses and need to be explicated here only as such. As far as the concept of velocity is concerned, this expression also sometimes acquires in usage a variable meaning. We say that the earth rotates on its axis more rapidly than the sun, because it does so in a shorter time, although the motion of the sun is much more rapid. The circulation of the blood of a small bird is much more rapid than that of a man, although the flowing motion in the bird doubtless has less velocity; and so it is also in the case of the vibrations of elastic matters. The brevity of the time of return, whether of a circular or of an oscillating motion, constitutes the ground of this usage, in which no wrong is done if only misinterpretation is otherwise avoided. For this mere increase in the speed of return without increase of spatial velocity has special and very important effects in nature; perhaps there has not yet been enough notice taken of this fact in regard to the circulation of the fluids of animals. In phoronomy we use the word "velocity" merely in a spatial signification, $C = \frac{S^{18}}{T}$.

485   EXPLICATION 3

Rest is permanent presence (*praesentia perdurabilis*) in the same place; permanent is what exists throughout a time, i.e., endures.

[18] [$Celeritas = \dfrac{Spatium}{Tempus}$, Velocity $= \dfrac{Space}{Time}$.]

Observation

A body that is in motion is for a moment in every point of the line that it traverses. The question is, now, whether it rests at the point or moves. Doubtless one will say the latter, for it is present at this point only insofar as it moves. But let us

$$A \qquad\qquad B \qquad a$$

suppose the motion in this way: O————O • • O, the body describes the line AB forwards [from A to B] and backwards from B to A with uniform velocity in such a way that, since the moment it is at B is common to both motions, the motion from A to B is described in half a second and that from B to A also in half a second but both together in a whole second, so that not the smallest portion of time has been expended on the presence of the body at B. And so without the least increase in these motions, the latter, which occurred in the direction BA, will be able to be changed into a motion in the direction Ba, which lies in a straight line with AB; accordingly, the body while it is at B must be regarded not as at rest but as moved. Therefore in the former oscillatory motion it would also have to be regarded as moved at the point B. But this is impossible because, in accordance with what has been assumed, only one moment belongs both to the motion AB and to the equal motion BA, which is opposed to the former and is conjoined with it in one and the same moment. Consequently, if complete lack of motion constitutes the concept of rest, then in the uniform motion Aa the fact that the body is at rest must hold at every point, e.g., at B; but this contradicts the above assertion [that the body is in motion at the point B]. On the other hand, let the line AB be represented as erected over the point A, so that a body rising from A to B, after having lost its motion by means of gravity at the point B, would fall back again from B to A. Now, I ask whether the body at B can be regarded as moved or as at rest? Doubtless one will say at rest, because all previous motion has been taken from it after it has reached this point, and then a uniform motion back is next to follow, but is not yet present; this lack of motion, one will add, is rest. However, in the first case of an assumed uniform motion, the motion BA could not begin otherwise than by the previous cessation of the motion AB and by the nonexistence of the motion from B to A, with the result that at B there was a lack of all motion; and according to the usual explication, rest would have to be assumed. But it must, nevertheless, not be assumed, because at a given velocity no body may be thought of as at rest in any point of its uniform motion. Upon what, then, is the claim of rest based in the second case, since this rising and falling are likewise separated from one another only by a moment? The ground for this claim lies in the fact that the latter motion is not thought of as uniform with the given velocity but as being at first uniformly retarded and afterwards uniformly accelerated, in such a way that the velocity at the point B is not wholly retarded, but only up to a degree that is smaller than any assignable velocity. If the body with such velocity were not to fall back but, rather, its line of fall BA were to be placed in the direction Ba, and hence if it were to be considered as still rising, then it would, as with a mere moment of velocity (the resistance of gravity being disregarded), traverse uniformly in any assignable time, however great, a space smaller than any assignable space. Hence it would not at all change its place (for any possible experience) in all eternity. Consequently, it is put into a state of enduring presence in the same place, i.e., of rest, although owing to the continuous influence of gravity, i.e., the change of this state, the rest is immediately abolished. To be in a permanent state and to persist therein (if nothing else disturbs this state) are two distinct concepts, and one does not impede the other. Therefore, rest cannot be explicated by lack of motion, which, as = 0, does not at all admit of being constructed but must be explicated by permanent presence in the same place. Since this concept can be con-

486

structed by the representation of a motion with infinitely small velocity throughout a finite time, it can therefore be used for the subsequent application of mathematics to natural science.

EXPLICATION 4

To construct the concept of a composite motion means to present a priori in intuition a motion insofar as it arises from two or more given motions united in one movable thing.

Observation

The construction of concepts requires that the condition of their presentation not be borrowed from experience, and hence that there not be presupposed certain forces whose   *487* existence is deducible only from experience, or, in general, that the condition of the construction must not itself be a concept which cannot at all be given a priori in intuition, as, for instance, the concept of cause and effect, or action and resistance, etc. Now, it is here especially noteworthy that phoronomy throughout has as its object primarily the construction of motions in general as quantities. Since phoronomy takes matter merely as something movable and hence does not at all consider any quantity of this movable thing, it must a priori determine these motions solely as quantities according to their velocity, as well as their direction, and indeed their composition. For this much must be determined entirely a priori and indeed through intuition on behalf of applied mathematics. For the rules of the connection of motions through physical causes, i.e., forces, never admit of being fundamentally expounded before the principles of their composition in general are previously mathematically laid down as a foundation.

PRINCIPLE

Every motion as object of a possible experience can be viewed at will either as motion of a body in a space that is at rest, or as rest of the body and motion of the space in the opposite direction with equal velocity.

Observation

To experience the motion of a body requires that not only the body but also the space in which it moves be objects of external experience—hence, that they be material. Therefore, an absolute motion, i.e., a motion referred to an immaterial space, is utterly incapable of being experienced and is hence nothing at all for us (even if one might want to grant that absolute space is something in itself). But in all relative motion the space itself, because it is assumed to be material, may be represented as at rest or as moved. The first[19] occurs when, beyond the space with reference to which I regard a body as moved, there is no more extended space that includes this space (as when in the cabin of a ship I see a ball moved on a table). The second occurs when outside this space there is another space that includes this one (as, in the case mentioned, the bank of the river), since with regard to the riverbank I can view the nearest space (the cabin) as moved and the body itself [the ball] as at rest. Now, respecting an empirically given space, however extended it may be, it is utterly impossible to determine whether or not this space is itself moved with reference to a still greater space enclosing it. Hence for all experience and for every inference from experience, it must be all the same whether I want to consider a body as moved, or else consider the body as at rest and the space as moved in the opposite direc-

488

---

[19] [The space represented as at rest.]

tion with an equal velocity. Furthermore, since absolute space is nothing for any possible experience, these concepts are equivalent: whether I say that a body moves with reference to this given [empirical] space in this direction with this velocity, or whether I think of the body as at rest and want to ascribe all the motion to this space, but in an opposite direction. For the one concept[20] is quite the same as the other, and there is no possible instance of the latter being different from the former; only with regard to the connection we want to give the latter in the understanding is it different [from the former].

Moreover, we cannot in any experience whatever specify a fixed point by reference to which there would be determined what absolute motion and absolute rest should mean. For everything given us in this way[21] is material, and is hence movable, and (since in space we know of no extreme limit of possible experience) is perhaps also actually moved without our being able to perceive this motion. Regarding the motion of a body in empirical space, I can assign one part of the given velocity to the body and the other part to the space, but in the opposite direction. The whole possible experience concerning the results of these two combined motions is equivalent to thinking of the body alone as moved with the entire velocity, or thinking of the body as at rest and the space as moved with the entire velocity in the opposite direction. I here assume all motions to be rectilinear. For as concerns nonrectilinear ones, whether I am warranted in regarding the body as moved (e.g., the earth in its daily rotation) and the surrounding space (the starry heavens) as at rest, or the latter as moved and the former as at rest, is not in all respects equivalent; this will be treated in particular in the sequel.[22] In phoronomy, then, where I consider the motion

---

[20] [Namely, the body moved and the space at rest.]

[21] [That is, in experience.]

[22] ["Phenomenology," Ak. 556–558, 560–562.]

of a body only in relation to space (upon whose motion or rest the body has no influence at all), it is quite undetermined and arbitrary whether I attribute to the body or to the space any or all or how much of the velocity of the given motion. Later in mechanics, where a moved body is to be considered in active relation to other bodies in the space of its motion, this[23] will be no longer so completely equivalent, as will be shown in the proper place.[24]

489   EXPLICATION 5

The composition of motion is the representation of the motion of a point as identical with two or more motions of the point combined.

Observation

Since in phoronomy I cognize matter by no other property than its movability and hence may consider matter itself only as a point, the motion can be considered only as the description of a space. But it is considered in such a way that I pay attention not merely to the space described, as in geometry, but also to the time involved therein and hence to the velocity with which a point describes the space. Phoronomy is, then, the pure doctrine (*mathesis*) of the quantity of motions. The determinate concept of a quantity is the concept of the production of the representation of an object through the composition of the homogeneous. Now, since nothing is homogeneous with motion except motion, so phoronomy is a doctrine of the composition of the motions of the same point according to their direction and velocity, i.e., the representation of a single motion as one that comprises within itself simultaneously two or even several motions, or else

---

23 [That is, whether the motion is attributed to the body or to the space.]
24 ["Mechanics," Ak. 544–550.]

the representation of two motions of the same point simultaneously insofar as they together constitute one motion (that
is, they are identical with this motion), and not insofar as
they produce the latter in the way that causes produce their
effect. In order to find the motion arising from the composition of several motions—or of as many as one wants—one
has only, as with the production of all quantities, first to
seek out that motion which is under given conditions compounded from two motions; thereupon this is compounded
with a third; and so on. Consequently, the doctrine of the
composition of all motions is reducible to the composition
of two. But two motions of one and the same point which
are found simultaneously at this same point can be distinguished in a twofold manner, and as such can be combined in three ways at the point. First, they occur at the same
time either in one and the same line or in different lines;
the latter are motions comprising an angle. Those occurring
in one and the same line are either contrary to one another
in direction or keep the same direction. Since all these motions are considered as occurring simultaneously, there results immediately from the relation of the lines, i.e., of the
spaces described by the motions in equal time, the relation
of the velocities also. Hence there are three cases. (1) Two
motions (they may be of equal or unequal velocities) combined in one body in the same direction are to constitute
a resultant composite motion. (2) Two motions of the same   *490*
point (of equal or unequal velocity) combined in opposite
directions are to constitute through their composition a third
motion in the same line. (3) Two motions of a point, with
equal or unequal velocities, but in different lines that comprise an angle, are considered to be compounded.

PROPOSITION

The composition of two motions of one and the same
point can only be thought of by one of them being repre-

sented in absolute space, but instead of the second motion being so represented, a motion of the relative space in the opposite direction and with the same velocity is represented as being identical with the first motion.

Proof

First case: Two motions in the same line and direction belong simultaneously to one and the same point.

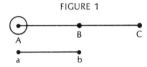

FIGURE 1

Let two velocities AB and ab be represented as contained in one velocity of the motion. Let these velocities be assumed for the time being to be equal, AB = ab; in this case I assert that they cannot be represented simultaneously at the same point in one and the same space (whether absolute or relative). For inasmuch as the lines AB and ab, which denote the velocities, are, strictly speaking, the spaces which are traversed in equal times; so the composition of these spaces AB and ab = BC, and hence the line AC (as the sum of the spaces), must express the sum of both velocities. But the parts AB and BC do not, individually, represent the velocity = ab; for they are not traversed in the same time as ab. Hence the double line AC, which is traversed in the same time as the line ab, does not represent the double velocity of the latter, as was nevertheless required. Hence the composition of two velocities in one direction in the same space cannot be presented intuitively.

491   On the other hand, if I represent the body A as moved in absolute space with the velocity AB and in addition I give to the relative space a velocity ab = AB in the opposite direction ba = CB, then this is the same as my having given the latter velocity to the body in the direction AB (Principle). But

the body in this case moves in the same time through the sum of the lines AB and BC, their sum being equal to 2ab, and in this time it would have traversed the line ab = AB only; and yet its velocity is represented as the sum of the two equal velocities AB and ab, which is what was required.

Second case: Two motions in exactly opposite directions are to be combined at one and the same point.

FIGURE 2

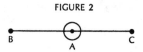

Let AB be one of these motions and AC the other in the opposite direction; we here assume the velocity of the latter motion to be equal to that of the first. In this case the very thought of representing two such motions in one and the same space at the very same point as simultaneous would be impossible, and hence the case of such a composition of motions would itself be impossible too, which is contrary to the assumption.

On the other hand, let the motion AB be thought of as in absolute space; and instead of the motion AC in this absolute space, let the opposite motion CA of the relative space be thought of with the very same velocity, which (according to our Principle) is fully equal to the motion AC and can hence be entirely substituted for it. In this case two exactly opposite and equal motions of the same point at the same time may very well be presented. Now, inasmuch as the relative space is moved with the same velocity CA = AB in the same direction with the point A; so this point, or the body present therein, does not change its place with regard to the relative space, i.e., a body moved in two exactly opposite directions with equal velocity rests, or, generally expressed, its motion is equal to the difference of the velocities in the direction of the greater one (and this fact easily follows from what has already been proved).

Third case: Two motions of the same point are repre-   *492* sented as combined according to directions that enclose an angle.

FIGURE 3

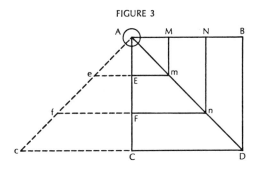

The two given motions are AB and AC, whose velocity and directions are expressed by these lines, but the angle enclosed by the latter is expressed by BAC (it may, as here, be a right angle, but it may also be any arbitrary oblique angle). Now, if these two motions are to occur simultaneously in the directions AB and AC and indeed in one and the same space, then they would not be able to occur simultaneously in both these lines AB and AC, but only in lines running parallel to these. It would therefore have to be assumed that one of these motions produced a change in the other (namely, the deviation from the given course), although the directions remained mutually the same. But this is contrary to the proposition's assumption, which indicates by the word "composition" that both the given motions are contained in a third and hence are identical with this third, and not that a third is produced by one of them changing the other.

On the other hand, let the motion AC be assumed as taking place in absolute space; but instead of the motion AB, let the motion of the relative space in the opposite direction be assumed. Let the line AC be divided into three equal parts, AE, EF, FC. Now, while the body A in absolute space traverses the line AE; the relative space, and with it the point E, traverses the space Ee = MA. While the body traverses the two parts together = AF; the relative space, *493* and with it the point F, describes the line Ff = NA. While, finally, the body traverses the whole line AC; the relative space, and with it the point C, describes the line Cc = BA. All this is the same as though the body A had traversed in these three divisions of time the lines Em, Fn, and CD = AM, AN, AB, and in the whole time in which it traverses AC had traversed the line CD = AB. Therefore, it is at the last moment at the point D and in this whole time is gradually at all points of the diagonal line AD, which, accordingly, expresses the direction as well as the velocity of the composite motion.

Observation 1

Geometrical construction requires that one quantity be identical with the other, or that two quantities in composition be identical with a third and not that they produce the third as causes, which would be mechanical construction. Complete similarity and equality insofar as they can be cognized only in intuition is congruity. All geometrical construction of complete identity rests on congruity. This congruity of two combined motions with a third (as the *motu compositio*[25] itself) can never take place when the two former are represented in one and the same space, e.g., relative space. Hence all attempts to prove the foregoing proposition in its three cases have always been mechanical solutions only, inasmuch, namely, as one let moving causes, by which a given motion was combined with another, produce a third motion. Such attempts, however, were not proofs that the former motions were identical with the latter motion and that because of this identity they admitted of being presented in pure intuition a priori.

[25] ["Composition of motion."]

Observation 2

When, for instance, a velocity AC is termed double, nothing else can be understood thereby but that it consists of two simple and equal velocities AB and BC (see Fig. 1). But if a double velocity be explicated by saying that it is a motion whereby a doubly great space is traversed in the same time, then something is here assumed which is not a matter of course, namely, that two equal velocities admit of being combined in the same way as two equal spaces. But it is not of itself obvious that a given velocity consists of smaller velocities and a speed of slownesses in the same way that a space consists of smaller spaces. For the parts of the velocity are not external to one another as the parts of the space are; and if the former are to be considered as quantity, then the concept of their quantity, since it is intensive, must be constructed in a way different from that of the extensive quantity of space. But this construction is possible in no other way than by the mediate composition of two equal motions, one of which is that of the body; the other, that of the relative space in the opposite direction, and just for this reason, completely identical with an equal motion of the body in the previous direction. For in the same direction two equal velocities do not admit of being combined in one body except through external moving causes, e.g., a ship carries the body with one of these velocities, while another moving force immovably combined with the ship impresses upon the body the second velocity, which is equal to the previous one. In all this it must always be assumed that the body maintains itself in free motion with the first velocity when the second velocity is added; this is a natural law of moving forces, and this law cannot at all come into consideration when the question is merely how the concept of velocity is constructed as a quantity. So much for the addition of velocities to one another. But when the question concerns the sub-

494

traction of one velocity from another, such substraction can indeed easily be thought of if the possibility of a velocity as quantity by addition has once been granted. But the concept of this subtraction cannot so easily be constructed. For to this end two opposite motions must be combined in one body; but how is this to happen? Immediately, i.e., with regard to the same resting space, there is no possibility of thinking of two equal motions in opposite directions in the same body. But the representation of the impossibility of these two motions in one body is not the concept of its rest but is the concept of the impossibility of the construction of this composition of opposite motions; nevertheless, this composition is assumed in the proposition to be possible. But this construction is not otherwise possible than by the combination of the motion of the body with the motion of the space, as has been proved. Finally, as concerns the composition of two motions whose direction encloses an angle, they likewise cannot be thought of in the body by reference to one and the same space unless one of the motions is assumed to be produced by an external, continuously inflowing force (e.g., a vessel bearing the body onward) and the other motion is assumed to maintain itself unaltered. Or to express it generally, one must have as a basis moving forces and the production of a third motion from two combined forces. This is indeed the mechanical execution of what a concept contains, but is not the mathematical construction of the composition. Such a construction should only make intuitive what the object (as quantum) is and not how the object may be produced by nature or art through certain tools and forces. In order to determine the relation of motions to other ones as quantity, their composition must take place according to the rules of congruity. This is possible in all three cases only by means of the space's motion which is congruent with one of the two given motions, whereby both are congruent with the composite motion.

495

Observation 3

Thus phoronomy, not as pure doctrine of motion, but merely as pure doctrine of the quantity of motion, in which matter is thought of according to no other property than that of mere movability, contains nothing but this single proposition, carried out in the three cases cited, concerning the composition of motion, and indeed concerning the possibility of rectilinear motion alone, not of curvilinear. For since in this latter the motion is continuously changed (in direction), a cause of this change, which cannot be merely space, must be introduced. But the fact that one usually understands by the designation "composite motion" only the single case where the directions of such a motion enclose an angle does some detriment to the principle of the division of a pure philosophical science in general, although not to physics. For as far as physics is concerned, all three cases treated in the above proposition can be presented adequately in the third case alone. For if the angle enclosing the two given motions is thought of as infinitely small, it contains the first case. But if the angle is represented as only infinitely little different from a single straight line, it contains the second case. Consequently, all three cases mentioned by us can indeed be given in the familiar proposition concerning composite motion as in a universal formula. But in this way one could not learn to comprehend a priori the quantitative doctrine of motion according to its parts; such comprehension is useful for many purposes.

If anyone wants to connect the aforementioned three parts of the phoronomic proposition with the schema of the division of all pure concepts of the understanding, namely, with that of the division of the concept of quantity, he will observe the following. Since the concept of quantity always contains the concept of the composition of the homogeneous, the doctrine of the composition of motions is at the same time the pure doctrine of quantity therein. And indeed this doc·

trine according to all three moments[26] furnished by space, namely, the unity of line and direction, the plurality of directions in one and the same line, and finally the totality of directions as well as of lines, according to which the motion can take place, contains the determination of all possible motion as quantum, although motion's quantity (in a movable point) consists merely in velocity. This observation is useful only in transcendental philosophy.

---

[26] [Cf. *Critique of Pure Reason*, B 106.]

SECOND
CHAPTER

Metaphysical Foundations of Dynamics

EXPLICATION 1

Matter is the movable insofar as it fills a space. To fill a space means to resist everything movable that strives by its motion to press into a certain space. A space that is not filled is an empty space.

Observation

This is, now, the dynamical explication of the concept of matter. This explication presupposes the phoronomic one but adds to it a property that is related as cause to an effect, namely, the capacity of resisting a motion within a certain space. This property could not come into consideration in the foregoing science, even when we dealt with the motions of one and the same point in opposite directions. This filling of space keeps a certain space free from the intrusion of any other movable thing when its motion is directed to any place within this space. Now, we must investigate what matter's resistance directed to all sides is based upon and what this resistance is. But one sees already from the preceding explication that matter is not here considered as resisting when it is driven from its place and is thus itself moved (this case will hereafter come into consideration as mechanical resist-

40

ance), but it is considered as resisting only when the space   *497*
of its own extension is to be diminished. One uses the words
"to occupy a space", i.e., to be immediately present in all
its points, in order to indicate thereby the extension of a
thing in space. But there is not determined in this concept
what action, or whether any action at all, arises from this
presence as it resists other presences that try to press into it;
or whether this concept signifies merely a space without
matter insofar as such a space is a sum total of several spaces,
just as one can say of every geometrical figure that it occupies a space (it is extended); or even whether there is
something in space necessitating another movable to penetrate deeper into this something (attracting others). Inasmuch, I say, as all of this is undetermined in the concept of
occupying a space, "to fill a space" is therefore a closer determination of the concept "to occupy a space".

PROPOSITION 1

Matter fills a space, not by its mere existence, but by a special
moving force.

Proof

Penetration into a space (in the initial moment this is called
the endeavor to penetrate) is a motion. The resistance to
motion is the reason why motion diminishes or even changes
into rest. Now, nothing can be combined with any motion
as lessening or destroying it but another motion of the same
movable thing in the opposite direction (phoronomic proposition). Consequently, the resistance offered by a matter[27]

---

[27] [Matter in particular usually means merely body. "A matter" as Kant
ordinarily employs this expression does not mean "a particular kind of matter" but "a piece of matter of any kind whatever". The context should make
clear whether "a matter" means "a piece of matter" or "a particular kind of
matter".]

in the space that it fills to all intrusion by another matter is a cause of the motion of this other matter in the opposite direction. But the cause of a motion is called moving force. Consequently, matter fills its space by moving force and not by its mere existence.

Observation

Lambert[28] and others called the property of matter by which it fills a space its solidity (a rather ambiguous expression) and maintained that such solidity must be assumed in everything which exists (substance), at least in the external sensible world. According to their concepts the presence of something real in space must by its very concept carry with it this resistance and hence does so according to the principle of contradiction, and must exclude the coexistence of anything else in the space in which such a real thing is present. But the principle of contradiction does not repel[29] any matter that advances in order to penetrate into a space in which another matter is to be found. Only when I attribute to that which occupies a space a force to repel every external movable thing that approaches it, do I understand how a contradiction is involved when the space which a thing occupies is penetrated by another thing of the same kind. Here the mathematician has assumed something as an initial datum of the construction of the concept of matter, but this something does not admit of being further constructed. Now, he can indeed begin his construction from any datum he pleases, without involving himself also in explicating this datum in turn; but he is nevertheless not thereby authorized to explicate this datum as something wholly incapable of any

498

[28] [Johann Heinrich Lambert (1728–1777) was a German mathematician, physicist, astronomer, and philosopher. He wrote *Photometry, Cosmological Letters, New Organon,* and other works.]

[29] [An example of Kantian wit.]

mathematical construction in order thereby to prevent a return to the first principles of natural science.

EXPLICATION 2

Attractive force is that moving force whereby a matter can be the cause of the approach of other matter to itself (or, equivalently, whereby it resists the withdrawal of other matter from itself).

Repulsive force is that whereby a matter can be the cause of making other matter withdraw from itself (or, equivalently, whereby it resists the approach of other matter to itself). The latter we shall also sometimes call driving force, and the former, drawing.

Note

These are the only two moving forces that can be thought of. For all motion which one matter can impress on another must always be regarded as imparted in the straight line between two points, since with respect to such motion each of these matters is considered merely as a point. But in this straight line only two kinds of motion are possible: one by which the above points recede from one another and a second by which they approach one another. But the force which is the cause of the first motion is called repulsive and that *499* of the second attractive. Consequently, there can be thought only these two kinds of forces, to which as such all the forces of motion in material nature must be reduced.

PROPOSITION 2

Matter fills its space by the repulsive forces of all its parts, i.e., by its own force of extension, which has a determinate degree, beyond which can be thought smaller or greater degrees to infinity.

Proof

Matter fills a space only by moving force (Proposition 1) and indeed by such a force as resists the penetration, i.e., the approach, of other matter. Now, this is a repulsive force (Explication 2). Therefore, matter fills its space only by repulsive forces, and indeed by the repulsive forces of all its parts, because otherwise a part of its space would not be filled (against the assumption) but would only be enclosed. But the force of something extended by virtue of the repulsion of all its parts is a force of extension (expansive). Therefore, matter fills its space only by its own force of extension; and this was the first point. Beyond every given force a greater must admit of being thought of, for that beyond which there is no greater possible would be one whereby in a finite time an infinite space would be traversed (which is impossible). Further, below every given moving force a smaller must admit of being thought of (for the smallest would be that by whose infinite addition to itself throughout any given time no finite velocity could be generated, but this means the lack of all moving force). Therefore, below every given degree of a moving force a still smaller degree must always be able to be given; and this is the second point. Hence the force of extension, whereby all matter fills its space, has its degree, which is never the greatest or smallest, but beyond which can be found greater as well as smaller to infinity.

500   Note 1

The expansive force of matter is also called elasticity. Now, since this force is the basis upon which rests the filling of space as an essential property of all matter, this elasticity must be termed original, because it cannot be derived from any other property of matter. All matter is, accordingly, originally elastic.

Note 2

There can be found beyond every extensive force a greater moving force which can work against the former and would thus diminish the space that the extensive force is striving to expand; in such a case this greater moving force would be termed a compressive one. Because of this fact, for every matter there must be able to be found a compressive force capable of driving this matter from every space that it fills into a smaller space.

EXPLICATION 3

A matter in its motion penetrates another when the former, by compression, completely abolishes the space of the latter's extension.

Observation

When the piston of an air pump's barrel that is filled with air is driven continually closer to the bottom, the air-matter is compressed. Now, if this compression could be carried so far that the piston completely touched the bottom (without the least bit of air escaping), then the air-matter would be penetrated. For the matters between which it is leave no space for it, and thus it would be found between the bottom and the piston without occupying a space. This penetrability of matter by external compressive forces, if anyone were willing to assume or even to think of such penetrability, would be termed mechanical. I have reasons for distinguishing, by such a limitation, this penetrability of matter from another

kind, the concept of which is perhaps just as impossible;
I may hereafter have occasion to make some mention of
this other kind of penetrability.[30]

501   PROPOSITION 3

Matter can be compressed to infinity; but it can never be
penetrated by other matter, regardless of how great the
pressing force of this other may be.

Proof

An original force whereby a matter endeavors to extend itself
everywhere in a given space that it occupies must be greater
when enclosed in a smaller space, and must be infinite when
compressed into an infinitely small space. Now, for any given
extensive force of matter there can be found a greater compressive force that drives this matter into a smaller space, and
so on to infinity; this was the first point. But in order to penetrate the matter, its compression into an infinitely small space
would be required, and hence an infinitely compressive force
would be required; but such a force is impossible. Consequently, a matter cannot be penetrated by the compression
of any other matter; this is the second point.

Observation

I have assumed at the very beginning of this proof that the
more an extensive force is constricted so much the more
strongly must it counteract. Now, this would not indeed
hold for every kind of elastic forces that are only derivative;
but this can be postulated of matter possessing essential

[30] [Cf. below, Ak. 530–532.]

elasticity insofar as it is matter in general filling a space. For expansive force exercised from all points toward all sides constitutes the very concept of elasticity. But the same quantum of expanding forces brought into a narrower space must in every point of the space repel so much the more strongly in inverse proportion to the smallness of the space in which a certain quantum of force diffuses its efficacy.

EXPLICATION 4

The impenetrability of matter resting on resistance, which increases proportionally to the degree of compression, I term relative; but that which rests on the assumption that   *502* matter, as such, is capable of no compression at all is called absolute impenetrability. The filling of space with absolute impenetrability may be called mathematical; that with merely relative impenetrability, dynamical.

Observation 1

According to the mere mathematical concept of impenetrability (which assumes no moving force as originally inherent in matter), no matter is capable of compression except insofar as it contains within itself empty spaces. Hence matter, insofar as it is matter, resists all penetration unconditionally and with absolute necessity. According to our discussion of this property, however, impenetrability rests on a physical basis; for the extensive force makes matter itself, as something extended filling its space, first of all possible. But this force has a degree which can be overcome, and hence matter's space of extension can be diminished, i.e., its space can be penetrated in a certain measure by a given compressive force, but only in such a way that complete penetration is impossible, inasmuch as such penetration would require an infinite compressive force; because of all this, the filling of space must be regarded only as relative impenetrability.

Observation 2

Absolute impenetrability is indeed nothing more or less than a *qualitas occulta*. For one asks, what is the reason why matters cannot penetrate one another in their motion? He receives the answer, because they are impenetrable. The appeal to repulsive force is free of this reproach. For although this force likewise cannot be further explicated according to its possibility and must hence be admitted as a fundamental one, it nevertheless yields the concept of an active cause and of the laws of this cause in accordance with which the effect, namely, the resistance in the filled space, can be estimated according to the degrees of this effect.

EXPLICATION 5

Material substance is that in space which of itself, i.e., separated from all else existing outside it in space, is movable.
503   The motion of a part of matter whereby it ceases to be a part [of that matter] is separation. The separation of the parts of matter is physical division.

Observation

The concept of substance signifies the ultimate subject of existence, i.e., that which does not itself in turn belong merely as predicate to the existence of another. Now, matter is the subject of everything in space that can be counted as belonging to the existence of things; for besides matter no subject would otherwise admit of being thought of except space itself, which is, however, a concept that does not contain anything at all existent but contains merely the necessary conditions of the external relation of possible objects of the external senses. Therefore, matter as the movable in space is substance therein. But just in the same way all parts of matter will likewise be substances insofar as one can say of them that they are themselves subjects and not merely predicates of other matters, and hence these parts themselves will in turn have to be called matter. They are themselves subjects if they are of themselves movable, and hence beside their association with other adjacent parts are also something existing in space. Therefore, the proper movability of matter or of any part thereof is at the same time a proof that this movable thing, and every movable part thereof, is substance.

PROPOSITION 4

Matter is divisible to infinity, and indeed into parts each of which is again matter.[31]

Proof

Matter is impenetrable by its original force of extension (Proposition 3), but this force of extension is only the consequence of the repulsive forces of each point in a space filled with matter. Now, the space that matter fills is mathematically divisible to infinity, i.e., its parts can be differentiated to infinity, although they cannot be moved and, consequently, cannot be separated (according to demonstrations of geometry). But in a space filled with matter every part of the space contains repulsive force to counteract on all sides all remaining parts, and hence to repel them and likewise be

---

[31] [This proposition, its proof, and the following two observations should be compared with the Second Antinomy in the *Critique of Pure Reason*, B 462–471, 518–535, 551–560.]

repelled by them, i.e., to be moved to a distance from them.
504   Hence every part of a space filled by matter is of itself movable and is therefore separable by physical division from the
remaining parts, insofar as they are material substance.
Consequently, as far as the mathematical divisibility of space
filled by a matter reaches, thus far does the possible physical
division of the substance that fills the space likewise reach.
But the mathematical divisibility extends to infinity, and
consequently also the physical, i.e., all matter is divisible
to infinity and indeed is divisible into parts each of which
is itself in turn material substance.

Observation 1

By the proof of the infinite divisibility of space, that of matter
is not by a long way proved, if one has not previously
shown that in every part of space there is material substance,
i.e., that parts movable of themselves are to be found. For
if a monadist might want to assume that matter consists of
physical points each of which (for this reason) has no movable parts but yet fills a space by mere repulsive force, he
would be able to grant that this space, but not the substance
acting in it, is at the same time divided, and hence that the
sphere of the substance's activity is divided, but not that the
active movable subject itself is at the same time divided by
the division of the space. Accordingly, he would compound
matter from physically indivisible parts and yet allow it to
occupy space in a dynamical way.

By the above proof, however, this subterfuge is completely
taken away from the monadist. For from this proof it is clear
that in a filled space there can be no point that does not
itself on all sides repel in the same way as it is repelled, i.e.,
as a reacting subject, of itself movable, existing outside of
every other repelling point; and it is clear that the hypothesis
of a point filling a space by mere driving force and not by
means of other likewise repulsive forces is completely im-

possible. In order to make this fact and thereby also the proof of the preceding proposition intuitable, let it be assumed that A is the place of a monad in space, that ab is the

FIGURE 4

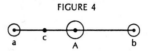

diameter of the sphere of its repulsive force, and hence that aA is the radius of this sphere. Thus between a, where the penetration of an external monad into the space occupied by the sphere in question is resisted, and A, the center of the sphere, a point c can be specified (according to the infinite divisibility of space). Now, if A resists whatever endeavors to penetrate into a, then c must resist both the points A and a, for if this were not so, they would approach each other unimpeded; consequently, A and a would meet in the point c, i.e., the space would be penetrated. Therefore, there must be something in c that resists the penetration of A and a, and thus repels the monad A as much as this something is repelled by the monad. Now, since repulsion is a motion, c is something movable in space, i.e., matter; and the space between A and a could not be filled by the sphere of the activity of a single monad, neither could the space between c and A, and so on to infinity.

505

Mathematicians represent the repulsive forces of the parts of elastic matters in their greater or lesser compression as increasing or decreasing in a certain proportion to their distances from one another, e.g., the smallest parts of air repel each other in inverse proportion to their distances from one another because their elasticity stands in inverse proportion to the spaces within which they are compressed. One completely mistakes their meaning and misinterprets their language when he attributes to the object of the concept what necessarily belongs to the process of the construction of the concept. For according to this process, all contact can be represented as an infinitely small distance; moreover, this must necessarily happen in those cases where a larger or smaller space is to be represented as completely filled by the same quantity of matter, i.e., by one and the same quantum of repulsive forces. Consequently, as regards something infinitely divisible, there can be assumed no actual distance of parts, which always constitute a continuum as regards all expansion of the space of the whole, although the possibility of this expansion can be made intuitable only under the idea of an infinitely small distance.

Observation 2

Mathematics can indeed in its internal practice be quite indifferent with regard to the chicanery of a mistaken metaphysics and rest in the certain possession of its evident assertions of the infinite divisibility of space, regardless of what objections a sophistry picking over mere concepts may introduce against such divisibility. But in the application of its propositions valid for space to substance filling space, it must nevertheless concern itself with a test according to mere concepts, and hence with metaphysics. The above proposition is already a proof of this. For although matter is infinitely divisible from a mathematical point of view, it does not necessarily follow that matter is physically divisible to infinity (even if every part of space is again a space and consequently always includes within itself parts external to one another) unless one can prove that in every possible part of this filled space there is substance as well, and that, consequently, this substance, separated from all other substances, exists as of itself movable. Therefore, something was lacking heretofore in the mathematical proof; without this something, such a proof could have no sure application 506 to natural science. This deficiency has been remedied in the proposition given above. But as for what concerns the remaining attacks of metaphysics upon the present physical proposition of the infinite divisibility of matter, the mathematician must cede these attacks entirely to the philosopher. The latter, anyway, by these objections, ventures into a labyrinth out of which it becomes difficult for him to find his way, even in questions immediately concerning him. He thus has enough to do on his own account, without the mathematician's being allowed to mix himself up in this business. If, namely, matter is infinitely divisible, then (concludes the dogmatic metaphysician) it consists of an infinite multitude of parts; for a whole must in advance already contain within itself all the parts in their entirety into which it can be divided. This last proposition is also indubitably certain of every whole as a thing in itself. Now, one cannot grant that matter, or even space, consists of infinitely many parts (because there is a contradiction involved in thinking of an infinite number as complete, inasmuch as the concept of an infinite number already implies that it can never be wholly complete). Therefore, one must resolve either to defy the geometer by saying that space is not divisible to infinity, or to irritate the metaphysician by saying that space is no property of a thing in itself and hence that matter is not a thing in itself but is the mere appearance of our external senses, just as space is their essential form.

Here the philosopher now comes into the strait between the horns of a dangerous dilemma. To deny the first proposition, that space is divisible to infinity, is an empty undertaking; for mathematics does not allow anything to be reasoned away. But yet to regard matter as a thing in itself and hence space as a property of things in themselves is identical with denying this first proposition. The philosopher sees himself thus forced to depart from the assertion that matter is a thing in itself and space a property of things in themselves, however common and suited to the common understanding this assertion may be. But of course he departs from this assertion only under the condition that in the event of his making matter and space appearances only (hence making space only the form of our external sensible intuition, and thus making both matter and space not things in themselves but only subjective modes of representation of objects in themselves unknown to us), he is then helped out of the difficulty of matter's being infinitely divisible even though it does not consist of infinitely many parts. That matter consists of infinitely many parts can indeed be thought by reason, even though this thought cannot be constructed and rendered intuitable. For with regard to what is actual only by its being given in the representation, there is not more given than is met with in the representation, i.e., as far as the progression of the representations reaches. Therefore, one can only say of appearances, whose division goes on to infinity, that there are as many parts of the appear-

507   ance as we give, i.e., however far we divide. For the parts insofar as they belong to the existence of an appearance exist only in thought, namely, in the division itself. Now, the division indeed goes on to infinity, but it is never given as infinite; and hence it does not follow that the divisible contains within itself an infinite number of parts in themselves, that are outside of our representation, merely because the division goes on to infinity. For it is not the division of the thing [*Ding*] but only the division of its representation that can indeed be infinitely continued. And even though in the objeck [*Objekt*] (that as thing in it-self is unknown) there is also a basis for the continuation of this division to infinity, nevertheless such division can never be entirely given. Therefore, any division of the representation proves no actual infinite multitude to be in the object (that a multitude would be an express contradiction). A great man[32] who perhaps contributes more than anyone else to maintain the reputation of mathematics in Germany has several times repulsed metaphysical presumptions of overturning the propositions of geometry concerning the infinite divisibility of space by the established reminder that space belongs only to the appearance of external things; but he has not been understood.

[32] [Alois Höfler, editor of the Akademie edition of the *Metaphysical Foundations of Natural Science*, suggests that Kant might mean either Leibniz, Wolff, Euler, Lambert, or Kästner.]

This proposition was taken as though it meant that space itself appears to us, and is otherwise a thing in itself or a relation of things in themselves, but the mathematician considers it only as it appears. Instead of this the proposition should have been taken to mean that space is no property appertaining to anything outside of our senses, but is only the subjective form of our sensibility. Under this form objects of our external senses appear to us, but we do not know them as they are constituted in themselves. We call this appearance matter. By the foregoing misinterpretation space was always thought of as a quality adhering to things even outside of our power of representation, but the mathematician thought of this quality only according to common concepts, i.e., confusedly (for appearance is commonly explained in this way). By this same foregoing misinterpretation one attributed the mathematical proposition of the infinite divisibility of matter, a proposition presupposing the highest clarity in the concept of space, to a confused representation of space, which the geometer laid as his foundation. In this way it remained open to the metaphysician to compound space of points and matter of simple parts and thus (according to his opinion) to bring distinctness into this concept of space. The ground of this aberration lies in a badly understood monadology, which does not at all belong to the explication of natural appearances but is a platonic concept of the world carried out by Leibniz. This concept is correct in itself insofar as the world is regarded not as an object of the senses but as a thing in itself, i.e., as merely an object of the understanding which nevertheless lies at the basis of the appearances of the senses. Now, the composite of things in themselves must certainly consist of the simple; for the parts must here be given before all composition. But the composite in the appearance does not consist of the simple, because in the appearance, which can never be given *508* otherwise than as composite (extended), the parts can be given only through division and thus not before the composite but only in it. Therefore, it was not Leibniz' intention, as far as I comprehend, to explicate space by the order of simple entities side by side, but rather to juxtapose this order as corresponding to space while yet belonging to a merely intelligible (for us unknown) world. And this is to assert nothing other than what was pointed out elsewhere, namely, that space, along with the matter whose form space is, comprises not the world of things in themselves but only the appearance of such a world, and is itself only the form of our external sensible intuition.

PROPOSITION 5

The possibility of matter requires a force of attraction, as the second essential fundamental force of matter.

Proof

Impenetrability, as the fundamental property of matter whereby it first reveals itself as something real in the space of our external senses, is nothing but matter's capacity of extension (Proposition 2). Now, an essential moving force by which parts of matter recede from one another cannot, firstly, be limited by itself, because matter is impelled by such a force to continuously expand the space that it occupies, and cannot, secondly, be fixed by space alone at a certain limit of extension. This second is so because even though space can indeed contain the ground of the fact that with the increase in the volume of a matter extending itself, the extensive force becomes weaker in inverse proportion; yet inasmuch as smaller degrees of every moving force are possible to infinity, space cannot anywhere contain the ground of the ceasing of such a force. Therefore, matter by its repulsive force alone (which contains the ground of its impenetrability), and if no other moving force counteracted this repulsive one, would be held within no limits of extension, i.e., would disperse itself to infinity, and no assignable quantity of matter would be found in any assignable space. Consequently, with merely repulsive forces of matter, all spaces would be empty; and hence, strictly speaking, there would be no matter at all. Therefore, forces which are opposed to 509 the extensive ones, i.e., compressive forces, are required for the existence of all matter. But these cannot in turn be sought for originally in the opposition of another matter, for this other itself requires a compressive force in order that it may be matter. Consequently, there must be assumed an original force of matter acting in an opposite direction to the repulsive, and hence acting for approach, i.e., an attractive force. Now, inasmuch as this attractive force belongs to the possibility of matter as matter in general, and consequently precedes all distinctions of matter; so this force must not be attributed merely to a particular species of matter, but to every matter generally and originally. Thus an original attraction belongs to all matter as a fundamental force appertaining to its essence.

Observation

Regarding the transition from one property of matter to another property specifically different from it, and yet equally belonging to the concept of matter, even though not contained in this concept, the attitude of our understanding must be more closely considered. If attractive force is itself originally requisite for the possibility of matter, why do we not equally make use of it with impenetrability as the primary sign of matter? Why is impenetrability given immediately with the concept of matter, while attraction is not thought in the concept but only attributed to it by inference? The fact that our senses do not let us perceive attraction so immediately as repulsion and the resistance of impenetrability cannot sufficiently answer the difficulty. For if we had

such a capacity, it is easy to comprehend that our understanding would nevertheless choose the filling of space in
order to designate thereby substance in space, i.e., matter,
just as in this filling of space, or, as it is otherwise called,
solidity, there is posited the characteristic of matter as a thing
distinct from space. Attraction, however well we might perceive it, would never reveal to us a matter of determinate
volume and shape, nor anything beyond the endeavor of our
perceiving organ to approach a point outside us (the central
point of the attracting body). For the attractive force of all
parts of the earth can affect us neither more nor otherwise
than if it were concentrated entirely in the center of the
earth and this point alone were what influenced our sense;
similarly with the attraction of a mountain, or of any stone,
etc. Now, we thereby obtain no determinate concept of any
object in space, since neither figure nor size nor even the
510   place where the object might be located can fall within the
range of our senses. (The mere direction of the attraction
would be able to be perceived, as in the case of weight; the
attracting point would be unknown, and I do not even see
how this point should be disclosed through inferences, without the perception of matter insofar as it fills space.) Thus
it is clear that the first application of our concepts of quantity to matter whereby there first becomes possible for us
the transformation of our external perceptions into the experiential concept of matter as object in general is founded
only on matter's property of filling space. By means of the
sense of feeling, this property provides us with the size and
shape of an extended thing, and hence with the concept of a
determinate object in space; this concept is laid at the foundation of all else that can be said about this thing. This is
doubtless the reason why, in spite of the clearest proofs that
attraction must belong to the fundamental forces of matter
equally as much as repulsion does, one nevertheless opposes
the former force so much, and wants to grant no other
forces at all besides those of impact and pressure (both by

means of impenetrability). For that whereby space is filled is substance, one says, and this is correct enough. But this substance reveals its existence to us by sense, whereby we perceive its impenetrability, namely, by feeling; hence it reveals its existence only in relation to contact, whose beginning (in the approach of one matter to another) is called impact, but whose continuation is called pressure. Because of this it seems as though the immediate action of one matter on another could never be anything else but pressure or impact, the only two influences we can immediately perceive; on the other hand, attraction, which in itself can give us either no sensation at all or at least no determinate object of sensation, is so difficult for us to think of as a fundamental force.

PROPOSITION 6

By mere attraction, without repulsion, no matter is possible.

Proof

Attractive force is that moving force of matter whereby it compels another to approach it; consequently, when such force is found among all parts of matter, then it endeavors by means of this force to diminish the distance of its parts from one another, and hence the space which they together occupy. Now, nothing can hinder the action of a moving force except another moving force opposed to it; but the force that is opposed to attraction is repulsive force. Therefore, by mere approach, and without repulsive forces, all parts of matter would approach one another without hindrance and diminish the space that matter occupies. Since, now, in the case assumed there is no distance of parts with regard to which a greater approach through attraction would be made impossible by means of repulsive force, the parts would

511

move toward one another until no distance between them would be found, i.e., they would coalesce in a mathematical point and the space would be empty and hence without any matter. Accordingly, matter is impossible by mere attractive forces without repulsive ones.

Note

That property upon which as a condition even the inner possibility of a thing rests is an essential element of its inner possibility. Therefore, repulsive force belongs just as much to the essence of matter as attractive force; and one cannot be separated from the other in the concept of matter.

Observation

Since one can think of no more than two moving forces in space, repulsion and attraction, it was previously necessary—so as to prove a priori the union of both in the concept of a matter in general—to consider each separately, in order to see what taken singly they could provide for the presentation of matter. It turns out, now, that whether one posits neither of them or assumes merely one, space always remains empty and no matter is found in it.

EXPLICATION 6

Contact in the physical sense is the immediate action and reaction of impenetrability. The action of one matter upon another outside of contact is action at a distance (*actio in distans*). This action at a distance, which is also possible without the mediation of matter lying in between, is called immediate action at a distance, or the action of matters on one another through empty space.

512

Observation

Contact in the mathematical meaning is the common boundary of two spaces and hence is within neither the one space nor the other. Therefore, straight lines cannot touch one another; but when they have a point in common, it belongs as much to the one as to the other of these lines when they are extended, i.e., they cut each other. But circle and straight line, circle and circle touch each other in a point, planes in a line, and bodies in planes. Mathematical contact lies at the basis of the physical but does not alone constitute it. In order that physical contact may arise from the mathematical, there must be thought in addition a dynamical relation—and indeed not a dynamical one of the attractive forces but of the repulsive ones, i.e., of impenetrability. Physical contact is the reciprocal action of repulsive forces at the common boundary of two matters.

PROPOSITION 7

The attraction essential to all matter is an immediate action through empty space of one matter upon another.

Proof

The original attractive force itself contains the ground of the possibility of matter as that thing which fills a space in a determinate degree, and hence contains the ground of the very possibility of a physical contact of matter. Therefore, this attractive force must precede the physical contact of matter; and its action must, consequently, be independent of the condition of contact. Now, the action of a moving force that is independent of all contact is also independent of the filling of space between the moving thing and the thing moved, i.e., such action must take place without the space between the moving thing and the thing moved being filled, and hence takes place as action through empty space. Therefore, the original and essential attraction of all matter is an immediate action of one matter upon another through empty space.

513   Observation 1

That the possibility of fundamental forces should be made conceivable is a completely impossible demand; for they are called fundamental forces precisely because they cannot be derived from any other force, i.e., they cannot be conceived.[33] But the original attractive force is not the least bit more inconceivable than the original repulsion. The original attractive force merely does not offer itself so immediately to the senses as impenetrability does in furnishing us concepts of determinate objects in space. Inasmuch as attraction is not felt but is only to be inferred, it therefore appears to be a derived force, just as though it were only a hidden play of moving forces produced by repulsion. Considering attraction more closely, we see that it cannot be further derived from any source, least of all from the moving force of matters through their impenetrability, since its action is just the opposite of impenetrability. The most common objection to immediate action at a distance is that a matter cannot directly act where it is not. When the earth directly influences the moon to approach it, it acts upon a thing many thousand miles removed from it, but nevertheless acts immediately; the

[33] [By "conceive" Kant here means to derive a concept (or concepts) from more fundamental ones. Those which cannot be derived from any others cannot be conceived but only assumed for one reason or another (for example, the concept of substance is an a priori category, whose possibility requires a transcendental deduction, or justification; we are made aware of repulsive force through the sensation of resistance, etc.). And so the possibility of matter in general as something possessing a definite degree of the filling of space can be conceived by deriving matter from the fundamental forces of repulsion and attraction, whose possibility cannot be conceived. See below, Ak. 524–525, 534.]

space between it and the moon may be regarded as entirely empty, for although matter may lie between both bodies, this fact does not affect the attraction. Therefore, attraction acts directly in a place where it is not—something that seems to be contradictory. But it is so far from being contradictory that one can say, rather, that everything in space acts on another only in a place where the acting thing is not. For if the thing should act in the same place where it is itself, then the thing upon which it acts would not be outside it; for "outside" means presence in a place where the other thing is not. If earth and moon touched each other, the point of contact would be a place where neither the earth nor the moon is; for both are removed from one another by the sum of their radii. Moreover, no part either of the earth or of the moon would be found at the point of contact; for this point lies at the boundary of both filled spaces, and this boundary constitutes no part either of the one or of the other. That matters, therefore, cannot immediately act on each other at a distance would be tantamount to saying that they cannot immediately act on each other without the intervention of the forces of impenetrability. Now, this would be tantamount to my saying that repulsive forces are the only ones by which matters can be active or are at least the necessary conditions under which alone matters can act upon one another. This would declare the force of attraction to be either wholly impossible or always dependent on the action of repulsive forces, but both are assertions without any foundation. The confusion of the mathematical contact of spaces _514_ and the physical contact through repulsive forces constitutes the ground of the misunderstanding here. To attract immediately outside of contact means to approach one another according to a constant law without the repulsive force's containing the condition of such approach; this must admit of being thought of, just as well as to repel one another immediately, i.e., to fly from one another according to a constant law without the attractive force's having any share therein. For both moving forces are wholly different in kind, and there is not the least foundation for making one dependent on the other and claiming that one is not possible without the intervention of the other.

Observation 2

No motion at all can arise from attraction in contact; for contact is the reciprocal action of impenetrability, which impedes all motion. There must, consequently, be some immediate attraction outside of contact, and hence at a distance; for otherwise even the forces of pressure and impact, which are to produce the endeavor to approach, could have no cause, or at least no cause lying originally in the nature of matter, inasmuch as they act with the repulsive force of matter in the opposite direction [to attraction]. One may call that attraction which occurs without the intervention of repulsive forces the true attraction, and that which proceeds merely in the other manner the apparent; for, strictly speaking, the body that another is striving merely in this latter way to approach exercises no attractive force whatever on this other body, because this other has been driven toward the first body from elsewhere by impact. But even these apparent attractions must nevertheless ultimately have a true one at their basis, because matter, whose pressure or impact is to serve instead of attraction, would not even be matter without attractive forces (Proposition 5); consequently, the mode of explicating all phenomena of approach by merely apparent attraction moves in a circle. It is commonly held that Newton did not find it necessary for his system to assume an immediate attraction of matters, but with the strictest abstinence of pure mathematics herein left the physicists full freedom to explain the possibility of such attraction as they might find good, without mixing up his propositions with their play of hypotheses. But how could he establish the proposition that the universal attraction of bodies, which they exercise equidistantly on all sides, is proportional to the quantity of their matter, if he did not assume that all matter exercises this motive force simply as matter and by its essential nature? For certainly in the case of two bodies, whether homogeneous or not as to matter, if one pulls the other, the mutual approach (according to the law of the equality of reciprocal action) must always occur in inverse proportion to the quantity of   *515* the matter. Nevertheless, this law constitutes only a principle of mechanics, not of dynamics, i.e., it is a law of motions following from attractive forces but not of the proportion of attractive forces themselves, and this law is valid for all moving forces in general. Therefore, if a magnet is at one time attracted by another identically similar magnet, and at another time is attracted by this same other magnet enclosed in a wooden box that is double this second magnet's weight, then in the latter case this second magnet will impart more relative motion to the first magnet than in the former case, although the wood, which increases the quantity of the matter of this second magnet, adds nothing at all to its attractive force and manifests no magnetic attraction of the box. Newton says (Cor. 2, Prop. 6, Lib. III, *Princip. Phil. N.*): "If the ether or any other body were without weight, it would, inasmuch as it differs from any other matter in nothing but form, be able to be transformed little by little through a gradual change of this form into a matter of the kind that has the greatest weight on earth; and, conversely, this latter by a gradual change of its form would be able to lose all its weight, which is contrary to experience, etc."[34] Thus he did

---

[34] [Kant has rendered Newton rather freely. Newton says, "If the ether, or any other body, were either altogether void of gravity or were to gravitate less in proportion to its quantity of matter, then, because (according to Aristotle, Descartes, and others) there is no difference between that and other bodies but in mere form of matter, by a successive change from form to form, it might be changed at last into a body of the same condition with those which gravitate most in proportion of their quantity of matter; and, on the other hand, the heaviest bodies, acquiring the first form of that body, might by degrees quite lose their gravity. And therefore the weights

not even exclude the ether (much less other matters) from the law of attraction. What kind of matter, then, could remain for him, by whose impact the approach of bodies to one another could be regarded as mere apparent attraction? Therefore, if we take the liberty of substituting for the true attraction, which he asserted, an apparent one, and of assuming the necessity of an impulse through impact in order to explicate the phenomenon of approach; then we cannot cite this great founder of the theory of attraction as our precursor. He rightly abstracted from all hypotheses in answering the question regarding the cause of the universal attraction of matter; for this question is physical or metaphysical, but not mathematical. And although in the advertisement to the second edition of his *Optics* he says, *ne quis gravitatem inter essentiales corporum proprietates me habere existimet, quaestionem unam de ejus causa investiganda subjeci,*[35] one can well note that the offense which his contemporaries and perhaps he himself took at the concept of an original attraction made him at variance with himself. For he absolutely could not say that the attractive forces of two planets, e.g., Jupiter and Saturn, which they manifest at equal distances of their satellites (whose mass is unknown), are proportional to the quantity of the matter of these heavenly bodies, unless he assumed that they merely as matter, and hence according to a universal property of the same, attracted other matter.

---

would depend upon the forms of bodies and, with those forms, might be changed, contrary to what was proved in the preceding Corollary." The preceding corollary says, "Hence the weights of bodies do not depend upon their forms and textures; for if the weights could be altered with the forms, they would be greater or less, according to the variety of forms, in equal matter, altogether against experience." *Mathematical Principles of Natural Philosophy,* Florian Cajori's revision of Andrew Motte's translation of 1729 (Berkeley and Los Angeles: University of California Press, 1962), Vol. II, pp. 413–414.]

[35] ["And to show that I do not take gravity for an essential property of bodies, I have added one question concerning its cause. . . ."]

EXPLICATION 7

A moving force by which matters can directly act on one another only at the common surface of contact, I call a superficial force; but that whereby one matter can directly act on the parts of another beyond the surface of contact, a penetrative force.

Note

Repulsive force, by means of which matter fills a space, is a mere superficial force. For the parts touching each other mutually limit each other's sphere of action; the repulsive force cannot move any more distant part except by means of those lying between, and an immediate action (passing right through these parts) of one matter upon another by means of the forces of extension is impossible. On the other hand, no intervening matter limits an attractive force. By means of such a force a matter occupies a space without filling it; thereby matter acts through empty space upon other distant matters, and no intervening matter limits the action of such a force. Now, it is thus that the original attraction, which makes matter itself possible, must be thought. Therefore, it is a penetrative force and for this reason alone is always proportional to the quantity of the matter.

PROPOSITION 8

The original attractive force, upon which the very possibility of matter as such is founded, extends itself directly throughout the universe to infinity, from every part of the universe to every other part.

Proof

Because the original attractive force, namely, to act immediately at a distance, belongs to the essence of matter, it also belongs to every part of matter. Now, let it be granted 517 that there is a distance beyond which the force of attraction does not reach; this limitation of the sphere of its efficacy would rest either on the matter lying within this sphere or merely on the magnitude of the space in which its influence is spread. The first does not take place, for this attraction is a penetrative force and acts directly at a distance, in spite of all intervening matters, through every space as an empty space. The second likewise does not take place. For inasmuch as every attraction is a moving force having a degree, beyond which ever smaller degrees to infinity can be thought; in the greater distance there would indeed lie a cause for diminishing the degree of attraction in inverse proportion to the amount of the diffusion of the force, but never for completely destroying it. Now, since there is hence nothing which might anywhere limit the sphere of the efficacy of the original attraction of any part of matter, this attraction reaches out beyond all assignable limits to every other matter, and hence reaches throughout the universe to infinity.

Note 1

From this original attractive force as a penetrative force exercised by all matter upon all matter, and hence in proportion to the quantity of matter and spreading its action throughout all possible regions—from this force, I say, in combination with its counteracting one, namely, repulsive force, the limitation of this latter, and hence the possibility of a space filled in a determinate degree, must admit of being derived. And thus would the dynamical concept of matter as the movable filling its space (in a determinate degree) be constructed.

But for this construction one needs a law of the relation both of original attraction and of original repulsion at various distances of matter and of its parts from one another. Since this relation rests solely on the difference of direction of both these forces (inasmuch as a point is driven either to approach others or to recede from them) and on the size of the space into which each of these forces diffuses itself at various distances, this law is a pure mathematical problem, with which metaphysics is no longer concerned. Metaphysics is not responsible if the attempt to construct matter in this way is not crowned with success. For metaphysics answers merely for the correctness of the elements of the construction that are granted our rational cognition; it does not answer for the insufficiency and limits of our reason in the execution of the construction.   *518*

Note 2

Since all given matter must fill its space with a determinate degree of repulsive force in order to constitute a determinate material thing, only an original attraction in conflict with the original repulsion can make a determinate degree of the filling of space, i.e., matter, possible. Now, it may be that the attraction involved in this determinate degree of the filling of space arises from the individual attraction of the parts of the compressed matter among one another or arises from the union of this compressed matter with the attraction of all the matter of the world.

The original attraction is proportional to the quantity of matter and reaches to infinity. Therefore, the determinate degree of the filling of space by matter cannot in the end be brought about without matter's infinitely reaching attraction; such a determinate degree of the filling of space can then be imparted to every matter in accordance with the degree of its repulsive force.

The action of universal attraction, which all matter exercises directly on all matter and at all distances, is called gravitation; the endeavor to move in the direction of the greater gravitation is weight. The action of the universal repulsive force of the parts of every given matter is called its original elasticity. Therefore, this elasticity and the aforementioned weight constitute the only a priori comprehensible universal characteristics of matter, the former being internal, the latter involving an external relation; for the possibility of matter itself rests upon these two foundations. When cohesion is explained as the reciprocal attraction of matter insofar as this attraction is limited solely to the condition of contact, then such cohesion does not belong to the possibility of matter in general and cannot therefore be cognized a priori as bound up with matter. This property would hence not be metaphysical but physical, and therefore would not belong to our present considerations.

Observation 1

I cannot forbear adding a small preliminary observation for the sake of any attempt that may perhaps be made toward such a possible construction.

519 1. One may say of every force which directly acts at different distances and which is limited as to the degree whereby it exercises moving force upon any given point at a certain distance from it only by the size of the space in which it must diffuse itself in order to act upon that point—of such a force one may say that in all spaces through which it is diffused, however small or great they may be, it always constitutes an equal quantum, but that the degree of its action upon that point in this space always stands in inverse proportion to the space through which it has had to diffuse itself in order to be able to act upon that point. So, for instance, light diffuses itself everywhere from an illuminating point in spherical surfaces that ever increase with the square of the distance, and the quantity of the illumination in all

these infinitely larger spherical surfaces is as a whole always the same. Whence it follows that an equal part in any one of these spherical surfaces must according to degree be so much the less illuminated as the diffusion surface of the same quantity of light is greater. And so it is with all other forces and laws according to which these forces must diffuse themselves either into surfaces or corporeal space in order to act according to their nature upon distant objects. It is better to represent the diffusion of a moving force from one point to all distances in this manner than it is to represent this diffusion in the ordinary way, as such representation occurs (being one among other such ways) in optics, by means of rays diverging in a circle from a central point. For lines drawn in this way can never fill the space through which they pass, nor therefore the surface which they reach, regardless of how many of them are drawn or plotted; this is the inevitable consequence of their divergence. Thus they only give occasion to troublesome inferences, and these to hypotheses which could very well be avoided if one were to consider merely the size of the whole spherical surface which is to be uniformly illuminated by the same quantity of light, and if one took the degree of the illumination of the surface in any one place as inversely proportional to the size of the whole surface, as is natural; and similarly with every other diffusion of a force through spaces of different sizes.

2. If the force is an immediate attraction at a distance, the lines of the direction of the attraction must still less be represented as rays diverging from the attracting point, but, rather, must be represented as converging at the attracting point from all points of the surrounding spherical surface (whose radius is the given distance). For the line of direction of the motion to this point, which is the cause and goal of the motion, already assigns the *terminus a quo,* from which the lines must begin, namely, from all points of the surface. These lines have their direction from this *terminus* to the attracting center, and not vice versa. For only the size of the surface

determines the number of lines; the center leaves them un-determined.[36]

520   3. If the force is an immediate repulsion, whereby a point (in its merely mathematical presentation) fills a space dynamically, and if the question is according to what law of infinitely small distances (which are here equivalent to contacts) an original repulsive force (whose limitation consequently rests solely on the space in which it is diffused) acts at different distances; then one can still less represent this force by diverging rays of repulsion coming from the as-

---

520   [36] It is impossible to represent surfaces at given distances as wholly filled with the action of lines spreading out from a point like rays, whether the action be that of illumination or attraction. Thus, by such diverging rays of light the inferior illumination of a distant surface would merely rest on the fact that between the illuminated places there remain those that are not illuminated, and these latter are so much the larger the farther away the surfaces are. Euler's hypothesis* avoids this inconvenience but has certainly so much the more difficulty in making the rectilinear motion of the light conceivable. But this difficulty comes from an easily avoidable mathematical representation of light-matter as an aggregation of particles; this aggregation would, according to its variously oblique position in the direction of impact, certainly produce a lateral motion of light. Instead of this, nothing prevents one's thinking of light-matter as originally and indeed thoroughly fluid, without being divided into fixed particles. If the mathematician wants to render intuitable the diminution of light with increasing distance, he makes use of rays diverging in a circle in order to exhibit on the spherical surface of their diffusion the size of the space in which the same quantity of light is to be uniformly diffused between these rays, i.e., the diminution of the degree of illumination. But he does not want these rays to be regarded as the only places of illumination, just as if there were always to be found places devoid of light between the rays, these unilluminated places becoming larger with increasing distance. If one wants to represent to himself every such surface as illuminated throughout, then the same quantity of illumination that covers the smaller surface must be thought of as uniformly covering the larger one. Therefore in order to indicate the rectilinear direction, straight lines must be drawn from the surface and all its points to the illuminating point. The action and its magnitude must be thought of beforehand and the cause thereupon specified. The same holds for rays of attraction, if one will so call them, and indeed for all directions of forces which from a point are to fill a space, be it even a corporeal space.

---

* [Leonhard Euler (1707–1783) propounded the wave theory of light. He was one of the few men in the eighteenth century to oppose Newton's particle theory, or emission theory as it is sometimes called.]

sumed repelling point, even though the direction of the motion has this point for a *terminus a quo*. The reason for this lies in the fact that the space in which the force must be diffused in order to act at a distance is a corporeal space that is to be thought of as filled. The way in which a point can fill a space corporeally by moving force, i.e., dynamically, is certainly capable of no further mathematical presentation; and diverging rays coming from a point cannot possibly represent the repelling force of a corporeally filled space. Rather, one would estimate the repulsion at various infinitely small distances of these mutually repelling points simply in inverse *521* proportion to the corporeal spaces that each of these points dynamically fills, and hence in inverse proportion to the cube of the distances of these points from one another, without one's being able to construct these points.

4. Therefore, the original attraction of matter would act in inverse proportion to the square of the distance at all distances and the original repulsion in inverse proportion to the cube of the infinitely small distances. By such an action and reaction of both fundamental forces, matter would be possible by a determinate degree of the filling of its space. For inasmuch as the repulsion increases in greater measure upon approach of the parts than the attraction does, the limit of approach beyond which by means of the given attraction no greater is possible is determined, and hence the degree of compression that constitutes the measure of the intensive filling of space is also determined.

Observation 2

I see well the difficulty of this mode of explicating the possibility of matter in general. This difficulty consists in the fact that if a point cannot directly drive another by repulsive force without at the same time filling the whole corporeal space up to the given distance by its force, then this space must, as seems to follow, contain several repulsive points.

This fact contradicts the assumption, but this fact was refuted above (Proposition 4) under the name of a sphere of repulsion of the simple in space. However, there is a distinction to be made between the concept of an actual space, which can be given, and the mere idea of a space, which is thought only for the determination of the relation of given spaces but which is in fact no space. In the case cited of a supposed physical monadology, there were to be actual spaces which were filled by a point dynamically, i.e., through repulsion; for they existed as points before any possible production of matter from these points, and they determined by the proper sphere of their activity that part of the space to be filled which could belong to them. Therefore, in the hypothesis in question, matter cannot be regarded as infinitely divisible and as continuous quantity; for the parts, which directly repel one another, have nevertheless a determinate distance from one another (the sum of the radii of the sphere of their repulsion). On the other hand, when we, as actually happens, think of matter as continuous quantity, no distance whatsoever of the directly mutually repelling parts obtains, and hence no increasing or decreasing spheres of their immediate activity. However, matters can expand or be compressed (like the air), and in this case one represents to himself a distance of their nearest parts, that can increase and decrease. But inasmuch as the closest parts of a continuous matter touch one another, whether it is further expanded or compressed, one thinks of their distances from one another as infinitely small, and this infinitely small space as filled in a greater or lesser degree by their force of repulsion. The infinitely small intermediate space is, however, not at all different from contact. Hence it is only the idea of space that serves to render intuitable the expansion of matter as continuous quantity; whether this idea is indeed in this way actual cannot be conceived. When it is said, then, that the repulsive forces of the directly mutually driving parts of matter stand in inverse proportion to the cube of their distances, this means only that they stand in inverse proportion to the corporeal spaces which one thinks of between parts that nevertheless immediately touch each other, and whose distance must just for this reason be termed infinitely small in order that such distance may be distinguished from all actual distance. Hence one must not from the difficulties of the construction of a concept, or rather from the misinterpretation of the construction, raise any objection to the concept itself; for otherwise the concept would concern the mathematical presentation of the proportion with which attraction occurs at different distances, as well as those distances through which each point in an expanding or compressed whole of matter directly repels another point. The universal law of dynamics would in both cases be this: the action of the moving force that is exercised by one point upon every other one external to it is in inverse proportion to the space in which the same quantity of moving force has had to diffuse itself in order to act directly upon this other point at the determinate distance.

From the law that the parts of matter originally repel one another in inverse cubic proportion to their infinitely small distances, there must necessarily follow a law of the expansion and compression of these parts that is entirely different from the law of Mariotte[37] regarding the air. Mariotte's law proves that the forces causing the closest parts of the air to flee from one another stand in inverse proportion to the distances of the parts, as Newton proves (*Princ. Ph. N.,* Lib. II, Propos. 23, Schol.). But one cannot regard the expansive force of the parts of the air as the action of originally repulsive forces; for this expansive force rests on heat, which compels the proper parts of the air (to which, moreover, actual distances from each other may be conceded) to fly from one another, and acts not merely as a matter interpen-

---

[37] [Edme Mariotte (1620–1684) was a French physicist. The law named after him appeared in his treatise *Concerning the Nature of the Air* (1679).]

etrating the parts but, to all appearance, through its vibrations. But that these vibrations must impart to the air's parts closest to one another a force that causes them to flee from one another and that stands in inverse proportion to the distances of the parts can be made readily conceivable according to the laws of the communication of motion through the vibration of elastic matters.

523   Yet I declare that I do not want the present exposition of the law of an original repulsion to be regarded as necessarily belonging to the aim of my metaphysical treatment of matter, nor do I want this treatment (for which it is enough to have presented the filling of space as a dynamic property of matter) to be mixed up with the disputes and doubts which might befall this exposition.

GENERAL NOTE TO DYNAMICS

If we review all our discussions of the metaphysical treatment of matter, we shall observe that in this treatment the following things have been taken into consideration: first, the *real* in space (otherwise called the solid) in its filling of space through repulsive force; second, that which, with regard to the first as the proper object of our external perception, is *negative*, namely, attractive force, by which, as far as may be, all space would be penetrated, i.e., the solid would be wholly abolished; third, the *limitation* of the first force by the second and the consequent perceptible determination of the degree of a filling of space. Hence we observe that the quality of matter has been completely dealt with under the moments of reality, negation, and limitation,[38] as much as such a treatment belongs to a metaphysical dynamics.

[38] [Cf. *Critique of Pure Reason*, B 106.]

GENERAL
OBSERVATION
ON DYNAMICS

The universal principle of the dynamics of material nature is this: all that is real in the objects of our external senses and is not merely a determination of space (place, extension, and figure) must be regarded as moving force. By this principle, therefore, the so-called solid, or absolute impenetrability, is banished from natural science as an empty concept, and in its stead repulsive force is posited. On the other hand, the true and immediate attraction is defended against all the sophistries of a metaphysics that misunderstands itself, and this attraction is explained as a fundamental force necessary even to the possibility of the concept of matter. From all this there arises the consequence that, should it be found necessary, space could be assumed to be at all events filled throughout and yet in varying degree, without distributing empty intermediate spaces within matter. For according to the originally varying degree of repulsive forces, upon which rests the first property of matter, namely, that of filling a space, the relationship of this property to original attraction (whether to the attraction of every matter of itself, or to the united attraction of all matter in the universe) can be thought   524
of as infinitely diverse. This is because attraction rests on the mass of matter in a given space, while the expansive force of matter rests on the degree to which the space is filled; this degree can be specifically very different (as the same quantity of air in the same volume exhibits more or less elasticity according to its greater or lesser heating). The general ground involved here is that by true attraction all parts of matter act directly on all parts of other matter; but by expansive force, only the parts in the surface of contact act, and thereby it is all the same whether behind this surface much or little of this matter is found. From all this a great

advantage arises for natural science, by its being relieved of the burden of building a world merely according to fancy out of fulness and emptiness. Rather, all spaces can be thought of as full and yet as filled in varying measure. By means of this, empty space at least loses its necessity and is reduced to the value of a hypothesis, since otherwise it might claim the title of a principle, under the pretext of being a necessary condition for the explication of the different degrees of the filling of space.

In connection with all this, the advantage of a methodically employed metaphysics to the detriment of principles that are also metaphysical but have not been brought to the test of criticism [Kritik] is apparently only negative. Nevertheless, indirectly the field of the investigator of nature is enlarged, because the conditions by which he previously limited his field and by which all original moving forces were philosophized away now lose their validity. But one must guard against going beyond what makes the universal concept of matter in general possible and against wanting to explain a priori the particular or even specific determination and variety of matter. The concept of matter is reduced to nothing but moving forces; this could not be expected to be otherwise, because in space no activity and no change can be thought of but mere motion. But who claims to comprehend the possibility of fundamental forces? They can only be assumed, if they inevitably belong to a concept concerning which there can be proved that it is a fundamental concept not further derivable from any other (such as is the fundamental concept of the filling of space).[39] These fundamental

---

[39] [This is to say that we can comprehend a priori the possibility of matter in general as composed of the two fundamental moving forces (as the foregoing part of dynamics has shown), but we cannot comprehend a priori the possibility of these original forces themselves nor can we explain a priori the specific varieties of matter as they are composed of various combinations of these forces. Compare below, Ak. 534: "Besides the ether, no law whatever of attractive or of repulsive force may be risked on a priori conjectures; but everything, even universal attraction as the cause of gravity, must, together

forces are the repulsive forces in general and the attractive forces in general (which counteract the repulsive ones). We can indeed judge well enough a priori concerning their connection and consequences; one may think of whatever relations of these forces among one another he wants to, provided he does not contradict himself. But he must not, therefore, presume to assume either of them as actual, because the authorization to set up a hypothesis irremissibly requires that the possibility of what is assumed be entirely certain. But in the case of fundamental forces, their possibility can never be comprehended. And because of this fact the mathematico-mechanical mode of explication has over the meta- *525*
physico-dynamical mode an advantage that the latter cannot provide, namely, from a completely homogeneous material, by means of the manifold shape of the parts, with empty intermediate spaces interspersed, this mathematico-mechanical mode can accomplish a great specific multiplicity of matters, according to their density as well as their mode of action (if foreign forces be superadded). For the possibility of the shapes as well as of the empty intermediate spaces can be proved with mathematical evidence. On the other hand, if the material itself is transformed into fundamental forces (whose laws we are not able to determine a priori, but still less are we able to reliably indicate a manifold of such forces sufficient for explicating the specific variety of matter), then all means are wanting for the construction of this concept

---

with the laws of such attraction, be concluded from data of experience. Still less will such conclusions in regard to chemical affinities be permitted to be tried otherwise than by means of experiment. For to comprehend original forces a priori according to their possibility lies generally beyond the horizon of our reason. Rather, all natural philosophy consists in the reduction of given forces apparently diverse to a smaller number of forces and powers sufficient for the explication of the actions of the former. But this reduction continues only to fundamental forces, beyond which our reason cannot go." However, in the *Transition from the Metaphysical Foundations of Natural Science to Physics* Kant explored these problems further, and claimed there that more can be comprehended a priori than he thought was possible here in the *Metaphysical Foundations of Natural Science*.]

and for presenting as possible in intuition what we thought universally. But a merely mathematical physics pays for the foregoing advantage doubly on the other side, in that it first of all must lay at its foundation an empty concept (that of absolute impenetrability), and secondly must give up all the proper forces of matter. In addition, with its original configurations of the fundamental material and its interspersion of empty spaces, it is afterwards required to make explications and must then allow the imagination more freedom in the field of philosophy—and indeed allow this freedom as a rightful claim—than can be consistent with the caution of philosophy.

I am unable to furnish an adequate explication of the possibility of matter and its specific variety from the fundamental forces; instead I shall, as I hope, completely present the moments to which its specific variety must all together admit of being reduced a priori (although I cannot conceive the possibility in the same way). The observations inserted between the definitions will elucidate the application of these definitions.

1. A *body*, in the physical signification, is a matter between determinate boundaries (and such matter therefore has a figure). The space between these boundaries, considered according to its magnitude, is the body's *content of space* (*volumen*). The degree of the filling of a space of determinate content is called *density*. (Otherwise the expression "dense" is also used absolutely for what is not hollow—vesicular, porous.) In this sense there is an absolute density in the system of absolute impenetrability, namely, if a matter contains no empty intermediate spaces at all. According to this concept of the filling of space one draws comparisons and calls one matter containing less emptiness within itself denser than another, until finally that matter no part of whose space is empty is termed perfectly dense. One can make use of the latter expression only in accordance with the merely mathematical concept of matter. But in the dynamical system of a merely

relative impenetrability there is no maximum or minimum of density, and any matter however thin can equally be called fully dense if it entirely fills its space without containing empty intermediate spaces, i.e., if it is a continuum and not an interruptum. But it is less dense, in the dynamical sense, in comparison with another matter if it entirely fills its space but not in an equal degree. However, even in the dynamical system it is unsuitable to think of a relation of matters according to their density unless they are represented as specifically homogeneous among one another, so that one can be produced from the other by mere compression. Now, since this last condition does not appear to be necessarily requisite to the nature of all matter in itself, no comparison can properly be permitted between heterogeneous matters with regard to their density, e.g., between water and quicksilver, although this is customary.

526

2. Attraction, insofar as it is thought as active merely in contact, is called *cohesion*. (Indeed one proves by very good experiments that the same force which in contact is called cohesion is found to be active also at a very small distance. But attraction is only called cohesion insofar as I think of it merely in contact, in accordance with common experience; with regard to such experience, attraction is scarcely perceived at small distances. Cohesion is commonly assumed to be an altogether universal property of matter, not as if one were led to this property already through the concept of matter, but because experience presents it everywhere. But this universality must not be understood collectively, as though every matter through this kind of attraction acted simultaneously upon every other matter in the universe—in the same way as gravitation—but merely disjunctively, namely, as though every matter through this kind of attraction acted upon one matter or another, of whatever kind these might be, that come in contact with it. Now, this attraction, as is provable on various grounds, is not a penetrating force but only a superficial one, inasmuch as it is not itself

as such determined everywhere according to density. For complete strength of cohesion one needs a preceding state of fluidity of the matters together with a subsequent solidification of them; and the closest fitting contact of broken but hard matters in the same surfaces in which they previously firmly cohered, e.g., a looking-glass where there is a crack, does not any way nearly admit the degree of attraction that these matters had from their solidification after being fluid. For all these reasons I hold this attraction in contact to be no fundamental force of matter, but to be only a derivative one. But more of this later.) A matter whose parts, notwithstanding their strong cohesion among one another, can yet be displaced past one another by every moving force, however small, is *fluid*. But parts of a matter are *displaced* past one another if, without diminishing the amount of contact, they are merely compelled to change their parts among themselves. Parts, and hence matters too, are *separated* if their contact with others is not merely changed, but is destroyed, or the amount of contact is diminished. A *solid*— better, a *rigid*—body (*corpus rigidum*) is one whose parts cannot be displaced past one another by any force; these parts, consequently, resist displacement with a certain degree of force. The hindrance to the displacement of matters past one another is *friction*. The resistance to separation of matters in contact is cohesion. Fluid matters, therefore, undergo no friction in their division; but where friction is found, the matters are assumed, at least in their smaller parts, to be rigid —in greater or lesser degree, the lesser being called viscosity (*viscositas*). The rigid body is *brittle* if its parts cannot be displaced past one another without breaking, and hence if the cohesion of the parts cannot be changed without this cohesion's being at the same time destroyed. The difference between fluid and solid matters is very incorrectly placed in the different degree of the cohesion of their parts. For to call a matter fluid does not depend on the degree of its resistance

527

to rupture, but only on that of its resistance to the displacement of its parts past one another. The former can be as great as one wants; the latter is always in a fluid matter $= 0$. Let us consider a drop of water. If a particle within the drop is drawn to one side by an ever so great attraction of the neighboring parts touching it, then it will be drawn just as much to the opposite side. And since the attractions mutually cancel their actions, the particle is just as easily movable as if it were in empty space, namely, the force that is to move it has no cohesion to overcome, but only the so-called inertia, which it would have to overcome in the case of all matter, even if the matter did not cohere at all. Therefore, a small microscopic animacule will move as easily within this drop as if there were no cohesion at all to separate. For it does not really have any cohesion of the water to destroy; nor any contact of the water within itself to diminish, but only to change. But think of this animacule as wanting to work its way through the outer surface of the drop. There is first to be noted the fact that the mutual attraction of the parts of this drop of water cause them to move themselves until they have arrived at the greatest contact among one another, and hence at the smallest contact with empty space, i.e., until they have constituted a globular shape. Now, if the said insect is trying to work its way beyond the surface of the drop, then it must change this globular shape and consequently bring about more contact of the water with the empty space and hence less contact of the parts of the water among one another, i.e., diminish their cohesion. And here   *528* the water for the first time resists the insect by its cohesion, but not by any cohesion within the drop, where the contact of the parts among one another is not at all lessened but only changed in their contact with other parts, i.e., they are not in the least separated but only displaced. Moreover, one may apply to the microscopic animacule what Newton says about the light ray, and indeed for similar reasons: that it is not reflected by dense matter but only by empty space.[40] It is therefore clear that the increase of the cohesion of the parts of a matter does not in the least affect its fluidity. Water coheres in its parts much more strongly than one commonly believes, as when one relies upon an experiment with a metal plate pulled off the surface of the water; this experiment decides nothing, because here the water does not break loose in the whole surface of the original contact, but in a much smaller surface finally attained by the displacement of its parts, much as a stick of soft wax can at first be drawn out thinner by an appended weight and must then break off in a much smaller surface than the original one. But what is quite decisive with regard to our concept of fluidity is this: fluid matters can be explicated as those whose every point seeks to move itself in all directions with just the same force with which it is pressed in any one direction. This is a property upon which the first law of hydrodynamics rests but which can never be attributed to an aggregation of smooth and also solid particles, as a very easy resolution of such an aggregation's pressure, according to the laws of composite motion, can show. By such a resolution the originality of the property of fluidity can be proved. Now, if the fluid matter were to suffer the least hindrance to displacement, and hence suffer even the smallest friction, then this friction would grow with the strength of the pressure with which its parts are pressed against one another, and finally a pressure would obtain with regard to which the parts of this matter would not admit of displacement past one another by any small force. For instance, take a bent tube with two arms, one of which may be as wide as one wants and the other as narrow as one wants (provided it is not a mere

---

[40] [There is no place in the *Optics* that says "only by empty space." However, Prop. VIII of Book II, Part III reads, "The cause of reflection is not the impinging of light on the solid or impervious parts of bodies, as is commonly believed."]

capillary). If one supposes both arms to be a few hundred feet high, then the fluid matter in the narrow arm would stand just as high as that in the wide, according to the laws of hydrostatics. But the pressure on the bottom of the tubes and hence also on the part joining both tubes (which stand in communication) can be thought of as ever greater to infinity in proportion to the heights. Because of this, if the least friction among the parts of the fluid took place, then one should be able to find a height of the tubes with regard to which a small quantity of water poured into the narrower tube would not displace the water in the wider tube from its position, and hence the column of water in the narrower tube would come to stand higher than that in the wider inasmuch as the lower parts in the narrower, with such great 529 pressure against one another, would no longer admit of displacement by means of so small a moving force as is provided by the added weight of the water. But this is contrary to experience and even to the concept of what is fluid. The same thing holds if instead of pressure by weight, the cohesion of the parts is posited, and the latter may be as great as one wants. The second definition of fluidity cited,[41] upon which the fundamental law of hydrostatics rests, says that fluidity is the property of a matter inasmuch as every part of the matter endeavors to move itself toward all sides with just the same force with which it is pressed in a given direction. This second definition follows from the first one[42] if there is combined with the first the fundamental principle of general dynamics. This principle says that all matter is originally elastic since it must endeavor to extend itself—i.e. (if the parts of a matter admit of being displaced without hindrance past one another by any force, as is actually the case with fluid matter) it must endeavor to move itself

41 [Cf. above, Ak. 528.]
42 [Cf. above, Ak. 526 ad fin.]

toward all sides of the space in which it is compressed with the same force with which the pressure in any given direction, whatever it may be, occurs. Therefore, it is only to rigid matters (whose possibility requires another ground of explication than that of the cohesion of parts) that one can, properly speaking, attribute friction; and friction already presupposes the property of rigidity. But certain matters, although they perhaps have a greater, or even a smaller force of cohesion than other fluid matters have, nevertheless very strongly resist displacement of their parts and therefore do not admit of separation otherwise than by the destruction of the cohesion of all parts in a given surface, thus giving the illusion of a superior cohesion. But why this is so, and hence how rigid bodies are possible, is still an unsolved problem, in spite of the ease with which ordinary natural science believes itself to dispose of it.

3. *Elasticity* (spring force) is the capacity of a matter to reassume its size or shape altered by another moving force when such a force has ceased. It is either expansive or attractive elasticity, the former in order after compression to assume the previously greater volume, the latter in order after expansion to assume the previously smaller volume. (Attractive elasticity, as the expression itself shows, is obviously derivative. An iron wire stretched by an appended weight springs back into its original volume when the connection is cut. In virtue of this attraction, which is the cause of the cohesion of the wire, or in the case of fluid matters, as when the heat is suddenly withdrawn from quicksilver, their matter would hasten to reassume the previously smaller volume. The elasticity which consists only in the recovery of the previous figure is always attractive, as in the case of a bent sword blade in which the parts on the convex surface, which are pulled away from one another, endeavor to assume their former proximity; and in the same way a small drop of quicksilver may be called elastic. But expansive elasticity may be original or it may be derivative. Thus the air has a derivative

530

elasticity by means of the heat's matter[43] that is most intimately united with it and whose elasticity is perhaps original. On the other hand, the fundamental material of the fluid which we call air must nevertheless, as matter in general, already have in itself elasticity that is called original. It is impossible to decide with certainty as to what kind a perceived elasticity may be in cases that present themselves.)

4. The action of moved bodies on one another through the communication of their motion is called *mechanical;* but the action of matters at rest insofar as they change the combination of their parts reciprocally by their own forces is called *chemical.* This chemical influence is called *solution* insofar as this influence has for its effect the separation of the parts of a matter (mechanical division, e.g., that by means of a wedge driven between the parts of a matter, is thus entirely different from chemical division, because the wedge does not act by its own force); but the influence that has for its effect the dissociation of two matters dissolved in one another is chemical *analysis.* The solution of specifically different matters in one another in which no part of one matter is found not united with a part of the other matter in the same proportion as that of the whole solution is absolute solution, and may also be called chemical penetration. Whether the dissolving forces that are actually to be found in nature are capable of effecting a complete solution may remain undecided. Here the question is only whether such a solution can be thought of. Now, it is obvious that as long as the parts of a dissolved matter are still particles (*moleculae*), a solution of them is not less possible than the solution of the larger parts. Indeed it is obvious that this solution, if the dissolving force continues, really must proceed until there is no part left that is not composed of the solvent and the matter to be dissolved in the proportion in which they each

[43] [Before the science of thermodynamics was developed in the nineteenth century, many thought that heat phenomena could be accounted for by positing the existence of a heat fluid, or caloric.]

stand to one another in the solution as a whole. Since, then, in such a case there can be no part of the volume of the solution that does not contain a part of the solvent, this solvent as a continuum must completely fill the volume. In the same way, since there can be no part of this volume of solution that does not contain a proportional part of the dissolved matter, this dissolved matter as a continuum must also fill the whole space constituting the volume of the mixture. But when two matters, and indeed each one of them, entirely fill one and the same space, they penetrate one another. Therefore, a perfect chemical solution would be a penetration of the matters. This chemical penetration would, nevertheless, be entirely different from the mechanical, since with regard to the latter one thinks that upon the closer approach of moved matters the repulsive force of the one could entirely outweigh that of the other, and one or both of these

531   forces could reduce the extension of these matters to nothing. On the other hand, in the case of chemical penetration the extension remains, but here the matters are not outside one another but within one another, i.e., by intussusception (as it is usually called) they together occupy a space proportional to the sum of their densities. It is difficult to oppose anything to the possibility of this perfect solution, and hence of chemical penetration, although such a solution does involve a complete division to infinity. Such a division, however, does not in this case contain any contradiction, because the solution takes place continuously throughout a time, i.e., through an infinite series of moments with acceleration. Moreover, by the division, the sums of the surfaces of the matters yet to be divided increase; and since the dissolving force acts continuously, the whole solution can be completed in a specifiable time. The inconceivability of such a chemical penetration of two matters is to be ascribed to the inconceivability of the divisibility to infinity of every continuum in general. If one departs from this complete solution, then one must assume the solution to extend only to

certain small particles of the matter to be dissolved, which swim in the solvent at fixed distances from one another, without one's being able to specify the least ground as to why these particles, since they are still divisible matters, are not also dissolved. For that the solvent does not act further may always be true enough in nature, as far as experience reaches. But the question here is about the possibility of a dissolving force that dissolves this particle and every other still remaining until the solution is completed. The volume occupied by the solution can be equal to the sum of the spaces occupied by the mutually dissolving matters before the mixture, or it can be smaller than this sum, or even larger than it, according to the way the attractive forces stand in relation to the repulsions. These mutually dissolving matters constitute in solution, each of itself and both combined, an elastic medium. This medium alone can provide a sufficient reason why the dissolved matter does not by its weight dissociate itself again from the solvent. For the latter's attraction, since it occurs equally strongly toward all sides, destroys the former's resistance. And to assume a certain viscosity in the fluid does not accord with the great force exercised by such fluids upon dissolved matters, e.g., acids diluted with water upon metallic bodies. Such bodies do not merely touch the acids, as must happen if they merely swam in their medium, but the acids with great attractive force separate these bodies from one another and disperse them throughout the entire space of the vehicle. Moreover, in case art [applied science, technical skill] might have in its power no chemical forces of solution of this kind to bring about a complete solution, nevertheless nature could perhaps exhibit such forces in its vegetal and animal operations and thereby could perhaps produce matters which, though indeed mixed, cannot be separated again by art. This *532* chemical penetration might even be found where one of the two matters is not separated by the other and in a literal sense dissolved, as, for instance, heat-matter [*Wärmestoff*] penetrates bodies because if it distributed itself only in the empty intermediate spaces then the solid substance itself would remain cold, since it could not absorb any of the heat. In the same way, an apparently free passage of certain matters through others could be thought of in such a manner as the passage of magnetic matter [through others], without preparing open pores and empty mediate spaces for such passage in all, even the densest, matters. However, this is not the place to point out hypotheses for particular phenomena but only the principle according to which such phenomena are all to be judged. Everything that relieves us of the necessity of having recourse to empty spaces is an actual gain for natural science. For these give far too much freedom to the imagination to supply by fiction the lack of intrinsic knowledge of nature. Absolute emptiness and absolute density are in the doctrine of nature approximately what blind chance and blind fate are in metaphysical science, namely, a barrier for the investigating reason, with the result that either fiction occupies the place of reason or else reason is lulled to sleep on the pillow of occult qualities.

As concerns the procedure in natural science regarding the foremost of all its problems, namely, the explication of a possible specific variety of matters extending to infinity, one can take only two ways: the mechanical way, by the combination of the absolutely full with the absolutely empty; or a dynamical way, opposed to the foregoing, by explicating all varieties of matter through the mere variety in the combination of the original forces of repulsion and attraction. The first has, as materials for its derivation, atoms and the void. An atom is a small part of matter that is physically indivisible. A matter is physically indivisible if its parts cohere with a force that cannot be overcome by any existing moving force in nature. An atom insofar as it is specifically distinguished from others by its figure is called a primary particle. A body (or particle) whose moving force depends upon its figure is called a machine. The mode of explication of the specific variety of matters by the nature and composition of their smallest parts as machines is the mechanical natural philosophy. But that mode of explication which derives the specific variety of matter not from matters as machines, i.e., as mere tools of external moving forces, but from the proper moving forces of attraction and repulsion originally belonging to these matters may be called the dynamical natural philosophy. The mechanical mode of explication, since it is very convenient for mathematics, has, *533* under the name of the atomistic or corpuscular philosophy, always maintained its authority and influence on the principles of natural science with little change from old Democritus to Descartes and even to our own times. Its essentials consist in the assumption of the absolute impenetrability of the primitive matter, in the absolute homogeneity of this matter, differences only being allowed in the shape, and in the absolute unconquerability of the cohesion of the matter in these fundamental particles themselves. Such were the materials for the production of specifically different matters in order not only to have at hand an unchangeable and yet variously shaped fundamental matter for the unchangeability of species and kinds, but also to explain mechanically nature's various actions as arising from the shape of these primary parts as machines (to which nothing more was wanting than an externally impressed force). The first and foremost credential of this system rests, however, on the ostensibly unavoidable necessity of employing empty spaces for the specific distinction of the density of matters; these spaces were assumed to be distributed within the matters and among the aforementioned particles in a proportion, as was found necessary for the sake of some appearances, even so large that the filled part of the volume (even of the densest matter) would be very nearly nothing as compared with the empty part. In order, now, to introduce a dynamical mode of explication (which is far more suited and more favorable to experimental philosophy inasmuch as it leads directly to the discovery of the moving forces proper to matters and the laws of such forces, but restricts the freedom of assuming empty intermediate spaces and fundamental particles of determinate shapes, neither of which can be discovered and determined by any experiment), it is not at all necessary to forge new hypotheses, but only necessary to refute the postulate of the merely mechanical mode of explication, namely, that it is impossible to think of a specific difference of the density of matters without the intermixture of empty spaces. One can refute this postulate by merely citing a way in which this specific difference of the density of matters can be thought of without contradiction. For if this postulate, upon which the merely mechanical mode of explication stands, were only first declared invalid as a fundamental principle, then it is obvious that this postulate must not be adopted as a hypothesis in natural science as long as there remains a possibility of thinking of the specific difference of densities without any intermediate spaces. But this necessity rests on the fact that matter does not (as the merely mechanical investigators of nature assume) fill its space by absolute impenetrability, but by repulsive force; this force has its degree, which can be different in different matters. And since the degree of the repulsive force has of itself nothing in common with the attractive force, which is proportional to the quantity

534   of the matter, the repulsive force can with regard to one and the same attractive force be originally different in degree in different matters. And consequently the degree of the extension of the matters may as regards the same quantity of matter and, conversely, the quantity of matter may as regards the same volume, i.e., density of the matter, admit originally of very great specific differences. In this way one would not find it impossible to think of a matter (as one perhaps represents the ether) that entirely filled its space without any void and yet with incomparably less quan-

tity of matter, at an equal volume, than any bodies we can subject to our experiments. The repulsive force in the ether must in relation to its proper attractive force be thought of as incomparably greater than in any other matter known to us. And the only reason why we merely assume such an ether, because it can be thought of, is as a foil to a hypothesis (that of empty spaces) which depends only on the assertion that such rarefied matter cannot be thought of without empty spaces. Besides the ether, no law whatever of attractive or of repulsive force may be risked on a priori conjectures; but everything, even universal attraction as the cause of gravity, must, together with the laws of such attraction, be concluded from data of experience. Still less will such conclusions in regard to chemical affinities be permitted to be tried otherwise than by means of experiment. For to comprehend original forces a priori according to their possibility lies generally beyond the horizon of our reason. Rather, all natural philosophy consists in the reduction of given forces apparently diverse to a smaller number of forces and powers sufficient for the explication of the actions of the former. But this reduction continues only to fundamental forces, beyond which our reason cannot go. And thus the investigation of metaphysics behind what lies at the basis of the empirical concept of matter is useful only for the purpose of leading natural philosophy as far as possible in the investigation of the dynamical grounds of explication, because these alone admit the hope of determinate laws, and consequently of a true rational coherence of explications.

This is all that metaphysics can ever accomplish for the construction of the concept of matter, and hence on behalf of the application of mathematics to natural science respecting the properties by which matter fills a space in determinate measure—namely, to regard these properties as dynamical and not as unconditioned original positions, such, for instance, as a merely mathematical treatment would postulate.

The familiar question as to the admissibility of empty spaces in the world may furnish the conclusion. The possibility of such spaces cannot be disputed. For space is required for all forces of matter; and since space also contains the conditions of the laws of the diffusion of these forces, it is
535   necessarily presupposed before all matter. Thus, attractive force is attributed to matter insofar as matter occupies a space around itself by attraction, yet without filling the space. Therefore space can, even where matter is active, be thought of as empty, inasmuch as the matter is not active by repulsive forces, and hence does not fill the space. But no experience, inference from experience, or necessary hypothesis for explicating empty spaces can justify us in assuming them as actual. For all experience gives us only comparatively empty spaces to cognize; these can be perfectly explicated from matter's property of filling its space by an expansive force greater or progressively smaller to infinity, in all possible degrees, without requiring empty spaces.

THIRD CHAPTER

Metaphysical Foundations of Mechanics

EXPLICATION 1

Matter is the movable insofar as it is something having a moving force.

Observation

Now, this is the third definition of matter. The merely dynamical concept could also regard matter as at rest. The moving force that was then taken into consideration concerned merely the filling of a certain space, without one's being permitted to regard the matter that filled the space as being itself moved. Repulsion was, therefore, an original moving force for imparting motion. On the other hand, in mechanics the force of a matter set in motion is regarded as present in order to impart this motion to another matter. But it is clear that the movable would have no moving force through its motion if it did not possess original moving forces, whereby it is active in every place where it exists before all proper motion. And it is clear that no uniform motion would be impressed on another matter by a matter whose motion lay in the path of the straight line in front of this other matter, unless both possessed original laws of repulsion; and that a matter could not by its motion compel another matter to follow it in the straight line (could not drag another after it), unless both possessed attractive forces. Hence all mechanical 537 laws presuppose dynamical ones; and a matter as moved can have no moving force except by means of its repulsion or attraction, upon which and with which it acts directly in its motion and thereby imparts its own motion to another matter. One will notice that I shall not make further mention here of the communication of motion by attraction (e.g., if perhaps a comet of stronger attractive power than the earth might in passing by the earth drag the earth after itself), but shall mention only the agency of repulsive forces, and hence such agency by pressure (as by means of tensed springs) or by impact. I shall do this because the application of the laws of repulsion in comparison with the case of attraction differs only with regard to the line of direction, but otherwise is the same in both cases.

EXPLICATION 2

The quantity of matter is the number of its movable [parts] in a determinate space. This quantity insofar as all its parts in their motion are regarded as simultaneously active (moving) is called the mass, and one says that a matter acts in mass when all its parts move in the same direction and at the same time exercise their moving force externally. A mass of determinate shape is called a body (in a mechanical sense). The quantity of motion (mechanically estimated) is what is estimated by means of the quantity of the moved matter and its velocity conjointly; phoronomically the quantity of motion consists merely in the degree of the moved matter's velocity.

PROPOSITION 1

The quantity of a matter can be estimated in comparison with every other matter only by its quantity of motion at a given velocity.

Proof

Matter is divisible to infinity; consequently, its quantity cannot be determined directly by means of the number of its parts. For if this occurs in the comparison of the given matter with a homogeneous one, in which case the quantity of the matter is proportional to the magnitude of the volume, then this is contrary to the requirement of the proposition, namely, that the quantity of the matter is to be estimated in comparison with every other (even specifically different) matter. Therefore matter can neither directly nor indirectly be validly estimated in comparison with every other matter as long as one abstracts from its proper motion. Consequently, there remains no other universally valid measure of the matter than the quantity of its motion. But in this the difference of the motion, which rests on the different quantity of the matters, can only be given when the velocity is assumed to be equal among the compared matters, therefore, etc.

538

Note

The quantity of the motion of bodies is in compound proportion to the quantity of their matter and their velocity, i.e., it is all the same whether I make the quantity of the matter of a body doubly as great and retain the velocity, or whether I double the velocity and retain just this mass. For the determinate concept of a quantity is only possible through the construction of the quantum. But this construction as regards the concept of quantity is nothing but the composition of the equivalent; consequently, the construction of the quantity of a motion is the composition of many motions equivalent to one another. Now, it is all the same according to the phoronomic propositions whether I impart to a movable thing a certain degree of velocity, or to many equally movable things all the smaller degrees of velocity that come from the given velocity divided by the number of movable things. Hereby arises at first an apparently phoronomic concept of the quantity of a motion as composed of many motions external to one another but yet composed in a whole of united movable points. If, now, these points are thought of as things having moving force by means of their motion, then the mechanical concept of the quantity of the motion arises. But in phoronomy it is not practicable to represent a motion as composed of many motions existing externally to one another. This is because the movable (which in phoronomy is represented as being without any moving force) in any com-

539 position with several of its own kind gives no distinction of the quantity of the motion other than that quantity which consists merely in the velocity. As the quantity of the motion of one body is related to the quantity of the motion of another, so likewise is the quantity of its action related (by "action" is to be understood its entire action). Those who assumed merely the magnitude of a space filled with resistance (e.g., the height to which a body with a certain velocity can rise against gravity, or the depth to which the same body can penetrate into soft matters) as the measure of the entire action brought forward another law of moving forces as regards actual motions, namely, that of the compound proportion of the quantity of the matters and the squares of their velocities. But they overlooked the quantity of the action in the given time in which the body traverses its space with less velocity, and this quantity can alone be the measure of a motion exhausted by a given uniform resistance. Hence there can be no difference between living and dead forces if mov-

ing forces are regarded mechanically, i.e., as those which bodies have insofar as they are themselves moved, and the velocity of their motion may be finitely or infinitely small (mere endeavor toward motion). Rather, one might far more appropriately call those forces with which matter (even if one entirely abstracts from its proper motion or even its effort to move itself) acts on other matters dead forces, and hence call the original moving forces of dynamics dead forces. And one might, on the other hand, call all mechanical moving forces, i.e., by means of motion proper, living forces, if one does not pay any regard to the difference of the velocity, whose degree may be infinitely small. All of this holds providing these designations of dead and living forces deserve to be retained at all.

Observation

In order to avoid diffuseness, we are going to condense the elucidation of the preceding three statements into one observation.

That the quantity of matter can only be thought of as the number of its movable parts (external to one another), as the definition [Explication 2] expresses it, is a remarkable and fundamental statement of universal mechanics. For thereby is indicated that matter has no other quantity than that which consists in the multitude of its manifold parts external to one another. Consequently, matter has no degree of moving force with given velocity such that this degree might be independent of the aforementioned multitude and might be 540 regarded merely as intensive quantity. Such would indeed be the case if matter consisted of monads, whose reality in every relation must have a degree that can be greater or smaller without being dependent upon a multitude of parts external to one another. As to what concerns the concept of mass in the same explication, it cannot, as is usually done, be taken to be the same as the concept of quantity. Fluid matters can act by their own motion in mass, but they can also act in flow. In the so-called water-hammer, the water in striking acts in mass, i.e., with all its parts simultaneously; the same thing occurs in water that has been enclosed in a vessel and that presses by means of its weight upon the scales on which it stands. On the other hand, the water of a millstream does not act in mass on the paddle of the struck water wheel, i.e., with all its parts rushing simultaneously against the wheel, but the parts act only successively. Therefore if here the quantity of matter that is moved with a certain velocity and that has moving force is to be determined, then one must first of all look for the body of water, i.e., such quantity of matter as can produce the same action when it acts in mass with a certain velocity (with its weight). Hence one usually understands by the word "mass" the quantity of matter of a solid body (the vessel in which a fluid is enclosed takes the place of its solidity). Finally, in regard to the proposition [Proposition 1] together with its appended note, there is something strange involved in the fact that according to the propostion, the quantity of the matter must be estimated by the quantity of the motion with given velocity, while according to the note, on the other hand, the quantity of the motion (of a body, because that of a point consists merely in the degree of its velocity) at the same velocity must be estimated by means of the quantity of the moved matter. All of this seems to revolve in a circle and to promise no determinate concept either of the one or of the other. This supposed circle would be actual if it were a reciprocal derivation of two identical concepts from one another. But it contains, on the one hand, only the explication of a concept and, on the other, the explication of the application of the concept to experience. The quantity of the movable in space is the quantity of the matter, but this quantity of the matter (the multitude of the movable) manifests itself in experience only by the quantity of the motion at equal velocity (e.g., by equilibrium).

There is yet to be noted that the quantity of matter is the

quantity of substance in the movable and, consequently, is not the magnitude of a certain quality of matter (of repulsion or attraction, which are cited in dynamics), and that the quantum of substance here signifies nothing but the mere number of the movable parts, which constitutes matter. For only this number of the moved parts can with the same velocity give a difference in the quantity of the motion. But the fact that   *541* the moving force which a matter possesses in its proper motion alone manifests its quantity of substance rests on the concept of substance as the ultimate subject (which is not a further predicate of another subject) in space; for this reason this subject can have no other quantity than that of the multitude of its homogeneous parts, being external to one another. Now, the proper motion of matter is a predicate which determines such motion's subject (the movable) and with regard to matter as a multitude of movable parts indicates the plurality of the moved subjects (at equal velocity in the same direction); this is not the case with dynamical properties, whose quantity can also be the quantity of the action of a single subject (e.g., a particle of air can have more or less elasticity). Because of all of this it is clear that the quantity of substance in a matter must be estimated mechanically, i.e., by the quantity of the proper motion of the matter, and not dynamically, by the quantity of its original moving forces. Nevertheless, original attraction as the cause of universal gravitation can indeed provide a measure of the quantity of matter and its substance (as actually happens in the comparison of matters by weighing), although there seems to be laid at the foundation here not the proper motion of the attracting matter but a dynamical measure, namely, attractive force. But in the case of this force, the action of one matter occurs with all its parts directly on all parts of another matter; and hence the action is (at equal distances) obviously proportional to the number of the parts. Because of this fact the attracting body itself thereby also imparts the velocity of its proper motion (by means of the resistance of the attracted body). This velocity is directly proportional, in equivalent external circumstances, to the number of the attracting body's parts; because of this the estimation takes place here, as a matter of fact, mechanically, although only indirectly so.

PROPOSITION 2

First law of mechanics: With regard to all changes of corporeal nature, the quantity of matter taken as a whole remains the same, unincreased and undiminished.

Proof

(In universal metaphysics there is laid down the proposition that with regard to all changes of nature, no substance either arises or perishes,[44] and here [in mechanics] there is only set forth what is substance in matter.) In every matter the movable in space is the ultimate subject of all the accidents inhering in matter, and the number of matter's movable parts external to one another is the quantity of substance. Hence the quantity of the matter according to its substance is nothing but the multitude of the substances of which it consists. Therefore the quantity of matter cannot be increased or diminished except by the arising or perishing of new substance of matter. Now, with regard to all change of matter, substance never arises or perishes. Hence the quantity of matter also is neither increased nor diminished thereby but remains always the same, as a whole, i.e., so that somewhere in the world matter continues to exist in the same quantity, although this or that matter may by the addition or subtraction of parts be increased or diminished.

542

[44] [Cf. *Critique of Pure Reason*, B 224–232.]

Observation

Substance is possible only in space and according to the conditions of space, and hence is possible only as object of the external senses. The essential thing which characterizes substance in this proof is that its quantity cannot be increased or diminished unless substance arises or perishes. Therefore, inasmuch as any quantity of an object that is possible only in space must consist of parts external to one another, these, if they are real (something movable), must necessarily be substances. On the other hand, that which is regarded as object of the internal sense can as substance have a quantity that does not consist of parts external to one another and whose parts are therefore not substances. The arising or perishing of this quantity, consequently, must not be the arising or perishing of substance; and the increase or diminution of such quantity is therefore possible without detriment to the principle of the permanence of substance. To wit, consciousness has a degree that may be greater or smaller without any substance needing to arise or perish. And hence the clarity of the representations of my soul has such a degree, and in consequence of this fact the faculty of consciousness, namely, apperception—and along with this faculty even the substance of the soul—has also such a degree. But inasmuch as a total disappearance of this faculty of apperception must finally ensue upon the gradual diminution of the same, even the substance of the soul would be subjected to a gradual perishing, even though the soul were of a simple nature, because this disappearance of its fundamental force could not ensue through division (separation of substance from a composite) but, as it were, by expiration, and even this not in a moment, but by the gradual remission of its degree, from whatever cause. The "I", the universal correlate of apperception and itself merely a thought, designates as a mere prefix a thing of indeterminate signification, namely, the subject of all predicates without any condition to distinguish this representation of the subject from that of a something in general, namely, substance; by the expression "substance", one has no concept as to what this substance is. On the other hand, the concept of a matter as substance is the concept of the movable in space. Hence it is no wonder if permanence of substance can be proved of matter but not of the soul. This is because in the case of matter there follows from its concept, namely, that it is the movable, which is only possible in space, the fact that what has quantity in matter contains a plurality of real parts external to one another, and hence contains a plurality of substances. Consequently, the quantity of matter can be diminished only by division, which is no disappearance; such disappearance would, according to the law of permanence, be impossible in the case of matter. The thought "I" is, on the other hand, no concept at all but only an internal perception. Therefore, from this thought, nothing at all can be concluded (except the complete distinction of an object of the internal sense from what is thought merely as object of the external senses); consequently, the permanence of the soul as substance cannot be concluded from the thought "I".

PROPOSITION 3

Second law of mechanics: Every change of matter has an external cause. (Every body remains in its state of rest or motion in the same direction and with the same velocity unless it is compelled by an external cause to forsake this state.[45])

Proof

(In universal metaphysics there is laid down the proposition

---

[45] [This is Newton's first law of motion.]

that every change has a cause;[46] here [in mechanics] there is only to be proved of matter that its change must always have an external cause.) Matter as mere object of the external senses has no other determinations than those of external relations in space and hence undergoes no changes except by motion. With regard to such change, insofar as it is an exchange of one motion with another, or of motion with rest, and vice versa, a cause of such change must be found (according to the principle of metaphysics). But this cause cannot be internal, for matter has no absolutely internal determinations and grounds of determination. Hence all change of a matter is based upon an external cause (i.e., a body remains etc.).

Observation   544

This mechanical law alone must be called the law of inertia (*lex inertiae*); the law that every action has an equal and opposite reaction cannot bear this name. For the latter says what matter does, but the former only what it does not do, and this is better adapted to the expression of inertia. The inertia of matter is and signifies nothing but its lifelessness, as matter in itself. Life means the capacity of a substance to determine itself to act from an internal principle, of a finite substance to determine itself to change, and of a material substance to determine itself to motion or rest as change of its state. Now, we know of no other internal principle of a substance to change its state but desire and no other internal activity whatever but thought, along with what depends upon such desire, namely, feeling of pleasure or displeasure, and appetite or will. But these determining grounds and actions do not at all belong to the representations of the external senses and hence also not to the determinations of matter as matter. Therefore, all matter as such is lifeless. The prop-

---

[46] [Cf. *Critique of Pure Reason*, B 232–256.]

osition of inertia says so much and no more. If we seek the cause of any change whatever of matter in life, we shall have to seek this cause at once in another substance different from matter, although bound up with it. For in natural knowledge it is necessary to know first the laws of matter as such and to clear them of the admixture of all other active causes before one connects these laws with such causes, in order to distinguish how and what each such law brings about of itself alone. The possibility of a natural science proper rests entirely upon the law of inertia (along with the law of the permanence of substance). The opposite of this, and therefore the death of all natural philosophy, would be hylozoism. From the very concept of inertia as mere lifelessness there follows of itself the fact that inertia does not signify a positive effort of something to maintain its state. Only living things are called inert in this latter sense, inasmuch as they have a representation of another state which they abhor and strive against with all their power.

PROPOSITION 4

Third mechanical law: In all communication of motion, action and reaction are always equal to one another.[47]

Proof

(The proposition that all external action in the world is reciprocal action must be borrowed from universal metaphysics.[48] Hence in order to stay within the bounds of mechanics, one only has to show that this reciprocal action—*actio muta*—is at the same time reaction—*reactio*. But the

[47] [This is Newton's third law of motion.]
[48] [Cf. *Critique of Pure Reason*, B 256–262.]

aforementioned metaphysical law of community cannot here be entirely left out without disrupting the completeness of the insight.) All active relations of matters in space and all changes of these relations insofar as they can be causes of certain actions must always be represented as reciprocal. That is, since all change of such relations is motion, no motion of a body with reference to one absolutely at rest which is thereby also to be set in motion can be thought of. Rather, this latter body must be represented only as relatively at rest with regard to the space to which it is referred; this body must be represented as moved, together with this space but in the opposite direction,[49] with the very same quantity of motion in absolute space as the moved body has in absolute space toward this one that is relatively at rest. For the change of relation (and hence the motion) is completely reciprocal between both bodies; by as much as the one body approaches every part of the other, by so much this other approaches every part of the first. And since the main thing here is not the empirical space surrounding both bodies but only the line lying between them (inasmuch as these bodies are considered merely in relation to one another according to the influence which the motion of the one can have on the change of state of the other, abstraction being made of all relation to empirical space), their motion is regarded as determinable only in absolute space, in which each of the two bodies must equally participate in the motion attributed to the one in relative space, since there is no ground for attributing more motion to one of them than to the other. On this footing, the motion of a body A toward another one B at rest, with regard to which the former can thereby be moving, is reduced to absolute space, i.e., the motion in question is considered to be a relation of efficient

---

[49] [That is, in the direction opposite to that of the motion of the first body toward the second body. This whole sentence becomes clearer when one refers to the discussion below, especially the construction of the communication of motion.]

causes referred merely to one another; and so the motion is considered as if both bodies equally participate in this motion, which in the appearance[50] is attributed only to the body A. This can occur only in the following way. The velocity which in the relative space is attributed only to the body A is divided between A and B in inverse proportion to their masses; A is given only its velocity in absolute space, while, on the other hand, B, together with the relative space in which it rests, is given its velocity in the opposite direction.

546 In this way the same appearance [*Erscheinung*] of the motion is perfectly retained. The action in the community of both bodies is constructed as follows. Let a body A be in

FIGURE 5

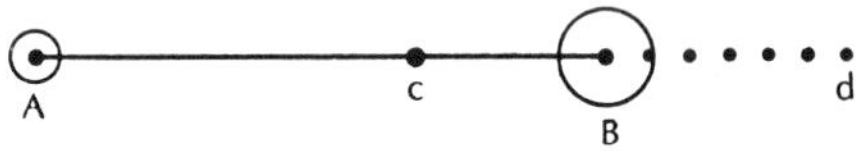

motion toward the body B with a velocity = AB with regard to the relative space; the body B is at rest with regard to the same space. Let the velocity AB be divided into two parts, Ac and Bc, which are related to one another inversely as the masses B and A. Represent A as moved with the velocity Ac in absolute space, but B with the velocity Bc in the opposite direction together with the relative space. Thus both motions are opposite and equal to one another; and since they mutually destroy one another, both bodies put themselves relatively to one another, i.e., in absolute space, in a state of rest. But, now, B together with the relative space was in motion with the velocity Bc in the direction BA; this velocity is exactly opposed to that of the body A, namely, AB. Hence if the motion of the body B is destroyed by impact, then the motion of the relative space is not therefore destroyed. Hence after the impact, the relative space with regard to both bodies A and B (which now rest in absolute space) moves in the direction BA with the velocity Bc, or, what is the same thing, both

---

[50] [*Erscheinung*, which can also be rendered as "phenomenon."]

bodies after the impact move with equal velocity Bd = Bc in the direction of the impacting AB. According to the foregoing, however, the quantity of motion of the body B in the direction and with the velocity Bc, and hence likewise the quantity of motion of B in the direction Bd with the same velocity, is equal to the quantity of motion of the body A with the velocity and in the direction Ac. Consequently, the effect, i.e., the motion Bd, which the body B receives by impact in relative space, and hence also the action of the body A with the velocity Ac, is always equal to the reaction Bc. The very same law (as mathematical mechanics teaches) suffers no alteration when, instead of the impact upon a resting body, an impact of the body upon a moved one is assumed; similarly, the communication of motion by impact is distinguished from that by traction only in the direction in which the matters oppose one another in their motions. Because of all this there follows that in all communication of   *547* motion, action and reaction are always equal to one another (that every impact can communicate the motion of one body to another only by means of an equal counterimpact, every pressure by means of an equal counterpressure, and, similarly, every traction only by an equal countertraction).[51]

---

[51] Inasmuch as the motion of a body was considered in phoronomy merely with regard to its space as change of relation in space, it was all the same whether I wanted to ascribe the motion to the body in space, or instead ascribe to the relative space an equal but opposite motion;* both gave fully the same appearance [Erscheinung]. The quantity of motion of the space was merely its velocity, and hence the quantity of motion of the body was likewise nothing but its velocity (for which reason the body could be regarded as a mere movable point). But in mechanics, a body is regarded as in motion toward another, respecting which it has a causal relation through its motion, namely, the relation that in the former's moving itself either by its approach through the force of impenetrability or by its withdrawal through the force of attraction, it comes into community with this other body. Because of this fact, whether I want to ascribe an opposite motion to one of these bodies, or to the space, is no longer all the same. For now another concept of the quantity of motion comes into play, namely, not that which is thought merely

---

* [See above, Ak. 487–488.]

548   ## Note 1

From the foregoing there follows the natural law, which is not unimportant for universal mechanics, that every body, however great its mass may be, must be movable by the impact of every other, however small its mass or velocity may be. For to the motion of A in the direction AB there necessarily corresponds an equal opposite motion of B in the direction BA. Both motions destroy one another in absolute space by impact. But thereby both bodies receive a velocity Bd = Bc in the direction of the impacting one; consequently, the body B is movable by every force of impact, however small.

Note 2

This is, then, the mechanical law of the equality of action and reaction. This law is based on the fact that no communication of motion takes place except insofar as a community

---

547   with regard to the space and consists only in the velocity, but that whereby at the same time the quantity of the substance (as moving cause) must be taken into consideration. And it is here no longer optional but necessary to assume both bodies as moved, and indeed moved with an equal quantity of motion in an opposite direction. But when the one body is relatively at rest with regard to its space, then it is necessary to attribute the requisite motion to this body together with its space. For the one cannot act on the other by this [first] one's own motion except by approach through repulsive force or by withdrawal through attractive force. Since, now, both forces always act equally and reciprocally in opposite directions, no body can act upon another body by means of these forces through its motion except just so much as the other body reacts with an equal quantity of motion. Hence no body can impart motion through its motion to an absolutely resting body, but this second body must be moved (together with its space) in the opposite direction with just that quantity of motion which is the same as that which it is to receive through the motion of the first body and in the direction of this first one. The reader will easily see that in spite of the somewhat unusual character which this mode of representation of the communication of motion has in itself, this representation can nevertheless be placed in the clearest light, if one does not shrink from the diffuseness of the explanation.

of these motions is presupposed. And so this law is based on the fact that no body strikes another that is at rest with regard to this first body, but, rather, the first body strikes the second body insofar as the second is at rest with regard to its space; and so the first strikes the second only insofar as the second together with its space moves in equal measure in the opposite direction with the motion which then falls to the first body as its relative share and which as a whole first of all gives the quantity of motion that we would attribute to this first body in absolute space.[52] For no motion [of a body] that is to be moving with regard to another body can be absolute; but if the motion is relative with regard to this other body, then there is no relation in space that is not reciprocal and equal. But there is yet another, namely, a dynamical, law of the equality of the action and reaction of matters, not insofar as one matter communicates its motion to another, but insofar as this first matter originally imparts its motion to the second one and by means of the second one's resistance the motion is at the same time produced in the first. This can be easily demonstrated in a similar way. For if the matter A attracts the matter B, then A compels B to approach A, or, what is the same thing, A resists the force with which B endeavors to withdraw. But inasmuch as it is all the same whether B withdraws from A or A from B, this resistance is at the same time a resistance which the body B exercises against A insofar as A endeavors to withdraw from B, and hence traction and countertraction are equal to one another.   *549*
In the same way, if A repels the matter B, then A resists the approach of B. But since it is all the same whether B approaches A or A approaches B, so B also resists just as much the approach of A; hence pressure and counterpressure are also always equal to one another.

---

[52] [This is an extremely difficult sentence to translate. Its meaning becomes clear when one refers to Kant's construction of the communication of motion above.]

Observation 1

This is, then, the construction of the communication of motion. This construction at the same time carries with it as its necessary condition the law of the equality of action and reaction. Newton did not at all trust himself to prove this law a priori, but appealed to experience to prove it. Other people for the sake of this law introduced into natural science a special force of matter under the name of the force of inertia (*vis inertiae*), first mentioned by Kepler, and thus they also really derived it from experience. Finally, still others posited the concept of a mere communication of motion which they regarded as a gradual transference of the motion of one body into another, whereby the moving body must lose exactly as much motion as it imparts to the moved one until it impresses no more motion on the latter (when, namely, it has arrived at an equality of velocity with the latter and its velocity is in the same direction as that of the latter).[53]

---

[53] The equality of the action with the—in this case falsely called—reaction turns out just as well when a person under the hypothesis of the transfusion of motions from one body into another allows the moved body A to give up its entire motion in one moment to the resting body. Consequently, the body A would rest after the impact; this situation would be inevitable as soon as both bodies were thought of as absolutely hard (a property that must be distinguished from elasticity). But inasmuch as this law of motion would in its application accord neither with experience nor with itself, one would know of nothing else to do but deny the existence of absolutely hard bodies. This would be tantamount to admitting the contingency of this law, inasmuch as it is to depend on the special quality of the matters which move one another. In our presentation of this law, on the other hand, it is quite the same whether one wants to think of the bodies that strike one another as absolutely hard or not. But it is quite inconceivable to me how the transfusionists of motion intend to explain in their way the motion of elastic bodies by impact. For it is clear that the resting body does not insofar as it is merely resting receive motion which the striking body loses, but that the resting body in impact exercises actual force in the opposite direction against the striking body, as though to compress a spring lying between them. To this end there is required on the part of the resting body just as much actual motion (but in the opposite direction) as the moving body on its part needs for this end.

In this way they actually destroyed all reaction, i.e., all really reacting force of the one strike against the one striking (which might perhaps be capable of tensing a spring). Moreover, *550* they do not prove what is actually meant in this aforementioned law, i.e., they did not at all explicate the communication of motion according to the possibility of such communication. For the words "transference of motion from one body to another" explicate nothing. And if one might not want to take this transference literally (since it is opposed to the principle, *accidentia non migrant e substantiis in substantias*[54]), as though motion were poured from one body into another, like water from one glass into another; then the problem here is how to make conceivable this possibility whose explication rests exactly on the same ground from which the law of the equality of action and reaction is derived. One cannot at all think how the motion of a body A must necessarily be connected with the motion of another one B except by one's thinking that there are forces belonging to both (dynamically) before all motion, e.g., repulsion. And now with these forces one can prove that the motion of the body A by approach toward B is necessarily connected with the approach of B toward A and, if B is regarded as at rest, is connected with the motion of B together with its space toward A, insofar as the bodies with their (original) moving forces are considered as in motion merely relatively to one another. This latter can thereby be fully comprehended a priori, viz., that whether the body B with respect to its empirically cognizable space be at rest or moved, it must be regarded as necessarily moved with respect to the body A and indeed as moved in an opposite direction. If this were not so, no influence of A upon the repulsive force of both bodies would occur; and without such an influence, no mechanical action whatever of matters on one another, i.e., no communication of motion by impact, is possible.

[54] ["Accidents do not wander from substances to substances."]

Observation 2

The designation force of inertia (*vis inertiae*) must, then, in spite of the famous name of its originator, be entirely dismissed from natural science. This must be done not only because this designation carries with it a contradiction in the expression itself, or because the law of inertia (lifelessness) might thereby be easily confused with the law of reaction in every communicated motion, but mainly because through this confusion the erroneous representation of those who are not correctly acquainted with the mechanical laws would be maintained and strengthened. According to this erroneous representation, the reaction of bodies, of which we are speaking under the name of the force of inertia, would consist in the fact that the motion in the world would be consumed, diminished, or destroyed. However, the mere communication of motion would not by such reaction be brought about, inasmuch as the moving body would have to expend a part of its motion merely to overcome the inertia of the resting one (such expense being pure loss), and with the remaining part alone could it set the latter in motion; but if no motion remained, then it would not by its impact bring the latter into motion because of the latter's great mass. Nothing but the opposite motion of another body can resist a motion, but this other's rest can in no way resist a motion. Here, then, inertia of matter, i.e., mere incapacity to move of itself, is not the cause of a resistance. A special and entirely peculiar force merely to resist, but without being able to move a body, would under the name of a force of inertia be a word without any meaning. The three laws of universal mechanics might, then, be more appropriately designated the law of the subsistence, the inertia, and the reaction of matters (*lex Subsistentiae, Inertiae et Antagonismi*), as regards all the changes of matters. That these laws, and hence all the propositions of the present science,

551

exactly answer to the categories of substance, causality, and community,[55] insofar as these concepts are applied to matter, requires no further discussion.

GENERAL
OBSERVATION
ON MECHANICS

The communication of motion takes place only by means of such moving forces as also inhere in a matter at rest (impenetrability and attraction). The action of a moving force on a body in one moment is the solicitation of the body. The velocity of the body brought about by its solicitation, insofar as this velocity can increase in equal proportion to the time, is the moment of acceleration. (The moment of acceleration must therefore contain only an infinitely small velocity, because otherwise the body would attain through the moment of acceleration an infinite velocity in a given time; but this is impossible. Moreover, the possibility of acceleration in general through a continuous moment of acceleration rests on the law of inertia.) The solicitation of matter by expansive force (e.g., of compressed air that bears a weight) occurs always with a finite velocity. But the velocity which is thereby impressed upon (or taken away from) another body can only be infinitely small; for expansive force is only a superficial force, or, what is the same thing, is the motion of an infinitely small quantum of matter, and such motion must, consequently, occur with finite velocity in order to be equal to the motion of a body of finite mass with infinitely small velocity (weight). On the other hand, attraction is a penetrating force by means of which a finite quan-

---

[55] [Cf. *Critique of Pure Reason*, B 106.]

tum of matter exercises moving force on a similarly finite
quantum of another matter. The solicitation of attraction
552   must, then, be infinitely small because it is equal to the moment of acceleration (which must always be infinitely small);
this is not the case as regards repulsion, where an infinitely
small part of matter is to impress a moment on a finite part.
No attraction with a finite velocity can be thought of without the matter's having to penetrate itself by its own attractive force. For the attraction which a finite quantity of matter
exercises on another finite quantity with a finite velocity must
in all points of the compression be superior to every finite
velocity with which the matter reacts by means of its impenetrability but only with an infinitely small part of the
quantity of its matter. If attraction is only a superficial force,
as one thinks of cohesion, then the opposite of this would
result. But it is impossible to think of cohesion in such a way,
if it is to be true attraction (and not merely external compression).

An absolutely hard body would be one whose parts attracted one another so strongly that they could not be separated by any weight nor be altered in their position with
regard to one another. Now, the parts of the matter of such
a body would have to attract one another with a moment of
acceleration that would be infinite as compared with the
moment of acceleration of gravity, but would be finite as
compared with the moment of acceleration of the mass that
is thereby put into motion. Because of this, resistance by
impenetrability as expansive force, since resistance always
occurs with an infinitely small quantity of matter, would have
to occur with more than finite velocity of solicitation, i.e.,
the matter would endeavor to extend itself with infinite
velocity; but this is impossible. Therefore, an absolutely hard
body, i.e., one that would oppose a body moved with finite
velocity and would do so in one moment with a resistance
on impact equal to the whole force of this latter body, is
impossible. Consequently, a matter produces by its impene-

trability or cohesion only an infinitely small resistance in one moment to the force of a body in finite motion. From this there follows, now, the mechanical law of continuity (*lex continui mechanica*), namely, in no body is the state of rest or motion—and in the latter, of velocity or direction—changed by impact in one moment, but only in a certain time through an infinite series of intermediate states whose difference from one another is smaller than that between the first and last such states. A moved body that strikes a matter is thus not brought to rest by the latter's resistance all at once but only by a continuous retardation, or a body that was at rest is set into motion only by a continuous acceleration, or a body is changed from one degree of velocity to another only according to the same rule. Similarly, the direction of a body's motion that is changed into such a direction as forms an angle with the former one does so only by means of all possible intermediate directions, i.e., by means of motion in a curved line (this law, for a similar reason, can   *553* also be extended to the change of state of a body by means of attraction). This *lex continui* is based on the law of the inertia of matter. On the other hand, the metaphysical[56] law of continuity must be extended to all change (internal as well as external) in general and hence would be based on the mere concept of a change in general, as quantity, and on the concept of the generation of such change (such generation necessarily proceeds continuously in a certain time, like time itself). And so this metaphysical law has no place here.

[56] [Kant might more appropriately have said "transcendental" here.]

FOURTH
CHAPTER

Metaphysical Foundations of Phenomenology[57]

EXPLICATION

Matter is the movable insofar as it can as such be an object of experience.

Observation

Motion, like everything that is represented through sense, is given only as appearance.[58] In order that the representation of motion may become experience, there is required in addition that something be thought through the understanding, namely, in addition to the way in which this representation of motion inheres in the subject, there is required further the determination of an object by means of this representation.

[57] [By "phenomenology" Kant means the doctrine of appearance (*Erscheinungslehre*). See Kant's footnote (71) below, Ak. 559–560.]

[58] [Cf. *Critique of Pure Reason*, trans. Norman Kemp Smith (London: Macmillan and Co., 1929, and St. Martin's Press: New York, 1964), B 34, p. 65: "The undetermined object of an empirical intuition is entitled *appearance*." This and the following quotations from the *Critique* are printed by permission of St. Martin's Press, Macmillan and Company Limited, and The Macmillan Company of Canada.]

Therefore, the movable as such becomes an object of experience when a certain object (here, a material thing) is thought as determined with regard to the predicate of motion. But motion is change of relation in space. There are, then, always two correlates[59] here. Firstly,[60] in the appearance, change can be attributed to one just as well as to the other of these correlates, and either the one or the other can be called moved inasmuch as both attributions are equivalent. Or, secondly,[61] one of these correlates must in the experience be thought as moved to the exclusion of the other. Or, thirdly,[62] both of these correlates must necessarily through reason be represented as moved at the same time. In the appearance, which contains nothing but the relation in the motion (according to the change of the relation), none of these determinations are contained. But when the movable as such, namely, according to its motion, is to be thought as determined, i.e., for the sake of a possible experience, then it is necessary to indicate the conditions under which the object (matter) must be determined in one way or another by the predicate of motion. Here the question is not of the transformation of illusion [Schein] into truth, but of appearance [Erscheinung] into experience. For as regards illusion, the understanding is always involved with its judgments determining[63] an object, although it is always in danger of taking the subjective for the objective; but in the appearance, no judgment at all of the understanding is to be

555

---

[59] [The two correlates of motion are matter and space.]

[60] [Cf. Proposition 1 below.]

[61] [Cf. Proposition 2 below.]

[62] [Cf. Proposition 3 below.]

[63] [Cf. *Critique of Pure Reason,* B 93, p. 105: "Judgment is therefore the mediate knowledge of an object, that is, the representation of a representation of it. In every judgment there is a concept which holds of many representations, and among them of a given representation that is immediately related to an object."]

found.[64] It is necessary to note this not only here but in the whole of philosophy, because otherwise there is always misunderstanding when the question is about appearances and this expression is taken as identical in meaning with that of illusion.

PROPOSITION 1

The rectilinear motion of a matter with regard to an empirical space, as distinguished from the opposite motion of this space, is a merely possible predicate. The rectilinear motion of a matter in no relation to a matter outside of itself, i.e., such rectilinear motion thought of as absolute, is impossible.

Proof

In the case of a body moved in relative space, whether this space is said to be at rest, or, conversely, this space is said to be moved with equal velocity in the opposite direction and the body to be at rest—in this case, I say, there is no disagreement as to what belongs to the object, but only as to what belongs to the relation of the object to the subject; and hence there is no disagreement concerning what belongs to the experience, but only to the appearance. For if the spectator puts himself in the same space that is at rest, then he says that the body is moved; if he puts himself (at least in thought) in another space enclosing the aforementioned one and the body is at rest with regard to this enclosing space, then the aforementioned relative space is said to be moved. Therefore, in experience (in a cognition that validly determines the object for all appearances), there is no difference what-

[64] [Cf. *ibid.*, B 350, p. 297: "It is therefore correct to say that the senses do not err—not because they always judge rightly but because they do not judge at all. Truth and error, therefore, and consequently also illusion as leading to error, are only to be found in the judgment, i.e., only in the relation of the object to our understanding."]

ever between the motion of the body in relative space and the resting of the body in absolute space with the equal but opposite motion of the relative space. Now, the representation of an object by one of two predicates that are equivalent regarding the object and different from one another only regarding the subject and his mode of representation is not a determination according to a disjunctive judgment, but is merely a choice according to an alternative one. (The disjunctive judgment assumes for the determination of the object one of two objectively opposed predicates to the exclusion of its contrary. But the alternative judgment assumes for the determination of the object one of two judgments that are indeed objectively equivalent, but are subjectively opposed to one another without the contrary's being excluded from the object—and hence assumes this one judgment by mere choice.[65]) This means that through the concept of motion as object of experience, there is no determination (and hence an equivalence) whether a body is represented as moved in relative space, or the relative space is represented as moved with regard to the body. Now, that which is in itself undetermined as regards two mutually opposed predicates is thus far merely possible. Therefore, the rectilinear motion of a matter in empirical space, in contradistinction to the equal and opposite motion of the space, is in experience a merely possible predicate. This was the first point in the proposition.

556

Further, a relation, and hence also a change of this relation, i.e., motion, can be an object of experience only insofar as both of motion's correlates[66] are objects of experience; but pure space, which is also called absolute space in contradistinction to relative (empirical) space, is no object of experience and is nothing at all. Because of this, rectilinear

---

[65] Concerning this distinction of disjunctive and alternative opposition, more in the general observation to this chapter. [Cf. Kant's footnote (71) below, Ak. 559–560.]

[66] [That is, matter and space.]

motion without reference to anything empirical, i.e., absolute motion, is utterly impossible. This was the second point in the proposition.

Observation

This proposition determines the modality of motion with regard to phoronomy.

PROPOSITION 2

557

The circular motion of a matter, in contradistinction to the opposite motion of the space, is an actual predicate of matter. On the other hand, the opposite motion of a relative space, taken instead of the motion of the body, is no actual motion of the body; if this opposite motion of a relative space is held to be an actual motion of the body, then such motion is a mere illusion [Schein].

Proof

Circular motion is (like every curvilinear motion) a continuous change of rectilinear motion; and since this change is itself a continuous change of relation with regard to external space, circular motion is a change of the change of these external relations in space and, consequently, is a continuous arising of new motions. Now, according to the law of inertia, a motion insofar as it arises must have an external cause. But the body at every point of this circle is (according to the very same law) endeavoring to proceed in the straight line touching the circle, and this motion acts against the aforementioned external cause. Hence every body in circular motion manifests by its motion a moving force. Now, the motion of the space, in contradistinction to the motion of the body, is merely phoronomic and has no moving force. Consequently, the judgment that here either the body is moved or else the space is moved in the opposite direction is a disjunctive one, by which, if the one member, namely, the motion of the body, is posited, then the other member, namely, the motion of the space, is excluded. Therefore, the circular motion of a body, in contradistinction to the motion of the space, is an actual motion. Even though according to the appearance [*Erscheinung*] the motion of the space agrees with the circular motion of the body, nevertheless in the complex of all appearances, i.e., of possible experience, the former motion conflicts with the latter; and hence the former is nothing but mere illusion [*Schein*].

Observation

This proposition determines the modality of motion with regard to dynamics. For a motion which cannot take place without the influence of a continuously acting external moving force proves directly or indirectly original moving forces of matter, either of repulsion or of attraction. By the way, on the present subject, one can refer to the latter part of Newton's scholium to the definitions with which he begins his *Mathematical Principles of Natural Philosophy*. From this it will become clear that the circular motion of two bodies around a common center (and hence also the rotation of 558 the earth on its axis) even in empty space, and hence without any possible comparison through experience with external space, can nevertheless be cognized by means of experience, and that therefore a motion, which is a change of external relations in space, can be empirically given, although this space itself is not empirically given and is no object of experience. This paradox deserves to be solved.

PROPOSITION 3

In every motion of a body whereby it is moving with regard to another body, an opposite and equal motion of this other body is necessary.

Proof

According to the third law of mechanics (Proposition 4), the communication of the motion of the bodies is possible only through the community of their originally moving forces, and this community is possible only through reciprocal opposite and equal motion. The motion of both bodies is therefore actual. However, the actuality of this motion does not rest (as in the second proposition[67]) on the influence of external forces, but follows immediately and inevitably from the concept of the relation of the moved in space to every other thing thereby movable; therefore, the motion of this latter is necessary.

Observation

This proposition determines the modality of motion with regard to mechanics. That these three propositions, moreover, determine the motion of matter with regard to its possibility, actuality, and necessity, and hence with regard to all three categories of modality,[68] is obvious of itself.

[67] [Of phenomenology.]
[68] [Cf. *Critique of Pure Reason,* B 106.]

GENERAL
OBSERVATION
ON PHENOMENOLOGY

Hence there are manifested here three concepts whose employment in universal natural science is unavoidable, and whose exact determination is for this reason necessary, although this determination is not so easy and comprehensible. They are, namely, the concept of motion in relative (movable) space; secondly, the concept of motion in absolute (immovable) space; thirdly, the concept of relative motion in general, in contradistinction to absolute motion. The concept of absolute space is laid at the foundation of all of them. But how do we come by this unusual concept, and upon what does the necessity of its employment rest? *559*

It cannot be an object of experience, for space without matter is no object of perception; and yet it is a necessary concept of reason, and is therefore nothing but a mere idea.[69] For in order that motion may be given even as appearance, there is required an empirical representation of space with regard to which the movable is to change its relation; but the space which is to be perceived must be material and hence, according to the concept of matter in general, must itself be movable. Now, in order to think of this space as moved, one can think of it only as contained in a space of greater compass and can assume this latter to be at rest. But this latter space admits of being arranged in just the same way as regards a still more enlarged space, and so on to infinity without ever by experience arriving at an immovable (immaterial) space with regard to which motion or rest could

[69] [See *ibid.*, B 366–377.]

be attributed absolutely to any matter. Rather, the concept of these relational determinations will have to be constantly changed according as the movable is considered to be related to one or the other of these spaces. Now, the condition for regarding something as at rest or moved is always again and again conditioned to infinity in relative space; from this fact the following things become clear. Firstly, all motion or rest can be merely relative and neither can be absolute, i.e., matter can be thought of as moved or at rest only in relation to matter and never as regards mere space without matter. Therefore, absolute motion, i.e., such as is thought of without any reference of one matter to another, is simply impossible. Secondly, for this very reason no concept of motion or rest in relative space and valid for every appearance is possible. But a space must be thought of in which this relative space can be thought of as moved; the determination of such a space does not further depend on any other empirical space and hence is not again conditioned—that is, an absolute space, to which all relative motions can be referred, must be thought of.[70] In such a space everything empirical is movable. Consequently, in it all motions of material things can be valid as merely relative to one another, and as alternatively-reciprocal;[71] but none can be valid as absolute

---

[70] [See *ibid.*, B 377–389.]

[71] In logic the "either-or" always denotes a disjunctive judgment; for if one member is true, the other must be false. For instance, a body is either moved or not moved, i.e., at rest; for one speaks there simply of the relation of the cognition to the object. It is different in the doctrine of appearance [*Erscheinungslehre*], where there is involved the relation to the subject in order to determine according to this relation the relation of the objects. For here the proposition that the body is either moved and the space at rest or vice versa is not a disjunctive proposition with an objective reference but only a subjective one, and both of the judgments contained in this proposition are alternatively valid. In this very same phenomenology, when motion is considered not merely phoronomically but, rather, dynamically, the disjunctive proposition is, on the other hand, to be taken with an objective meaning, i.e., instead of the rotation of a body I cannot assume the rest of the body and, on the other hand, the opposite motion of the space. But even

motion or rest (since, inasmuch as one is called moved, the   560
other, with reference to which this former is moved, is nevertheless represented as absolutely at rest). Absolute space is,
then, necessary not as a concept of an actual object but as
an idea that is to serve as a rule for considering all motion
therein only as relative.[72] All motion and rest must be reduced to absolute space if the appearance of these is to be
transformed into a determinate concept of experience (all
appearances being united by this concept).

Thus the rectilinear motion of a body in relative space is
reduced to absolute space when I think of the body as in
itself at rest but think of the relative space as moved in the
opposite direction in absolute space (which does not fall under the senses). Representing such rectilinear motion in this
way gives exactly the same appearance.[73] By means of this
representation all possible appearances of rectilinear motions which a body might simultaneously have are reduced
to that concept of experience which unites them all together,
namely, the concept of merely relative motion and rest.

Inasmuch as circular motion can, according to the second
proposition, be given as actual motion in experience even
without reference to an external, empirically given space, it
does indeed seem to be absolute motion. For relative motion
with regard to an external space (e.g., the rotation of the
earth on its axis relative to the stars of the heavens) is an
appearance in whose stead the opposite motion of this space

---

when motion is considered mechanically (as when a body rushes toward another that is apparently at rest), even then the disjunctive form of the judgment as regards the object is to be used distributively; and so the motion must
not be attributed either to the one body or to the other, but an equal share
must be attributed to each. This distinction of alternative, disjunctive, and
distributive determination of a concept as regards contrary predicates has its
importance, but cannot be further discussed here.

[72] [See *Critique of Pure Reason*, B 670–696.]

[73] [Gives the same appearance as thinking of the body as moved in a space
that is at rest.]

(of the heavens) in the same time can be posited as fully equivalent to the former motion. But according to this second proposition, in experience the latter motion must never
561 be posited instead of the former, and hence the aforementioned rotation is not to be represented as externally relative, and thus it sounds as though this kind of motion is assumed to be absolute.

But it is well to note that here the question is about the true (actual) motion, which does not seem to be such. And hence if one might want to judge of this motion merely according to empirical relations to space, then it could be regarded as rest. In other words, the question is about the true motion, in contradistinction to illusion, but is not about the motion as absolute, in contrast to relative. And hence even though circular motion exhibits in its appearance no change of place, i.e., no phoronomic change of the relation of the moved to (empirical) space, it exhibits, nevertheless, a continuous dynamic change of the relation of matter within its space and this change is provable by experience; for instance, there is manifested as an effect of circular motion a constant diminution of the attraction by an endeavor to escape, and thereby circular motion certainly indicates its difference from illusion. One can, for instance, represent the earth as rotated about its axis in infinite empty space and can prove this motion by experience, although neither the relation of the parts of the earth among one another nor their relation to the space outside the earth is changed phoronomically, i.e., in the appearance. For nothing on the earth or in it changes its position with regard to the first space, which is empirical; with reference to the second space, which is completely empty, no external changed relation, and hence no appearance of a motion, can ever occur. However, if I represent to myself a deep hole descending to the center of the earth, and let a stone fall into this hole, but find that although at every distance from the center gravity is always directed thereto yet the falling stone continuously diverges from the vertical direction in its fall, and indeed from west to east; then I conclude that the earth is rotated on its axis from evening to morning. Or if outside I put the stone at some distance from the surface of the earth and the stone does not remain over the same point of the surface but wanders from west to east, then I shall draw the same conclusion as to the aforementioned rotation of the earth on its axis. Either perception[74] is an adequate proof of the actuality of this circular motion, but the change of the earth's relation to external space (the starry heaven) is inadequate inasmuch as this change is a mere appearance which can proceed from two actually opposed causes, and is not a cognition derivable from the ground of explication of all appearances of this change, i.e., from experience. But this motion, even though it is no change of relation to empirical space, is nevertheless no absolute motion but a continuous change of the relations of matters to one another, although it is represented in absolute space and hence is actually only relative motion and, for just this reason alone, is true motion. The fact that this circular motion is true rests upon the representation of the reciprocal continuous withdrawal of each part of the earth (outside of the earth's axis) from every other part that lies *562* at an equal distance from the center of the circle [that is perpendicular to the earth's axis] in the line of this circle's diameter that runs through both of these parts.[75] For this rotation is actual in absolute space inasmuch as by means of this circular motion the withdrawal of the parts at the distance in question, which gravity of itself alone would pull together to one body if there were indeed no dynamical

[74] [That is, the deviation of the stone falling down the hole or falling from a point above the surface of the earth.]

[75] [That is, given a point off the earth's axis of rotation, pass a plane through this point so that this plane is perpendicular to the axis. This plane and the earth's surface intersect in a circle. The "other part" Kant talks about is the point lying opposite the first point in the diameter that runs through the two points and lying at the same distance from the earth's axis (center of the circle) as the first point.]

repulsive cause (as can be seen from the example chosen by Newton in the *Mathematical Principles of Natural Philosophy,* page ten, edition of 1714[76]), is continuously restored; and hence this withdrawal is restored by means of an actual motion referred to the space enclosed within the moved matter (namely, referred to the center of this matter) but not referred to the external space.[77]

As to the case of the third proposition, in order to show the truth of the reciprocally opposed and equal motion of both bodies even without reference to empirical space, there is no need for an active dynamical influence (of gravity or of a stretched string) given through experience, though this was necessary in the case of the second proposition. Rather, there is carried with the mere dynamical possibility of such an influence insofar as this influence is a property of matter (repulsion or attraction)—this very possibility, I say, carries with itself, as regards the motion of the one matter, the equal and opposite motion of the other matter at the same time; and indeed such action and reaction stem from

[76] He there says: *Motus quidem veros corporum singulorum cognoscere et ab apparentibus actu discriminare difficillimum est: propterea, quod partes spatii illius immobilis, in quo corpora vere moventur, non incurrunt in sensus. Causa tamen non est prorsus desperata.** Hereupon he lets two spheres connected by a cord rotate about their common center of gravity in empty space and shows how the actuality of their motion together with its direction can nevertheless be found by experience. I have also tried to show this under somewhat altered circumstances with regard to the earth as moved about its axis.

[77] [That is, the actuality of the earth's rotation rests upon the tendency of the parts of the earth on opposite sides of the axis of rotation to recede from each other. The rotation is actual in absolute space inasmuch as this rotation is referred to the space within, and not to that outside of, the rotating body.]

* ["It is indeed a matter of great difficulty to discover, and effectually to distinguish, the true motions of particular bodies from the apparent; because the parts of that immovable space, in which those motions are performed, do by no means come under the observation of our senses. Yet the thing is not altogether desperate." Florian Cajori's revision of Andrew Motte's translation of 1729 (Berkeley and Los Angeles: University of California Press, 1962), Vol. I, p. 12. Kant must mean, incidentally, the edition of 1713, not 1714. The first edition appeared in 1686, the second in 1713, and the third in 1725–1726.]

mere concepts of a relative motion when this motion is re-garded as in absolute space, i.e., according to truth. There-fore, this third proposition is, like everything adequately provable from mere concepts, a law of an absolutely nec-essary countermotion.

There is, then, also no absolute motion even if a body in absolute space is thought of as moved with regard to an-other body. The motion of both is here not relative to the space surrounding them but only to the space between them, which alone determines their external relation to one an-other, when this space is regarded as absolute; and hence this motion is again only relative. Absolute motion would, then, be only that motion which belongs to a body without a relation to any other matter. Such a motion would be solely the rectilinear motion of the universe, i.e., of the sys-tem of all matter. For if outside of a matter there were still any other matter, even separated from the former by empty space, then the motion would certainly be relative. For this reason, every proof of a law of motion having as its result the fact that the contrary of this law must imply a rectilinear motion of the whole universe is an apodeictic proof of the *563* truth of this law, simply because absolute motion would follow from the contrary of this law, and such motion is utterly impossible. Of this kind is the law of antagonism in all community of matter by means of motion. For every divergence from this law would move the common center of gravity of all matter, and hence the whole universe, from its place. On the other hand, this would not happen if one were to represent the universe as rotated on its axis; there-fore, it is always possible to think of such rotation, although to assume it, as far as one can see, would be quite without any conceivable use.

The various concepts of empty space also have their reference to the various concepts of motion and moving forces. Empty space in a phoronomic respect, also termed absolute space, should properly not be called empty space.

For it is only the idea of a space in which I abstract from all particular matter (that makes it an object of experience) in order to think in such a space the material, or every empirical, space still as movable, and thereby to think of motion not merely unilaterally as an absolute predicate but always reciprocally as a merely relative one. Such space is, then, nothing at all belonging to the existence of things; but it belongs merely to the determination of concepts, and hence no empty space exists. Empty space in a dynamic respect is that which is not filled, i.e., that in which nothing else movable resists the penetration of the movable, consequently, in which no repulsive force acts. And such space may be either the empty space within the world (*vacuum mundanum*), or, if the world is represented as bounded, then the empty space outside of the world (*vacuum extramundanum*). The empty space within the world may, moreover, be represented either as dispersed (*vacuum disseminatum*, which constitutes only a part of the volume of matter) or as accumulated empty space (*vacuum coacervatum*, which separates bodies, e.g., heavenly bodies, from one another). This distinction is not essential inasmuch as it rests only on the difference of places assigned to empty space in the world; but it is nevertheless used for a distinct purpose: firstly, in order to derive the specific difference of density; secondly, to derive the possibility of a motion in the universe that is free of all external resistance. That it is not necessary to assume empty space for the first purpose has already been shown in the general observation on dynamics;[78] but that empty space is impossible can in no way, from the mere concept of such space, be proved according to the principle of contradiction. However, even if no merely logical ground for its rejection might here be found, there might nevertheless be a general physical ground for banishing it from the doctrine of nature, namely, the ground of the pos-

[78] [Cf. above, Ak. 523–525, 532–535.]

sibility of the composition of a matter in general (if such composition were only better comprehended). To this end, let the attraction which is assumed for the explication of the cohesion of matter be only apparent and not true at- *564* traction—let it be merely the action of compression by means of external matter (the ether) distributed everywhere in the universe. This external matter is itself brought to this pressure only by means of a universal and original attraction, namely, gravitation.[79] This supposition is supported by many reasons, and upon it empty space within matters would be impossible—even if not logically impossible, yet dynamically and hence physically so—because every matter would expand of itself into the empty spaces assumed to be within it (since nothing here resists its expansive force) and would keep these spaces always filled up. An empty space outside of the world would, if by "world" is understood the sum total of all principal attractive matters (the sum total of the large heavenly bodies), be impossible for the very same reasons: namely, according as the distance from these large bodies increases, the attractive force on the ether (which encloses all these bodies and, driven by this attractive force, maintains them in their density by compression) decreases in inverse proportion, and hence this ether itself would only infinitely decrease in density but would nowhere leave the space entirely empty. Nobody need be surprised that this elimination of empty space is in the meantime quite hypothetical; the assertion that there is empty space does not fare any better. Those who venture to decide this controversial question dogmatically, whether they do so affirmatively or negatively, rely ultimately on nothing but metaphysical suppositions, as may be seen in the dynamics; but it was at least necessary to show here that these people cannot at all decide the problem in question. Thirdly, concerning empty space in a mechanical respect, such is the accumulated emptiness

[79] [Cf. above, Ak. 514–515].

within the universe in order to provide the heavenly bodies with free motion. It is easily seen that the possibility or impossibility of such emptiness does not rest on metaphysical grounds but on nature's difficultly disclosed secrets as to why matter sets limits to its own force of extension. Nevertheless, if what was said in the general observation on dynamics as to the possible greater expansion to infinity of specifically different matters with the same quantity of matter (as regards its weight) is granted, then there might indeed be no necessity to assume an empty space for the sake of the free and lasting motion of the heavenly bodies, because the resistance, even in entirely filled spaces, can be thought of as being as small as one wants.

———

And so ends the metaphysical doctrine of body with the empty and therefore with the inconceivable, wherein this doctrine has the same fate as all other attempts of reason when, in going back to principles, it aspires to the first causes of things. Reason's nature is such that it can never conceive 565 anything except insofar as the latter is determined under given conditions. Consequently, inasmuch as it can neither rest with the conditioned nor make the unconditioned comprehensible, nothing remains for it, when thirst for knowledge invites it to grasp the absolute totality of all conditions, but to turn back from objects to itself in order to investigate and determine the ultimate boundary of the capacity given it, instead of investigating and determining the ultimate boundary of things.[80]

---

[80] [Cf. *Critique of Pure Reason*, B 349–398.]

The Unity
of Kant's Thought
in His Philosophy
of Corporeal Nature

INTRODUCTION

In Kant's Preface to the *Metaphysical Foundations of Natural Science,* he claims that this metaphysics of corporeal nature can be presented as a complete system "inasmuch as the object [matter] must . . . be compared with all the necessary laws of thought [and so this metaphysics] must furnish a definite number of cognitions, which can be fully exhausted."[1] The table of categories to be found in the early part of the *Critique of Pure Reason* provides the schema for the elaboration of this metaphysical system of corporeal nature.[2]

Quite obviously Kant takes his architectonic very seriously, and consequently the reader of the *Metaphysical Foundations of Natural Science* cannot understand in the fullest sense what is going on in that treatise unless he is also familiar with the "Transcendental Analytic" of the *Critique of Pure Reason.* Kant develops his system of corporeal nature in the following way. He starts in the *Critique* with the most formal act of human cognition, called by him the transcendental unity of apperception, and its various aspects, called the logical functions of judgment. He then proceeds to the pure categories of the understanding, and then to the schematized categories, and finally to the transcendental principles of

---

[1] Above, Ak. 473. References to the translation will be made to the (marginal) Akademie edition page numbers.

[2] See above, Ak. 474–476: "Under the four classes of quantity, quality, relation, and finally modality, all determinations of the universal concept of a matter in general and, therefore, everything that can be thought a priori respecting it, that can be presented in mathematical construction, or that can be given in experience as a determinate object of experience, must be capable of being brought. There is no more to do in the way of discovery or addition. . . ."

nature in general. In the *Metaphysical Foundations* he is at long last ready to consider the metaphysical principles of corporeal nature. There is a progression from what is most formal (and so least empirical) to what is less formal (and so more empirical). The *Metaphysical Foundations* is, therefore, a subsequent stage of an elaborate architectonic. The present essay is intended to show how the metaphysics of corporeal nature fits into this grand architectonic scheme, and I must accordingly spend more time talking about the *Critique* than the *Metaphysical Foundations*. I must assume, therefore, that the reader is familiar with both treatises; if he is not, then this essay will not be very enlightening.

As mentioned above, Kant takes his architectonic quite seriously (though many of his commentators do not). Unfortunately, he did not always make clear how the gears of this grand machine mesh (perhaps one reason why so many of his commentators do not take it seriously). In the following essay I shall try to make clear the workings of this architectonic, which is the very core of Kant's philosophy of corporeal nature. If my efforts are blessed with even moderate success, this essay will have some excuse for being.

Few if any philosophers have excited so much comment— both favorable and unfavorable—as has Kant. Even among those critics who profess a great admiration and respect for Kant's efforts, often many reservations are expressed. "Like all great pioneering works in philosophy the *Critique* is full of mistakes and confusions. It is a misunderstanding to think that a supreme philosopher cannot have erred badly and often: the *Critique* still has much to teach us, but it is wrong on nearly every page."[3] It is difficult to see how a man who supposedly has made so many mistakes and been the victim of so much confusion could be worthy of any respect or admiration at all. It may be, of course, that much of the con-

[3] Jonathan Bennett, *Kant's Analytic* (Cambridge: Cambridge University Press, 1966), p. viii.

fusion lies in the critic's mind; if so, then Kant is vindicated.

With regard to Kant's confusion specifically in his architectonic and the role the categories are supposed to play
in that architectonic, Schopenhauer speaks out quite boldly
when he says that the

table of categories is now supposed to be the guiding line
along which every metaphysical, and in fact every scientific,
speculation is to be conducted (*Prolegomena,* §39). In fact, it
is not only the foundation of the whole Kantian philosophy,
and the type according to which its symmetry is carried
through everywhere, as I have already shown above, but it has
also really become the Procrustean bed on to which Kant
forces every possible consideration by means of a violence
that I shall now consider somewhat more closely. . . . But in
every inquiry conducted by Kant, every quantity in time and
space, and every possible quality of things, physical, moral,
and so on, is brought under those category-titles, although
between these things and those titles of the forms of judging
and thinking there is not the least thing in common, except
the accidental and arbitrary nomenclature. We must be mindful of the high esteem due to Kant in other respects, in order
not to express our indignation at this procedure in harsh
terms. The pure physiological table of general principles of
natural science at once furnishes us with the nearest example.
What in the world has the quantity of judgements to do with
the fact that every perception has an extensive magnitude?
What has the quality of judgements to do with the fact that
every sensation has a degree? On the contrary, the former
rests on the fact that space is the form of our external perception, and the latter is nothing more than an empirical, and
moreover quite subjective, observation or perception drawn
merely from the consideration of the nature of our sense-
organs. . . . Several examples, if possible even more glaring,
are furnished by the table of the *categories of freedom* in the
Critique of Practical Reason; further by the *Critique of Judgement,* first book, which goes through the judgement of taste
according to the four titles of the categories; finally by the
Metaphysical Rudiments [Foundations] of Natural Science
which are cut out entirely in accordance with the table of
categories. Possibly the false, which is mixed up here and
there with what is true and excellent in this important work,
was mainly brought about precisely in this way. Let us see,

at the end of the first chapter [of the *Metaphysical Foundations*], how the unity, plurality, and totality of the directions of lines are supposed to correspond to the categories, so named according to the quantity of the judgements.[4]

Aware of all these rumblings, I embark on this voyage to explore the workings of Kant's architectonic not without some trepidation.

I. THE TRANSCENDENTAL UNITY OF APPERCEPTION

Kant maintains that the "synthetic unity of apperception is therefore that highest point, to which we must ascribe all employment of the understanding, even the whole of logic, and comformably therewith, transcendental philosophy. Indeed this faculty of apperception is the understanding itself."[5] He very likely took the rather high-sounding term "apperception" from Leibniz;[6] it means consciousness. Kant thus holds consciousness to be the very beginning of all speculative philosophy, just as Descartes held the *cogito* in his *Meditations*. Now, the representations contained in consciousness can be viewed in two ways, as merely the contents of our consciousness, or as referring beyond themselves to the objects which they purport to represent.

[4] *The World as Will and Representation*, trans. E. F. J. Payne (Indian Hills, Colorado: The Falcon's Wing Press, 1958), Vol. I, pp. 470–471.

[5] *Critique of Pure Reason*, trans. Norman Kemp Smith (London: Macmillan and Co., 1929, and St. Martin's Press: New York, 1964), B 134 note, p. 154. This and the following quotations from the *Critique* are printed by permission of St. Martin's Press, Macmillan and Company Limited, and The Macmillan Company of Canada.

[6] Leibniz says, "Thus it is well to make distinction between the perception, which is the inner state of the monad representing external things, and apperception, which is consciousness or the reflective knowledge of this inner state; the latter not being given to all souls, nor at all times to the same soul." "Principles of Nature and of Grace, Based on Reason," published 1714, in *Leibniz Selections*, ed. Philip P. Wiener (New York: Charles Scribner's Sons, 1951), p. 525.

According to the first way it "must be possible for the 'I think' to accompany all my representations; for otherwise something would be represented in me which could not be thought at all, and that is equivalent to saying that the representation would be impossible, or at least would be nothing to me."[7] Thus he asserts the unity of consciousness—that all my representations are bound up together as the thoughts of one mind.[8] This pure apperception is an act of spontaneity and as such is different from sensibility, which is a passive receptivity for intuitions. This means that the representation "I think" is simple and in itself entirely empty of any content. No manifold is given through the "I think"; rather, every manifold is given to the "I think" to be determined. Accordingly, we do not know our noumenal selves, as Kant claims Descartes taught. Rather, the self

> is known only through the thoughts which are its predicates, and of it, apart from them, we cannot have any concept whatsoever, but can only revolve in a perpetual circle, since any judgment upon it has always already made use of its representation. And the reason why this inconvenience is inseparably bound up with it, is that consciousness in itself is not a representation distinguishing a particular object, but a form of representation in general, that is, of representation in so far as it is to be entitled knowledge; for it is only of knowledge that I can say that I am thereby thinking something.[9]

This is to say that the self becomes aware of itself and gains cognition of itself only by bringing to self-consciousness (through an act of synthesis) the manifold of intuitions afforded by sensibility. Accordingly, the self knows itself only phenomenally.

[7] *Critique of Pure Reason,* B 131–132, pp. 152–153.

[8] Cf. *ibid.,* B 132, p. 153: "For the manifold representations, which are given in an intuition, would not be one and all *my* representations, if they did not all belong to one self-consciousness. As *my* representations (even if I am not conscious of them as such) they must conform to the condition under which alone they *can* stand together in one universal self-consciousness. . . ."

[9] *Ibid.,* B 404, pp. 331–332.

In the second place, representations refer beyond themselves to the objects which they purport to represent. Although human apperception is spontaneous, it is not creative. A creative (or intuitive) understanding would be one which could through its self-consciousness supply to itself the manifold of intuition.[10] Such an understanding would create the objects of its representations through its own self-consciousness. The human understanding does not intuit; it synthesizes the manifold which sensibility intuits. Indeed synthesizing the manifold of sensible intuition is exactly what is meant by saying that apperception is an act of spontaneity. For the moment, let us say that such synthesizing activity of the mind means that unity can be bestowed upon a manifold of perceptions by the mind's going through that manifold, taking it up, and connecting it according to a concept which serves as a rule. For example, the concept of cause and effect can serve as a rule for synthesizing a manifold, e.g., the perceptions involved in observing a stove's heating a room. I shall have much more to say about synthesis later on when the logical forms of judgment and the categories are treated.

The two preceding paragraphs have spoken of two unities. Let us call the unity treated in the first the subjective unity of consciousness, and that treated in the second the objective unity of consciousness. Actually these two unities are merely two sides of the same synthetic unity of representations. Kant states that the principle of the subjective unity of consciousness "is itself, indeed, an identical, and therefore analytic, proposition. . . ."[11] This principle merely says that all my representations are my representations. Correlatively, let us ask how it is that the consciousness of given representations can determine in a definite way the thoroughgoing unity of self-consciousness in the consciousness of my representations. The answer is that I think this or that. Only thus do I

[10] Cf. *ibid.*, B 138–139.
[11] *Ibid.*, B 135, pp. 154–155.

have a determinate thought. My thinking is differentiated by objects. And so the necessity of a relationship of my representations to objects is expressed in the "I think". The analytic principle of the subjective unity of thought "nevertheless . . . reveals the necessity of a synthesis of the manifold given in intuition, without which the thoroughgoing identity of self-consciousness cannot be thought. For through the 'I', as simple representation, nothing manifold is given; only in intuition, which is distinct from the 'I', can a manifold be given; and only through *combination* in one consciousness can it be thought."[12] And so the subjective unity of consciousness expresses an objective unity of consciousness. The "I think" synthesizes a given manifold of intuition to yield cognition of an object. For obvious reasons, Kant sometimes calls the objective unity of self-consciousness the synthetic unity of self-consciousness.

I mentioned earlier (p. 142) that the human understanding is not intuitive; it is discursive by means of concepts.[13] We do not know objects immediately; we cognize objects mediately through concepts. A concept is the consciousness of the determinate relationship of given representations to an object; and in this concept the manifold of given representations is united, e.g., the concept "horse" applies to Bucephalus.[14] Kant calls the operation by which given representations (e.g., spruce, willow, linden) are transformed into

[12] *Ibid.,* B 135, p. 155.

[13] Cf. *ibid.,* B 92–93, p. 105: "The understanding has thus far been explained merely negatively, as a non-sensible faculty of knowledge. Now since without sensibility we cannot have any intuition, understanding cannot be a faculty of intuition. But besides intuition there is no other mode of knowledge except by means of concepts. The knowledge yielded by understanding, or at least by the human understanding, must therefore be by means of concepts, and so is not intuitive, but discursive."

[14] Cf. *ibid.,* B 93, p. 105: "Whereas all intuitions, as sensible, rest on affections, concepts rest on functions. By 'function' I mean the unity of the act of bringing various representations under one common representation. Concepts are based on the spontaneity of thought, sensible intuitions on the receptivity of impressions."

a concept (e.g., tree) an analytic one; the form (universality) of a concept arises analytically; the specific unity of representations that is thought in the concept is an analytic unity.[15] And so we have not only a synthetic unity of consciousness but also an analytic unity of consciousness. The analytic unity presupposes the synthetic.

> The analytic unity of consciousness belongs to all general concepts, as such. If, for instance, I think red in general, I thereby represent to myself a property which (as a characteristic) can be found in something, or can be combined with other representations; that is, only by means of a presupposed possible synthetic unity can I represent to myself the analytic unity. A representation which is to be thought as common to *different* representations is regarded as belonging to such as have, in addition to it, also something *different*. Consequently it must previously be thought in synthetic unity with other (though, it may be, only possible) representations, before I can think in it the analytic unity of consciousness, which makes it a *conceptus communis*.[16]

In contrast to our discursive understandings we can (at least problematically) think of an intuitive understanding.

> It is, in fact, a distinctive characteristic of our understanding, that in its cognition . . . it moves from the *analytic universal* to the particular, or, in other words, from conceptions to given empirical intuitions. In this process, therefore, it determines nothing in respect of the multiplicity of the particular. . . . But now we are also able to form a notion of an understanding which, not being discursive like ours, but intuitive, moves from the *synthetic universal,* or intuition of a whole as a whole, to the particular—that is to say, from the whole to the parts.[17]

And so Kant distinguishes an analytic universal concept, which is discursive, from a thinkable synthetic universal concept, which is intuitive. The latter concept is the intuition of a whole as a whole; the necessary correlate of such a concept

---

[15] Cf. *ibid.,* B 102.

[16] *Ibid.,* B 133–134 note, p. 154.

[17] *Critique of Teleological Judgement,* trans. J. C. Meredith (Oxford: Oxford University Press, 1928), p. 63 (Ak. 407).

is not our discursive concept of an object in general (which is a simple and entirely contentless representation), but is the intuition of the totality of objects. In our discursive cognition by means of universal concepts our self-consciousness is not related to the whole of the manifold of representations (the totality of objects) collectively, but is related only to an object in general, and hence to the totality of objects merely distributively.

And so a discursive concept (*conceptus communis*) is at the same time both a universal representation and a representation of a part—it is not a universal representation insofar as it is the representation of a whole as a whole. This means that all our concepts are marks, or partial representations; and as such they are analytic grounds of cognition. To say that a concept is a partial representation involves what is meant when a concept is said to have a content; to say that it is an analytic ground of cognition involves what is meant when it is said to have a range (or sphere). Content and range are inversely proportional. The concept with the widest range is that of an object in general, i.e., gold, silver, metal, movable thing, and everything else fall under it. But it has no content, i.e., it represents no given thing. The concept of gold has a narrower range, but it has more content. Concepts are subordinated to one another according to their increasing ranges (or decreasing contents), e.g., gold, metal, movable thing, object in general. Inasmuch as all concepts are general, they only partially represent particular objects. Intuitions are particular and immediately related to individual things.[18]

We now know what the objective unity of self-consciousness is and what a concept in general (i.e., the analytic unity of consciousness) is. And we know that analysis presupposes

---

[18] Cf. *Critique of Pure Reason*, B 93, p. 105: "Since no representation, save when it is an intuition, is in immediate relation to an object, no concept is ever related to an object immediately, but to some other representation of it, be that other representation an intuition, or itself a concept."

synthesis. Concepts are made by analysis, but prior to any such analysis there must be a synthetic activity of the mind. This act of synthesis is judging. And so judgment, rather than conception, is the fundamental activity of the mind; indeed Kant regards concepts as predicates of possible judgments.[19] He explains a judgment as the "manner in which given modes of knowledge [*Erkenntnisse*] are brought to the objective unity of apperception."[20]

Such objective unity of given representations is to be contrasted with a subjective unity of representations. The former is necessary insofar as knowledge is to be acquired by means of the relation of the given representations.

> Only in this way does there arise from this relation a *judgment,* that is, a relation which is *objectively valid,* and so can be adequately distinguished from a relation of the same representations that would have only subjective validity—as when they are connected according to laws of association. In the latter case, all that I could say would be, 'If I support a body, I feel an impression of weight'; I could not say, 'It, the body, is heavy'. Thus to say 'The body is heavy' is not merely to state that the two representations have always been conjoined in my perception, however often that perception be repeated; what we are asserting is that they are combined *in the object,* no matter what the state of the subject may be.[21]

To say that a judgment is objectively valid is to say that it is true, i.e., representations are so related in a judgment that

---

[19] Cf. *ibid.*, B 94, p. 106: "Now we can reduce all acts of the understanding to judgments, and the *understanding* may therefore be represented as a *faculty of judgment.* For, as stated above, the understanding is a faculty of thought. Thought is knowledge by means of concepts. But concepts, as predicates of possible judgments, relate to some representation of a not yet determined object. Thus the concept of body means something, for instance, metal, which can be known by means of that concept. It is therefore a concept solely in virtue of its comprehending other representations, by means of which it can relate to objects. It is therefore the predicate of a possible judgment, for instance, 'every metal is a body'." Cf. also *Prolegomena,* § 22.

[20] *Ibid.*, B 141, p. 159.

[21] *Ibid.*, B 142, p. 159. Cf. *Prolegomena,* §'s 18–22.

this relation is ontologically valid and thus true of things.

One must note that the logical form of *every* judgment consists in the original synthetic unity of apperception. The content, or matter, of a judgment consists in the representations to be related to one another in the judgment. The form of the judgment consists in the way these given representations are related to one another in the objective unity of apperception. According to content a judgment may be either analytic or synthetic, depending on whether the predicate-concept is something which is already thought in the subject-concept, or the predicate-concept is indeed somehow connected with the subject-concept but not contained in it (e.g., "All bodies are extended" is analytic, while "All bodies are heavy" is synthetic). But according to logical form, even the form of an analytic judgment consists in the synthetic unity of apperception.[22] This refutes those commentators who have emphatically claimed that the form of an analytic judgment consists in the analytic unity of consciousness and the form of a synthetic judgment in the synthetic unity of consciousness. Kant *says* that the distinction between analytic and synthetic judgments is a question of the *content* of the judgments, while the *form* of both kinds of judgments consists in the synthetic unity of apperception. Indeed the "synthetic unity of apperception is therefore that highest point, to which we must ascribe all employment of the understanding, even the whole of logic, and conformably therewith, transcendental philosophy. Indeed this faculty of apperception is the understanding itself."[23]

[22] Cf. *ibid.*, B 131 note, p. 152: "Whether the representations are in themselves identical, and whether, therefore, one can be analytically thought through the other, is not a question that here arises. The *consciousness* of the one, when the manifold is under consideration, has always to be distinguished from the consciousness of the other; and it is with the synthesis of this (possible) consciousness that we are here alone concerned." Cf. also *Prolegomena*, §2, Ak. 266.

[23] *Ibid.*, B 134 note, p. 154.

II. THE LOGICAL
FORMS OF JUDGMENT

The logical form of a judgment consists in the way that the given representations are combined in the synthetic unity of apperception. What are the various ways in which the given representations are so combined? This, of course, is a question of the famous table of the logical functions of judgment and especially of that table's completeness—one of the thorniest problems in all of Kant's philosophy. It is of the utmost importance in our consideration of the architectonic, because the completeness of the table of categories depends entirely upon the completeness of the table of logical functions. Where did Kant get this table and can it lay any claim at all to completeness? Unfortunately, Kant himself gives us very little direct help in the *Critique of Pure Reason;* we shall see why at the end of this Part Two. One must search through the unpublished manuscripts on logic and metaphysics found after his death (*Der handschriftliche Nachlaβ* of the Academy edition), and through the notes taken on his lectures (which have just appeared in the Academy edition). Also, this search must be guided by a great deal of *Kantgefühl.*

In the first half of this Part Two let us consider the question of where the table comes from; in the last half, the question of the table's completeness. The answer usually given to the first question is that Kant gleaned the table empirically from the logic textbooks in use at his time.[24] This is undoubtedly

[24]Kant does say, "But in order to discover such a principle, I looked about for an act of the understanding which comprises all the rest and is differentiated only by various modifications or moments, in bringing the manifold of representation under the unity of thinking in general. I found this act of the understanding to consist in judging. Here, then, the labors

the way in which he first became aware of the separate logical forms. But the logic books he might have been famil-

of the logicians were ready at hand, though not yet quite free from defects; and with this help I was enabled to exhibit a complete table of the pure functions of the understanding, which were however undetermined in regard to any object. I finally referred these functions of judging to objects in general, or rather to the condition of determining judgments as objectively valid; and so there arose the pure concepts of the understanding, concerning which I could make certain that these, and this exact number only, constitute our whole cognition of things from pure understanding." *Prolegomena to Any Future Metaphysics,* Mahaffy-Carus translation extensively revised by James W. Ellington (Hackett Publishing Co.: Indianapolis, 1977), pp. 65–66 (Ak. 323–324). But this hardly amounts to a confession that he raked the list together haphazardly without following any a priori principle. Cf. Hegel, *Encyclopaedia of the Philosophical Sciences,* Part I, The Science of Logic, trans. William Wallace (Oxford: Oxford University Press, 1892), p. 87: "Kant, it is well known, did not put himself to much trouble in discovering the categories. 'I', the unity of self-consciousness, being quite abstract and completely indeterminate, the question arises, how are we to get at the specialized forms of the 'I', the categories? Fortunately, the common logic offers to our hand an empirical classification of the kinds of *judgment.* Now, to judge is the same thing as to *think* of a determinate object. Hence the various modes of judgment, as enumerated to our hand, provide us with the several categories of thought." Even a sympathetic critic like Wilhelm Windelband finds serious problems. Compare his "The Principles of Logic," trans. Ethel Meyer, in *Encyclopaedia of the Philosophical Sciences,* eds. William Windelband and Arnold Ruge, Vol. I (London: Macmillan and Co., 1913), p. 29: "But we arrive at the same result through a criticism of the division of judgments as they were taken over by Kant in his well-known table as the result of the dogmatic structure of Formal Logic. Since the investigations of Sigwart and Lotze, however, it can no longer pretend to be obviously true, as it did in the last century." Also *ibid.,* p. 40 note: "We must not, therefore, reproach Kant because he sought in the relation of the categories to the kinds of judgment a ground of common principles for the two parts of his Logic — the formal and the transcendental: we must hold firmly to the inner connexion between the two. The defect of the 'transcendental analytic' is only that the 'table of categories' is 'raked together' entirely historically. For the division is neither derived nor derivable from the essence of the judgment, but was taken over empirically from the scholastic Logic and trimmed up into a symmetrical trichotomy." Cf. also Josiah Royce, *Lectures on Modern Idealism* (New Haven: Yale University Press, 1919), p. 47 ". . . [Kant] obtained his table of the categories of the understanding in a somewhat more superficial way, viz., from a consideration of the traditional classification of judgments that the textbooks of formal logic contained. In any case, his list of the forms essential to our intelligence looks rather empirical. He gives us no reason why just these forms and no others *must* result from the very nature of a self such as ours. No one principle seems to define the whole list. His forms appear in his account without any statement of their genesis and with no acceptable discussion of the reasons for holding his list to be exhaustive."

iar with present grounds for various possible lists, and the question is why he chose the list he did rather than some other one. A person with nothing more than a little bit of *Kantgefühl* would doubtless hazard the guess that Kant's reasons for choosing his list are a priori rather than a posteriori.

I thought about this problem for many years, and reading widely in the commentaries—Vaihinger, Smith, de Vleeschauwer, Paton, et alia—gained no satisfactory answers. Finally Klaus Reich's *Die Vollständigkeit der kantischen Urteilstafel* (*The Completeness of the Kantian Table of Judgments,* Berlin: Richard Schoetz, 1932) came to my attention. It was like walking into a brightly lighted room, if I may say of this what Goethe is reputed to have said about the *Critique of Pure Reason.* All the pieces of the puzzle fell into place. Through Reich's help I have come as close as I shall very likely ever be to the very truth itself regarding this thorny problem in Kant's philosophy. In this Part Two, therefore, I shall draw freely on Reich's work, and can obviously make no claim to originality here. But the truth should be the property of all men. In what ensues I have made no effort to follow the exact order of Reich's arguments, but have drawn on his book freely as suits my purposes at this stage of our exploration of Kant's architectonic.

Where does the list come from? Its origins are a priori inasmuch as it can be shown to follow analytically from the above-mentioned explication of a judgment in general (p. 146). A judgment relates representations in such a way that the relation is ontologically valid and, accordingly, true of things. This characteristic of a judgment is its modality. We relate representations in such a way that this relationship is thought of as being objectively valid.[25] However, it will be

[25] Cf. *Critique of Pure Reason,* B 99–100, p. 109: "The *modality* of judgments is a quite peculiar function. Its distinguishing characteristic is that it contributes nothing to the content of the judgment . . . but concerns only the value of the copula in relation to thought in general."

more convenient in enumerating the various logical functions of thought to begin with the categorical form of relation. We shall see later (p. 165) that the modal forms and the relational ones are intertwined, and so we may exercise an option here. Mindful of the fact that modality is the very first characteristic of our explication of a judgment in general, let us nevertheless first try to see how the categorical form is contained in our explication. The convenience in so beginning will become apparent as the various functions issue forth from our explication.

Concepts are the given materials that are brought together in the objective unity of apperception.[26] Our explication says that given concepts are united in a judgment in such a way that they stand in relation to original pure apperception and its necessary unity. This means that the given concepts must be so related to one another that they represent an object. Kant calls this the *relation* of a judgment.

We saw earlier (p. 145) that concepts taken in themselves have an analytic relationship to one another. This is their subordination, e.g., gold, metal, body, object in general. Every judgment involves this relationship simply because concepts are the matter of judgments. But this is not the relationship according to which concepts are combined in the transcendental unity of apperception to yield knowledge of objects. A concept taken in itself is entirely general; the concept "tree" represents what is common to an oak, beech, linden, etc.—namely, an object having roots, trunk, branches, leaves—and it is just for this very reason that "tree" can represent not only oak, beech, linden but larch, birch, spruce, etc. as well. The application of a concept has to be determined in such a way as to give us definite knowledge. By itself a concept swims in the vast ocean of possibility. How can it be fixed in order to yield some actual cognition of objects?

---

[26] Cf. *ibid.*, B 322, p. 280: "In any judgment we can call the given concepts logical matter (i.e., matter for the judgment), and their relation (by means of the copula) the form of the judgment."

We have just seen in the preceding paragraph that concepts are the only materials we have for the act of judging. Therefore, in order for a judgment to be made, concepts must be subordinated in such a way that they can be thought of as belonging together so as to represent an object. As far as the analytic subordination of concepts is concerned, the only requirement is that the range of one concept be contained in the range of another—i.e., gold, metal; but not metal, gold. The synthetic requirements for objective knowledge presuppose this analytic subordination, to be sure; but there is a further demand that the concepts be subordinated in such a way as to give cognition of an object (or objects). In other words, one concept must be thought of as the condition of the application of another in order that we may acquire objective knowledge, e.g., all oaks are trees (the application of "tree" is conditioned by "oak"). The concept serving as the condition has the function of the subject, while the other has the function of the predicate—i.e., S is P. Such a synthesis of two given concepts is called the function of the *categorical* judgment.

Let us now consider briefly how this account of the categorical judgment meets the restriction of pure general logic that only the form of knowledge be treated and not the content.[27] The formal unity of a judgment in general is the objective unity of consciousness. Since concepts of themselves do not provide us with knowledge of things, their objective employment is possible only on the supposition that certain given concepts are to be related in the objective unity of consciousness. What is the condition for the objective employment of concepts? A concept taken in itself expresses nothing more than the analytic unity in the consciousness of my representations. A concept so taken is completely

[27] Cf. *ibid.*, B 79, p. 95: "General logic . . . abstracts from all content of knowledge . . . and considers only the logical form in the relation of any knowledge to other knowledge; that is, it treats of the form of thought in general."

indeterminate as regards its objective reference. Accordingly, the analytic unity of consciousness expressed by the form of a concept (see pp. 143–144, above) does not have objective validity. What imparts this objective validity to a concept? It is the presence of another concept that specifies a *condition* for the former concept's application, as a predicate to a subject or the application of a rule to what is subsumed under it. We have come to this notion of the condition of a judgment *analytically* by considering nothing but the form of a judgment in general (its objective validity) and the form of a concept in general (which does not by itself have objective validity). If a concept is to function in such a way as to make a judgment possible, then it must acquire objective validity. Such validity is acquired when a condition for its application is supplied; this purely formal requirement therefore properly belongs to pure general logic since it borrows nothing from the matter (or content) of thought. And so the function of the categorical judgment is already present in the form of a judgment in general.

Two given concepts cannot be related so as to have objective validity by any function of judgment other than the categorical. But now after gaining the categorical function of judgment, we have not only concepts but also categorical judgments as possible matter for other functions of judgment. Can two categorical judgments be related in apperception in such a way as to give us further objective knowledge? We can at least have many truths (objectively valid categorical judgments), for such judgments can be conjoined (e.g., "There is a perfect justice and the obstinately wicked are punished"); but as far as the objective unity of consciousness is concerned, the conjunction is merely additive (i.e., one can just as easily say, "The obstinately wicked are punished and there is a perfect justice"). Such a conjunction involves no new form of knowledge and so is not another form of judgment. Similarly, a disjunction of categorical judgments involves no new form of knowledge unless the disjunction is such that its components determine the totality of some knowledge, as we shall see later (pp. 156–158). Now, the form of a judgment in general involves a *thorough-going* objective unity of apperception in the consciousness of my representations.[28] If we have nothing but categorical judgments, then it will be impossible for us to have truth taken formally as the reference of given thoughts (either concepts or judgments) to the thoroughgoing unity of objective consciousness. Since this "principle of apperception is the highest principle in the whole sphere of human knowledge,"[29] we may therefore conclude that distinct categorical judgments must admit of combination in an objective unity of their consciousness.

How are such judgments to be combined? Very much like the way in which two concepts (the one serving as the subject and the other as the predicate) were related to one another through the categorical form of thought so as to constitute truth. In the present case one judgment may be the condition for using the other one in such a way as to attain possible truth, i.e., the one may be the condition of the actual reference of the other to an objective situation. In such a relationship of categorical propositions, it makes a great deal of difference whether I say, "If there is a perfect justice, then the obstinately wicked are punished", or say, "If the obstinately wicked are punished, then there is a perfect justice". When our two categorical judgments are so combined in the objective unity of consciousness, they serve as the mat-

---

[28] Cf. *ibid.*, B 133–135, pp. 153–155: "This thoroughgoing identity of the apperception of a manifold which is given in intuition contains a synthesis of representations, and is possible only through the consciousness of this synthesis. . . . This principle of the necessary unity of apperception . . . reveals the necessity of a synthesis of the manifold given in intuition, without which the thoroughgoing identity of self-consciousness cannot be thought. For through the 'I', as simple representation, nothing manifold is given; only in intuition, which is distinct from the 'I', can a manifold be given; and only through *combination* in one consciousness can it be thought."

[29] *Ibid.*, B 135, p. 154.

ter for a new form of judgment. Since logic abstracts from the content of knowledge and considers only the form of thought, we must abstract from the fact that the constituent concepts of the two judgments have already been referred to apperception through the categorical function of thought. This means that the truth of both categorical judgments is here left undecided except as it is conditioned by their connection in the new judgment.[30] This connection is the function of the *hypothetical* judgment, which is expressed by "if ..., then ...". The one categorical judgment serving as the condition has the function of the antecedent, and the other has the function of the consequence.

We have just seen that in the case of the hypothetical judgment the relationship of concepts thought in the constituent categorical judgments is left undetermined as regards objective validity (truth) because of the requirements of formal logic. The thought of leaving objective validity undetermined is necessary (through the function of the categorical judgment) for the form of truth in general. Initially we discerned the objective validity of a relationship of concepts in the categorical judgment. The form of a judgment in general then required a relationship no longer merely of concepts but of judgments. This function of the hypothetical judgment did make objective knowledge possible, i.e., the logical sequence was true. But this fact implies that it must be possible to leave the truth of the constituent categorical judgments undetermined. A (categorical) judgment thought in this form is called a *problematic* judgment.

At first glance the notion of a problematic judgment might strike one as being a bit strange. From the explication of a

---

[30] Cf. *ibid.*, B 98–99, p. 109: "The hypothetical proposition, 'If there is a perfect justice, the obstinately wicked are punished', really contains the relation of two propositions, namely, 'There is a perfect justice', and 'The obstinately wicked are punished'. Whether both these propositions are in themselves true, here remains undetermined. It is only the logical sequence which is thought by this judgment."

judgment in general as a synthesis of representations in the transcendental unity of apperception, it might seem that any judgment ought to be an objectively valid synthesis of representations. But through the problematic function of thought nothing is "judged"; by the very form of this function the truth of a connection of representations is left undetermined. The connection between subject and predicate as expressed in a problematic categorical judgment is only subjectively valid. But we have just seen from our consideration of the hypothetical judgment that the problematic function of thought does necessarily belong to the form of a judgment in general. And so we must conclude that such problematic validity of a connection of subject and predicate must have a determinate relationship to the objective validity of this connection in the form of judging in general—i.e., there must be some function of thought that determines the truth or falsity of a problematic judgment. We shall see next what this function is.

By itself the problematic function of thought leaves truth undecided. We have seen above that the hypothetical function of thought can bestow objective validity on the connection of two such judgments.[31] But this function says nothing about the truth or falsity of the single problematic judgments (serving as the logical matter for the hypothetical one) when they are considered in themselves; this function tells us only that the antecedent can be false without the consequence having to be so, and that the consequence can be true without the antecedent having to be so. There must be a special function of thought that determines the objective validity of

---

[31] Cf. *ibid.*, B 100, p. 110: "Thus the two judgments, the relation of which constitutes the hypothetical judgment (*antecedens et consequens*) . . . are one and all problematic only. In the above example ['If there is a perfect justice, the obstinately wicked are punished'], the proposition, 'There is a perfect justice', is not stated assertorically, but is thought only as an optional judgment, which it is possible to assume; it is only the logical sequence which is assertoric. Such judgments may therefore be obviously false, and yet, taken problematically, may be conditions of the knowledge of truth."

the single problematic judgment inasmuch as arbitrary problematic judgments do not of themselves determine anything
more than their subjective validity. This function cannot be
something lying outside of the given problematic judgments;
for it must be what first refers the given problematic judgments as such to the objective unity of apperception, since
a judgment in general is explained as the way in which given
representations (concepts) or thoughts (judgments) are
brought to the objective unity of consciousness. This is to
say that the required function must follow analytically from
the form of a judgment in general. And so the given problematic judgments must themselves constitute this function.
In their totality (in community) must they determine the
truth. Since no part of this totality is given in itself as true,
they must reciprocally determine one another in such a way
that the truth is thereby determined.

The *disjunctive* function of thought (expressed by means
of the "either . . . or") conjoins its constituent problematic
judgments in just such a reciprocally determinant objectively
valid relationship.[32] The sense of the disjunction is that one
of the parts is true without a definite one of the parts being
thought as true, as will be shown in detail on pp. 160–162, below. The parts determining the totality of the knowledge are
what is conditioned in this relationship; the totality (whole)
determined through the parts is the condition.[33] The disjunc-

---

[32] Cf. *ibid.*, B 100–101, p. 110: "[The] judgments the reciprocal relation of
which forms the disjunctive judgment (members of the division), are one
and all problematic only. . . . Thus the judgment, 'The world exists by blind
chance [or through inner necessity, or through an external cause]', has in the
disjunctive judgment only problematic meaning, namely, as a proposition that
may for a moment be assumed."

[33] Cf. *ibid.*, B 99, p. 109: "Finally, the disjunctive judgment contains a
relation of two or more propositions to each other, a relation not, however,
of logical sequence [as in the hypothetical judgment], but of logical opposition, in so far as the sphere of the one excludes the sphere of the other, and
yet at the same time of community, in so far as the propositions taken together occupy the whole sphere of the knowledge in question. The disjunctive
judgment expresses, therefore, a relation of the parts of the sphere of such

tion consists in the unity of the conditioned and its condition as regards the use of merely problematically given judgments as such so as to attain objective knowledge. We now have the three *relational* moments of thought: subject-predicate, antecedent-consequence, and whole-parts.

As Kant says in the last footnote, the constituent problematic judgments are thought of in such a way that, since the sphere of each part is a complement of the sphere of the others, they determine the true knowledge when they are taken together. But this means that this connection of merely problematic judgments determines some one of them as being objectively valid (true). In Kant's example, "The world exists through blind chance, or through inner necessity, or through an external cause", one of the constituent judgments must be true, though the disjunction certainly does not tell us which one.[34] Since we have derived the form of the disjunctive judgment analytically from the form of judging in general, it is quite clear that we have gained another function of thought—namely, the *necessity* of a judgment. In the disjunctive function one of the members thereby related must be true; logical necessity is, then, the objective

---

knowledge, since the sphere of each part is a complement of the sphere of the others, yielding together the sum-total of the divided knowledge. Take, for instance, the judgment, 'The world exists through blind chance, or through inner necessity, or through an external cause'. Each of these propositions occupies a part of the sphere of the possible knowledge concerning the existence of a world in general; all of them together occupy the whole sphere. To take the knowledge out of one of these spheres means placing it in one of the other spheres, and to place it in one sphere means taking it out of the others. There is, therefore, in a disjunctive judgment a certain community of the known constituents, such that they mutually exclude each other, and yet thereby determine *in their totality* the true knowledge. For, when taken together, they constitute the whole content of one given knowledge."

[34] Cf. *ibid.*, B 100–101, p. 110: "Thus the judgment, 'The world exists by blind chance', has in the disjunctive judgment only problematic meaning, namely, as a proposition that may for a moment be assumed. At the same time, like the indication of a false road among the number of all those roads that can be taken, it aids in the discovery of the true proposition."

validity which is assumed with the merely problematic validity under given conditions.

Necessary validity, actual validity, and problematic validity comprise the *modal* moments of thought. "The *modality* of judgments is a quite peculiar function. Its distinguishing characteristic is that it contributes nothing to the content of the judgment . . . but concerns only the value of the copula in relation to thought in general."[35] Through the *assertoric* function an objectively valid relationship of thoughts is judged to be actually existent.

We have gained these relational and modal functions of thought by analyzing the form of a judgment in general (the thoroughgoing objective unity of apperception in the consciousness of one's representations). This procedure is in keeping with the nature of pure general logic. "For since general logic abstracts from all content of knowledge, the sole task that remains to it is to give an analytical exposition of the form of knowledge [as expressed] in concepts, in judgments, and in inferences, and so to obtain formal rules for all employment of understanding."[36] These various logical forms of judgment are rules for combining representations in the objective unity of consciousness. We were able to distinguish them only insofar as we could see how they were associated with one another. Quite obviously the modal functions and the relational ones are intertwined (see p. 165, below).

Are there any more distinctions to be gained from our explication of a judgment in general? As far as relation and modality are concerned our functions are complete, for reasons which we shall consider later (see pp. 167–170). Of course various combinations of the modal and relational functions can be made, e.g., assertoric categorical, apodeictic

[35] *Ibid.*, B 99–100, p. 109.
[36] *Ibid.*, B 171–172, p. 177.

hypothetical, etc. In looking for other original functions, we must return to the general form of judging. We have not yet considered one of this form's necessary aspects referred to by Kant when he claims that the logical functions of judgment are the clue to the discovery of the categories of the understanding: "The same understanding, through the same operations by which in concepts, by means of analytical unity, it produced the logical form of a judgment. . . ."[37] We briefly touched on the matter of judgments when we considered the categorical function of thought (see p. 151). We must now consider this logical matter, i.e., the concepts contained in a judgment insofar as they are concepts in general (representations to which the analytic unity of consciousness belongs). In so doing we must consider how it is that the unity of a judgment characterized by modality and relation determines the internal form of the logical matter of such a judgment.

Let us consider the disjunctive judgment characterized by the modal function of necessity. It is obvious from our discussion of the disjunctive judgment (pp. 156–158) that since the given problematic judgments which function as the parts of the disjunctive one are all categorical, the problematic ones all have the same subject. Now, let us ask how it happens that "in concepts by means of analytical unity"[38] problematic judgments all having the same subject reciprocally determine one another in such a way that a true judgment necessarily results. We have seen (p. 145) that the analytic unity in the relationship of given concepts consists in the determination of their subordination relationship to one another according to their range (sphere) and content. Since the disjunction has to be a reciprocal determination of problematic judgments, the concepts P, P', P'', etc. as predicates of the same subject S cannot be subordinated to one another

[37] Ibid., B 105, p. 112.

[38] Ibid., B 105, p. 112. See the preceding paragraph.

according to their range. If they could be, then by means of
the truth or falsity of one predicate-concept of S we could
by derivation determine forthwith the truth or falsity of its
other predicate-concepts; in this case the determination
would not be reciprocal but unilateral.[39] Since the predicates
are related coordinately (rather than serially), their relationship cannot be one of agreement (compatibility). In the disjunctive judgment the relationship is clearly one of the disagreement (opposition) of the predicate-concepts; if one of
them can be asserted of the subject-concept, then the others
taken together necessarily cannot be so asserted because
they constitute the opposite of the one that can. This distinction is called the *quality* of a judgment; *affirmation* or *negation* are functions of a judgment in general. Since this qualitative distinction was won analytically from the form of the
disjunctive judgment, it belongs to the objective unity of
consciousness.

Now, let us consider how in the disjunctive judgment the
community of given representations expresses itself through
the relationship of opposition (one of the qualitative functions) "in concepts by means of analytical unity". In the
disjunctive judgment a relationship of the parts of the sphere
of the subject-concept is thought of in such a way that the
sphere of each part is a complement of the sphere of the
other parts, while together the spheres of each part constitute
the whole sphere of the proper knowledge of the subject (see
Kant's remarks above, note 33). This means that in the disjunctive judgment one thinks of a relationship between the
whole sphere of a concept and the parts of that sphere. In

[39] Cf. *ibid.*, B 112, p. 117: ". . . we must observe that in all disjunctive judgments the sphere (that is, the multiplicity which is contained in any one judgment) is represented as a whole divided into parts (the subordinate concepts),
and that since no one of them can be contained under any other, they are
thought as co-ordinated with, not subordinated to, each other, and so as
determining each other, not in one direction only, as in a series, but reciprocally, as in an aggregate—if one member of the division is posited, all the
rest are excluded, and conversely."

Kant's example in the just mentioned note 33, he talks on the one hand about the parts "of the sphere of the possible knowledge concerning the existence of a world in general" and on the other hand about the whole sphere of this possible knowledge, i.e., on the one hand about the relationship of the concepts "blind chance", "inner necessity", and (external) necessity by reference to "an external cause" and on the other hand about the modality of existence in general insofar as such modality touches the subject, namely, the actuality of a world in general. The disjunctive relationship of the parts of the sphere of the subject and the whole sphere of the subject is thought as being actually in the logical matter, i.e., "in concepts by means of analytical unity". This disjunctive relationship is the form in which the relationship between the parts of the sphere of a concept and the whole sphere of that concept is thought as referred to the objective unity of apperception. This means that the forms of the *universal* and *particular* judgments are derived from the form of the disjunctive judgment. In the universal judgment the sphere of the subject is entirely included within the sphere of the predicate, while in the particular judgment a part of the sphere of the subject is included in the sphere of the predicate; these are the functions of the *quantity* of a judgment. (To relate a predicate to a subject in a restricted sphere presupposes negation. Therefore quality had to be treated before quantity.)

The various logical forms of thought have now been gained by analyzing the form of a judgment in general. The question as to where the logical functions come from (see pp. 148, 150) has now been answered.

One of the main concerns of general logic is to analyze the synthetic unity of consciousness into its various logical functions of judging. In the preceding sketch[40] these logical

---

[40] The general outlines of this sketch were suggested by K. Reich, pp. 46–55. (See p. 150, above.)

functions have been presented in an order starting first with the interconnections of the relational and modal ones and then proceeding to the qualitative and quantitative ones. According to Kant, "since general logic abstracts from all content of knowledge, the sole task that remains to it is to give an analytical exposition of the form of knowledge [as expressed] in concepts, in judgments, and in inferences, and so to obtain formal rules for all employment of understanding."[41] In the "Paralogisms of Pure Reason" he states that the analytical exposition (as far as the functions of judgment are concerned) proceeds in the order, modality, relation, quality, quantity.[42] Yet in the famous table of the logical functions of judgment given in the *Critique of Pure Reason*, B 95, he proceeds from quantity, to quality, to relation, to modality. Why so? At this point in the *Critique* the table of the logical forms of judgment serves as the clue for discovering the table of the pure categories of the understanding. And the *Critique* proceeds synthetically rather than analytically (progressively from condition to conditioned rather than regressively from conditioned to condition).[43] Accordingly, in several places in

[41] *Critique of Pure Reason*, B 171–172, p. 177.

[42] "If, on the other hand, we should proceed *analytically*, starting from the proposition 'I think', as a proposition that already in itself includes an existence as given, and therefore modality, and analysing it in order to ascertain its content, and so to discover whether and how this 'I' determines its existence in space or time solely through that content, then the propositions of the rational doctrine of the soul would not begin with the concept of a thinking being in general, but with a reality, and we should infer from the manner in which this reality is thought, after everything empirical in it has been removed, what it is that belongs to a thinking being in general. This is shown in the following table: 1. *I think* [modality], 2. *as subject* [relation], 3. *as simple subject* [quality], 4. *as identical subject in every state of my thought* [quantity]." *Ibid.*, B 418–419, pp. 375–376.

[43] Cf. "That work being completed, I offer here such a plan which is sketched out after an analytical method, while the *Critique* itself had to be executed in the synthetical style, in order that the science may present all its articulations, as the structure of a peculiar cognitive faculty, in their natural combination." *Prolegomena to Any Future Metaphysics*, Mahaffy-Carus translation extensively revised by James W. Ellington (Hackett Publishing Co.: Indianapolis, 1977), p. 8 (Ak. 263).

the *Critique* he rearranges and modifies the usual orders of general logic to suit the purposes of transcendental logic.[44] In the latter, quantity, quality, relation, modality are the headings of the thought of an object in general in the synthetic order. It is clear from the mere concepts that, for example, the concept of the substance-accident relationship (relation) presupposes the concept of the real (quality), and further that the thought of the existence of an object (modality) presupposes a concept of what the object is, this being specified by means of the three preceding heads, quantity, quality, relation.

On the other hand, in general logic the doctrine of judgment must dissect the operation of judging into its various functions. In the preceding sketch there was an implicit claim that the analytic order (belonging as it does to the very nature of formal logic) must be followed in ordering the various functions of thought in judgment as regards their connections with one another. This means that from something determinate laid down as a basis, something else de-

---

[44] In the preceding sketch of the logical functions of judgment when quality and quantity were treated, no mention was made of the infinite and singular functions, though these appear in the table given in the *Critique* at B 95. But compare the following: "If, therefore, we estimate a singular judgment (*judicium singulare*), not only according to its own inner validity, but as knowledge in general, according to its quantity in comparison with other knowledge, it is certainly different from general judgments (*judicia communia*), and in a complete table of the moments of thought in general deserves a separate place—though not, indeed, in a logic limited to the use of judgments in reference to each other. . . . In like manner *infinite judgments* must, in transcendental logic, be distinguished from those that are *affirmative*, although in general logic they are rightly classed with them, and do not constitute a separate member of the division. General logic abstracts from all content of the predicate (even though it be negative); it enquires only whether the predicate be ascribed to the subject or opposed to it. But transcendental logic also considers what may be the worth or content of a logical affirmation that is thus made by means of a merely negative predicate, and what is thereby achieved in the way of addition to our total knowledge." *Critique of Pure Reason*, B 96–97, pp. 107–108. More will be said (pp. 171–172) about infinite and singular judgments when we come to consider the completeness of the table of logical functions.

terminate can be gained analytically. This is exactly the procedure we followed in starting first with the general form of a judgment, whereby given concepts are so united that they are related to original pure apperception and its necessary unity, and from this form deriving the various functions in an analytic order from one another.

Can this list lay any claim to being complete? This, of course, is the second question to be answered in this Part Two (see p. 148).[45] That there are only these four heads (modality, relation, quality, quantity) follows from the explication of a judgment in general. Let us first note that there is a division between modality and relation on the one hand, and quality and quantity on the other.[46] We have seen earlier (p. 146) that the logical form of *every* judgment consists in the original synthetic unity of apperception. This means that representations are so united in a judgment that this judgment is objectively valid, i.e., true. This characteristic of a judgment, which precedes all other characteristics, refers to modality. "The *modality* of judgments is a quite peculiar function. Its distinguishing characteristic is that it contributes

---

[45] In answering this question I shall follow fairly closely the solution given by Reich in pp. 88–95 of his book. However, much of the answer in what follows was worked out by me before my discovery of Reich's book. Warner Wick once suggested that I use Kant's concepts of reflection, which I did in my own work on the problem. Reich also uses the concepts of reflection; his solution is somewhat neater than the one I succeeded in gaining.

[46] In speaking of the categories Kant remarks that "while it [table of categories] contains four classes of the concepts of understanding, it may . . . be divided into two groups; those in the first group [quantity, quality] being concerned with objects of intuition, pure as well as empirical, those in the second group [relation, modality] with the existence of these objects, in their relation either to each other or to the understanding. The categories in the first group I would entitle the *mathematical*, those in the second group the *dynamical*. The former have no correlates; these are to be met with only in the second group. This distinction must have some ground in the nature of the understanding." *Critique of Pure Reason*, B 110, p. 116. This same division must hold for the logical forms of judgment since the categories "are concepts of an object in general, by means of which the intuition of an object is regarded as determined in respect of one of the logical functions of judgment", B 128, p. 128.

nothing to the content of the judgment . . . but concerns only the value of the copula in relation to thought in general."[47] And so relation presupposes modality—we relate representations in such a way that this relationship is thought as objectively valid. Accordingly, a relationship of representations is rendered necessary by means of modality's original moment of objective validity. Relation leads to quality and quantity by means of the form of the disjunctive judgment. Can there be any more heads? The division just noted between the heads gives us the answer. Modality and relation belong fundamentally together. Since a judgment is an objectively valid (modality) relationship (relation) of concepts by means of the analytic unity of consciousness, quality and quantity follow. We have seen (p. 145) that a concept is by its very form a partial representation and as such is an analytic ground of knowledge. When modality and relation are considered with reference to concepts insofar as they are analytic grounds of knowledge, then the quality and quantity of a judgment are determined. The explication of a judgment is now complete—a judgment is an objectively valid (modality) relationship (relation) of concepts, which are partial representations (resulting in quality) and are therefore analytic grounds of knowledge (resulting in quantity). This is to say that any act of knowing involves at the very minimum (in the case of the categorical function) a combination—*relation*— of representations (concepts)—these through their analytic unity, or subordination, involving *quality* and *quantity*—in the transcendental unity of apperception. These immediate judgments of the understanding called categorical can be combined in apperception—*relation*—through the hypothetical and disjunctive functions to yield more complex immediate judgments. (These immediate judgments of understanding are to be distinguished from the mediate judgments of reason, or syllogisms.) Further, such immediate judgments

[47] *Ibid.*, B 99–100, p. 109.

have a special relationship to the mind that holds them—
modality. There are no other heads possible. The foregoing
explication of a general immediate judgment of understanding characterizes the primordial act of cognition—the transcendental unity of apperception.

Are the moments under the four heads complete? Kant
provides the principle for answering this question in the following terse statement:

> There are therefore three logical functions [elementary and
> not derivative] under a certain head, and hence three cate-
> gories also: two of the functions manifest the unity of con-
> sciousness as regards two opposites, but the third function
> mutually connects the consciousness again. No more kinds of
> the unity of consciousness can be thought. For there is (a) one
> consciousness which combines a manifold, (b) another con-
> sciousness which combines in an opposite way, and so (c) is
> the combination of (a) and (b).[48]

[48] *Reflections on Metaphysics,* No. 5854, to be found in Vol. XVIII, p. 370 of
the Akademie edition. Erich Adickes dates it in the 1780's. Cf. *Critique of
Aesthetic Judgement,* trans. J. C. Meredith (Oxford: Oxford University Press,
1911), p. 39 note (Ak. 197): "It has been thought somewhat suspicious that
my divisions in pure philosophy should almost always come out threefold.
But it is due to the nature of the case. If a division is to be *a priori* it must
be either analytic, according to the law of contradiction—and then it is always
twofold (quodlibet ens est aut A aut non A)—or else it is *synthetic.* If it is
to be derived in the latter case from *a priori* concepts (not, as in mathematics,
from the *a priori* intuition corresponding to the concept,) then, to meet the
requirements of synthetic unity in general, namely (1) a condition, (2) a conditioned, (3) the concept arising from the union of the conditioned with its
condition, the division must of necessity be trichotomous." Also, *Critique of
Pure Reason,* B 110–111, pp. 116–117: "Secondly, in view of the fact that
all *a priori* division of concepts must be by dichotomy, it is significant that
in each class the number of the categories is always the same, namely,
three. Further, it may be observed that the third category in each class always
arises from the combination of the second category with the first. Thus
allness or *totality* is just plurality considered as unity; *limitation* is simply
reality combined with negation; *community* is the causality of substances
reciprocally determining one another; lastly, *necessity* is just the existence
which is given through possibility itself. It must not be supposed, however,
that the third category is therefore merely a derivative, and not a primary,
concept of the pure understanding. For the combination of the first and second
concepts, in order that the third may be produced, requires a special act of
the understanding, which is not identical with that which is exercised in the

How does this principle apply to the completeness of the functions of modality? In what way are the forms of the problematic and the assertoric judgments opposed to one another? In the *Critique of Pure Reason*, B 100–101 (pp. 109–110), Kant claims that "problematic judgments are those in which affirmation or negation is taken as merely possible (optional)." The problematic judgment "is thought only as an optional judgment, which it is possible to assume. . . . The problematic proposition is therefore that which expresses only logical (which is not objective) possibility—a free choice of admitting such a proposition, and a purely optional admission of it into the understanding." In the note at B 101 (p. 110) he says, "Just as if thought were in the problematic a function of the understanding [the faculty of concepts]" and not yet a function of the faculty of judgment [*Urteilskraft*]. We have seen earlier (p. 151) that concepts are the matter of a judgment. From what Kant has just said in the note at B 101, it is clear that problematic validity provides nothing more than "matter" for judging. On the other hand, assertoric (objective) validity involves the logical "form" of a judgment in general—i.e., the assertoric judgment refers the concepts contained in it to the transcendental unity of apperception. When the assertoric validity is determined by the conditions given through the merely problematic validity, apodeictic validity results; this is to say that the apodeictic combines the other two.

Under relation how are the forms of the categorical and hypothetical judgments opposed to one another? Through the former we think an "internal" relationship of concepts, while in the latter an "external" relationship of judgments. In

---

case of the first and the second. Thus the concept of a *number* (which belongs to the category of totality) is not always possible simply upon the presence of concepts of plurality and unity (for instance, in the representation of the infinite); nor can I, by simply combining the concept of a cause and that of a substance, at once have understanding of *influence,* that is, how a substance can be the cause of something in another substance. Obviously in these cases, a separate act of the understanding is demanded; and similarly in the others."

a categorical judgment we think of the predicate-concept as itself belonging to the subject-concept. We know that the subject serves as the condition for referring the predicate to the transcendental unity of apperception (see p. 152). The predicate is internally connected with the subject for the very reason that the subject does have this function of referring the predicate to truth. The relationship between antecedent and consequence is external. We have already seen (p. 155) that the truth of both categorical judgments making up the hypothetical one must be left undetermined, and their truth must be thought of as founded on their reference to possible truth through their connection in the hypothetical one. The hypothetical function of thought externally relates (the antecedent can be false without the consequence having to be so, and the consequence can be true without the antecedent having to be so) the two categorical judgments in such a way that they together constitute one objectively valid thought. The disjunctive judgment combines the internal and the external as follows. The constituent, single problematic judgments are externally related to one another: if S is P, then S is not one of the P', P'', etc.; and if S is not P, then S is one of the P', P'', etc. But at the same time this (external) relationship of problematic judgments determines the true knowledge of S; this is to say that the disjunction itself belongs internally to the objectively valid cognition of S.

In order to prove the completeness of the functions under modality and relation, we have used the concepts of reflection called matter-form and internal-external. But we have not used these concepts to discover the functions. We take the functions as already given through our earlier derivation of them (pp. 150–162); we now apply the concepts of reflection to them in order to prove their completeness.[49] In this way

---

[49] Cf. *Critique of Pure Reason*, B 317, p. 277: "Now the relations in which concepts in a state of mind can stand to one another are those of *identity* and *difference* [quantity], of *agreement* and *opposition* [quality], of the *inner* and the *outer* [relation], and finally of the *determinable* and the *determination* (matter and form) [modality]."

we heed the injunction laid down by Kant in "The Amphiboly of the Concepts of Reflection"[50] as to the misuse of these concepts. We have used the concepts of reflection merely to learn which two functions under a head are opposites in the sense that they synthesize representations in opposite ways.

What happens when the qualitative functions and the quantitative ones are compared according to those concepts of reflection called agreement-opposition and identity-difference?[51] In an affirmative judgment, what is thought in the predicate-concept is judged as being in agreement with what is thought in the subject-concept, while in a negative one, as being in opposition. In a universal judgment, what falls under the subject-concept is judged as being identical in reference to the predicate-concept, while in a particular one, as being different. But even though the negative judgment involves an opposition of concepts, this is not to say that the opposition is an analytic opposition of the concepts as such; nor is the identity thought in the universal judgment an analytic identity of the concepts. The *form* of both judgments consists in the *synthetic* unity of apperception; according to the *content* (or matter) of the judgments there is an *analytic* opposition of concepts in the negative judgment and an *analytic* identity of concepts in the universal one (see p. 147). Regarding the completeness of the functions under the qualitative and quantitative heads, Kant claims that for general logic affirmative and negative are the only functions under quality, and universal and particular are the only ones under quantity. "Logic does not consider content, i.e., the determination of a concept [and so infinite judgments are excluded from

---

[50] Cf. *ibid.*, B 316–349.

[51] Cf. *ibid.*, B 317–318, p. 277: "Before constructing any objective judgment we compare the concepts to find in them *identity* (of many representations under one concept) with a view to *universal* judgments, *difference* with a view to *particular* judgments, *agreement* with a view to *affirmative* judgments, *opposition* with a view to *negative* judgments, etc."

logic], but considers only the form of the relationship: agreement or opposition."[52] Also, "according to the principle of excluded middle the sphere of one concept relative to that of another is either exclusive or inclusive."[53] As to quantity, he says that "according to quantity there are only universal and particular judgments; for the subject is either completely included in or excluded from the notion of the predicate, or else it is partially included in or excluded from the predicate."[54]

How does our foregoing principle of completeness (see p. 167) square with the qualitative and quantitative functions? We have just seen that there is an opposition between two functions under each head. In the case of both modality and relation there was a third function which combined the other two opposite functions. How is one to think of such a combination under quality and quantity? We have already seen (pp.160–162) that these heads within the confines of pure general logic are concerned with the merely analytic unity that belongs to concepts as such when they are related in the objective unity of consciousness. What does one think of when he combines affirmation and negation in a separate thought (function of the infinite judgment), and universality and particularity in a separate thought (function of the singular judgment)? The results are puzzling. How is one to think of affirmation (in the infinite judgment) when there is no possibility of employing a determinate (finite) partial representation (concept); how is one to think of universality (in the singular judgment) when there is no possibility of employing a relationship of the spheres of concepts (see p. 145)? And so within the confines of pure general logic such combinations are empty. As we have already seen (p. 164

---

[52] *Reflections on Logic*, No. 3063 ad fin., Vol. XVI, p. 638 of the Akademie edition. Adickes dates it toward the end of the 1770's.

[53] *Ibid.*, No. 3072, Vol. XVI, p. 641. It dates from the 1790's.

[54] *Ibid.*, No. 3084, Vol. XVI, p. 650. It dates from about 1770.

note), Kant includes the singular and infinite functions in the table given at B 95 of the *Critique;* but he does so with an eye on the completeness of the table of the categories soon to come. We shall see (pp. 173–175) that transcendental logic is concerned with the forms of knowledge in general, and such knowledge involves not only concepts but pure intuitions as well. General logic, on the other hand, abstracts from all content of knowledge.

And so within the province of pure general logic no more additions can be made to our list of the logical functions of judgment; there are no other elementary functions of thought through concepts by means of the analytical unity of consciousness. The table of the pure general logical functions of unity in judgments as given at B 95 in the *Critique* is therefore complete. At B 94 (p. 106) Kant says that the "functions of the understanding [categories] can, therefore, be discovered if we can give an exhaustive statement of the functions of unity in judgments. That this can quite easily be done will be shown in the next section." And at B 105 (p. 113) he claims that "these [logical] functions [in all possible judgments] specify the understanding completely, and yield an exhaustive inventory of its powers." But yet in the *Critique* he merely sets forth the table of judgments in the synthetic order (see pp. 163–165) with an eye on the table of categories soon to follow; he does not work out the systematics of these logical functions nor does he justify their completeness. Why not?

Under Section VII (B 24–30) of the "Introduction" of the *Critique* he distinguishes a system of pure reason from a critique of pure reason. The former "would be the sum-total of those principles according to which all modes of pure *a priori* knowledge can be acquired and actually brought into being" (B 24–25, p. 58). The latter is merely a propaedeutic to such a system of pure reason; this propaedeutic merely examines the sources and limits of pure reason. The critique is concerned only with the complete examination of that knowledge which is a priori and synthetic. "I entitle *tran-scendental* all knowledge which is occupied not so much with objects as with the mode of our knowledge of objects in so far as this mode of knowledge is to be possible *a priori*. A system of such concepts might be entitled transcendental philosophy" (B 25, p. 59). And "if this critique is not itself to be entitled a transcendental philosophy, it is solely because, to be a complete system, it would also have to contain an exhaustive analysis of the whole of *a priori* human knowledge" (B 27, p. 60). Such a system "is still, at this stage, too large an undertaking. For since such a science must contain, with completeness, both kinds of *a priori* knowledge, the analytic [and hence such a science must contain an exhaustive analysis of the a priori knowledge developable in pure general logic] no less than the synthetic, it is, so far as our present purpose is concerned, much too comprehensive" (B 25, p. 59). Hence for the purposes of the *Critique* it is enough merely to set forth the table of logical judgments. However, transcendental philosophy would presuppose that an exhaustive analysis of the forms of thought, i.e., the whole of logic, had first been developed from the original synthetic unity of self-consciousness; the system of transcendental philosophy could then be elaborated. "The synthetic unity of apperception is therefore that highest point, to which we must ascribe all employment of the understanding, even the whole of logic, and conformably therewith, tran-scendental philosophy" (B 134 note, p. 154).

III. THE CATEGORIES OF THE UNDERSTANDING

We saw earlier when we discussed singular and infinite judgments (pp. 164 note, 171–172) that such judgments are meaningless within the confines of general logic, which is concerned with nothing but the form of our knowledge. However, transcendental logic does not abstract from all content (or matter) of our knowledge but only from all empirical content.[55] Singular and infinite judgments are important from the point of view of knowledge in general, involving as it does both concepts and intuitions. If we may anticipate just a bit, the categories of totality and limitation are based on the logical functions of thought in singular and infinite judgments, and hence these forms of judgment are quite significant for transcendental logic. For example, Kant says of the infinite judgment,

> by the proposition, 'The soul is non-mortal', I have, so far as the logical form is concerned, really made an affirmation. I locate the soul in the unlimited sphere of non-mortal beings. Since the mortal constitutes one part of the whole extension of possible beings, and the non-mortal the other, nothing more is said by my proposition than that the soul is one of the infinite number of things which remain over when I take away all that is mortal. The infinite sphere of all that is possible is thereby only so far limited that the mortal is excluded from it, and that the soul is located in the remaining part of its extension. But, even allowing for such exclusion, this extension still remains infinite, and several more parts of it may be taken away without the concept of the soul being thereby in the least increased, or determined in an affirmative man-

[55] Cf. *Critique of Pure Reason,* B 79–80, pp. 95–96: "General logic, as we have shown, abstracts from all content of knowledge, that is, from all relation of knowledge to the object, and considers only the logical form in the relation of any knowledge to other knowledge; that is, it treats of the form of thought in general. But since, as the Transcendental Aesthetic has shown, there are pure as well as empirical intuitions, a distinction might likewise be drawn between pure and empirical thought of objects. In that case we should have a logic in which we do not abstract from the entire content of knowledge. This other logic, which should contain solely the rules of the pure thought of an object, would exclude only those modes of knowledge which have empirical content. It would also treat of the origin of the modes in which we know objects, in so far as that origin cannot be attributed to the objects. General logic, on the other hand, has nothing to do with the origin of knowledge, but only considers representations, be they originally *a priori* in ourselves or only empirically given, according to the laws which the understanding employs when, in thinking, it relates them to one another. It deals therefore only with that form which the understanding is able to impart to the representations, from whatever source they may have arisen."

ner. These judgments, though infinite in respect of their logical extension, are thus, in respect of the content of their
knowledge, limitative only, and cannot therefore be passed
over in a transcendental table of all moments of thought in
judgments, since the function of the understanding thereby
expressed may perhaps be of importance in the field of its
pure a *priori* knowledge.[56]

And so transcendental logic is very much concerned to show
that concepts are meaningful only when they have an intuitive content.[57]

Kant says that the categories "are concepts of an object
in general, by means of which the intuition of an object is
regarded as determined in respect of one of the logical functions of judgment."[58] In Part Two we have seen that the table
of the logical forms of judgment given in the *Critique* at B 95
is complete (see pp. 165–173). In the light of a category's
characterization just cited, the table of categories given at
B 106 must be complete too. This agreement of the categories
with the logical functions is the basis for the *metaphysical
deduction* of the categories.[59] In fact this metaphysical deduction provides the complete enumeration of the twelve
categories.[60] The *transcendental deduction* shows that these

---

[56] *Ibid.,* B 97–98, p. 108.

[57] Cf. *ibid.,* B 102, p. 111: "Transcendental logic . . . has lying before it a
manifold of a *priori* sensibility, presented by transcendental aesthetic, as material for the concepts of pure understanding. In the absence of this material
those concepts would be without any content, therefore entirely empty." Also,
B 75, p. 93: "Thoughts without content are empty, intuitions without concepts
are blind."

[58] *Ibid.,* B 128, p. 128.

[59] Cf. *ibid.,* B 159, p. 170: "In the *metaphysical deduction* the a *priori* origin
of the categories has been proved through their complete agreement with the
general logical functions of thought. . . ."

[60] No more ultimate account of why there are just these twelve categories
is possible; they are the cognizing correlates of the logical functions of judgment, which were differentiated by analyzing the nature of judging in general.
Cf. *ibid.,* B 145–146, p. 161: "This peculiarity of our understanding, that it can
produce a *priori* unity of apperception solely by means of the categories, and
only by such and so many, is as little capable of further explanation as why
we have just these and no other functions of judgment, or why space and
time are the only forms of our possible intuition." Cf. also *Prolegomena,* § 36, Ak. 318.

twelve categories can relate a priori to objects, but it contains no principle for the enumeration of the categories. The table of the logical functions of judgment provides the basis for enumerating the categories, the transcendental principles of pure understanding, the metaphysical principles of corporeal nature, and the principles contained in the *Transition from the Metaphysical Foundations of Natural Science to Physics.*

The categories are

concepts of an object in general, by means of which the intuition of an object is regarded as determined in respect of one of the logical functions of judgment. Thus the function of the categorical judgment is that of the relation of subject to predicate; for example, 'All bodies are divisible'. But as regards the merely logical employment of the understanding, it remains undetermined to which of the two concepts the function of the subject, and to which the function of predicate, is to be assigned. For we can also say, 'Something divisible is a body'. But when the concept of body is brought under the category of substance, it is thereby determined that its empirical intuition in experience must always be considered as subject and never as mere predicate. Similarly with all the other categories.[61]

The pure categories are rules according to which a manifold of intuition is synthesized to yield knowledge of an object in general. Kant refers to the categories as the pure concepts of the understanding. Since they are pure, they cannot be pictured; they are functions of thought which impose a unity on a manifold (or variety) of sensible intuition, which can be pictured.

Since the categories are a priori and are therefore not abstractions from sense perceptions, they owe their origin to

---

[61] *Ibid.,* B 128–129, p. 128. Cf. also *ibid.,* B 143, p. 160: "But that act of understanding by which the manifold of given representations (be they intuitions or concepts) is brought under one apperception, is the logical function of judgment. . . . All the manifold, therefore, so far as it is given in a single empirical intuition, is *determined* in respect of one of the logical functions of judgment, and is thereby brought into one consciousness. Now the *categories* are just these functions of judgment, in so far as they are employed in determination of the manifold of a given intuition."

the very nature of the mind itself. But they are not mere subjective conditions of thought; they have objective validity. Thought imposes upon objects certain categorical characteristics, and objects insofar as they are objects known to us must have these characteristics. Thus we can have a priori knowledge of objects in general. But yet this knowledge is limited to objects that can be given in sensible intuition; we can know a priori that all substances are permanent, but not that the soul is a substance and so immortal. *The transcendental deduction of the categories* is concerned with their objective validity, the extent of their employment, and the limits of their legitimate use. For the purposes of this essay there is no necessity to enter into the details of this deduction. For those interested, I might remark that Kant fleshed out this deduction far more fully than he did the metaphysical one; in fact, he provided the world with two different versions of it.

In order for the pure categories to have objective validity (and not merely subjective validity) they must be related to sensibility. The

> categories have this peculiar feature, that only in virtue of the general condition of sensibility can they possess a determinate meaning and relation to any object. Now when this condition has been omitted from the pure category, it can contain nothing but the logical function for bringing the manifold under a concept. By means of this function or form of the concept, thus taken by itself, we cannot in any way know and distinguish what object comes under it, since we have abstracted from the sensible condition through which alone objects can come under it. Consequently, the categories require, in addition to the pure concept of understanding, determinations of their application to sensibility in general (schemata). Apart from such application they are not concepts through which an object is known and distinguished from others, but only so many modes of thinking an object for possible intuitions, and of giving it meaning, under the requisite further conditions, in conformity with some function of the understanding, that is, *of defining it.* But they cannot themselves be defined. . . . The pure categories are nothing but representations of things in general, so far as

the manifold of their intuition must be thought through one or other of these logical functions. Magnitude is the determination which can be thought only through a judgment which has quantity (*judicium commune*); reality is that determination which can be thought only through an affirmative judgment; substance is that which, in relation to intuition, must be the last subject of all other determinations. But what sort of a thing it is that demands one of these functions rather than another, remains altogether undetermined. Thus the categories, apart from the condition of sensible intuition, of which they contain the synthesis, have no relation to any determinate object, cannot therefore define any object, and so do not in themselves have the validity of objective concepts.[62]

From what Kant says here one can see that the logical forms of judgment and the *pure* categories are really the same synthetic functions; yet the pure categories are potentially functions of knowing objects whenever the understanding is directed to the determination of a manifold of intuition, while the logical forms abstract completely from intuition and are both potentially and actually merely pure forms of thought of any objects whatsoever. The pure categories are empty insofar as their contents are the empty forms of thought; they refer merely to an object in general and would hence *seem* to apply even to noumena, to the extent that we can think about noumena at all.[63] From this same passage we can see that the schematized categories apply only to sensible objects.

What, now, are the transcendental schemata? Whenever

---

[62] *Ibid.*, A 244–246, pp. 263–264. Cf. *Prolegomena,* §'s 20–22.

[63] Cf. *ibid.*, B 309, pp. 270–271: "If I remove from empirical knowledge all thought (through categories), no knowledge of any object remains. For through mere intuition nothing at all is thought, and the fact that this affection of sensibility is in me does not [by itself] amount to a relation of such representation to any object. But if, on the other hand, I leave aside all intuition, the form of my thought still remains—that is, the mode of determining an object for the manifold of a possible intuition. The categories accordingly extend further than sensible intuition, since they think objects in general, without regard to the special mode (the sensibility) in which they may be given."

a general concept is thought to represent an object, there must be a certain homogeneity between the concept and the object.[64] Since all concepts are partial representations (see p. 145), how do they represent objects? Intuitions are immediately related to individual objects; whenever we picture to ourselves a man, we have an *image* of him as possessing some particular height, hair color, eye color, etc. But a concept abstracts from such particular qualities and thus makes possible the thought of many men at once by means of their common characteristics. A concept represents an object by means of a *schema*. When I think of a man, I generate an image according to a rule. In my imagination I delineate in a general manner the figure of a two-footed upright animal, and am not limited (as in the case of an image) to any single determinate figure. Kant defines a schema as a "representation of a universal procedure of imagination in providing an image for a concept."[65] So much for empirical concepts. In the case of pure mathematical concepts, much the same holds. To construct a triangle the rule says to draw a plane figure having three straight sides which meet at three vertices. And there are infinitely many images which can be generated in accordance with this rule.

But what about the categories? He asserts that "the schema of a *pure* concept of understanding can never be brought into any image whatsoever."[66] In other words, for the categories there are no corresponding given intuitions (images) with which these concepts are homogeneous; empirical concepts are homogeneous with empirical intuitions, and mathematical concepts with the pure sensible intuitions of time and space. At B 174 (p. 179) of the *Critique* he speaks of "the rule (or rather the universal condition of rules), which is given in the pure concept of understanding." A universal

[64] Cf. *ibid.*, B 176.

[65] *Ibid.*, B 179–180, p. 182.

[66] *Ibid.*, B 181, p. 183.

condition of rules would be a rule for rules. The category of substance is related to the concept of man as the latter in turn is related to the image of a particular man. Since the categories are rules for rules, it is impossible to give images for them. The category of causation, to cite another example, gives the rule for particular empirical concepts of causal connection, which are usually called causal laws; these empirical laws (e.g., fire burns, water cools) give the rules for connecting particular phenomena and hence can have images.

What must the schema of a category be like in order that the category may be connected with intuition? The schema must be pure, or else the connection would be empirical; and it has to be homogeneous with both the category and the intuition. It must be intellectual (i.e., a product of spontaneity) in order to be homogeneous with the category. It has to be sensible in order to be homogeneous with intuition. To be both sensible and yet pure, it must be connected with the pure form of intuition; Kant turns to time as the pure form of intuition required. Since the pure category is a concept of the pure synthetic unity of an intuitive manifold in general, the pure synthetic unity of the manifold of time must come under it. Not only does time contain in itself a manifold of pure intuition; it is also the form of inner sense and is accordingly the formal condition of the synthesis of all representations whatsoever.[67] A transcendental determination of time is homogeneous with the category since such a determination is universal and rests on an a priori rule; it is also homogeneous with appearances since time is contained in every empirical representation of an object. Therefore the transcendental determination of time is the me-

---

[67] Cf. *ibid.*, B 177, p. 181: "Time, as the formal condition of the manifold of inner sense, and therefore of the connection of all representations, contains an *a priori* manifold in pure intuition." Also, *ibid.*, A 99, p. 131: "All our knowledge is thus finally subject to time, the formal condition of inner sense. In it they must all be ordered, connected, and brought into relation."

diating representation which makes possible the application of the categories to appearances, and as such this determination is identified with the transcendental schema.[68]

Imagination has an intermediate position between sensibility and understanding. It is the synthesizing faculty directly related to intuitions; it represents an object in intuition even when the object is not present.[69] The synthesis of the manifold of sensible intuition under the form of time is the work of imagination. It is a figurative synthesis (*synthesis speciosa*) and is to be distinguished from the purely intellectual synthesis (*synthesis intellectualis*) of understanding.[70] But yet it is a transcendental synthesis which is a priori and is also the condition of the possibility of a priori knowledge. Since all human intuition is sensible, imagination is therefore connected with sensibility. Imagination is in the service of understanding when it synthesizes the sensible manifold in accordance with the pure concepts of understanding. This transcendental synthesis of imagination is the first working of understanding upon sensibility and is the first application of understanding to objects of human experience. The expressions "transcendental synthesis of imagination" and "transcendental synthesis of apperception" indicate two different aspects (pointing out the degree of removal of spontaneity from passive sensibility) of one and the same transcendental synthesis. "It is one and the same spontaneity, which in the one case, under the title of imagination, and in the other case, under the title of understanding, brings combination into the manifold of intuition."[71] In such synthetic activity imagination is said to be productive. (It is reproductive when its synthesis is entirely subject to empirical laws of association, and such synthesis is empirical. The reproduc-

[68] Cf. *ibid.*, B 177–178.

[69] Cf. *ibid.*, B 151.

[70] Cf. *ibid.*, B 151.

[71] *Ibid.*, B 161 note, pp. 171–172.

tive synthesis is treated in psychology rather than in transcendental philosophy.) Now, the transcendental schemata are the ways in which a given manifold of intuition is combined in one time by the transcendental synthesis of productive imagination. The transcendental schemata are, then, products of the transcendental synthesis of productive imagination.[72]

Every pure category can be characterized as the concept of the synthesis of a manifold of intuition in the cognition of some object. Every schematized category can be characterized as the concept of this synthesis in time. The synthesis involved in both is the same, but the schematized category can be applied to nothing but a manifold of intuition given through the form of time. I pointed out earlier (p. 178) that the pure categories relate only to objects in general and would seem to apply necessarily to all objects whatsoever (even to noumena). But the schematized categories contain within themselves transcendental determinations of the pure intuition of time, and so their application is limited to objects of human experience (phenomena).

Having started with the transcendental unity of apperception, we have now discerned quite a few distinguishable aspects of that original act. At this point it might be helpful briefly to make explicit what the various logical functions of judgment, pure categories, schematized categories, and transcendental schemata are.[73] We shall consider these in the synthetic order (see pp. 163–165, above).

Under the head of quantity the pure categories are derived from the logical forms of judgment "This S is P", "Some S is P", "All S is P". These pure categories of unity, plurality, totality may be described as concepts of the synthesis of the homogeneous, for in these quantitative judgments the ob-

---

[72] Cf. *ibid.*, B 179–180.

[73] For this I have found very helpful H. J. Paton's *Kant's Metaphysic of Experience* (London: George Allen and Unwin Ltd., 1936), Vol. II, pp. 42–65.

jects referred to by the subject-concept are regarded as being homogeneous with one another. The schematized categories are concepts of the synthesis of the homogeneous in time and space; as such they are the categories of extensive quantity. The transcendental schemata which are the products of this synthesis are all number.

Under the head of quality the pure categories are derived from the logical forms of judgment "S is P", "S is not P", "S is non-P". These pure categories of reality, negation, limitation are concepts of the synthesis of being, not-being, being and not-being. The schematized categories are concepts of the synthesis of being, not-being, being and not-being in time and space; as such they are the categories of intensive quantity. The transcendental schemata which are the products of this synthesis are all degree (both of sensation and of what corresponds to sensation).

Real, experiential objects have not only quantity and quality; they also have a fixed position in one common time and space and stand in definite relations to one another. As we saw earlier (p. 176), in the merely logical categorical judgment the subject and the predicate can be interchanged; but in that pure category which is the synthesis of subject and predicate the subject is regarded as a subject which can never be a predicate. The schematized category is the concept of the synthesis of the unchanging subject to which the changing predicates belong and is usually called by Kant the category of substance and accident. Permanence is the transcendental schema which is the product of this synthesis. The second pure category of relation is the concept of the synthesis of antecedent and consequence, corresponding to the hypothetical judgment. The schematized category is the concept of this synthesis of antecedent and consequence in which the consequence succeeds the antecedent in time and is called the category of cause and effect. Necessary succession in time is the transcendental schema which is the product of this synthesis. The third pure category of relation, which corresponds to the disjunctive form of judgment, is that of community and is the concept of the synthesis of ultimate subjects according to which the predicates of one subject have their ground in another and vice versa. The schematized category is the concept of the synthesis of unchanging substances according to which the changing accidents of one substance have their cause in another and vice versa, and it is called the category of interaction. The transcendental schema which is the product of this synthesis is the necessary coexistence of the accidents of one substance with those of another.

The schematized categories of quantity and quality determine the intuitive manifold provided by objects, while those of relation determine objects as enduring substances and the relationships of objects to one another. The schemata of modality are not concerned with the necessary traits of objects but rather with their relation to the mind that knows them. The pure categories of possibility, actuality, and necessity correspond to the problematic, assertoric, and apodeictic forms of judgment. These pure categories are nothing but concepts of the synthesis which is present in every judgment. The pure category of possibility is the concept of that synthesis which is self-consistent according to the formal laws of thought. The schematized category is the concept of productive imagination's transcendental synthesis insofar as this synthesis involves the forms of intuition. The transcendental schema which is the product of this synthesis is the agreement of different representations with the conditions of time in general. The pure category of actuality is the concept of that synthesis which is present in every judgment that claims to determine a real object. The schematized category is the concept of productive imagination's transcendental synthesis insofar as this synthesis involves the matter of intuition given at a determinate time. Existence at a determinate time is the transcendental schema which is the product of this synthesis. The pure category of necessity is

the concept of that synthesis which is present in every judgment that follows logically from other concepts or judgments according to the formal laws of thought. The schematized category is the concept of productive imagination's
transcendental synthesis insofar as this synthesis determines
the given manifold with respect to the whole of time. Existence at all times is the transcendental schema which is the
product of this synthesis.

The schemata, then, are sensible characteristics which
must belong to all objects insofar as the sensible manifold of
these objects is combined in one time. Kant's conclusion
is that the schemata are a priori determinations of time in
accordance with rules. These rules relate (in the synthetic
order of the categories) to the time-series, the time-content,
the time-order, and the totality of time in respect of all possible objects of experience.[74]

In view of the course of thought of this essay, it scarcely
need be said that these logical functions of thought, pure
categories, schematized categories, and transcendental schemata are merely distinguishable aspects of the original synthetic unity of apperception. Any judging of objects of
possible experience is a combination of representations in
the original synthetic unity of self-consciousness. This synthesizing activity of understanding has various aspects distinguished according to the different ways the subject and the
predicate are combined in apperception, or two or more
judgments are combined in apperception, or various judgments are related to the whole knowing faculty of the mind
in apperception. In the empirical judgment "All trees have
branches", the aspects of the form of uniting the representations "trees" and "branches" in apperception which are involved are the categorical, universal, affirmative; and the
modality (depending as it does on how the judgment is held
by the mind) may be problematic, assertoric, or apodeictic.

[74] Cf. *Critique of Pure Reason*, B 184.

This judgment involves the pure categories of inherence and subsistence, totality, reality, possibility, actuality, and necessity. The schemata involved which make possible the application of these categories to the representations contained in this judgment are permanence, number, degree, the agreement of the synthesis of "trees" and "branches" with the conditions of time in general, existence at a determinate time, and existence at all times. Any other judgment (empirical or pure, analytic or synthetic) would involve all the heads, though the moments under the heads are alternatives (but one and the same judgment may involve all three of the modal moments[75]).

IV. THE TRANSCENDENTAL PRINCIPLES OF NATURE

"Transcendental philosophy has the peculiarity that besides the rule (or rather the universal condition of rules), which is given in the pure concept of understanding, it can also specify a priori the instance to which the rule is to be applied."[76] Therefore we can have a transcendental science of nature. The laws of this science, which state the ways in which phenomena must be synthesized in all experience, are called by Kant the Principles (Grundsätze) of Pure Understanding. These show how the schematized categories must apply to all objects of experience. We saw earlier (note 46) that the categories of quantity and quality go together, as do those of relation and modality. The principles likewise are

[75] Cf. ibid., B 101, p. 110: "Since everything is thus incorporated in the understanding step by step—inasmuch as we first judge something problematically, then maintain its truth assertorically, and finally affirm it as inseparably united with the understanding, that is, as necessary and apodeictic—we are justified in regarding these three functions of modality as so many moments of thought." I shall have more to say about modality when we come to the Postulates of Empirical Thought (see pp. 192–194, below).

[76] Ibid., B 174–175, p. 179.

divided into mathematical and dynamical.[77] The quantitative principles are called the Axioms of Intuition and the qualitative ones the Anticipations of Perception; the relational ones the Analogies of Experience and the modal ones the Postulates of Empirical Thought. The mathematical principles are concerned with the objects of intuition, while the dynamical ones are concerned with the existence of these objects in relation either to one another or to the understanding.[78]

The Axioms of Intuition tell us that the intuitions of phenomena are extensive magnitudes. To have sense perception of an object as an appearance, we must synthesize the pure and homogeneous manifold of the determinate space and time which it occupies. Therefore the synthetic unity of the pure and homogeneous manifold of the determinate space and time is one condition that must be fulfilled if we are to perceive an object. But such synthetic unity is exactly what is thought in the schematized category of extensive quantity through the schema of number. Therefore all objects as appearances must fall under this category, and this means that phenomenal objects must be extensive quantities. And hence the application of pure mathematics to objects of experience is justified.

An object is something more than the space which it occupies and the time through which it lasts. It is real insofar as it fills a determinate space and time, and as such it must have intensive quantity, or degree. Experiential objects, then, have intensive matter as well as extensive form. This matter for some object in general is that through which an object is represented as existing in space and time, and such matter is the real of sensation. Since a continuous change is

---

[77] Cf. *ibid.*, B 197–202. Cf. also *Prolegomena*, §'s 24–25.

[78] In what follows I shall briefly summarize some of the main points of Kant's discussion of these principles and shall make no attempt to detail his proofs of them. For the particulars of the *Grundsätze*, see the *Critique*, B 202–274, *Prolegomena*, §'s 24–33, and Paton's *Kant's Metaphysic of Experience*, Vol. II, pp. 111–371.

possible between pure intuition and sense perception (which is empirical consciousness), there is possible a synthesis that produces a ouantity (a more or less) of sensation, starting from pure intuition (complete absence of any sensation) and arriving at any particular quantity of sensation given through sense perception. Sensation thus has an intensive quantity. Since the sensible perception of objects always involves sensation(as well as intuitions of time and space), a corresponding intensive quantity must be ascribed to objects. Hence color, sound, taste, and even resistance and weight must have intensive quantity. This, briefly, is what the Anticipations of Perception tell us.

While the Axioms and Anticipations are concerned with homogeneous elements of experience which do not necessarily belong to one another, the Analogies of Experience are concerned with relations of heterogeneous elements which do necessarily belong to one another. The relations involved are those of substance and accident, cause and effect, and reciprocal causality among substances (this last combining the first two). The pure categories of relation apply to appearances through their schemata, which are deteᴗrminations of time. Permanence, succession, and coexistence are the correlates of substance, causality, and community. The principles which show how the schematized relational categories apply to all phenomena are rules for all the time-relations of appearances; in accordance with these rules the existence of every appearance with regard to the unity of all time can be determined. These rules are prior to experience and give us the necessary conditions under which alone experience is possible. The unity of the time in which all phenomena exist is founded on the unity of apperception, which is manifested only in synthesizing representations according to these rules. The temporal position of objects is determined solely by their relations to one another in time; this determination is brought about by means of a priori rules that are valid for any and every time.

The First Analogy treats of the permanence of substance. Since the time with which Kant is concerned is a condition of experience, it is the one time in which all objective determinations of time have their being. All objective determinations of time (whether of succession or of simultaneity) must be constituted by referring representations to an object in which they are related; only in this way can objective relations of time be distinguished from merely subjective or from imaginary ones. Time itself is not an object. An objective time-order is constructed by setting a representation in objective time-relations to other representations. And so time itself cannot be perceived, and because of this fact experience must have a permanent object and ultimately one permanent substratum for the whole objective world of phenomena. Change (coming into existence and passing out of it) is nothing but a way in which the permanent exists; the permanent is not merely one among many appearances but is the substratum of all appearances. A change is a way of existing that follows upon another way in which the same thing exists; there is an exchange of one state of a thing for another state of that thing, but the thing itself must remain the same thing.

The Second Analogy contains Kant's famous treatment of efficient causation.[79] According to this principle all changes of phenomena take place in conformity with the law of the connection of cause and effect. The succession of appearances is nothing but a change of permanent substances. All objects that are given to us through the forms of time and space must have a characteristic according to which they can be judged by the hypothetical form of judgment. That characteristic is the schema of necessary succession in time. The pure category of antecedent and consequence receives its experiential significance when it is translated into terms of

---

[79]Cf. Robert Paul Wolff, *Kant's Theory of Mental Activity* (Cambridge, Mass.: Harvard University Press, 1963), p. 260: "The Second Analogy is undoubtedly one of the most powerful pieces of philosophy ever written." For a thoroughly penetrating and enlightening treatment of the Analogies, see Arthur Melnick, *Kant's Analogies of Experience* (Chicago, University of Chicago Press, 1973).

time and is thereby transformed into cause and effect. Thus transformed the cause is a ground which must precede the effect (actually the cause is the ground of the existence of the effect), although a merely logical antecedent does not necessarily precede its consequence. (Compare p. 176, above, where Kant says that when the subject in a categorical judgment is subsumed under the category of substance, then subject and predicate cannot be interchanged.) What, now, is the nature of this necessary succession? We have already seen (pp. 140–142) that representations have a double nature; they may be considered simply as contents of consciousness or may be considered as representing objects. Knowledge is a connection of representations *qua* objective and not of representations *qua* subjective (see pp. 145–147, above). The only sort of relation which all representations have to one another is a time-relation inasmuch as time is the form of inner sense (see p. 180, above). Therefore representations can be arranged in a subjective time-order or in an objective one. The two orders may be quite different. In the *Critique* (at B 235–236) Kant gives the example of the parts of a house, which are perceived successively but yet objectively coexist. Hence in order to have knowledge through perceptions, we must connect them in their objective time-relations. Even a singular object is a special way of synthesizing our representations, i.e., it is not something distinct from the representations of it (an unknowable thing in itself); furthermore, the object must serve as the ground for the objective connection of our representations. So the house as an object is the synthetic reworking of the manifold of perceptions. Now, if we have a succession of objects or a succession of events, much the same sort of reworking takes place. If event A (glowing stove) precedes event B (warm room) objectively, then we must think of A as preceding B or else be wrong. It makes no difference whether we perceive A first and then B, or B first and then A in our subjective consciousness. There is no necessity in the order of our subjective consciousness, but there is necessity in our synthetic reorganization of it. We think objective succession through the schematized category of cause and effect. We saw earlier (pp. 179–180) that the categories are rules for rules. Accordingly, the universal law of efficient causation is imposed a priori by the mind upon objects, while particular causal laws can be known only a posteriori. All such empirical laws are merely particular determinations of the one universal law.[80]

The Third Analogy tells us that substances stand in a relation of reciprocal causality with respect to their accidents. This Third Analogy arises from a combination of the other two (see p. 167 and note 48), but is not derivative from them. Though we can show that substance and causality are necessary conditions of experience, we cannot conclude that substances mutually influence one another. Kant argues for such influence by pointing out that some sense perceptions can follow one another reciprocally (we can see first the moon and then the earth, or vice versa), while in the case of the Second Analogy, where one has an objective unilinear succession of perceptions, this reciprocity cannot hold. Since our representations qua objective are perceptions of objects (or permanent substances, which are not things in themselves), we can say that inasmuch as our perceptions of certain objects follow one another reciprocally, the objects are coexistent. This reversibility of our representations is a criterion for distinguishing objective coexistence from objective

---

[80] Cf. *Critique of Pure Reason*, B 165, p. 173: "Nature, considered merely as nature in general, is dependent upon these categories as the original ground of its necessary conformity to law (*natura formaliter spectata*). Pure understanding is not, however, in a position, through mere categories, to prescribe to appearances any a priori laws other than those which are involved in a *nature in general*, that is, in the conformity to law of all appearances in space and time. Special laws, as concerning those appearances which are empirically determined, cannot in their specific character be *derived* from the categories, although they are one and all subject to them. To obtain any knowledge whatsoever of these special laws, we must resort to experience; but it is the a priori laws that alone can instruct us in regard to experience in general, and as to what it is that can be known as an object of experience."

unilinear succession. Also, we can say that if the objects perceived coexist, then the succession of our representations must be reversible. Now, a sense perception is not something lying between us and the object; it is an object's state, which is immediately present to our minds. The object is made up of such possible or actual perceptions bound up in a necessary synthetic unity. If the reciprocal succession of our perceptions is grounded on coexistent objects, then the reciprocal succession of the states, or determinations, must be grounded on coexistent objects. If the objects were things in themselves, then it might be argued that their coexistence could determine the reversibility of our perceptions; but it could not be argued that the states of the two coexistent objects must therefore be reciprocally determined by the two objects. Since objects are not things in themselves, we can infer from the coexistence of objects that they must interact. And so coexistent objects must mutually determine one another's states; accordingly, we can know that the order of our representations must be reversible, and we can know that the objects coexist. The necessity involved here is imposed by a concept of the relation of substances in which one substance contains states whose ground is contained in the other; the relation is one of causal action of one substance upon another and is furthermore reciprocal. The pure category of community so schematized is that of interaction. It is the concept of functional interdependence, expressed in such equations as the laws of motion, and is of the utmost importance for science. The world as science knows it is a system of functional relations between measurable quantities.

The Postulates of Empirical Thought are concerned with the existence of objects in relation to the mind. Up till now I have shown that if an object is to be an object of experience, then it must have in itself certain necessary traits, or determinations; it must have extensive and intensive quantity, and must be a substance (with changing accidents) in causal interaction with all other such substances. The concept of the object when it is considered only in itself does not contain possibility, actuality, and necessity; these are determinations of an object in a sense different from the aforementioned ones. The Postulates add to the concept of an object nothing more than the cognitive faculty in which the concept originates and has its seat. But Kant is not concerned with merely logical possibility, actuality, and necessity; rather, he explains real possibility, actuality, and necessity by reference to experience. Possibility depends on the form of experience, actuality mainly on the matter of experience, and necessity (as is to be expected from p. 167 and note 48) on the combination of the two. The First Postulate says that if things are to be possible, then the concept of these things must agree with the forms of intuition (time and space) and with the transcendental unity of apperception. The Second Postulate states that what is connected with the material conditions of experience (viz., sensation) is actual. This means that we must have sense perception in order to have knowledge of the actuality of things. The Third Postulate says that the necessary is that whose connection with the actual is determined in accordance with the universal conditions of experience (namely, the Analogies). The necessity involved here is hypothetical (not absolute) by means of the causal law expressed in the Second Analogy. Such necessity applies only to the changing states of substances and not to the substances themselves, inasmuch as substances endure and do not come to be and pass away. If the cause is actual, then the effect must exist; if we have actual experience of the cause of something, then by thought we can affirm the necessary existence of objects.[81] These Postulates must apply to all experiential objects; accordingly, every object of experience is possible, actual, and necessary—but in different respects. An object has different relations to the mind because of

[81] Cf. *ibid.*, B 239.

the different aspects of the object which were just discussed. Every object has a form imposed by the mind, and the object is possible because of this form. Every object has a matter that is given to the mind and synthesized under that form; thereby is the object actual. Every object is a combination of form and matter, i.e., it is a substance whose accidents are causally determined; thereby is the object necessary. Accordingly, possibility is no wider than actuality, and actuality is no wider than necessity.[82]

It is not surprising that the (modal) Postulates conclude the Principles of Pure Understanding. After all, one cannot talk about the existence of an object (modality) without first having a concept of what the object is; and what it is, is specified by means of quantity, quality, relation. Throughout the Principles Kant has appealed to the possibility of experience, and so to the possibility of experiential objects. In the Analogies he argued that what is objective, or actual, can be distinguished from what is merely subjective or merely imaginary, because the actual is governed by necessity. In the Postulates he considers this possibility, actuality, and necessity. He has shown in the Axioms, Anticipations, and Analogies what objects must be if they are given to intuition and if they exist in relation to one another in a common space and time. In the Postulates he shows what relations they must have to the mind that knows them.

In view of the preceding course of thought, I scarcely need say that these various Principles are simply distinguishable aspects of the one synthesis contained in the transcendental unity of apperception (see pp. 185–186, above). The Axioms are concerned with the synthesis of the form of intuition; the Anticipations with the synthesis of the matter of intuition; the Analogies with the synthesis of the form and the matter of intuition; and the Postulates with the relations of all these syntheses to the mind that produces them. *All* the Principles apply to *each and every* object of experience.

[82] Cf. *ibid.,* B 282–285.

V. THE METAPHYSICAL PRINCIPLES OF NATURE

Part of the "General Note on the System of the Principles" in the *Critique* heralds the *Metaphysical Foundations of Natural Science:*

> . . . in order to understand the possibility of things in conformity with the categories, and so to demonstrate the *objective reality* of the latter, we need, not merely intuitions, but intuitions that are in all cases *outer intuitions.* When, for instance, we take the pure concepts of *relation,* we find, firstly, that in order to obtain something *permanent* in intuition corresponding to the concept of *substance,* and so to demonstrate the objective reality of this concept, we require an intuition in space (of matter). . . . Secondly, in order to exhibit *alteration* as the intuition corresponding to the concept of *causality,* we must take as our example motion, that is, alteration in space. . . . For alteration is combination of contradictorily opposed determinations in the existence of one and the same thing. Now how it is possible that from a given state of a thing an opposite state should follow, not only cannot be conceived by reason without an example, but is actually incomprehensible to reason without intuition. The intuition required is the intuition of the movement of a point in space. The presence of the point in different locations (as a sequence of opposite determinations) is what alone first yields to us an intuition of alteration. . . . Lastly, the possibility of the category of *community* cannot be comprehended through mere reason alone; and consequently its objective reality is only to be determined through intuition, and indeed through outer intuition in space. For how are we to think it to be possible, when several substances exist, that, from the existence of one, something (as effect) can follow in regard to the existence of the others, and *vice versa;* in other words, that because there is something in the one there must also in the others be something which is not to be understood solely from the existence of these others? For this is what is required in order that there be community; community is not conceivable as holding between things each of which, through its subsistence, stands in complete isolation. . . . [A] community of substances is utterly inconceivable as arising simply

from their existence. We can, however, render the possibility of community—of substances as appearances—perfectly comprehensible, if we represent them to ourselves in space, that is, in outer intuition. For this already contains in itself *a priori* formal outer relations as conditions of the possibility of the real relations of action and reaction, and therefore of the possibility of community. Similarly, it can easily be shown that the possibility of things as *quantities,* and therefore the objective reality of quantity, can be exhibited only in outer intuition. . . .[83]

Indeed the word "space" occurs as frequently in the *Metaphysical Foundations of Natural Science* as "time" does in "The Analytic of Principles" in the *Critique*. The former treatise is an important step in the direction of the empirical; in it are to be found instances for the extremely abstract transcendental concepts and principles of the latter.[84]

The principles of pure understanding (see Part Four above) comprise the transcendental doctrine of the objects of a pos-

---

[83] *Ibid.,* B 291–293, pp. 254–256.

[84] In the Preface to the *Metaphysical Foundations* (above, Ak. 477–478) Kant says that the general doctrine of body (i.e., the *Metaphysical Foundations*) "facilitates the uniform progress of this science [system of general metaphysics as contained in the *Critique*] toward its goal, if, in all cases where the general doctrine of body is needed, one can call upon the separate system of such a doctrine without encumbering the larger system of metaphysics in general. . . . Furthermore, it is indeed very remarkable (but cannot here be thoroughly entered into) that general metaphysics in all cases where it requires instances (intuitions) in order to provide meaning for its pure concepts of the understanding must always take such instances from the general doctrine of body, i.e., from the form and principles of external intuition; and if these instances are not at hand in their entirety, it gropes, uncertain and trembling, among mere meaningless concepts. Hence there are the well-known disputes, or at least the obscurity in questions, concerning the possibility of an opposition of realities, the possibility of intensive magnitude, etc., with regard to which the understanding is taught only through instances from corporeal nature what the conditions are under which the concepts of the understanding can alone have objective reality, i.e., meaning and truth. And so a separate metaphysics of corporeal nature does excellent and indispensable service to general metaphysics, inasmuch as the former provides instances (cases *in concreto*) in which to realize the concepts and propositions of the latter (properly, transcendental philosophy), i.e., to give to a mere form of thought sense and meaning."

sible experience in general. The general doctrine of body takes as its subject the empirically given concept of matter and determines this concept by means of transcendental predicates already familiar to us as the categories.[85] In this general doctrine of body

> the concept of matter had to be carried out through all the four functions of the concepts of the understanding (in four chapters), in each of which a new determination of matter was added. The fundamental determination of a something that is to be an object of the external senses must be motion, for thereby only can these senses be affected. The understanding leads all other predicates which pertain to the nature of matter back to motion; thus natural science is throughout either a pure or an applied doctrine of motion. *The Metaphysical Foundations of Natural Science* may be brought, then, under four main chapters. The first may be called *Phoronomy;* and in it motion is considered as pure quantum, according to its composition, without any quality of the matter. The second may be termed *Dynamics,* and in it motion is regarded as belonging to the quality of the matter under the name of an original moving force. The third emerges under the name of *Mechanics,* and in it matter with this dynamical quality is considered as by its own motion to be in relation. The fourth is called *Phenomenology;* and in it matter's motion or rest is determined merely with reference to the mode of representation, or modality, i.e., as an appearance of the external senses.[86]

[85] Cf. above, Ak. 469–470: "But either it [metaphysics of nature] can treat of the laws which make possible the concept of a nature in general even without reference to any determinate object of experience, and therefore undetermined regarding the nature of this or that thing of the sense-world— and in this case it is the transcendental part of the metaphysics of nature—or it occupies itself with the special nature of this or that kind of things, of which an empirical concept is given in such a way that besides what lies in this concept, no other empirical principle is needed for cognizing the things. For example, it lays the empirical concept of a matter . . . at its foundation and searches the range of cognition of which reason is a priori capable regarding [this object]. Such a science must still be called a metaphysics of nature, namely, of corporeal . . . nature; however, it is then not a general but a special metaphysical natural science (physics . . .), in which the aforementioned transcendental principles are applied to [this] species of [sense-object]."

[86] Above, Ak. 476–477.

And so we discern a progression from the most formal to what is less formal—from the transcendental unity of apperception with its aspects called the logical functions of judgment, to the pure categories, to the schematized categories, to the transcendental principles of nature in general, and now to the metaphysical principles of corporeal nature. Or one might say that we have a progression from what is not empirical at all to what is empirical to a certain extent. Similarly, in Kant's moral philosophy one proceeds from the categorical imperative, which holds for all rational beings, i.e., beings whose actions can be determined by reason rather than by the inclinations of the senses, to the various metaphysical imperatives, which hold for human beings, whose physical nature and moral nature must be considered in elaborating the system of duties contained in the *Metaphysics of Morals*. In his theoretical philosophy he analyzes experience by considering how the form of thought synthesizes the manifold of intuition as provided by time through inner sense in the *Critique* and now especially by space through the external senses in the *Metaphysical Foundations*.

Kant says that

> the completeness of the metaphysics of corporeal nature may be confidently expected. The reason for this is that in metaphysics the object is considered merely as it must be represented in accordance with the universal laws of thought, while in other sciences, as it must be represented in accordance with data of intuition (pure as well as empirical). Hence the former, inasmuch as the object must always be compared with all the necessary laws of thought, must furnish a definite number of cognitions, which can be fully exhausted; but the latter, inasmuch as such sciences offer an infinite manifold of intuitions (pure or empirical), and therefore of objects of thought, can never attain absolute completeness but can be extended to infinity, as in pure mathematics and the empirical doctrine of nature.[87]

The empirical sciences are built up through observation and experiment, and hence their working out is endless. Also, pure mathematics is endless, since it constructs its concepts

[87] Above, Ak. 473.

in the pure intuitions of time and space, and such constructions can be infinitely many. Now, mathematics can be
applied to physical phenomena insofar as such appearances
are considered as quantities (see p. 187). Certainly its applications in empirical sciences such as astronomy are infinite.
What is the relationship between the metaphysics of nature
and mathematics? "Pure rational cognition from mere concepts is called pure philosophy, or metaphysics; on the other
hand, that pure rational cognition which is based only upon
the construction of concepts by means of the presentation
of the object in an a priori intuition is called mathematics."[88]

[88] Above, Ak. 469. Cf. also *Critique of Pure Reason*, B 741–744, pp. 577–578:
"*Philosophical* knowledge is the *knowledge gained by reason from concepts;*
mathematical knowledge is the knowledge gained by reason from the *construction* of concepts. To *construct* a concept means to exhibit a *priori* the
intuition which corresponds to the concept. For the construction of a concept
we therefore need a *non-empirical* intuition. The latter must, as intuition, be
a *single* object, and yet none the less, as the construction of a concept (a
universal representation), it must in its representation express universal validity for all possible intuitions which fall under the same concept [see this
essay, p. 179, above]. . . . Thus, philosophical knowledge considers the
particular only in the universal, mathematical knowledge the universal in the
particular, or even in the single instance, though still always a *priori* and by
means of reason. . . . The essential difference between these two kinds of
knowledge through reason consists therefore in this formal difference, and
does not depend on difference of their material or objects. Those who propose to distinguish philosophy from mathematics by saying that the former
has as its object *quality* only and the latter *quantity* only, have mistaken the
effect for the cause. The form of mathematical knowledge is the cause why it
is limited exclusively to quantities. For it is the concept of quantities only that
allows of being constructed, that is, exhibited a *priori* in intuition; whereas
qualities cannot be presented in any intuition that is not empirical. Consequently reason can obtain a knowledge of qualities only through intuition. . . .
The shape of a cone we can form for ourselves in intuition, unassisted by
any experience, according to its concept alone, but the colour of this cone must
be previously given in some experience or other. I cannot represent in intuition
the concept of a cause in general except in an example supplied by experience;
and similarly with other concepts. . . . Philosophy confines itself to universal
concepts; mathematics can achieve nothing by concepts alone but hastens
at once to intuition, in which it considers the concept *in concreto*, though
not empirically, but only in an intuition which it presents a *priori*, that is,
which it has constructed, and in which whatever follows from the universal
conditions of the construction must be universally valid of the object of the
concept thus constructed."

Now, a

> pure philosophy of nature in general, i.e., one that only investigates what constitutes the concept of a nature in general [in the *Critique*], may indeed be possible without mathematics; but a pure doctrine of nature concerning determinate natural things (doctrine of body . . .) is possible only by means of mathematics. And since in every doctrine of nature only so much science proper is to be found as there is a priori cognition in it, a doctrine of nature will contain only so much science proper as there is applied mathematics in it.[89]

To cognize anything a priori means to know it from its mere *possibility*, while to cognize anything a posteriori means to know it from its *actuality* through an empirical intuition (see pp. 192–194). The transcendental doctrine of nature, as we have already seen (p. 196), cognizes its phenomenal objects in general from mere concepts. But the metaphysical doctrine of body lays the concept of a determinate natural object (matter) at its foundation. And

> the possibility of determinate natural things cannot be cognized from their mere concepts; from these concepts the possibility of the thought (that it does not contradict itself) can indeed be cognized, but not the possibility of the object as a natural thing, which can be given (as existing) outside of the thought. Therefore, in order to cognize the possibility of determinate natural things, and hence to cognize them a priori, there is further required that the intuition corresponding to the concept be given a priori, i.e., that the concept be constructed. Now, rational cognition through the construction of concepts is mathematical.[90]

The expressions "determinate natural objects" and "phenomenal objects in general" do not indicate two different kinds of things but, rather, aspects of differing degrees of generality of the same things. If the object is a determinate natural one rather than a phenomenal object in general, then the intuition corresponding to the concept of the object must be given. If this intuition is given empirically through sensation, then the *actuality* of this determinate object is known a

[89] *Metaphysical Foundations of Natural Science*, above, Ak. 470.

[90] Above, Ak. 470.

posteriori as in the empirical sciences. If this intuition is given a priori, then the *possibility* of this determinate object is known a priori as in the metaphysics of corporeal nature.[91] Since natural science (as experiential knowledge) does not conceive its objects spontaneously but, rather, receives them in intuition and describes them in accordance with determinations of time and space, the metaphysics of corporeal nature must in its reference to experience have reference to intuition. And hence this metaphysics must make use of mathematics.

Now,

> in order to make possible the application of mathematics to the doctrine of body, which can become natural science only by means of such application, principles of the construction of concepts that belong to the possibility of matter in general must precede. Hence a complete analysis of the concept of a matter in general must be laid at the foundation of the doctrine of body. This is the business of pure philosophy, which for this purpose makes use of no particular experiences but uses only what it finds in the separated (although in itself empirical) concept [of matter] with regard to pure intuitions in space and time (according to laws which already depend essentially on the concept of nature in general); hence such a doctrine is an actual metaphysics of corporeal nature.[92]

The *Metaphysical Foundations of Natural Science* is, then, concerned with the principles of the construction of concepts belonging to the possibility of matter in general. These principles constitute a complete system when the concept of matter is determined by the schematized categories. And so even though mathematics is used in the metaphysical doctrine of body, this use does not render this doctrine a system comprising infinitely many propositions.

The sort of construction Kant has in mind is, for example, that when two motions of one material body (considered as a math-

---

[91]Cf. Francis J. Zucker's translation of C.F. von Weizsäcker, *The Unity of Nature* (New York: Farrar, Straus, Giroux, 1980), pp. 337–339. Here v. Weizsäcker (following the insights of a former student, Peter Plaass) carefully distinguishes (transcendental) possibility from (metaphysical) objective reality.

[92]*Metaphysical Foundations of Natural Science*, above, Ak. 472.

ematical point) are represented by two lines (each expressing velocity and direction) which enclose an angle, then the composite motion of the point can be represented by the diagonal (expressing velocity and direction) of the parallelogram produced by drawing lines parallel to the original two lines.[93] And so in this example we have exhibited a priori the single intuition which corresponds to the concept of such a composite motion of the point. And yet this parallelogram is a rule (or *schema*) for generating infinitely many *images* involving all manner of angles between the lines and all lengths of the lines. This single schema, inasmuch as it is the construction of a concept (a universal representation), must express in its representation universal validity for all possible intuitions which fall under the concept of such a composite motion of the point. Here we have considered the universal in the particular (see above, p. 199 note), i.e., the concept *in concreto* (though not empirically). This schematic (or metaphysical) construction is a precondition for the subsequent mathematical constructions describing the actual motions of material objects.

The transcendental doctrine of nature, on the other hand, considers only the phenomenal objects of a possible experience in general, and the knowledge involved is cognition from concepts.[94] Here the concern is with logical possibility and not with the real possibility of objects. Accordingly, it does not need to construct its concepts of such phenomenal objects in general, because here the concern is not with schematized categories but with pure categories of the understanding and hence no constructions are encountered. Indeed it is impossible mathematically to provide an a priori intuition corresponding to a concept of such general phenomenal things. In the case of the Third Analogy of Experience (see pp. 191–192), what sort of

[93]Cf. above, Ak. 492.

[94]Cf. Lothar Schäfer, *Kants Metaphysik der Natur* (Berlin: Walter de Gruyter & Co., 1966), pp. 30–38, where transcendental synthesis, metaphysical construction, and mathematical construction are carefully distinguished. So far this study is the best available commentary on the *Metaphysical Foundations*. Cf. also C.F. von Weizsäcker, *op. cit.*, p. 338 note.

construction is one to make for the fact that substances stand in a relation of reciprocal causality with regard to their accidents? The Third Law of Mechanics (which is the metaphysical analogue of the Third Analogy) says that in all communication of motion, action and reaction are always equal to one another; and this communication can be constructed (see above, Ak. 546). But this is not to say that the *Metaphysical Foundations of Natural Science* contains nothing but schematic constructions. It contains also philosophical cognitions *from* concepts and even empirical examples of metaphysical concepts.[95]

Kant claims that mathematical physicists could not develop their mathematical systems of nature without metaphysical principles, but that they nevertheless did not organize these principles in a separate system. Instead they postulated such metaphysical laws without investigating their a priori sources.[96] His accomplishment will be to gather these metaphysical laws in a system called the *Metaphysical Foundations of Natural Science.*

This system indicates (among other things) which mathematical constructions are appropriate and useful for application to natural phenomena and which are inappropriate.[97] For example (above, Ak. 518–519), a force that diffuses itself through space so as to act on a distant body is appropriately represented in analogy with the diffusion of the illumination of a light through space by means of concentric spherical surfaces that ever increase with the square of the distance from the light source— any one of these infinitely larger spheres is uniformly illuminated, while the degree of illumination of any one of them is inversely proportional to its distance from the light source. On

[95]Cf. *Metaphysical Foundations*, above, Ak. 474–476: "Under the four classes of quantity, quality, relation, and finally modality, all determinations of the universal concept of a matter in general and, therefore, everything that can be thought a priori respecting it, that can be presented in mathematical construction, or that can be given in experience as a determinate object of experience, must be capable of being brought."

[96]Cf. above, Ak. 472–473.

[97]Cf. above, Ak. 485–486, 493–495, 503–508, 518–523.

the other hand, an inappropriate mode of representation (often used) involves letting rays diverge from a central point (the seat of the force) so that an infinite number of concentric spherical surfaces is thereby indicated; this is inappropriate because the rays so drawn can never, because of their divergence, fill the space through which they pass nor fill the spherical surface they reach. Another interesting example (above, Ak. 503–508) concerns the infinite divisibility of matter. Since space is infinitely divisible mathematically, the matter that fills space is likewise infinitely divisible mathematically. But this fact does not permit one to go on and say that since the spatial representation of matter is infinitely divisible, matter in itself consists of infinitely many parts. Any actual physical division of matter can never be completed and hence can never be entirely given. Therefore, the fact that the spatial representation of matter is infinitely divisible does not prove that matter in itself is composed of an infinite multitude of simple parts, as the atomists claim. Matter (as appearance) is potentially divisible to infinity, but matter (as thing in itself) is never actually infinitely divisible into an infinite set of simple parts.

Metaphysics is therefore an architectonic science that determines the legitimate role that mathematics may play in our natural knowledge; or, as Kant would say, the principles of the *Metaphysical Foundations* make possible a subsequent system of the mathematical principles of corporeal nature. But the task of metaphysics is not that of discovering applications of mathematics to phenomena; mathematical physics does that.[98] Metaphysics, rather, has the function of criticism.

Let us now briefly consider the system of these metaphysical principles of nature. We know (see p. 197) that the "fundamental determination of a something that is to be an object of the external senses must be motion, for thereby only can these senses be affected.[99] The understanding leads all other predi-

[98]See above, Ak. 517–518, 521–523.
[99]Cf. Lothar Schäfer, *op. cit.,* p. 28.

cates which pertain to the nature of matter back to motion; thus natural science is throughout either a pure or an applied doctrine of motion."

In phoronomy nothing but motion is considered. Accordingly, movability in space is the only property attributed to matter, which is then considered as a mathematical point. Motion is regarded as a quantum which is measured by velocity and direction. Only rectilinear motions are considered in phoronomy, because curvilinear ones require the addition of a cause by means of which there is a continuous change of direction; hence such motions cannot be treated merely in terms of quantity, for they need relation (cause) as well. Simple rectilinear motions can be considered as the description of a space; in this description one must pay attention not only to the space described (direction) but also to the time involved (velocity).

> Phoronomy is, then, the pure doctrine (*mathesis*) of the quantity of motions. The determinate concept of a quantity is the concept of the production of the representation of an object through the composition of the homogenous. Now, since nothing is homogeneous with motion except motion, so phoronomy is a doctrine of the composition of the motions of the same point according to their direction and velocity, i.e., the representation of a single motion as one that comprises within itself simultaneously two or even several motions, or else the representation of two motions of the same point simultaneously insofar as they together constitute one motion (that is, they are identical with this motion), and not insofar as they produce the latter in the way that causes produce their effect.[100]

The composition of ever so many motions is reducible to the composition of two—i.e., find that motion which under given conditions is composed of two motions, then compound this with a third, and so on. But two motions of one and the same point which are simultaneously found at this same point can be differentiated in two ways. Either they occur simultaneously in one and the same line, or else in different lines comprising an angle. Those motions occurring in the former way are either

[100]*Metaphysical Foundations*, above, Ak. 489.

contrary to one another in direction or else keep the same direction.

> Hence there are three cases. (1) Two motions (they may be of equal or unequal velocities) combined in one body in the same direction are to constitute a resultant composite motion. (2) Two motions of the same point (of equal or unequal velocity) combined in opposite directions are to constitute through their composition a third motion in the same line. (3) Two motions of a point, with equal or unequal velocities, but in different lines that comprise an angle, are considered to be compounded.[101]

These three cases are proved by letting one of the motions be represented in absolute space; the other motion is represented by a motion of the relative space in a direction that is the opposite of what this other motion would have in absolute space, but the relative space moves with the same velocity as this other motion would have in absolute space.

> If anyone wants to connect the aforementioned three parts of the phoronomic proposition with the schema of the division . . . of the concept of quantity [that is, with the categories of unity, plurality, totality], he will observe the following. Since the concept of quantity always contains the concept of the composition of the homogeneous, the doctrine of the composition of motions is at the same time the pure doctrine of quantity therein. And indeed this doctrine according to all three moments furnished by space, namely, the unity of line and direction, the plurality of directions in one and the same line, and finally the totality of directions as well as of lines, according to which the motion can take place, contains the determination of all possible motion as quantum, although motion's quantity (in a movable point) consists merely in velocity.[102]

These phoronomic principles are the metaphysical analogues of the Axioms of Intuition. In phoronomy motion in space is regarded simply as an extensive magnitude.

In dynamics matter is considered as the movable insofar as it fills a space. This dynamical explication of the concept of matter presupposes the phoronomic one of matter as the movable

[101]Above, Ak. 489–490.
[102]Above, Ak. 495.

in space, but adds to matter the property of being able to resist a motion within a certain space. Dynamical resistance concerns the diminution of the spatial extension of matter (compressibility). Matter dynamically resists when the space it fills is diminished (which is quite different from the mechanical resistance—inertia—involved when matter is driven from its place and is thus itself moved). Matter fills a space by means of a special moving force and not by its mere existence. Only two moving forces can be thought of. All the motion that one matter can impress upon another (both matters being considered as points) must be imparted in the straight line connecting the two points. In this straight line only two kinds of motion are possible: one by which the points recede from one another, and a second by which they approach one another. The force which causes the first is called repulsive, and that which causes the second, attractive. Now, matter fills its space by the repulsive forces of all its parts, i.e., by its own force of extension, beyond which can be thought lesser or greater degrees to infinity. But if there were no other moving force to counteract this repulsive one, matter would disperse itself to infinity; all spaces would be empty, and there would be no matter at all. If matter is to exist, there must be an attractive force acting in an opposite direction to repulsion. And hence an original attraction belongs to all matter as a fundamental force appertaining to its essence. "Kant argues that space-filling presupposes two sorts of forces: attraction and repulsion. This argumentation is transcendental, i.e., it specifies what must be the case if there is to be such a thing as matter. It thereby stands in sharp contrast to the idea that the necessity of these fundamental forces must first be understood in terms of their essence, and the existence of matter deduced therefrom. Kant says: 'That the possibility of fundamental forces should be made conceivable is a completely impossible demand; for they are called fundamental forces precisely because they cannot be derived from any other force, i.e., they cannot be conceived (Ak. 513).' In other words, as soon as we realize that matter, in the sense of that which fills space, is possible only on the basis of the fundamental forces, the material exist-ence of matter tells us *that* these forces are possible; *how* they are possible is for us a meaningless question in that we cannot think up any possible answers."[103]

Repulsion (or impenetrability) is immediately thought in the concept of matter, while attraction is attributed to matter by in-ference. By means of sensation, impenetrability provides us with the size, shape, and location of an extended thing, i.e., a determinate object in space. But attraction by itself can give us no determinate object of sensation, i.e., no matter of determi-nate volume and shape; attraction reveals only the endeavor of our body to approach a point outside us (the central point of the attracting body). Thus, as we have seen that there would be no matter by repulsion alone, likewise would there be none by mere attraction; for without repulsion, all matter would coalesce in a mathematical point, and space would be empty. And so the one force cannot be separated from the other in the concept of matter. Matter as that thing which fills a space in a determinate degree is possible only by means of the attractive force's limiting the repulsive one, i.e., matter is possible only by the combination of weight and original elasticity.

If this dynamical (metaphysical) concept of matter were to be mathematically constructed, then one might do so according to the law that

> the original attraction of matter would act in inverse proportion to the square of the distance at all distances and the original repulsion in inverse proportion to the cube of the infinitely small distances. By such an action and reaction of both fundamental forces, matter would be possible by a determinate degree of the filling of its space. For inasmuch as the repulsion increases in greater measure upon approach of the parts than the attraction does, the limit of approach beyond which by means of the given attraction no greater is possible is determined, and hence the degree of compression that constitutes the measure of the inten-sive filling of space is also determined.[104]

[103]C.F. von Weizsäcker, *op. cit.*, pp. 340–341.
[104]*Metaphysical Foundations*, above, Ak. 521.

The attractive force (weight) depends on the mass of the matter in a given space; however, the expansive (or repulsive) force (elasticity) rests on the degree to which the space is filled, and this degree can be specifically very different (as the same quantity of air in the same volume exhibits more or less elasticity according to its greater or lesser heating). This is to say that the repulsive force can with regard to one and the same attractive force be originally different in degree in different matters. And so the degree of the extension of various matters may admit of very great specific differences with regard to the same quantity of matter; conversely, the quantity of matter may as regards the same volume (i.e., its density) admit of very great differences. Hence every space can be thought of as full and yet as filled in varying measure. And specific empirical matters can be as rare as the ether or as dense as osmium.

> If we review all our discussions of the metaphysical treatment of matter, we shall observe that in this treatment the following things have been taken into consideration: first, the *real* in space (otherwise called the solid) in its filling of space through repulsive force; second, that which, with regard to the first as the proper object of our external perception, is *negative*, namely, attractive force, by which, as far as may be, all space would be penetrated, i.e., the solid would be wholly abolished; third, the *limitation* of the first force by the second and the consequent perceptible determination of the degree of a filling of space. Hence we observe that the quality of matter has been completely dealt with under the moments of reality, negation, and limitation, as much as such a treatment belongs to a metaphysical dynamics.[105]

These dynamic principles are the metaphysical analogues of the Anticipations of Perception. Repulsive force has degrees and hence intensive magnitude; accordingly, repulsive force can with regard to one and the same attractive force be originally different in degree in different matters, and so matter in general fills space in varying measure.

In mechanics matter is regarded as the movable insofar as it is something having a moving force. According to the dynamical

[105]Above, Ak. 523.

explication, matter could be regarded as being at rest as well as in motion. The moving force there considered enabled matter to fill a certain space, but this force was not there regarded as actually causing any matter to move. Repulsion there was an original moving force potentially capable of imparting motion. Mechanics, on the other hand, is concerned with matters that have been set in motion, and the force of a moving matter is regarded as present in it in order to impart its motion to another matter (either at rest or moving). But yet mechanics depends upon dynamics, because one matter moving in a straight line toward another matter could impress no uniform motion on this other matter unless they both possessed original repulsive forces. Similarly, one matter could not compel another to follow it in the straight line connecting the two unless both possessed original attractive forces; (in mechanics Kant considers only cases of repulsion because these differ from cases of attraction only in the line of direction of the forces). And so a matter as moved can have no moving force except by means of its repulsion or attraction, upon which and with which it acts directly in its motion and thereby imparts its own motion to another matter.

We saw earlier (p. 206) that the dynamical explication of matter as the movable insofar as it fills a space presupposes the phoronomic one of matter as the movable in space. Thus Kant builds up his definition of matter in the *synthetic order* (see above, pp. 163–165, 194) by determining the universal concept of a matter in general under quantity, quality, and now relation, all of which are merely aspects of the one objective unity of self-consciousness.

The three mechanical laws state that (1) in all changes of corporeal nature the quantity of matter taken as a whole remains the same, unincreased and undiminished,[106] (2) every change of matter has an external cause, (3) in all communication of mo-

---

[106]Cf. above, Ak. 543: " . . . permanence of substance can be proved of matter but not of the soul." Therefore, matter is eternal, but the soul cannot be shown to be immortal.

tion, action and reaction are always equal to one another. Quite obviously these three laws are the metaphysical analogues of the transcendental Analogies of Experience.

> The three laws of universal mechanics might . . . be . . . designated the law of the subsistence, the inertia, and the reaction of matters (lex Subsistentiae, Inertiae et Antagonismi), as regards all the changes of matters. That these laws, and hence all the propositions of the present science, exactly answer to the categories of substance, causality, and community, insofar as these concepts are applied to matter, requires no further discussion.[107]

In phenomenology matter is regarded as the movable insofar as it can as such be an object of experience. Here the concern is with the relations matter has to the mind that knows it. Now, the "fundamental determination of a something that is to be an object of the external senses must be motion, for thereby only can these senses be affected. The understanding leads all other predicates which pertain to the nature of matter back to motion . . ."[108] Accordingly, the discussions in phenomenology center primarily on motion itself. We have seen (pp. 140–142) that representations can be regarded as merely the contents of our consciousness or as referring beyond themselves to the objects which they purport to represent. The representation of motion is given to us merely as an appearance, i.e., as the undetermined object of an external empirical intuition. "In order that the representation of motion may become experience [i.e., objective knowledge], there is required in addition [to representation by mere sense] that something be thought through the understanding, namely, in addition to the way in which this representation of motion inheres in the subject, there is required further the determination of an object by means of this representation."[109] The movable as such becomes an object of experience when matter is determined by the predicate of motion. Motion is change of relation in space. And thus motion always has two correlates: matter and space. With regard to the appearance of

[107]Above, Ak. 551.
[108]Above, Ak. 476–477.
[109]Above, Ak. 554.

motion, change can be attributed to matter just as well as to space; and either matter or space can be said to be moved. Accordingly, the first proposition of phenomenology says that the "rectilinear motion of a matter with regard to an empirical space, as distinguished from the opposite motion of this space, is a merely possible predicate. The rectilinear motion of a matter in no relation to a matter outside of itself, i.e., such rectilinear motion thought of as absolute, is impossible."[110] Clearly this "proposition determines the modality of motion with regard to phoronomy."[111]

With regard to the transformation of appearance into experience, either matter or space must be thought of as moved to the exclusion of the other. The second proposition states that the "circular motion of a matter, in contradistinction to the opposite motion of the space, is an actual predicate of matter. On the other hand, the opposite motion of a relative space, taken instead of the motion of the body, is no actual motion of the body; if this opposite motion of a relative space is held to be an actual motion of the body, then such motion is a mere illusion."[112] Does the earth rotate on its axis or is it still while the heavens rotate about it? Phoronomically (in the appearance) one cannot tell. But dynamically the actuality of the earth's rotation can be experienced. Drill a hole to the center of the earth. Drop a stone into this hole. The force of gravity acts on the stone at every distance from the earth's center, but yet the stone continuously diverges from the vertical direction (diverges from west to east) in its fall. This fact proves that the earth rotates on its axis from west to east. This second proposition "determines the modality of motion with regard to dynamics."[113]

According to the third proposition both matter and space must necessarily be represented as moved at the same time. It

[110]Above, Ak. 555.
[111]Above, Ak. 556.
[112]Above, Ak. 556–557.
[113]Above, Ak. 557.

declares that in "every motion of a body whereby it is moving with regard to another body, an opposite and equal motion of this other body is necessary."[114] Finally, "this proposition determines the modality of motion with regard to mechanics. That these three propositions, moreover, determine the motion of matter with regard to its possibility, actuality, and necessity, and hence with regard to all three categories of modality, is obvious of itself."[115] These principles are the metaphysical analogues of the Postulates of Empirical Thought.

VI. THE TRANSITION FROM THE METAPHYSICAL PRINCIPLES OF NATURE TO THE PHYSICAL PRINCIPLES OF NATURE

In the dynamics of the *Metaphysical Foundations of Natural Science*, which was published in 1786, between the two editions of the *Critique of Pure Reason* (1781 and 1787), Kant says:

> But one must guard against going beyond what makes the universal concept of matter in general possible and against wanting to explain a priori the particular or even specific determination and variety of matter. The concept of matter is reduced to nothing but moving forces; this could not be expected to be otherwise, because in space no activity and no change can be thought of but mere motion. But who claims to comprehend the possibility of fundamental forces? They can only be assumed, if they inevitably belong to a concept concerning which there can be proved that it is a fundamental concept not further derivable from any other (such as is the fundamental concept of the filling of space). These fundamental forces are the repulsive forces in general and the attractive forces in general (which counteract the repulsive ones). We can indeed judge well enough a priori concerning their connection and consequences; one may think of

[114]Above, Ak. 558.
[115]Above, Ak. 558.

whatever relations of these forces among one another he wants to, provided he does not contradict himself. But he must not, therefore, presume to assume either of them as actual, because the authorization to set up a hypothesis irremissibly requires that the possibility of what is assumed be entirely certain. But in the case of fundamental forces, their possibility can never be comprehended. . . . [If] the material itself is transformed into fundamental forces (whose laws we are not able to determine a priori, but still less are we able to reliably indicate a manifold of such forces sufficient for explicating the specific variety of matter), then all means are wanting for the construction of this concept and for presenting as possible in intuition what we thought universally.[116]

Again,

Besides the ether, no law whatever of attractive or of repulsive force may be risked on a priori conjectures; but everything, even universal attraction as the cause of gravity, must, together with the laws of such attraction, be concluded from data of experience. Still less will such conclusions in regard to chemical affinities be permitted to be tried otherwise than by means of experiment. For to comprehend original forces a priori according to their possibility lies generally beyond the horizon of our reason. Rather, all natural philosophy consists in the reduction of given forces apparently diverse to a smaller number of forces and powers sufficient for the explication of the actions of the former. But this reduction continues only to fundamental forces, beyond which our reason cannot go. And thus the investigation of metaphysics behind what lies at the basis of the empirical concept of matter is useful only for the purpose of leading natural philosophy as far as possible in the investigation of the dynamical grounds of explication, because these alone admit the hope of determinate laws, and consequently of a true rational coherence of explications.[117]

From these remarks one might expect that the next step in our knowledge of nature would be empirical science—we have investigated completely the a priori forms of natural knowledge and now have come finally to the matter of knowledge, at which point we must leave philosophy and go to empirical sci-

---

[116]Above, Ak. 524–525.
[117]Above, Ak. 534.

ence. But Kant conceived of a *Transition from the Metaphysical Foundations of Natural Science to Physics.*

Between 1790 and 1803 Kant was, among other things, busy working on what is now called the *Opus Postumum*, part of which is the *Transition.* At his death the *Opus* survived as a stack of handwritten pages, which were eventually gathered into thirteen fascicles (*Convolute*). The *Opus Postumum* appears in Volumes XXI and XXII of the Academy edition of Kant's works. Sections of it constitute coherent wholes, others provide illustrations, and still others are just repetitions. Erich Adickes wrote a critical exposition of it entitled *Kant's Opus Postumum*, in which he produced a coherent account of the work; this appeared as Supplementary Volume Number 50 of the *Kant-Studien* (Berlin, 1920).

In the *Metaphysical Foundations* the pure, formal structure of motion (admitting of mathematical construction) was studied. We know a priori that in general the motion of matter is caused by the fundamental forces of repulsion and attraction. We have seen (just above) that the specific variety and behavior of matter can be accounted for in no other way than by appealing to particular forces known only through experience. The variety, intensity, and laws of these forces are studied by empirical physics. For Kant the ideal of a science is a system necessarily exhaustive of our cognitions of an object. This ideal is satisfied in the *Metaphysical Foundations*, where motion is treated abstractly by considering its pure spatio-temporal relations (which are constructed without any appeal to actual experience in the pure intuitive forms given by sensibility itself, and which are, accordingly, necessarily and exactly determinable by means of pure thought alone).

But the case is quite different as regards physics. How is it to effect a rational unity of the multiplicity of forces provided by empirical observation? In order for physics to become a science there must be the possibility of anticipating a priori the totality and order of these empirical forces. Actual perception (experience) cannot do the job. It merely gives us the forces without guaranteeing an exhaustive enumeration of them or a systematic form in which they are ranged. From this we conclude that either physics cannot be a science or else we must look for a way to reduce to a system the empirical forces which determine the particular nature and behavior of matter as given in experience.[118] Kant chooses the latter alternative. The matter of experience cannot be anticipated; only the form of it can be. Therefore we must set up in an a priori way the formal schematism of matter's constitutive forces, which experience reveals to us and which physics studies in their concrete realizations. Kant calls this science a physiology. It will serve as a propaedeutic for physics by preordering and prearranging the empirical search for forces in their actual realization. In the *Metaphysical Foundations*, motion *in abstracto* could be treated purely mathematically. But natural motions, dependent as effects upon causes called forces, cannot be so treated. Mathematics can serve as an instrument for calculating the quantitative value of the play of forces which is revealed by experience, but it cannot serve to discover the forces themselves.[119] The science mediating the *Metaphysical Foundations* and empirical physics is to be an entirely philosophical one made up of cognitions from concepts instead of through the construction of concepts (see pp. 199–202). It will point out in an a priori manner how the formal conditions of cognition serve as the clue for the discovery of all the empirical forces that physics encounters in its work.

The *Transition* is developed in two stages. In the first stage the a priori system of possible forces manifested by experience is fixed; in the second the general properties of matter are established. Finally, Kant sets up the foundation of the unity of experience and matter by the deduction of the ether; this last operation is independent of the other two.

[118]Cf. *Opus Postumum*, Vol. XXI of the Akademie edition, pp. 161–165, 174–180, 284–294, 481–488, 524–527, 616–625, 630–645, for example.

[119]Cf. *ibid.*, Vol. XXI, pp. 203–204, 209, 238–239, 241–245, 488, for example.

The possibility of the realization of empirical representations (perceptions) in a subject are necessarily conditioned by the subject's forms of receptivity (time and space) and synthetic functions of thought. This means that perceptions are determined by the forms of sensibility and the synthetic functions of the understanding. If a force is to mean anything to us, it must be perceived and hence must be determined by these forms and functions. These synthetic functions are comprised in the table of the categories. By means of the categories, then, one can set up a priori the schema of all the possible forces that can affect us and be perceived by us in experience. Various sketches of this schema are to be found in the *Transition*; there is some difficulty in telling which one Kant might have settled on as being the final one. In general, the various sketches contain classifications already familiar to us—repulsive and attractive, superficial and penetrative, etc.

The formal schema of the general properties of matter is deduced in a similar fashion. Such a property is nothing but the dynamical behavior of a synthetic combination of forces. Every synthesis is the activity of a subject and must be conducted in accordance with the possible a priori forms of synthesis in general. The table of the categories presents us with all the possible forms. Accordingly, every empirical property that we can know anything about must conform to the categories; therefore this table provides us with a sufficient basis for setting up a priori a schema of the properties of matter. Again, there are various sketches of this schema. In general, the *quantity* of matter with regard to its moving forces concerns the ponderability of individual matter as made possible by means of an imponderable matter called the ether. Under *quality* is treated (1) fluidity and solidity, (2) drop formation and capillary action, (3) crystallization and melting. Under *relation* is treated (1) cohesion, (2) rubbing and polishing, (3) the luster of metals. *Modality* is concerned with the moving forces in a world system.

These schemata in no way replace experience. We are unable by means of them to foretell or predetermine what concrete forces or what empirical properties will affect us here and now or which ones will be given us by experience. But these schemata provide us with a clue and a sure guide for exploring the empirically real; they enable us to classify in a necessary way every possible object of physics until experience gives us the actual presence of some one of these forces or properties.

The third part of the *Transition* treats of the ether. In the *Metaphysical Foundations* (Ak. 534), Kant thought that one might be justified in assuming the existence of the ether as a more acceptable alternative to the hypothesis (which he found unacceptable) of impenetrable atoms and absolutely empty space. But in the *Transition* he was not quite so cautious. He thought that the unity of physics was not sufficiently guaranteed by the a priori possibility of a manifold of forces and properties of matter. In the ether he found a unitary element coextensive with both the unity of matter and the unity of experience. The theory of the ether, whose existence is treated in Convolute X, XI, and XII of the *Opus,* figures in all the inquiries of the *Transition.* It is a matter that occupies absolutely every part of space, that penetrates the whole material domain, that is identical in all its parts, and that is endowed with a spontaneous and perpetual motion. He bases his proof of its existence upon the unity of experience. The form of all experience is space, which is unitary; hence experience is unitary. Experience is a system made up of a manifold of perceptions synthesized by the understanding in space. The source of these perceptions lies in the actions of the material forces which fill space. Accordingly, the forces of matter must collectively be capable of constituting a system in order to conform to the unity of possible experience. Such a system is possible only if one admits as the foundation of these forces the existence of an ether having the properties listed above. Therefore, the existence of the ether is the a priori condition of the system of experience.[120]

The *Transition* as it has come down to us is merely a series of

[120]Cf. J. N. Findlay, *Kant and the Transcendental Object* (Oxford: Oxford University Press, 1981), pp. 264–268.

sketches for a work that was never finished. Accordingly, it suggests about as many unanswered questions as it provides solutions. I have discussed it only to indicate the place it occupies in Kant's system of corporeal nature.

CONCLUSION

Our exploration of the architectonic constituting the very core of Kant's philosophy of corporeal nature is now at an end. Kant himself did not always make clear the workings of this architectonic. My hope is that this essay, to some extent, succeeds in clarifying them.

JAMES ELLINGTON

GERMAN-ENGLISH APPENDIX OF TERMS USED IN THE *METAPHYSICAL FOUNDATIONS OF NATURAL SCIENCE*

A

Äther ether
Akzeleration acceleration
Allheit totality
Anschauung intuition
Anziehung attraction
Anziehungskraft force of attraction
Apperzeption apperception
Atom atom
Auflösung solution
Ausdehnung extension

B

Bebung trembling
Begriff concept
Berührung contact
Beschaffenheit quality, characteristic
Beschleunigung acceleration
Bestrebung endeavor
Beweglichkeit movability
Bewegung motion
Bewußtsein consciousness

C

Chemie chemistry

Construction, mathematische construction, mathematical

D

Denken thought
Dichtigkeit density
Ding an sich thing in itself
Druck pressure
durchdringen penetrate
Durchdringung penetration
Dynamik dynamics

E

Eigenschaft property
eindringen penetrate into, intrude
eindrücken impress
Einfache, das simple
Einheit unity
Elastizität elasticity
Empfindung sensation
entfernen withdraw
Erfahrung experience
Erscheinung appearance
Erzeugung production

F

fest solid

flüssig fluid

G

Gärung fermentation
Gegenwirkung reaction
Gemeinschaft community
Geschwindigkeit velocity
Gestalt shape
gleichartig homogeneous
gleichförmig uniform
Größe quantity
Grundsatz principle

H

Hydrodynamik hydro-
dynamics
Hydrostatik hydrostatics
Hylozoismus hylozoism
Hypothese hypothesis

I

Intussuszeption intussusception

K

Kategorie category
Kausalität causality
Klebrigkeit viscosity
Kongruenz congruence
Körper body
Kraft force

L

Leben life

Leblosigkeit lifelessness
Leere, das void
Logik logic

M

Masse mass
Materie matter
Mathematik mathematics
Mechanik mechanics
Metaphysik metaphysics
Modalität modality
Möglichkeit possibility
Monade monad
Monadologie monadology

N

Natur nature
Naturwissenschaft natural
science
Negation negation

O

Ort place

P

Phänomenologie phenom-
enology
Phoronomie phoronomy
Physik physics
Punkt point

Q

Qualität quality

R

Raum space
Raumesinhalt volume
Reibung friction
Richtung direction
Ruhe rest

S

Scheidung analysis
Schein illusion
Schwere weight
Seele soul
Sollizitation solicitation
spröde brittle
starr rigid
Stetigkeit continuity
Stoff material
Stoß impact
Substanz substance

T

Teilbarkeit divisibility
Teilung division
Trägheit inertia
Trennung separation

U

Undurchdringlichkeit
  impenetrability
Unteilbarkeit indivisibility
Ursache cause
Urteil judgment

V

Veränderung change,
  alteration
Vernunft reason
Verschiebung displacement
Verstand understanding
Vielheit plurality
Voraussetzung assumption

W

Wärme heat
Wahrnehmung perception
Wechselwirkung reciprocal
  action
Wesen essence
Widerstand resistance
Wirklichkeit actuality
Wirkung action, effect
Wirkung in die Ferne
  action at a distance
Wissenschaft science

Z

Zeit time
Zitterung vibration
Zug traction
Zurückstoßung repulsion
Zurückstoßungskraft
  force of repulsion
zurücktreiben repel
Zusammendrückung
  compression
Zusammenhang cohesion
Zusammensetzung
  composition

INDEX

223